AN ACCOUNT
OF THE
MUTINIES IN OUDH
AND OF
THE SIEGE
OF THE LUCKNOW RESIDENCY.

AN ACCOUNT

OF THE

MUTINIES IN OUDH

AND OF

THE SIEGE

OF THE LUCKNOW RESIDENCY.

WITH SOME OBSERVATIONS ON THE CONDITION OF THE PROVINCE OF OUDH, AND ON THE CAUSES OF THE MUTINY OF THE BENGAL ARMY

MARTIN RICHARD GUBBINS

GYAN

Published by

GYAN

Gyan Publishing House
5, Ansari Road
Daryaganj, New Delhi-110002
Phone: 011-47034999, 9811692060
E-mail: books@gyanbooks.com

Distribution Network
gyanbooks.com
India, USA, Canada, UK, Australia

ISBN: 978-93-6433-241-5 (HB)

First Published, 1858

2nd Impression 2024

Printed at: Gyan Press, Delhi.

AN ACCOUNT OF THE MUTINIES IN OUDH AND OF THE SIEGE OF THE LUCKNOW RESIDENCY

Author: MARTIN RICHARD GUBBINS

AN ACCOUNT

OF THE

MUTINIES IN OUDH,

AND OF

THE SIEGE

OF THE LUCKNOW RESIDENCY.

TOMB OF THE MOTHER OF SAADUT ALY KHAN

TOMB OF NEWAUB SAADUT ALY KHAN

CUPOLAS OF THE KAISUR BAUGH

VIEW OF THE KAISUR BAUGH PALACE.

AND PART OF THE CITY OF LUCKNOW.

London Richard Bentley, New Burlington Street, 1858

Hullmandel & Walton, Lith.

AN ACCOUNT

OF THE

MUTINIES IN OUDH,

AND OF

THE SIEGE

OF THE LUCKNOW RESIDENCY;

WITH SOME OBSERVATIONS ON THE CONDITION
OF THE PROVINCE OF OUDH, AND ON THE CAUSES OF THE MUTINY
OF THE BENGAL ARMY.

BY

MARTIN RICHARD GUBBINS,

OF THE BENGAL CIVIL SERVICE,
FINANCIAL COMMISSIONER FOR OUDH.

SECOND EDITION.

LONDON:
RICHARD BENTLEY, NEW BURLINGTON STREET,
Publisher in Ordinary to Her Majesty.
1858.

PREFACE.

THE writer of these pages entered Oudh at the period of its annexation to the Anglo-Indian Empire, as a Member of the British Commission. During the fourteen months' administration of Oudh, which preceded the breaking out of the Mutinies, he was in the habit of daily intercourse with the natives. Several of the chief officers of the former native Government were his constant visitors; and his door was open to all who desired to make any communication, whenever business permitted.

During the cold season of 1856–57, he completed a tour through the whole of Oudh, with the object of testing the summary settlement of the Land Revenue, which had been completed; in order to ensure its moderation. To accomplish this duty successfully there was only one effectual means. This was to mix familiarly with the people; to enter their villages alone, or attended by a single horseman; to sit down among them, and let themselves speak out their grievances. This was done in many quarters. The writer conversed with the people of Oudh in their villages, at their ploughs, freely, and without restraint. No native official interposed between him and them.

The result of his tour was a very large reduction of the Land Revenue, imposed by several of the district officers.

Nor was it with the villagers only that he conversed. Wherever he went, the native chiefs and talooqdars attended. These were always courteously received, and patiently listened to; and wherever they appeared to have been hardly dealt with, arrangements were made for re-investigating their claims, and redressing their grievances. It was thus that the writer became personally acquainted with most of the chiefs and talooqdars in Oudh. All the chief bankers and the native nobility of the city were personally known to him; and he does not scruple to call one of them, Newaub Ahmed Aly Khan Monowurooddowlah, his friend.

Again, from the first moment when the sighing of the gale was heard, which ushered in the fearful tempest which has desolated Upper India, he was the intimate adviser and confidant of the late lamented Sir Henry Lawrence. Until the electric telegraph wires were cut, every message received or sent went through his hands. He managed the Intelligence Department by desire of Sir Henry Lawrence, until the British position at Lucknow was beleaguered; when all means of obtaining intelligence ceased.

It is true that latterly, when Sir Henry Lawrence's health had failed, some difference of opinion took place; the writer strongly advocating the disarming of the remnants of the native regiments at the capital, to which step Sir Henry Lawrence was opposed. Perhaps in consequence of some change of feeling which may have thence arisen, for a few days prior to the investment of the Residency, he was not made cognizant of every measure that was taken; especially he neither knew of, nor was consulted respecting, the advance against the enemy at Chinhut.

During the siege, from first to last, the writer necessarily took a conspicuous part. His house and enclosing compound was one of the most exposed outposts; and its defences and batteries were mainly erected by himself, his servants, and native followers; with the aid of the other officers of his own garrison.

Having kept a journal of events from the first, and finding on the arrival of General Havelock's force, considerable misapprehension to exist on several matters of importance, especially concerning the condition of Oudh; he employed the comparative leisure afforded during the blockade of Generals Outram and Havelock, in preparing an account of the Oudh mutinies and the siege. In this he received every encouragement from the late lamented General Havelock, with whose friendship he was honoured. The General promised him the plans of the Battle of Cawnpoor; and Lieutenant H. M. Havelock, his son, dictated, while recovering from his wound, to the writer, a highly graphic and animated account of his father's campaign, in which he himself bore a conspicuous part.

The transmission of the manuscript to England for publication was delayed by severe illness, which attacked the writer on his arrival at Cawnpoor with Sir Colin Campbell's army. It was not, consequently, despatched until February, when the first part was forwarded by the Peninsular and Oriental Company's steamer Ava, and the second part by the Bentinck; the writer himself being compelled to make the long voyage, *viá* the Cape, for the recovery of his health.

The Ava, it is known, was wrecked; in lieu, therefore, of finding his work in print on his arrival in England, the writer has had to reproduce the missing portion from his original journal, which remained with him. He has to regret, however, that two valuable parts of it cannot be restored; viz. the narrative of his father's campaign by Lieutenant H. M. Havelock, and an account of the engagement of Chinhut, in the words of Captain Hamilton Forbes, 1st Bengal Light Cavalry, who commanded the advanced guard on that disastrous occasion.

He has also to regret the loss of many admirably-executed illustrations of the scenes around the Residency by the pencil of Colonel Vincent Eyre, Bengal Artillery, and Captain W. H. Hawes, of the 5th O. I. Infantry. One of the former was fortunately preserved, and appears in this work, which also contains a sketch of the Gateway of the Alum Bagh, for which the author has to thank Lieutenant E. C. Wynne, H.M.'s 90th Light Infantry: and one of the Residency, for which he is indebted to the kindness of Mr. S. N. Martin of the Bengal Civil Service. The illustration which portrays a part of the city of Lucknow is taken from a photograph in possession of the author, executed by a native of Lucknow, the Darogha Azim Alee Khan, who attained to great excellence in this beautiful art.

Despite the delay in putting this Work to press, which has allowed public curiosity to be in some degree satisfied by the publication of other accounts, it is hoped that it will not be altogether without interest. Many particulars, which have not yet been laid before the public, will be found in its pages. More especially a succinct account of the occurrences which marked those days of never-to-be-forgotten anxiety and alarm, which preceded the actual mutiny.

The writer has availed himself of the unexpected delay which has taken place in the publication of his own work, to examine the other narratives of this memorable siege, which have appeared in the interim. He desires to acknowledge the advantage which he has derived from a comparison of his own notes with the careful and accurate record of facts, which has been prepared by Captain F. P. Wilson, of the 13th N. I., in the Diary of a Staff Officer, and by Lieutenant M'Leod Innes (Engineers), in his "Rough Notes."

BRIGHTON,
June 3, 1858.

PREFACE TO THE SECOND EDITION.

Two additions have been made to this Edition, which will, it is hoped, be found of interest. In Appendix No. 9 will be found the narrative given of her escape by one of the ladies who fled from Sultanpoor. And Major Eyre's account of the glorious little Arrah campaign forms the tenth Appendix.

August 7th, 1858.

CONTENTS.

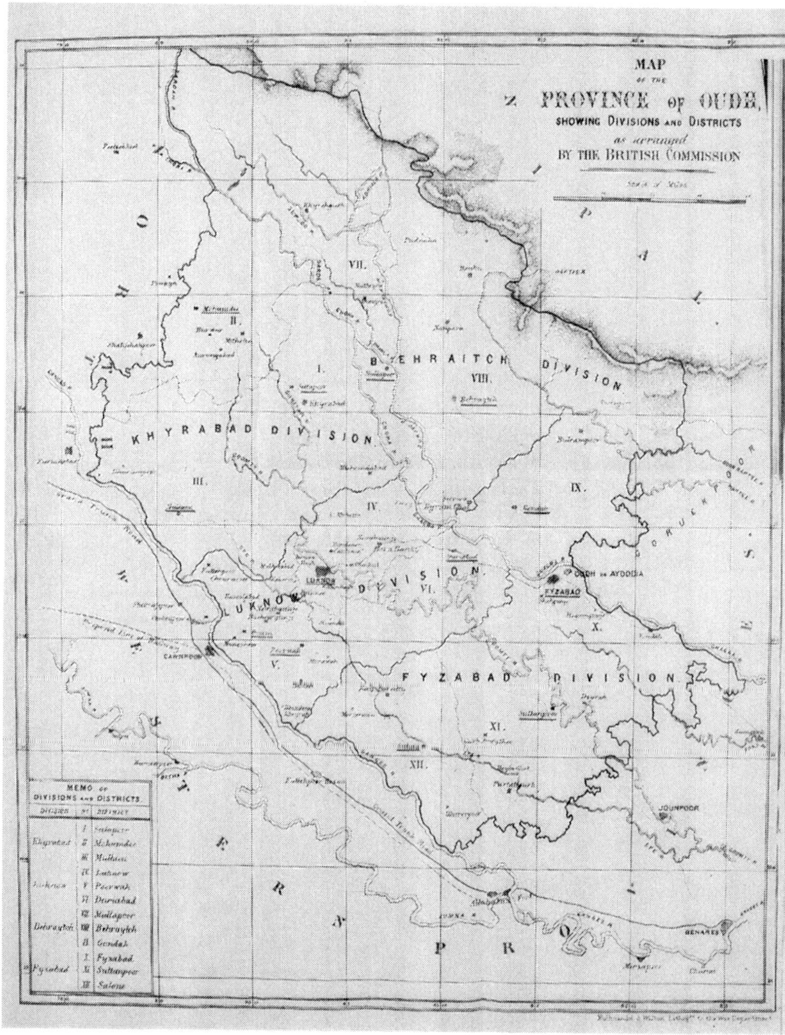
MAP OF THE PROVINCE OF OUDE,
SHOWING DIVISIONS AND DISTRICTS
as arranged
BY THE BRITISH COMMISSION
KHYRABAD DIVISION
BEHRAITCH DIVISION
LUKNOW DIVISION
FYZABAD DIVISION
LUKNOW
CAWNPOOR
FYZABAD
OUDH or AYODHA
JOUNPOOR
BENARES
GORUCKPOOR
MEMO OF DIVISIONS AND DISTRICTS
Mullapoor
Behraytch
Gondah
Fyzabad
Sultanpoor
Salone

ERRATA.

Page 23, lines 8 and 23, *for* Seiks *read* Sheiks
„ 24, line 11, *for* Kudduum *read* Kuddum
„ 38, line 31, *for* his horse *read* the horse
„ 72, note, *for* Taseen-khan *read* Yaseen-khan
„ 81, line 1, *for* Countenance these *read* Countenance, then
„ 85, line 32, *for* these were *read* this was
„ 101, line 14 of contents of Chapter VII., *for* them *read* him
„ 114, line 32 of contents of Chapter VIII., *for* Black *read* Block

AN ACCOUNT

OF THE

MUTINIES IN OUDH.

CHAPTER I.

THE FIRST ALARM OF MUTINY AT LUCKNOW.—APRIL.

Month of April at Lucknow.—Uneasiness respecting the allegiance of the native soldiery.—News of their repugnance to the new cartridges, and of the mutiny of the 19th N. I.—Accounts from Amballa of the disaffection there.—Sir Henry Lawrence's arrival.—His conciliatory demeanour and general affability to the natives.—Untoward occurrence in the 48th N. I. hospital from Dr. Wells' mistaken conduct.—Dr. Wells' bungalow fired.—Disaffection of the 48th N. I. becomes suspected.—Sir Henry Lawrence concentrates his military resources.—Their previous faulty disposition explained.—Position of the Residency.—Financial and Judicial Commissioners' residences, Bailey Guard.—Location of H. M.'s 32nd Foot.—Powder magazine.—Lines of the military police.—Tara Kotee.—Position of the Dowlut Khana and Sheesh Muhul.—Head-quarters of the Oudh Irregular Force.—Military magazine.—Position of the Oudh Irregular Infantry Regiments at the Moosa Bagh.—The Muriaon cantonments described.—Artillery lines, Regular, and belonging to the Oudh Irregular Force.—The cavalry cantonment at Moodkeepoor.—Troops quartered in both cantonments.—Position of the 2nd Regt. of O. I. Cavalry at the Chukker Kotee.—Necessity for this faulty distribution.—Alterations made in it by Sir Henry Lawrence.—Condition of Oudh at this time.—General tranquillity.—Police.—Revenue arrangements.

In the month of April, 1857, uneasiness first began to be felt by the authorities at Lucknow respecting the allegiance of the native soldiery quartered at that capital. During the two preceding months, the newspapers had made known the general repugnance felt by the sepoys to the use of the new cartridges. We had heard of the mutiny of the 19th Regt. of Native Infantry at Berhampoor, and its disbandment at Barrackpoor. The feeling of the disbanded soldiers was known to be anything but friendly; and, as many of them resided in Oudh, no good effect was expected to result from their return to the Province. It was known also, that serious disaffection prevailed in other regiments at the Presidency. We were aware that the feeling of the native troops at Amballa was far from good. At that station a school of musketry instruction had been formed, where the sepoys were to be taught the use of the Enfield rifle cartridge. Detachments from a large number of regiments were there collected, including those quartered at Lucknow. And from the officers so detached, the accounts which reached us of the disaffection of the soldiery, particularly of the 60th N. I., and the alarm manifested by them at the introduction of the new fire-arms, were nowise calculated to allay the apprehension which had been aroused in Bengal.

Towards the close of March, Sir Henry Lawrence arrived at Lucknow, in the capacity of Chief Commissioner; and the influence of his kind and conciliatory demeanour towards the native community was soon felt. No one was more calculated to win the esteem and regard of the native gentry than Sir Henry Lawrence. Affable, and easily approached, deeply sympathizing with all who had lost consideration, or the means of respectable maintenance by the British annexation of the Province, he was eminently calculated to soothe the public mind. The native gentry hastened to wait upon him; all returned from the interview satisfied and hopeful. All congratulated themselves on having found a ruler so well disposed to listen to their grievances, and to remedy them, so far as was in his power.

Sir Henry Lawrence, indeed, was essentially a friend of the natives. He had long been habituated to cultivate a free intercourse with them; and to free himself more than most men from the trammels of native subordinates. He thought that Europeans were too apt to overvalue themselves and their own Government, and to undervalue the native Governments of the country. He thought that the people had many just causes for complaint; and he was desirous, in ordering the administration over which he had been appointed to preside, to remove these grievances as far as possible.

Early in April an occurrence took place, which showed sufficiently the jealousy which then existed in the minds of the native soldiery on the subject of their caste and religion. One of the three regiments stationed at the capital was the 48th N. I. This corps had long been reputed to be one of the finest in the service. Sir H. M. Wheeler, the General commanding at Cawnpoor, had long been its colonel; and for several years it had been commanded by an officer second to none in Upper India, Colonel Colin Troup. It was now commanded by Lieutenant-Colonel Palmer. Dr. Wells, the surgeon of the regiment, having occasion to visit the medicine store of the hospital, and feeling at the time indisposed, incautiously applied to his mouth a bottle taken from the hospital medicines containing a carminative. This act was in contravention of the rules of Hindoo caste. No high-caste Hindoo could afterwards have partaken of the medicine contained in the polluted bottle. The native apothecary, who attended Dr.

Wells, was unfortunately on bad terms with him, and informed the sepoys in hospital of what had been done. The consequence was an outcry among them, and a refusal to touch any of the medicines prescribed for them. Colonel Palmer assembled the native officers, and in their presence destroyed the bottle which the surgeon had touched with his lips, besides subjecting Dr. Wells to a deserved rebuke.

It was hoped that these measures would have satisfied the sepoys, and that the matter would have been forgotten. But it was not so. The men in hospital, indeed, no longer persisted to refuse their medicines; but the doctor's offence was not forgiven. A few nights after, the bungalow* in which he resided was fired, and Dr. Wells escaped, but with the loss of most of his property. It was well known that the incendiaries belonged to the 48th N. I., but as no proof could be obtained, punishment could not be inflicted.

Not long after it became known that the regiment was disaffected. Some of the native officers were reported by the police to be intriguing with one Rookunooddowlah, and Moostufa Alee, relatives of the ex-King of Oudh, residing in the city. It was believed that they had proposed that some member of the Royal Family of Oudh should place himself at their head. Not long after this, Captain Adolphus Orr, commanding one of the regiments of military police, reported that an attempt had been made by some sepoys of the 48th, to tamper with a native guard of his regiment. Despite all these reports, however, the officers of the regiment maintained the most unshaken confidence in the fidelity of their

* Thatched house.

men, and indignantly rejected all suspicion of their disaffection.

Seeing this state of things, Sir Henry Lawrence vigorously applied himself to concentrate his military resources. The faulty and imperfect arrangement of these, indeed, had struck him on his first arrival, and must be here described.

The head-quarters of the Chief Commissioner were at the Residency, situated in the city, close to the river Goomtee, and about a quarter of a mile from the iron bridge. About the Residency were closely clustered several substantial buildings of solid masonry, which formed the residences and contained the offices of the judicial and financial commissioners, the civil surgeon, and others. Here also were the Treasury, the Hospital, and Thuggee Department Gaol. A company of Native Infantry, weekly relieved from the cantonments, guarded the Residency and Treasury. The sepoys occupied a curved line of buildings outside the principal gate leading to the Residency, as well as some others close to the Treasury, to which the name of "*Bailey Guard*" was applied. About a mile and a half to the eastward was placed the only European infantry which we had in the Province—H. M.'s 32nd Regt., the depôt, and many women belonging to which were at Cawnpoor. The men occupied a cruciform building, called the "Chowpeyrah Istubul," as their barracks. The officers were scattered about the neighbourhood. Colonel Inglis and others occupied detached houses along the road leading directly from the Chowpeyrah Istubul towards the Martiniere. The rest lived still further from their men in apartments of the Chuttermunzil Palace, between which and the soldiers' barracks was the strong building, called the "Khoorsheydmunzil," which was the mess-house, where a few officers resided. Directly north of the barracks, and close to the river, stood an old tomb, where was preserved a stone brought from Mecca, supposed to bear the impress of the foot of the Prophet. It was hence called the Kuddum Rusool.* This had been repaired, and converted into a powder-magazine, and was protected by a native sepoy guard. In this neighbourhood were the lines of the head-quarters of the 3rd Regt. of Military Police, which furnished all the civil guards at the capital. The Tara Kotee, or Observatory, where now were concentrated all the local courts of civil justice, adjoins the 32nd mess, and was protected by a regular guard of Native Infantry, while several European officials—the Commissioner, Major Banks; the Deputy-Commissioner, Mr. S. N. Martin; the Superintendent of Canals, Lieutenant J. C. Anderson—occupied detached residences in this locale.

About a mile from the Residency up stream through the city were the Dowlut Khana and Sheesh Muhul, which had belonged to a former palace of one of the Kings of Oudh. The head-quarters of Brigadier Gray, who commanded the Oudh Irregular Force, were in the former. In the latter was the magazine, where a considerable number of stand of arms, as well as many native guns belonging to the late Oudh Government, were deposited. About two miles further up stream, and near the Moosa Bagh Garden Palace, were cantoned the 4th Regt. of O. I. Infantry, commanded by Captain Hughes; and a mile beyond them, again, were the lines of the 7th Regt. of O. I. Infantry, temporarily commanded by Lieutenant J. T. Watson; the officers of both corps residing in the Moosa Bagh.

* Foot of the Prophet.

Such was the disposition of the troops on the south side of the river.

Three miles from the Residency, on the north of the Goomtee, was the old British military cantonment, called by the natives Muriaon. Here the officers resided, in rows of thatched bungalows, each surrounded by a separate enclosure, called in India "compound," while the native troops occupied rows of low thatched huts fronting their several parades. Between the native lines and the parade ground stood the bells of arms, each containing the arms of one company; one building, larger than the rest, on the right of the bells of arms, being the regimental magazine. On the right of the entrance to the cantonment from the city side were the lines of the company of European Artillery, and also of Major Simonds' Regular Native Battery and their guns. Beyond the Native Infantry lines were those of two newly-raised Oudh Irregular batteries, commanded by Lieutenants D. C. Alexander and Ashe. At a distance of one and a half mile further on, and beyond the race-course, was the new cavalry cantonment of Moodkeepoor, where was stationed the 7th Regt. of Light Cavalry (native). The whole force in the Muriaon and Moodkeepoor cantonments was the following:—

European Artillery . . 1 light horse battery.
Regular Native Artillery 1 ditto bullock battery.
Oudh Irregular Artillery 2 ditto horse batteries.
Regular Native Cavalry . 1 regiment.
Ditto Native Infantry . 3 regiments, viz. the 13th, commanded by Major Bruere; the 48th, by Lieutenant-Colonel Palmer; and the 71st, by Lieutenant-Colonel Halford.

It remains only to mention the location of the 2nd

Regiment of O. I. Cavalry, commanded by Major Gall, of the Madras army. This was at the Chukker Kotee, or old King's Race-course, on the left bank of the river nearly opposite to the Secunder Bagh, and about three miles from the Residency.

This very faulty and irregular distribution of troops and military stores had mainly arisen from the necessities attending our first occupation of Oudh at an advanced period of the year 1856. The hot weather was then rapidly setting in: there was not time to erect new buildings, and therefore the most suitable ones which were found ready to hand were appropriated to our several requirements, although often inconveniently placed. Sir Henry Lawrence lost no time in addressing himself to arrange matters so as to place the British force in a more effective military position. He moved up four of Simonds' guns from the Muriaon cantonment to the lines of H. M.'s 32nd, and anxiously looked about for a place of strength in which he could collect together in one his scattered military stores.

At this time the condition of the Province of Oudh was perfectly tranquil. No breeze ruffled the serenity of the still waters. The single proclaimed robber who had given us any trouble, and whose previous deep-dyed offences under the native Government had excluded him from pardon, had been destroyed. There was in Oudh no more of heavy crime than was found in the best-managed districts of the North-Western Provinces. The country had been distributed into four divisions and twelve districts, the former presided over by a Commissioner, the latter each by a Deputy-Commissioner. The police arrangements appeared to give satisfaction to the people. The revenue system certainly did so, in so far as the limitation of its amount is concerned. The land revenue of the districts of two divisions, Khyrabad and Bareytch, had been admirably settled by the intelligent exertions of the two experienced Commissioners, Messrs. G. J. Christian and C. J. Wingfield. In the two remaining divisions the assessment, originally fixed too high, had been carefully revised and reduced. The reduction had been notified to the people by public proclamation, which appeared on the 1st of April, and had given general satisfaction.

CHAPTER II.

THE MONTH OF MAY.—THE FIRST APPEARANCE OF MUTINY.

Mutiny of the 7th Regt. of O. I. Infantry.—Objection taken by them to ordinary cartridges.—Attempt to tamper with the 48th N. I.—Military arrangements to quell the mutiny.—Mutiny quelled.—Court of inquiry held. Sir Henry Lawrence endeavours to conciliate the native soldiery.—Attempt of emissaries from the city to tamper with the 13th N. I. discovered.—Men of the 48th and 13th N. I. rewarded at a public durbar.—Sir Henry's address.—Demeanour of the native officers.—Remarks by the soldiery.—Anxiety respecting the conduct of the 3rd Light Cavalry at Meerut.—News of the outbreak at Meerut reaches Lucknow.—Sir Henry disposes of the mutineers of the 7th O. I. Infantry.—What punishment was awarded.—A second telegraphic message received, announcing the fall and mutiny of the troops at Dehli.—Anxiety felt about the Residency Treasury.—Captain Hayes and Mr. Gubbins recommend that a European guard be placed over it.—Sir Henry Lawrence consents.—Delay.—European Infantry and Artillery placed over the Treasury on the 16th.—The rest of the 32nd Regt. move to cantonments.—Their position described.—European officers residing near the abandoned European lines leave their houses.—Regular payment of land revenue.

SUCH was the state of things at the beginning of May, 1857. The state of the soldiers now became daily the subject of more and more anxiety. On the 7th of May mutiny first appeared in one of our regiments, the 7th O. I. Infantry, stationed at Moosa Bagh. Captain Graydon, the Commandant, had gone on sick leave to the hills, and the regiment was temporarily commanded by Lieutenant J. T. Watson. The recruits of this regiment refused to use their cartridges, objecting that the sepoys of their regiment declared that the cartridges had been tampered with. In effect nothing could have been more groundless than the objection. It was blank cartridge which they were using, of precisely the same make and appearance with that which they had always used. Their officers endeavoured to persuade the men to return to obedience, and hoped at first that they had succeeded. Some of the native officers promised to set the example next day of firing the obnoxious cartridges. Next day, however, when the men were drawn out for this purpose several of the sepoys called out to the native officer, who was preparing to fire, that it was useless, for even if he used the cartridge they would not. Hearing this he also desisted, and the whole corps being manifestly in a state of mutiny, the fact could no longer be concealed, and came to the knowledge of Sir Henry Lawrence. Immediately Brigadier Gray received orders to parade the regiment, make every possible explanation, and induce the sepoys, if possible, to return to their duty. This was done, but the attempt failed. When called upon to state what was their objection to use the cartridge, the men replied that other regiments had taken objection to them and so must they.

All attempts to restore the regiment to obedience having failed, Sir Henry Lawrence resolved to employ force against them, and to disarm them. This was the more necessary, for the mutineers lost no time in seeking the aid and support of the 48th N. I. in cantonments. On the morning of the 16th they addressed a missive to that regiment, and sent it to one of the soobahdars. It was stated in the Hindoo letter that they had taken this step from religious considerations, and they called on the 48th as their "elders" or "superiors" to support them. Fortunately no one was found immediately who could read the note; and it fell into the hands of the young sepoy who was writer in the office of the Adjutant Lieutenant Smith. Perceiving its seditious import he told the soobahdar that it could not be read aloud, and then both proceeded to deliver it up to the adjutant and commanding officer. It was now evidently necessary to act with decision. Accordingly Sir Henry Lawrence ordered the European Infantry and guns, two regiments of N. I., and the 7th Light Cavalry, with Gall's Horse, to march upon the mutineers. The orders were issued late on Sunday, the 10th of May, and it was not till past nine o'clock at night that the force assembled at the lines of the mutineers. These, after proceeding to the extreme of insolence, threatening their officers with violence, and arming themselves, had afterwards lowered their tone, when they learned the preparations which were being made to coerce them.

We found them drawn up by a bright moonlight in line. The guns were placed opposite to them, and they and the European Infantry were so disposed as to be able to turn their fire upon the regular native regiments should they fail in their duty. Sir Henry Lawrence with his staff occupied the space between the guns and the mutineers. Some little delay occurred while the last-arrived corps were closing into their place, during which, by some mistake, one of the artillery serjeants lighted a port fire. The guns were loaded, and standing as we were with Sir Henry Lawrence between them and the mutineers, our position was not exactly comfortable. In the uncertain light of the moon some mistake might have occurred. Certainly so thought the mutineers, for not many moments elapsed after the lighting of the port fire before they were seen to be running. Gaps first appeared here and there in the line, and then the great mass of the regiment broke and fled. About 120 men stood still. A squadron of the 7th Light Cavalry galloped off to intercept the fugitives. Sir Henry rode up to the men that remained, and bade them lay down on the ground their muskets and accoutrements. The order was at once obeyed: the men laid down their pieces and took off their cross-belts, with subdued exclamations of "Jye Company ki,"* "Jye Company Bahadoor ki."† They were then told to go to their lines, guards of the 4th O. I. Infantry and Gall's I. Cavalry, both of which had behaved well, were placed: and the affair was over. Before two in the morning the troops had returned to their several lines. During the next few days a court of inquiry sat to investigate the causes and particulars of this mutiny; but were able to discover little. The European officers indeed could indicate those men who took the most conspicuous part in the outbreak, and these were put in irons. The weather having greatly increased in heat, Sir Henry Lawrence now left the Residency, and removed to a bungalow belonging to the Chief Commissioner in the cooler Muriaon cantonments.

Having thus vigorously put down the first overt act of mutiny, Sir Henry applied himself to conciliate the native soldiery by every means in his power. Instructions were addressed to the civil officers to give precedence of hearing to those cases in which a sepoy was a party, and the Chief Commissioner himself not unfrequently visited the native lines and hospitals, and conversed familiarly with the men. A few days previously a sepoy of the 13th N. I. had shown marked fidelity. Two natives from the city had gone down to cantonments, and endeavoured to tamper with the men of the 13th N. I. They recommended them to mutiny, and said that

* "Victory to the Company."

† "Victory to the illustrious Company."

there were those in the city who would reward them well. The sepoy pretended to consent, and to accompany them to the city; but leading them by the house of his officer, Captain Germon, he made them prisoners, and reported their treason. It was resolved to reward publicly this man, and the soobahdar and men of the 48th, who had surrendered the letter addressed to the regiment by the mutineers of the 7th O. I. Infantry. A public durbar was accordingly held at the Chief Commissioner's residence in cantonments, on the 12th of May, which was attended by all the chief civil and military officers. Chairs were provided in the garden grounds for all the native officers of the troops in cantonments, who were addressed by Sir Henry in a speech well suited to the occasion. They were reminded of the paternal care with which the British Government had always treated them, and how carefully all interference with their religion had been avoided. Mussulman rulers at Dehli have persecuted Hindoos, said Sir Henry, Hindoo rulers at Lahore have persecuted the Mussulmans; but the British Government has ever extended equal toleration to all. The history of a hundred years, said he, should teach them the falsehood of those who would now deceive them with assertions that the Government entertained designs against their caste. He pointed out the vast power of England; and lastly, appealed to them not to endamage the glory and good name borne by the Bengal army for a hundred years. Dresses of honour and purses of money were then bestowed upon those persons who had merited reward. After which the durbar rose, and we mixed with the native officers, forming various groups, and discussing the momentous events of the time. The bearing of these men was then decidedly favourable. Most of them eagerly declared their own attachment, and the part which they either had taken, or were willing to have taken, in the suppression of the recent mutiny. A number of sepoys were standing round the space appropriated to the durbar. We subsequently learnt that the remarks which they were overheard to make, were of a different character; and that they attributed the whole proceeding to our fears.

During the first days of the month we had heard of the refusal of the 3rd Light Cavalry at Meerut to use the cartridges which had been served out to them early in the month. It was known that a reference was pending on the subject, and some anxiety was felt as to the result; when on the 13th of May, a message from the Lieutenant-Governor at Agra by electric telegraph, announced the fact of a serious mutiny having taken place. All the native regiments at the station were stated to have mutinied, and after committing incendiarism and murder, to have marched towards Dehli. This news was indeed appalling. It was felt that a great crisis was at hand, in which the capital which we held was sure to be involved. Sir Henry's thoughts were mainly occupied in revolving how best to turn to advantage the priority of information which had thus been gained by aid of the telegraph; how best to anticipate the ill effect which that intelligence, when it became generally known, would have on the minds of the native soldiery.

It appeared to him necessary at once to dispose of the case of the 7th O. I. Infantry which was on hand, and to reassure the minds of the majority of the men of the regiment, whom he had decided not to punish with severity. The Court of Inquiry had elicited little. The native officers and men appeared to be too closely banded together to afford hope of further discovery. The Chief Commissioner, therefore, disposed of it himself. The ringleaders, to the number of about forty, were kept in irons, and the rest of the mutineer regiment was paraded at the Moosa Bagh in company with the 4th O. I. Infantry, the first of course without arms; the latter carrying their muskets. There they were harangued by Sir Henry, who reduced all the native officers, dismissing most of them, and promoting a few who had behaved well. The rest of the men he pardoned, and directed that they should, till further orders, do duty without arms. Their arms he promised should be restored to them when they had deserved it by their good conduct. The 4th O. I. Infantry were praised, and several native officers of that regiment were promoted.

Sir Henry Lawrence's mode of treating this first case of mutiny was, in my judgment, eminently judicious. To have dismissed the privates would have served no good purpose. The parties most to blame were the native officers, and these were all reduced or dismissed, the ringleaders being kept for severe punishment.

Up to this time no change had taken place in the disposition of the troops as before described. A company of sepoys still guarded the Treasury containing thirty lacs of rupees in specie, besides a still larger amount of deposited Company's paper. A second telegraphic message, received on the 14th, had brought us the still more alarming intelligence of the seizure of the city of Dehli, with its treasury and magazine, and of the defection of all the troops at that station. We heard at the same time of the murder of several European officers and ladies, and that the King of Dehli had put himself at the head of the mutineers.

To myself, therefore, and to Captain Fletcher Hayes, Military Secretary to the Chief Commissioner, it appeared that the time had arrived for taking effective measures to protect the Residency and the treasure at Lucknow. It was still entirely in the hands of the sepoys. The European Infantry were still in their barracks a mile and a half distant. The European Artillery were in cantonments. The Treasury might be plundered, and the Europeans residing about the Residency destroyed, before aid could be received from either quarter. After communicating our sentiments, we resolved to press the subject on Sir Henry Lawrence, and, accordingly, on the 15th of May, we earnestly urged upon him the necessity of moving up a party of Europeans and artillery to the Residency. To this measure we found Sir Henry Lawrence much opposed. It would, he thought, alarm the sepoys, and provoke the dreaded outbreak. He clung still to the hope of conciliating them, and urged the necessity of treating them with confidence. After much anxious debate, however, he partly yielded his assent, and I received his authority to address Colonel Inglis, to inquire whether the Colonel had any objection to detach a party of the 32nd Regt. to the Residency. Colonel Inglis's reply disclaimed any objection, provided that the detachment were not less than 100 men. Nothing, however, was effected on that day.

Next morning the question was again discussed at my house by Sir Henry with Brigadier Handscomb, with whom the chief military command then lay. It was admitted that it was necessary to adopt some precautionary measures to secure the Residency and Treasury; and also to protect the European officers in cantonments, whose only defence from the native troops, by whom they were surrounded, was a weak company of European Artillery. Finally, it was decided that a party of European Infantry and some guns, with the women and sick of the 32nd Regt., should be brought up to the Residency, and that the rest of the regiment should be moved down under canvas to the Muriaon cantonment. This consultation was held on Saturday the 16th of May; the move was fixed for Monday the 18th. Meanwhile preparation was to be made, and I was charged with clearing the Residency buildings for the reception of the troops. The latter measure was immediately commenced. The furniture of the many rooms of the Residency was collected together into a few, and the detached building, termed the Banqueting Hall, which was occupied by the clerks' establishment and Records of the Chief Commissioner's Office, was emptied: the records, &c., being removed to the buildings which formed the Offices of the Judicial and Financial Commissioners.

I had strongly opposed the delay of two days in moving the troops, which had been resolved on; and now, while superintending these arrangements, my opinion of the inexpediency of the delay was confirmed. The Treasury lay directly adjoining and below the Banqueting Hall, and it was impossible to conceal from the sepoy guard the preparations which were being made. They saw the building immediately above them being cleared out, and it was well known that this was being done to admit European soldiers. No words could have evidenced our distrust of themselves more clearly than these acts. What was there to prevent them, so soon as it was known that the Europeans would not move till the Monday, from rising during the two nights and the Sunday which would intervene, and making the Treasury their own? The danger seemed imminent. If the Treasury were lost, what chance of successful resistance should we have? I despatched, therefore, a horseman to Sir Henry Lawrence in cantonments, with a note urging these considerations, and entreating that the Residency might be occupied by the Europeans before night. My messenger returned with a few hurried lines from Sir Henry, authorizing me to order up a party of Europeans without delay. This was forwarded at once to Colonel Inglis. Before nightfall on that day 120 Europeans of the 32nd Regt., under Captain Lowe, with the women and sick, and four guns of Simonds' Battery, marched into the Residency enclosure, and the Treasury was safe.

The women were placed in the tykhana or underground story of the Residency, the sick in the Banqueting Hall, and the men were distributed partly in the lowest story of the Residency and in the Banqueting Hall, from the plateau of which they looked down directly on the heads of the sepoy guards below.

On the next morning, Sunday, the rest of the regiment marched down to the cantonment, and there encamped. The terrific heat of the weather, however, told severely upon the men, as had been feared. And after a few days the officers of the 13th N. I. surrendered their mess-house for the use of the Europeans, and some other buildings having been obtained close by, the whole were ere long placed under shelter. The position of the Europeans was close to that of the European battery, at the right entrance or city side of the cantonments. The withdrawal of the European force from the Chowpeyrah barracks rendered the whole of that vicinity insecure. Accordingly, the Commissioner of Lucknow, Major

Banks, who occupied an exposed building on the Dilkoosha Road, abandoned it, and removed with his family to my house. Mr. S. N. Martin, the Deputy-Commissioner of Lucknow, also removed his family from the house which he occupied in the same quarter, and obtained shelter for them in the Residency. The ladies of the 32nd Regt. were kindly received by Sir Henry Lawrence in his cantonment residence.

On the 1st of May, the first of the summer instalments of Land Revenue fell due in the Province. The payment of this tax is as good a test as can be selected of the feeling as well as of the condition of the people. No difficulty was experienced in the collection. No measures of *duresse* were found necessary. The revenue flowed in with the greatest regularity, and all the district treasuries were soon full.

CHAPTER III.

MAY 17.—MUCHEE BHOWUN.

Sir Henry Lawrence, casting about for a place of strength, fixes on the Muchee Bhowun.—Occupied and garrisoned, and repairs begun on the 17th May.—Muchee Bhowun described.—Military stores removed into it.—Adjacent buildings removed.—Mr. Gubbins begins fortifying his own house.—Objections made to remove adjacent buildings.—Description of Mr. Gubbins' compound, or enclosure.—Sir Henry Lawrence invested with full military powers, as Brigadier-General.—Accounts received by the telegraph, which passed through Mr. Gubbins' hands, from Mr. Colvin at Agra, from Sir Hugh Wheeler at Cawnpoor.—Detachment of Europeans sent to aid Sir Hugh Wheeler at Cawnpoor, accompanied by Captain Fletcher Hayes.—Expedition up the Grand Trunk Road projected and undertaken by Hayes.—Mutiny of the cavalry with Hayes.—Murder of Mr. R. Fayrer, Hayes, and Lieutenant Barbor.—Carey's escape.—Faithful conduct of the Seikh Naib Risaldar Sheyresingh.—Visit paid to Lucknow by the Nana of Bithoor in April.—Suspicions regarding it.—Communicated to Sir Hugh Wheeler, but disregarded.—Alarm communicated from Cawnpoor on the occasion of the Eed.—Precautions taken.—Symptoms of ill-feeling among the native soldiery.—Incendiarism.—Lines of the 13th and 48th Regts. of N. I. burned down.—Placards.—Ladies removed from the cantonment on the 26th May.—Located in various houses at the Residency.—Sir Henry Lawrence calls for written opinions on the proposal for increasing the pay of the sepoys of the line.—Majority opposed to the measure. —Abandoned in consequence.—Continued ill reports by telegraph from Agra.—Mr. Colvin requests aid of a party of Irregular Horse.—Departure of Gall's expedition intended to move up the Grand Trunk Road.—Symptoms of mutiny among the infantry of Gall's force at Cawnpoor.—Its return.—Captain H. Forbes' escape.—Alarms at Allahabad.—Captain Hardinge, with a wing of his regiment, deputed there.—Continued tranquillity in Oudh.—Incipient symptoms of disturbance in the province, on the part of some of the talooqdars.—The same shown by the zemindars of Mulheabad.—Captain Weston deputed to coerce them.—Major Burmester's moveable column, accompanied by Major Marriott and Lieutenant Hutchinson, sent towards Futtehgurh. —Mutinies on the way.—Burmester, Farquharson, N. Martin, and Staples slain.—Captain Boulton escapes into Sir Hugh Wheeler's intrenchment.—Beginning of defences about the Residency.—Additional

troops moved up there.—Treasure brought in from several of the districts.—Attempt to bring it in from Duriabad fails.—Intercourse of Mr. Gubbins with native gentlemen of the city at this time described. —Sir Henry Lawrence meets them.—Copy of Mr. Colvin's proclamation reaches Lucknow.—Sir Henry Lawrence issues a similar one in Oudh.—Telegraphic message from the Governor-General.—Also from Sir Hugh Wheeler on the 26th May—and from the Lieutenant-Governor.—Disarmament of sepoys discussed.—Why abandoned.—Captain Hardinge arrives with a wing of the 3rd O. I. Cavalry at the capital.—Sir Henry Lawrence's untiring exertions.—His health fails.

I HAVE before mentioned that Sir Henry Lawrence was casting about for a place of strength in which to concentrate his ammunition and military stores, and to serve as a place of refuge in case of attack. The position and buildings of the Muchee Bhowun had attracted his attention early in the month, and he had consulted the Chief Engineer, Major Anderson, as to the possibility of putting the place into an efficient state of repair in time. Major Anderson did not think that the very extensive repairs required could be effected within the period which seemed available, and the project had been deferred. Now, however, Sir Henry resolved to put it into execution. On the 17th of May, he directed that the repairs of this post should immediately be commenced under the superintendence of Lieutenant M. Innes of the Engineers; and a garrison, European and Native, was placed in it under command of Major Francis, of the 13th N. I. Some description of this post is required.

Proceeding on the main road, leading from the Residency towards the Dowlutkhana and Hoseynabad, up and parallel to the stream of the Goomtee, you pass under the walls of the Muchee Bhowun, which from this and some other positions on the river has an imposing appearance. It comprised three plateaus, of which the lowest was little above the level of the road, and the highest towered above the neighbouring buildings. The high road skirted the whole length of the position, and followed the level of the ground, which rose naturally from the lowest eastern plateau to that of the highest on the west side. From the road on that, *i. e.* the west extreme of the position, a short but steep ascent led to the main gateway. The highest plateau was covered with the "bhowuns" or pavilions originally built by the Seikhs of Lucknow, which were in a very dilapidated condition, and contained the modern residence of one of the ex-King's brothers, Newaub Yuheea ali Khan. On the second plateau stood a handsome baradurree,* and a few smaller buildings. The lower plateau was an open square, surrounded by low ranges of masonry sheds. There was no gate leading directly from the outside into the second plateau; but two opened into the lower, one at the east end, the second from the main road on the north side. There was no appearance of military defence in the character of the buildings, except in the high and buttressed wall, which rose from the main road to the bhowuns of the highest plateau.

When the Seikhs held Lucknow in times long gone by, it had been their stronghold, but for many years under the Oudh dynasty it had been used as a receptacle of stores, old tents, &c. On the south side the ground was of the same level as that on which the Muchee Bhowun was built, and was thickly covered with native buildings, which extended up to the walls of the place itself, and overlooked completely the second and lower plateaus. From the upper plateau of the Muchee Bhowun, the stone bridge over the Goomtee was completely commanded. The buildings it contained, when all put into repair, might accom-

* Open arcaded pavilion.

modate at most about 350 Europeans and the same number of natives. So soon as it was determined to convert this into a place of strength, Lieutenant Thomas, of the Madras Artillery, was directed to remove into it the magazine and stores from the Sheesh Muhul near the Dowlutkhana; and the civil authorities received orders to value and pull down the adjacent buildings on the north and east; those on the south were too extensive to be interfered with. Some days later, the gunpowder was removed from the Kudduum Rusool Tomb, and placed in the Muchee Bhowun. The O. I. Light Horse Battery, commanded by Lieutenant D. C. Alexander, was also removed from the Muriaon cantonment, and added to the garrison.

About this time I commenced fortifying my own house. It comprised two stories, and was solidly built of masonry, and stood in a pretty garden of no great extent. Being exposed on three sides to the city, it appeared to me not unlikely that it would be one of the first points attacked in case of an insurrection of the city people, against which it was necessary at once to make provision. The roof was flat, and a narrow spiral staircase led to it from the ground-floor, the entrance to which could easily be defended. I accordingly proposed, in case of alarm, to take refuge on the roof, and there to defend ourselves. For this purpose masonry parapets, pierced with loopholes, were erected all around the roof, and the verandahs and doorways of the lower story were similarly protected with walls of masonry: and strong doors, cased with sheet iron on the outside, were fixed upon the entrances on the ground-floor.

The compound or enclosure in which the house stood presented a surface of some unevenness, for it

On Stone by W. L. Walton. V. Eyre, delt. Printed by Hullmandel & Walton.

M^CGUBBINS' HOUSE, LUCKNOW.

London: Richard Bentley, New Burlington Street, 1858.

sloped from the house down to the enclosing wall on the south. On that side the ground inside was low; considerably lower, indeed, than the level of the lane outside, which separated the compound from the Goindah Lines.

There were two porticos, one on the west, the principal one on the south side. The latter was overhung by a magnificent forest tree, which rose high above the upper story of the house, affording a grateful shade. It was a beautiful tree. The native name I have forgotten, but it is of a kind peculiar to Oudh: at least I have never seen one out of the Province. In the spring it was covered with large bunches of pale yellow blossom, together with which a few leaves appeared. The blossom presently withered, and the tree was by that time covered with a gorgeous furniture of pendant leaves.

It was on the south side, as will be seen, that we became during the siege most exposed to the enemy's artillery. One gun alone used generally to salute us with seven or eight shots at daybreak. We called it the Lane Gun. The trunk and massive branches of the tree I have spoken of were interposed between the house and the fire of this gun: and many a round shot have they intercepted. Gradually the boughs were shot away, till at length little but the stem and a few main branches remained, which are shown in the illustration by the pencil of Colonel Eyre. The Seikh Risaldar Sheyresingh, on the occasion of one of them being cut away, and falling with a crash near us, once wittily remarked to me that the tree had done its duty well: or, as he expressed it, "it has well repaid all 'the Company's salt.'" Poor tree! its roots were in the ground; and from its battered trunk leaves and blossom have doubtless once more sprung, and it is now green again amidst that scene of ruin! So is the eye of Faith raised to behold the more splendid glories above of those noble soldiers of God and of their country who, faithful before in peace, and faithful doubly in that fearful struggle, left their shattered earthly frames to moulder in the neighbouring churchyard.

On the north side, the houses of the city approached so closely that a narrow lane only separated my house from them. I was anxious that they should be removed; but at the time I could not effect it. Major Anderson, the Chief Engineer, could not at this period realize the possibility of our houses being seriously assaulted. Indeed, he thought that if they were attacked it would be found sufficient to have demolished the upper parapet wall and upper floors of the houses which threatened us. Sir Henry Lawrence, on the other hand, shrunk from the idea of doing needless injury to any one, and the buildings remained.

Along part of the west and south sides, my compound was bounded by a line of out-offices, stables, and servants' houses. These were of masonry, and had flat roofs. Along these also I erected parapet walls pierced with loopholes. For about 100 yards on the south front a low and weak brick wall bounded the compound; and as the ground outside was much higher than the garden within, any one standing outside overlooked the wall, and completely commanded the enclosure. This wall carried you on to a high square flat-roofed building, which was untenanted, and belonged to a native who was absent from Lucknow. I now took possession of it; caused ladders to be made for reaching the roof, and erected a parapet wall around it. It subsequently received the name of Grant's Bastion, from being usually the post of an officer of that name, who was killed during the siege.

At this time I was the only one who seriously contemplated the possible attack of the Residency; and my preparations were not carried on without provoking the mirth of some of my neighbours.

Until the middle of May, the chief military authority in Oudh was vested in Brigadier Handscomb, who commanded the regular troops in the Province, and resided in the Muriaon cantonment. He was subordinate to the Major-General commanding the Division at Cawnpoor, Sir Hugh Massey Wheeler. After the suppression of the mutiny of the 7th O. I. Infantry, Sir Henry Lawrence applied to Government to be invested with full military powers. This was immediately acceded to, and the rank of Brigadier-General was conferred upon him; in virtue of which, about the 20th of May, he assumed command of all the British troops in Oudh.

The telegraph was at this time very busy, and messages were constantly passing and repassing between Sir Henry Lawrence and the Lieutenant-Governor N. W. Provinces at Agra, and Sir Hugh Wheeler commanding at Cawnpoor. The telegraph office was at the Residency, and Sir Henry resided three miles off, in cantonments: all messages therefore, to and fro, were made to pass through me. I received them, and after perusal forwarded them by a horseman to cantonments. The accounts received from Mr. Colvin at Agra were unfavourable. Boolundshuhur had been abandoned. At Alligurh the 9th N. I. had mutinied; the civil authorities had fled from that station, and from the adjoining one of Eytah, situate on the Grand Trunk Road. The

Goojurs had broken out into every excess of violence and plunder, and the people had thrown off all restraint of civil authority. In Mr. Colvin's words, the districts were disorganized; and he requested Sir Henry, if he could spare it, to assist him with a party of Irregular Horse to protect the Trunk Road, and to restore the disturbed districts to order. Not much more favourable were the messages from Sir Hugh Wheeler. The 2nd Light Cavalry, he informed us, were disaffected, but he hoped that the N. I. Regts. would remain firm.

At midnight of the 20th—21st of May, I was aroused by Sir Henry Lawrence, who had received an urgent application for aid from Cawnpoor. It was resolved to despatch immediately a party of Europeans and of Irregular Cavalry to aid General Wheeler. All the post carriages were accordingly collected; and by great exertion, fifty men of the 32nd Regt. under Captain Lowe were put into the carriages, and sent off at an early hour of the 21st. They were accompanied by a squadron of Gall's I. Cavalry and a second of Daly's Cavalry, under command of Lieutenant Barbor, and the brother of the Residency Surgeon, Mr. R. Fayrer, volunteered to accompany him. The party was also accompanied by Captain Fletcher Hayes, Military Secretary to the Chief Commissioner, who went by Sir Henry Lawrence's desire to communicate personally with Sir Hugh Wheeler. Hayes was to have returned after staying a day; but Sir Hugh Wheeler detained him for further communication. Finding that the cavalry was not wanted by the General at Cawnpoor, and knowing how much aid of that description was wanted along the Trunk Road, Hayes projected an expedition up the road with his cavalry, and telegraphed to

Lucknow for permission. Sir Henry Lawrence accorded his sanction in reply, and Hayes marched from Cawnpoor on the 27th May with the Irregular Cavalry, commanded by Lieutenant Barbor, with Mr. Fayrer. They were joined by Lieutenant T. Carey, of the 17th N. I., who was proceeding to the north-west. Gallant fellow as he was, Hayes burned to achieve some distinguished service, and but for the unlooked-for treachery of his men would, I have no doubt, have succeeded in so doing. The last letter which I received from him was dated the 30th of May from Mynpoory, and well expressed the noble spirit which animated him. He thought that too much alarm was generally shown by Europeans, and was persuaded that a bold front and daring would best assist the cause of order. He instanced his own unmolested march from Cawnpoor, along a line of road supposed then to be impassable, and informed me of his intention of pushing up the road as far as Eytah, and reducing to obedience, if possible, the rebellious Raja of that place. Alas! poor fellow, it was ordered otherwise.

On the morning of the 1st of June, Hayes and Lieutenant Carey left Mynpoory to rejoin the detachment, which was marching up the Trunk Road. Before starting Hayes had been warned that treachery was intended; but he did not credit the informant. He reached the detachment at Kerowlee, just as the treachery had broken out into action. Young Fayrer, while in the act of drinking water at a well, was cut down by one of the troopers with a sword blow on the neck. One of the native officers rode up, and warned Hayes and Carey of their danger, and they at once turned their horses and fled. Hayes was a bad rider, and his horse was tired. He was soon overtaken, cut down, and killed. Carey, an excellent horseman and well mounted, distanced his enemies, who pursued him for several miles, and got safe into Mynpoory. The commander of the party, Lieutenant Barbor, seeing what was taking place, galloped off in the direction of Alligurh, but was intercepted by the advance guard of his own men. He endeavoured to charge through them, and wounded two of the mutineers severely, but fell, overpowered by numbers. The troopers then drew up, and the chief Risaldar * proclaimed that Hindoos and Mussulmans were all one, and the King of Dehli was their sovereign, and to him they would march. A Naib Risaldar,† a Seikh of Daly's Horse named Sheyresingh, with a Seikh trooper, feigning illness, presently lagged behind and got away, and assisted in conveying the bodies of the slain, with the aid of the police and Hayes' servants, to Mynpoory, whence a messenger was immediately despatched down the road to give warning to a second party of Irregular Horse under Major Gall, which was then expected from Cawnpoor.

I must here mention a visit which was made to Lucknow, in April, by the Nana of Bithoor, whose subsequent treachery and atrocities have given him a pre-eminence in infamy. He came over on pretence of seeing the sights at Lucknow, accompanied by his younger brother and a numerous retinue, bringing letters of introduction from a former Judge of Cawnpoor, to Captain Hayes and to myself. He visited me, and his manner was arrogant and presuming. To make a show of dignity and importance, he brought six or seven followers with him into the

* Native captain of a squadron.

† Native lieutenant of a troop.

room, for whom chairs were demanded. One of these men was his notorious agent Azimoolla. His younger brother was more pleasing in appearance and demeanour. The Nana was introduced by me to Sir Henry Lawrence, who received him kindly, and ordered the authorities of the city to show him every attention. I subsequently met him parading through Lucknow, with a retinue more than usually large. He had promised before leaving Lucknow, to make his final call on the Wednesday. On the Monday, we received a message from him that urgent business required his attendance at Cawnpoor, and he left Lucknow accordingly. At the time his conduct attracted little attention: but it was otherwise when affairs had assumed the aspect which they did at Cawnpoor, by the 20th of May. His demeanour at Lucknow, and sudden departure to Cawnpoor, appeared exceedingly suspicious, and I brought it to the notice of Sir Henry Lawrence. The Chief Commissioner concurred in my suspicions, and by his authority I addressed Sir Hugh Wheeler, cautioning him against the Nana, and stating Sir Henry's belief that he was not to be depended on. The warning was unhappily disregarded: and on the 22nd of May a message was received, stating that "two guns and three hundred men, cavalry and infantry, furnished by the Maharaja of Bithoor, came in this morning."

The Mahomedan festival of the Eed fell on the 24th of May, and considerable apprehension was felt of an outbreak on that day. At eleven o'clock on the night of the 23rd, a telegraphic message arrived from General Wheeler, stating that "it is almost certain that the troops will rise to-night." Accordingly, the inmates of my house passed the night on the roof, whither our arms were conveyed, and we listened for sounds of artillery from the direction of Cawnpoor. Nothing, however, occurred; and the Eed passed off without any disturbance. Still the telegraphic messages, which came twice and often three times a day, showed that the rising of the troops was hourly apprehended. They had arranged a place of rendezvous, the church at Cawnpoor, in which the ladies took refuge at night; and those of Sir Hugh Wheeler's family went into it on the night of the 23rd.

Up to the 25th no further overt act of mutiny had been committed by the sepoys at Lucknow. But there were abundant symptoms of ill-feeling, leading to the belief that it could not be long delayed. Incendiarism had everywhere marked the first movements of the mutineers at other stations, and from the beginning of the month this had shown itself at Lucknow. Attempts were made to fire several bungalows by shooting arrows at the thatch wrapped with burning tow. But these had failed. The lines of two regiments, the 13th N. I. and the 48th N. I., had been burnt down. And it was clear that the fires were not accidental. Incendiary placards, calling upon all true Hindoos and Mussulmans to rise and exterminate the "Feringhees," were posted up at night in several places. Reports that the 71st Regt. was in actual mutiny had more than once got about, and on one occasion Sir Henry Lawrence and the military staff had been called down to the lines in the middle of the day by an alarm of the kind. It was believed that a rise of the troops at Cawnpoor would be immediately followed by one at Lucknow. It was, therefore, thought necessary that the ladies should leave cantonments, and take shelter in the Residency and adjacent houses. Accordingly, on the 25th, they all came up, and in the midst of much confusion and alarm were accommodated in the Residency, and in the houses of Dr. Fayrer, and the Judicial Commissioner, Mr Ommanney. My house was filled; Mrs. Couper, Mrs. Inglis, Mrs. Hayes, Mrs. Brydon, besides the former inmates, having found refuge with us.

Sir Henry Lawrence still clung to the hope of averting the threatening storm by conciliation, and thought that the offer of increased pay might yet enlist the native soldiery on our side. On the morning of the same day on which the ladies came up, I was instructed to summon a number of officers named, who were most in Sir Henry Lawrence's confidence, including Major Banks, Mr. Ommnaney, Captain Carnegie, and others, and require from them written answers to two proposals. The first of these was, to increase materially the pay of the regular native troops of the line; and the second, to raise the pay of the Irregulars and Oudh local regiments to an equality with that of the line. In laying these proposals before us, Sir Henry observed, that he was aware that the adoption of this measure on his part would necessitate its extension by the Government of India to the whole regular army; but he thought that the smaller number of native regiments, which would hereafter be employed, would more than counterbalance the increase of the rate of pay.

We were all agreed that the pay of the Oudh Irregulars should be raised. They performed the same duties as the regiments of the line, had hitherto generally evinced a better spirit, and it had been the general opinion that their scale of pay had originally been fixed too low. This measure was accordingly adopted by the Chief Commissioner, and orders were issued notifying the same. The first proposal to raise the pay of the Regulars found no seconder but in the Secretary, Mr. Couper. It was the general opinion, that the offer to increase the fixed pay of the native army, which had been so long established, would be attributed to fear, and would fail of the object desired. Sir Henry Lawrence probably came to the same conclusion, for the idea was abandoned.

There was, among thinking men in the garrison at this time, a growing opinion that the time when a conciliatory policy might have proved successful had gone by. It had manifestly failed. And now all further concessions to the native soldiery were viewed by themselves as nothing more than so many fresh signs indicating our sense of our own weakness and of their strength. Public feeling found expression in attaching to the mutineer sepoys the ironical terms of "babes" and "darlings;" which came into such general vogue in common conversation, that I have heard Sir Henry Lawrence himself make use of them with a smile. Indeed, in my garrison this appellation was throughout the siege more used than any other. By the natives themselves, the rebels, including mutineer sepoys, and all others who had joined them, were designated by the general name of "budmâsh," or bad characters.

The Lieutenant-Governor's messages from Agra continued to tell of little but the delay in the advance of the Commander-in-Chief upon Dehli, and of the disorganized condition of the districts of the Dooab, which latter state of things began seriously to affect the feeling of the people of our Oudh districts, bordering on the Ganges. Our border magistrates also reported that the utmost disorder prevailed on the other side of the river, and that its contaminating effect was already felt among their villages. Sir Henry

Lawrence accordingly resolved on sending a force of artillery, cavalry, and infantry, up the Grand Trunk Road to assist in restoring order. On the 26th of May, consequently, a force marched for Cawnpoor, under command of Major Gall. It consisted of a squadron of Gall's Irregular Cavalry, under his own command, assisted by a volunteer, Mr. Macrae; four companies of the 4th O. I. Infantry, under Captain Hughes, to which was added one company of the 1st O. I. Infantry; and two light-horse battery guns, under Lieutenant Ashe. The force encamped at Chillanwa, eight miles from Lucknow, on that day. About noon I received an order from Sir Henry to despatch a messenger to countermand Major Gall's advance. This was done, but the horseman brought back an earnest entreaty from Major Gall to be allowed to go on. All the men were described as being in the highest spirits. The commander's request was supported by myself. The force had moved out: its recall would be attributed to alarm: it might at all events march on to Cawnpoor. Sir Henry Lawrence acquiesced in the representation made, and I carried his order to advance to the camp that evening. It was received by all the European officers, Major Gall and Mr. Macrae, Captain Hughes, Lieutenant Soppit, and Dr. Partridge, with loud cheers, and in twenty minutes the force was on the march. It was not destined to accomplish anything. On reaching Cawnpoor, the company of the 1st O. I. Infantry demurred to proceeding further. The whole infantry, therefore, all but forty men, were sent back across the river to Onao. And the cavalry and artillery made one march up the Trunk Road; when they fortunately received intelligence from Mynpoorie, of the disaster which had befallen Hayes' party, and returned. General Wheeler, being short of artillery, retained Lieutenant Ashe, with his guns, at Cawnpoor. Major Gall, Captain Hughes, and the other officers, with the cavalry and infantry, returned to Lucknow. Captain H. Forbes, acting-commandant of Daly's Horse, had at the same time a narrow escape. He had proceeded to Cawnpoor, in order to overtake and take command of the squadron of his regiment on duty with Captain Hayes, and was travelling up the Trunk Road, in advance of Gall's party, in a post-carriage. He was fortunately seen and stopped by the Seikh Naib Risaldar Sheyresingh, who was returning from the scene of Hayes' disaster, just in time to save him from destruction; for a few miles only in advance, the road was covered with mutineers, horse and foot, from whom escape would have been impossible.

About this time the conduct of the troops at Allahabad had caused great uneasiness there, which was communicated by the magistrate, Mr. Court, to Sir Henry Lawrence. The importance of preserving that fortress and magazine was so great, that the Chief Commissioner directed Captain Hardinge to send a wing of his regiment, the 3rd O. I. Cavalry, cantoned at Purtabgurh, to Allahabad. This was done. Hardinge's men behaved well; and for some days kept in check the mutinous 6th Regt. of N. I.

25th of May. Up to this time, despite the disorganized condition of the north-western districts, no overt act of lawlessness and insurrection had manifested itself in Oude. Now, however, some of the disaffected began to manifest their ill-feeling. Some of the worst-disposed talooqdars began to repossess themselves of the villages which they had lost, and especially the Zemindars of Mulheeabad and its neighbourhood, distant about eighteen miles west of Lucknow, manifested marked disaffection. They are descendants of Afredees, originally from the Khybur mountains, greedy, poor, and idle. They began assembling in their villages, and threatened the local treasury at Mulheeabad. To repress them, Captain Weston, with a party of military police, was detached, with apparent good effect.

Sir Henry Lawrence now thought that a demonstration by a small military force moving through the country on our Ganges border might be useful, and as Major Marriott, pension-paymaster at Lucknow, was required to repair to Futtehgurh to disburse the military pensions there, it was resolved that a force should accompany him. The Light and Rifle Companies of the 48th N.I., under Major Burmester and Lieutenant Farquharson, with a squadron of the 7th Light Cavalry, under Captain Staples, with two subalterns, Lieutenants Boulton and Norman Martin, were accordingly ordered out, and marched from the capital on the 28th of May. The force was accompanied by Major Marriott and by Lieutenant Hutchinson, Engineers, in a political capacity, with Lieutenant Tulloh as his assistant, —and the last-named three officers had a special guard of twenty Seikh Irregular Horse. For the first few days, the sepoys and Regular Cavalry behaved well. When, however, the detachment neared the station of Mullaon, tidings of the mutiny at Lucknow reached the men, who soon became insubordinate. They refused to proceed on the road towards Futtehgurh, and took that leading to the Mehndeeghat Ferry over the Ganges, which is on the direct line towards Dehli, taking their officers along with them. Arrived at the ghaut, an effort was made to stay them, and with success. The men agreed to cross the river, and march not to Dehli, but to Cawnpoor, and thence return to Lucknow. About fifty of the worst of them broke away, and started for Dehli. The force was about to cross on the following day, when news of the Cawnpoor mutiny came in, and then all order was at an end. The whole of the men revolted. Lieutenants Hutchinson and Tulloh, with Major Marriott, withdrew under the protection of their twenty Seikhs, who remained staunch, after advising the other officers to come with them. But their advice was declined. Major Burmester and Captain Staples still hoped that their men might be reclaimed to obedience, and resolved to accompany them. The subalterns, of course, remained with their commanders.

That this conduct was mainly dictated by that blind and unwise confidence in the attachment of the native soldiers, which has cost the life of so many a brave officer, is no doubt true. Still it is impossible not to admire the devotion of the soldiers who thus put their lives to peril. Alas! none of these brave men survived. The mutineers marched to Chobeypoor, which is within twelve miles of Cawnpoor, and there made overtures to the Nana. Having arranged the terms for entering his service, they set about the destruction of their officers. These were seated outside their tents in the afternoon, when a party of the riflemen of the 48th and of the troopers approached and fired a volley into them. Burmester, Farquharson, and Norman Martin, fell slain. Boulton seized his horse, assisted his wounded commander, Staples, to mount behind him, and galloped off. He was pursued and fired upon by the mutineers, and Captain Staples fell from his horse killed. Boulton made good his escape into Cawnpoor, and threading his way at night through the lines of the mutineers, sought Wheeler's intrenchment. Early in the gray dawn of the following morning, a single horseman was seen by the beleaguered garrison to approach. The possibility of its being an European did not at first occur to them, and he was fired upon. Presently he was recognised, and welcomed into that sad scene of hopeless suffering and endurance. And there in a few days he found a grave.

Towards the end of May, some slight defensive works were began about the Residency and adjacent compounds; but they were slight, and confined to the most exposed positions, and were chiefly intended as a protection against any insurrectionary movement by the city people. The remainder of Ashe's battery, under Lieutenant Bryce, was also brought up from the cantonment, and placed in the Post-office compound, completely commanding the Treasury and its guard. Orders had also been issued to provision the Muchee Bhowun and the Residency, but no great progress had been made in storing grain. A large amount of treasure had been collected during the month of May, which was now lying out in the district treasuries, and which it was desired to bring in. Parties of the 7th Light Cavalry were sent out to Mullaon and to Oonao, and safely performed this duty. The treasure from Seetapoor and Sultanpoor also arrived safely. At Duriabad was a treasure of nearly threc lacs of rupees, guarded by the 5th Regt. of O. I. Infantry, which Captain W. H. Hawes commanding that corps was ordered to bring in. He attempted to accomplish this, but the fidelity of the regiment failed when the treasure began to be removed, and their conduct became so mutinous that the attempt was abandoned.

During this time I continued to see much of the chief native gentlemen of the city. Newaub Ahmedallee Khan Monowurooddowlah, the nephew of the well-known minister, Hukeem Mehndee;

Newaub Mirza Hosseyn Khan Ikramooddowlah, uncle-in-law to the ex-King; Mohamed Ibrahim Shurfooddowlah, lately the King's minister; Raja Balkishen, the late finance minister; Mirza Hyddur, grandson of the Buhoo Begum* of Fyzabad; Newaub Moomtauzooddowlah, a relative of the Royal Family; Shurfooddowlah Gholam Ruza, a large contractor under the native Government; Mohsunooddowlah, a near relation of the ex-King, and several of the city bankers, constantly attended. Most of these now began to exhibit considerable alarm. They were afraid of popular insurrection, and of the loss which they would suffer from plunder; and were glad to hear of measures of defence being taken. Towards the end of May I was requested by Sir Henry Lawrence to assemble all the respectable native gentry at my house, where he met them, and conveyed his sanction to their arming themselves and followers, and making every preparation for defence. They professed their inability to do much. Monowurooddowlah, indeed, who is a fine manly character, a sportsman and a soldier, and possessed a splendid English battery of guns and rifles by all the best London makers, assured us that he was ready to defend his house. Mohsunooddowlah, on the other hand, who was distinguished by his part adoption of the European style of dress, and by his affecting European society, used to turn almost of a green hue with fear whenever the mutinies were spoken of. Balkishen, a non-combatant Hindoo by profession, and a Kayth by caste, avowed that he dared not look upon a drawn sword, and that for him to fight was impossible.

At this time all the accounts which we received from native sources described the people of Lucknow

* Known in the time of Warren Hastings as the Bhow Begum.

to be in the main well affected towards us. Suffering among some classes, and discontent among many others, we knew to exist; but the mass of persons of influence and of substance, we were told, were on our side. It was suggested that the opinion of Captain Savary, an invalid officer of the Bengal Native Infantry, who had long resided in the city, and had mixed familiarly with native society, should be sought. Accordingly, by Sir Henry Lawrence's desire, the Judicial Commissioner requested a visit from that officer. Captain Savary attended a meeting at my house, at which Mr. Ommanney and myself were present. He was in the European costume, and was manifestly suffering, and out of health. His opinion confirmed that which we had previously received; for Captain Savary thought that there was a preponderance of well-affected persons in Lucknow. He told us, however, what we already knew, that the tax on the retail of opium was very unpopular; and that from the delay in the issue of the promised pensions many of the native gentry were suffering want. He shared our alarm respecting the progress of the mutinies; but hoped that if the rebel troops could be kept out of the capital, the city might remain quiet. Having satisfied our inquiries, Captain Savary returned to his home in the city, and I never saw or heard of him again. I entertain no doubt that when the investment of the Residency suddenly took place on the 30th of June, Captain Savary, as well as some other Europeans, were surprised by that event, and slain.

A copy of the proclamation issued by Mr. Colvin, the Lieutenant of Agra, promising immunity from punishment to all sepoys not concerned in murderous attacks upon Europeans, now reached Lucknow. Sir Henry

Lawrence did not disapprove of it; and directed the Judicial Commissioner to prepare and cause to be issued a notification throughout the Province of Oudh, holding out promises of clemency, not inferior to those promised by Mr. Colvin, to all revolted sepoys who should return to their duty.

Mr. Colvin's proclamation has attained a general notoriety. That issued by Sir Henry Lawrence will probably be first brought to the notice of the English public in the present work. The former state paper has been mercilessly condemned; and if the condemnation so pronounced be just, it must be extended to the still more lenient proclamation issued by Sir Henry Lawrence. I must not, however, conceal my opinion that the public censure upon Mr. Colvin has been undeservedly severe. At the time, at Lucknow, though myself and others considered the spirit of both proclamations to be too lenient, we did not regard the clemency to be so great as to be dangerous, and did not attach much importance to their issue. We never interpreted Mr. Colvin's proclamation so as to include those sepoys who had shared the murder of their officers, although it must be confesed that the words "private persons" were used unhappily. We, however, understood the meaning which they were intended to convey by Mr. Colvin, and should have been glad if his notification had availed anything to detach from the more dangerous and determined mutineers, those who had joined the rebel ranks, "because they could not get away." However myself, and I believe others, expected little benefit from it. We felt that the conspiracy which had given rise to such fearful outbreaks in the soldiery could not be stayed by so mild a measure. It might, indeed, detach a few from the mutineer ranks, but no general effect could be expected to follow; and, as already stated, little attention was paid to its issue, or to that which was put forth at Lucknow.

Such were the feelings prevalent upon the subject at the time, and near the spot where the proclamation was issued. Viewing the question after a considerable interval of time and space, I find little reason to find fault with Mr. Colvin, or to impugn the justice and policy of this palliative measure, which was adopted in the fearful crisis of the month of May, 1857. A faint hope still existed that the appalling danger might be warded off, and that the dreaded combination of the native troops might be stopped by timely conciliation. If there ever existed just ground for such a hope, which every ruler was bound to entertain as long as it was possible, it was then, when a semblance of order was preserved by the troops at Agra and at Lucknow. A few days later, and that semblance was gone, and open and defiant mutiny glared upon us.

Nor should it be forgotten, that no sooner was Mr. Colvin certified that it was no longer possible to repose confidence upon the native regiments at Agra, than he no longer hesitated, but at once disarmed them: a bold and decided line of conduct, which assuredly merits praise.

By the telegraph we learnt that reinforcements of European troops were being pushed up from Calcutta as fast as the defective means of conveyance allowed. On the 25th of May the Governor-General telegraphed as follows:—"It is impossible to place a wing of Europeans at Cawnpoor in less time than twenty-five days. The Government dawk, and the dawk companies, are fully engaged in carrying a company of the 84th to Benares, at the rate of eighteen men a dawk. A wing of the Madras Fusiliers arrived yesterday, and starts to-day by bullock train, part by steamer. The bullock train can take 100 men a day, at the rate of thirty miles a day. The entire regiment of the Fusiliers, about 1000 strong, cannot be collected at Benares in less than nineteen or twenty days. One hundred and fifty men who go by steamer will scarcely be there so soon. I expect that from this time forward troops will be pushed upwards at the rate of 100 men a day from Calcutta; each batch taking ten days to reach. From Benares they will be distributed as most required. The regiments from Pegu, Bombay, and Ceylon, will be sent up in this way. Every bullock and horse that is to be had, except just enough to carry the post, is retained; and no troops will be sent by steamer which can be sent more quickly by other means. This is the best I can do for you. I look anxiously for the recovery of Dehli. I fear the Commander-in-Chief cannot be there before Tuesday."

On the 26th of May Sir Hugh Wheeler telegraphed the following more favourable account from Cawnpoor:—"All well, very well, and I think likely to continue so, unless some startling event should occur. Captain Hayes' services, freely given, have been extremely valuable. The police under Major Parker admirable, not a single robbery. Electric telegraph from Benares, May 25th, intimates that detachments of Her Majesty's 84th Foot, which had just arrived there, were being forwarded by dâk garrie, as each succeeding detachment would be, as fast as the carriages can take them. Thanks for your aid, which has been so promptly given on every occasion. But I hope we may consider the crisis passed; though the disease is by no means cured. I shall return the men of the 32nd Foot, as soon as 150 men of Her Majesty's 84th arrive; and

I shall be ready to aid and support you, as you have me. Letters tell that all look to Cawnpoor."

Before the month closed, the Lieutenant-Governor had telegraphed to us the disarmament at Lahore of the mutinous native regiments, and later that himself had followed the same course at Agra with success. More than once I discussed with Sir Henry Lawrence the propriety of following the same course at Lucknow. Sir Henry admitted that it was quite possible to disarm the native troops at the capital where there was an European force, and seemed to incline to the measure, had the capital only been to be cared for. It was feared, however, and justly, that the adoption of this measure, though beneficial to ourselves, might precipitate an outbreak of the troops stationed at Cawnpoor, and at the out-stations of Oudh: and on this account the idea of adopting it was relinquished.

About the end of the month Captain Hardinge arrived at the capital with a wing of his regiment, the 3rd O. I. Cavalry, from Purtabgurh, where it would have been of little use. The second wing remained at Allahabad. A wing of the 15th Irregular Cavalry (Fisher's) under Captain Gibbings, had also come in from Seetapoor, escorting treasure.

During all this month Sir Henry Lawrence had been untiring in his exertions. He generally visited the Muchee Bhowun every morning, and any other post that called for his attention. From breakfast until dark he was consulting with his military subordinates, closeted with native officers, or at work with his pen. Under this weight of anxiety and exertion his health had greatly failed. When he came to us in March he was ill. His medical attendant had certified the necessity of his revisiting Europe, and he had reached Bombay *en route* to England, when he received the request of Government that he would remain. He accordingly retraced his steps to Lucknow, to take charge of the Chief Commissionership. The ordinary labours of his office had fully tried his strength; but the intense anxiety attending his position at the present crisis would have worn the strongest frame. At first he was able to ride about a good deal, but now he drove about in his carriage. He lost appetite and sleep, and his changed and careworn appearance was painfully visible to all.

CHAPTER IV.

CAUSES OF THE MUTINY.

Mr. Gubbins' opinion asked as to the causes of the mutiny.—Concurred in by Sir Henry Lawrence.—Causes which are usually assigned, viz.—1st. Russian intrigue; 2nd. A long-matured conspiracy on the part of the Mahomedans; 3rd. Viewed by some as a national revolt; 4th. Attributed by some to the annexation of Oudh; 5th. By others as a religious outbreak, from interference with their prejudices and religion; 6th. By others to the absence of a European force, and mismanagement, loss of discipline, and discontent of the Bengal army.—First cause not capable of investigation.—Second supposed cause prevalent in Bengal.—Its correctness discussed and questioned.—Third supposed cause, viz. a general national revolt, examined and combated.—Apathy of the people noticed and explained.—Want of information rendered by the people noticed.—Outrages committed by city people upon our women and children.—Attributable to the budmâshes.—Their habits explained.—Behaviour of the gentry.—Mahomedan gentry chiefly depend on service.—Their dislike to our Government explained.—Improvement in the native service by Lord William Bentinck.—Its insufficiency.—Some cases of their ingratitude noticed.—Newaub of Jhujjur.—Raja of Bullubgurh.—Good conduct of the Newaub of Rampoor noticed.—Much allowance necessary in considering the conduct of the gentry.—Their ignorance of our resources.

DURING the seven or eight weeks of alarm which had now elapsed, no question more agitated men's minds than that which sought to solve what really were the causes of the mutiny. Could they be clearly developed, it might be possible to apply a remedy. Communications upon this all-engrossing topic were passing in all directions; and, among others, Mr. Colvin, the Lieutenant-Governor at Agra, had inquired my opinion. Before despatching my reply, in which I entered fully into the question, I showed it to Sir Henry Lawrence, who added a memorandum expressive of his concurrence. The condition of the Bengal Native Army had of late years attracted much of the attention of that distinguished officer, and he had published two excellent articles upon the subject, which appeared in the "Calcutta Review." I have therefore the less hesitation in introducing my opinion of the subject in the present work. It would be impossible, indeed, to avoid doing so; for by many persons, both in India and in this country, who are not well acquainted with affairs in Oudh, the annexation of that Province has been assigned as a chief cause of the mutinies. Believing this wide-spread opinion to be founded on error, it would be impossible, in a work treating of the mutinies in Oudh, to avoid examining it. At any rate it would be right to adduce such facts respecting the actual condition of the sepoy in Oudh, as affected by the introduction of the British rule, as may enable the public to form a judgment upon the question. At the same time, as affecting ourselves specially located at the capital of Oudh, the state of feeling of the people of the Province, generally, will have to be described.

The following, then, embrace all the causes that have been adduced, so far as I have heard or read, to account for this wide-spread and unlooked-for mutiny.

First. It has been attributed to Russian intrigue.

Secondly. To a long-matured conspiracy on the part of the Mahomedans.

Thirdly. It is viewed by others as a national revolt.

Fourthly. Not a few attribute the mutinies to the British annexation of the Province of Oudh.

Fifthly. Some regard it to be a religious outbreak of the soldiery, aroused by our interference with their prejudices and religion, in which the people sympathized.

Lastly. It is regarded by others as chiefly attributable to the absence of a sufficient European force; to the condition and management of the Bengal army having been unsound and bad; and to the sepoy having been too much freed from the bonds of discipline, and having become discontented.

Now the first of these supposed causes need not here be investigated, for we had no means of forming an opinion upon it in India. Suffice it to say, that suspicion was present to our minds, but nothing certainly occurred in the Province of Oudh to give support to it. And if the suspicion be well-founded, it appears strange that during those anxious days, when everybody's attention was fixed upon the subject, no evidence at all pointing to Russia should have been obtained.

I pass, therefore, to the second opinion, which prevails a good deal in the Lower Provinces of Bengal, and at the Presidency. Prior to the arrival of Havelock's force, it had not found expression at Lucknow. We had considered the alarm as having been taken by the Hindoo religionists, which the Mahomedans had taken advantage of, had carefully fostered, and had turned to their own ends. And this I really believe to have been the right view of the case. Had the mutinies had their origin in a Mahomedan conspiracy, the first symptoms of disaffection would have manifested themselves among that class at the foci of Mahomedanism in India—Dehli, Agra, Patna, or Lucknow. Such is, however, far from having been the case. Murmurs of discontent among the sepoy regiments stationed in Bengal were first heard in January, and gradually swelled into the uproar of open mutiny. In these regiments the Hindoos exceed the Mussulmans in the proportion of five to one. With us at Lucknow, up to the end of May the sepoy regiments only had shown disaffection. We still trusted the Irregular Cavalry, in which Mahomedans prevailed. Hayes and his comrades had not yet fallen, and we had not yet learnt the bitter lesson that all arms of the service had become untrue. The fact is undeniable that mutiny did show itself first among the Hindoos, and though the Mahomedans joined the conspiracy, they were not the first to begin it. Moreover, were it true that a conspiracy of the Mahomedans was at the bottom of this mutiny, there would assuredly have been more evidence of combination and of design. But there is positively next to none. The most powerful Mahomedan chief in India, the Nizam of Hydrabad, has remained firm, and his contingent, comprising an *élite* Mahomedan cavalry, has not deserted us. To the north and west, the Mahomedan chiefs of Caubul, Candahar, and Beloochistan, have nowise molested our frontier. And even the fanatic Moslem bigots who inhabit the hills around Peyshawur, far from joining any general conspiracy against us, have enlisted in our service, and have remained faithful. The city of Patna, supposed to be the hotbed of Mussulman intrigue, has been little moved, even though the sepoy brigade in the neighbouring cantonment of Dinapoor succeeded in their tardy mutiny.

People have no doubt been misled by the King of Dehli having put himself at the head of the rebellious movement, and endeavoured to revive his fallen dynasty. I apprehend that his conduct will have been found to have been the effect and not the cause of the mutinies. Exasperated by severe usage, and doubtless already leagued with many others in the plot of an intended insurrection, it is probable that the Meerut mutineers looked about for some person of eminence who might head their revolt, and give to their cause the prestige of ancient authority and power. Within thirty miles of them resided the representative of Mahomedan power in India, the descendant of a long line of kings, who maintained within the fortified palace of his ancestors the semblance of imperial dignity. Naturally they turned to him, and their overtures were well received.

The supporters of this opinion lay much stress on a document said to have been found in the Palace of Dehli, being a communication from the Shah of Persia, inciting the King of Dehli to raise the standard of Islaâm. That such a letter should have been received from Persia during our lengthened differences with that State by the chief Mahomedan Court in India, which was known to be unfriendly to us, and unforgetful of its former power, is not surprising. But even taking for granted that the imperial family of Dehli had long been disaffected and meditated treason, it certainly affords no evidence that the Mussulmans originated this fearful outbreak. That they disliked us more than did the Hindoos is both natural and true. The latter had been long accustomed to subjection: the first could not forget that where we now rule, they had long been masters.

Nor will those who support this opinion have succeeded in making out their case, even if the suspicions which ascribed to the minions of the ex-King of Oudh a share in exciting this mutiny be founded on fact. The ex-King himself is an imbecile, who would long ago have been glad to resign the toilsome cares of royalty for the enjoyment of a wealthy retirement, devoted to debauchery and excess, if the minions who surrounded him had permitted. He, therefore, can personally lie under no suspicion. But few men have been ever surrounded by a Court more tainted with crime and villany than Wajid Alee Shah. All the men who composed it had reason enough to hate the British name and power; and nothing is more probable than that they, and the ex-Minister, Alee Nuckee Khan, in particular, should have fanned the rising flame, and done their utmost to excite and maintain the spirit of mutiny which they saw rising in our native soldiery. This fact, however, is quite insufficient to prove that the "fons et origo mali" was Mahomedan. On the contrary, it shows only what we are ready to admit, viz. that the Mahomedans, who dislike our rule in India the most, viewed with satisfaction the disaffection of the Hindoo soldiery, fanned the flame, joined in the movement, and endeavoured, with characteristic energy, to turn it to their own advantage.

Nor is it more just to regard this terrible outbreak in the light of a national revolt. The supposition does violence to all the facts before us. For five months the Anglo-Indian mind had been racked with anxiety. For the fear of what? was it of the people? Had local outbreaks indicated national discontent? Had isolated planters living by themselves, without protection, been cut off? Had the high roads been plundered and postal communication been interrupted, or the telegraph wire been cut? Were the rivers unsafe, and was merchandize no longer carried on the boats which crowd the waters of the Ganges and the Jumna? Had the payment of Government revenue been suspended, and the collector been driven away unsatisfied from any turbulent village? Not so. All these questions must be answered in the negative. The country was quiet; the high roads and rivers were covered with traffic; the post was never interrupted;

justice was administered as usual; revenue was regularly paid—until what? Until the army mutinied. But then it is objected that the people rapidly fell away, and made no stand for their rulers; that they soon broke into acts of violence and robbery; and that even when the cause of the mutineers seemed failing, they testified no good-will, but withheld the information we wanted, and often misled us. These facts are undoubtedly true, and the circumstances under which they occurred deserve consideration.

And first, it must be observed, that affection is a feeling which we have no right to challenge from our native subjects in India. Aliens as we are from them in blood, in feeling, in religion; nowise mingling with them in social intercourse, and interchanging few kindly offices, we have no right to expect from them love and sympathy: least of all, active assistance and support. Even supposing that our government of them were far better than it is, that it was not marked by the many faults and blemishes which undoubtedly disfigure it, still their obligation as subjects would have been discharged, if, in return for a just and equitable rule, they had rendered a faithful and regular payment of their tribute and a quiet and contented obedience. But in India the mass of the people have for centuries been habituated to trouble themselves little about who governs. The villager pays his land-tax to the ruler of the day. Conqueror after conqueror has swept over the country, without touching much the condition of the village communities, who form the great mass of the people. The villager has in turn paid his quota of revenue to Hindoo, to Pathan, to Mogul, and to Mahratta. They passed away; and he paid it to us. True our demand has been moderate, our faith has been good;

but what had he in connection with us that should induce him to lend us active aid, or to imperil life and property to maintain our rule? One good reason he had for not so doing. So long as anarchy prevailed, the peasant paid nothing to any one. He remembered in some quarters the good old times when such had been the case, and was not sorry that they had returned.

We do not, on the other hand, find that the people generally took part with or aided the mutineers. On the contrary, those tribes who from their wild and predatory habits did us most injury, the Goojurs and Meywatties, stopping the posts and robbing the high roads, committed their depredations alike upon the mutineers. No distinction was made: all travellers were equally plundered, whether coming from the camp of the mutineers or from the British cantonment. If it be true, as has been often asserted, that the enemy could always get information of our troops, while the country people were silent as to the movements of the mutineers, it must, I conceive, be attributed to other causes. The enemy was always ready to extort the required information by severities from which we would shrink. He would not hesitate to inflict death or mutilation, if information were withheld from him; we could not thus act. Again, the native is always better competent to gain information in India than the best-informed European. He has often connections, friends, clansmen, living on the spot. But with us, not only are such sources of information closed, but those are not unfrequently selected to procure intelligence, who possess little knowledge or experience of the native habits or character.

Again, the horrible outrages committed by the inhabitants of some of the largest cities in Upper

India, upon defenceless women and children, so soon as the revolt of the native armed force had left them at their mercy, has encouraged the idea of a general disaffection and revolt. It is, however, well known that these atrocities were not shared by the masses of the citizens, but were the work of the "budmâshes," or loose characters, who abound in all large native towns. Budmâsh means strictly a man of bad livelihood. They are more generally Mahomedans, though Hindoos are found among their number. They live by gambling, thieving, and swindling; or by extorting money out of the more respectable natives by threatening insult and abuse. They pass much of their time in our gaols, but too generally escape punishment by availing themselves of our legal technicalities. They revel in a time of riot or disorder; and it is not surprising, that, as soon as civil power was at an end, we should have suffered so severely at their hands.

It must be admitted that the native gentry and local noblemen and chiefs have shown little attachment to our rule; but nothing has transpired to show that these were leagued together in any conspiracy before the army mutiny broke out. When that event took place, the defection of the upper classes was almost universal. It cannot be denied that the native gentry of Hindoostan have not much to thank us for. In the early years of our rule, many old families were ruined by the severity of our assessments. In later times the settlement operations, while they greatly remedied the first defect, have yet much diminished the power and consequence of the talooqdars,* by transferring a large number of the

* Talooqdar meaning "holder of a tâlooqua," or large collection of villages.

villages which they held, to the rightful village proprietors. Of the general justice of this measure there can, I conceive, be no doubt; yet the lengthened period during which it was delayed, twenty or thirty years, caused it to be viewed by the sufferers as a hardship, and gave rise to much discontent among that class.

Again, the native gentry, especially the Mahomedan portion of it in India, look chiefly to the service of the State for a means of subsistence. But as all the chief offices in British India are monopolized by Europeans, the minor ones only are open to them. In fixing the remuneration of those, we have too much followed the scale of pay we found to prevail in the native Governments which we succeeded; forgetting that with them bribes and pecuniary gratifications were not forbidden. Under our system they could not openly be received: and in consequence several departments of the public service have been grossly underpaid. In the police service this was so particularly the case, that it has been found difficult to induce natives of good family to enter it at all. Our revenue service was better paid, and a native officer, responsible for collecting 20,000*l*. per annum, might receive a salary of 20*l*. per month. The natives complained, and with some justice, that in the earlier years of our government we had shown more liberality; and that a native collector had then been used to receive a commission of 10 per cent. on his collections, which would give him ten times the salary which has been latterly allowed.

There is no doubt that since the changes effected in 1832, by Lord William Bentinck, a great improvement had taken place in our native service. That statesman's wise liberality greatly increased the field of native employment, and attached to many branches of the service a liberal reward; yet for all that, the measure of relief was not sufficient: the native gentry were becoming daily more reduced, were pinched by want of means, and were therefore discontented.

It may, however, not unfairly be questioned, whether any measure of generosity would have secured the attachment of the Indian gentry, with the examples of ingratitude and disloyalty which we have before us. Since Dehli was taken, the Newaub of Jujjhur has been hanged for treason. Himself and his family owed their all to us. His ancestor had commanded a body of Irregular Horse under Lord Lake, and had been rewarded by a jagheer, which, if well managed, would have yielded more than twelve lacs of rupees per annum. Neglected and mismanaged, it gave him nine or ten lacs. Several successions had taken place in the family, and the next of kin had regularly succeeded to this valuable inheritance in virtue of the British grant. Yet no sooner did our native army mutiny, and the puppet king raise his standard at Dehli, than our Jujjhur vassal forgot his faith and joined our enemies! Very similar is the story of the Raja of Bullubgurh, who has also lately paid the penalty of his treason at Dehli. He, however, belonged to an old family, anciently settled at Bullubgurh, but had ever been treated by us with kindness and consideration.

Many other cases of like miserable defection might be instanced. Few, very few, in the disturbed districts have kept to their faith. One noble exception, indeed, I should not here omit to mention, Yoosufalee Khan, Newaub of Rampoor in Rohilcund, the representative of one of the original Rohilla chiefs, who, enjoying under British guarantee a valuable territory worth eight or nine lacs per annum, has remained loyal throughout.

Much allowance should, no doubt, be made in considering the conduct of the Indian gentry at this crisis, on account of their want of power to resist the armed and organized enemy which had suddenly risen against us. That enemy always treated with the utmost severity those among their countrymen who were esteemed to be friends of the British cause. Neither their lives nor their property were safe. Fear, therefore, no doubt, entered largely into the motives which induced many to desert us. Again, among the educated gentry even, few had any just idea of our resources. The Asiatic is generally influenced by what he sees. He saw in the North-Western Provinces only a handful of European troops, everywhere threatened with destruction by thousands of the enemy. He did not believe in the existence of the tens of thousands of our countrymen who would hasten to our succour from across the seas. He beheld us everywhere staggering from the shock. He thought our cause was hopeless, and deserted us.

But it is time to consider the fourth cause which has been assigned for the mutinies, viz. the British annexation of Oudh. As, however, in order properly to examine the grounds of this opinion, it will be necessary to describe the condition of this Province at the time when it came under British rule, as well as when the mutinies began, it is necessary to devote to this question a separate chapter.

CHAPTER V.

CAUSES OF THE MUTINY CONTINUED.—CONDITION OF OUDH.

The sepoy class form the peasantry of Oudh.—It had long been oppressed.—Its characteristic feature, viz. that of village communities.—Land-tax, how assessed.—Subdivision of land causes many to seek service.—The chief enemy of the sepoy class has been the talooqdar.—He had an enemy, also, in the revenue official of the native Government.—Extreme poverty and wretchedness of the people of the Province.—Chiefly attributable to the talooqdars, who sought to acquire the right of property belonging to the villagers.—The talooqdarree system saved trouble to the native Government.—Origin of talooquahs.—It answered sufficiently well before it was abused.—Its abuse.—How effected.—Fraud and violence practised by talooqdars.—Gives rise to violence among the people.—The expelled villager becomes a dacoit.—Hundreds of such when we entered Oudh.—How they ceased.—The peasantry under the native rule sought the aid of British authority against this injustice.—Each family made a point of having a relative in our army.—Theory of those who attribute the sepoy mutiny to the annexation of Oudh—explained and refuted.—The sepoy class was that most benefited by the introduction of the British rule.

The sepoy class form the peasantry of Oudh. In considering, therefore, how the sepoys were affected by our annexation of the Province, it is manifestly necessary to possess some just idea of the condition of the peasantry. This had been long in a lamentable state, from the exactions and venality of the King's officials, and from the oppression and violence of the talooqdars. Oudh, though long governed by Mahomedan sovereigns, is essentially a Hindoo province, its population is chiefly Brahmin, and chutree, or rajpoot: and Hindoo institutions form the characteristic of the country. Of these the most marked and universal feature is that of the village communities. The brotherhood which resides in each village is the only real proprietor of the soil, and among its members the ancestral fields are divided. The only person competent to alienate the right in each field, whether by sale, gift, or mortgage, is the individual sharer whose patrimony it is; and each village forms in itself a complete community, or, as the late Lord Metcalfe justly termed it, a separate little republic. Every village has its accountant, and its public servants, the priest, the carpenter, the smith, the washerman, and the watchman, who are generally paid by dues claimable from the grain produce of each shareholder. The payment of a land-tax is one of the oldest institutions of the country. It is levied from the several shareholders, by a rate upon the land, the shares, the ploughs, or the grain produce, and is paid to the Government officer through the head man of the village. The tenacity with which the Hindoo sharer clings to his ancestral fields, and his affection for the soil which he inherits, is unsurpassed in any country. As the numbers of these communities increase, their land no longer affords them a sufficient maintenance, and numbers leave their villages to seek service, returning on leave of absence to visit their families; and retiring when pensioned to live and die in their ancestral home. Such are the features which distinguish the class from which our sepoys are drawn. They are, it will be observed, proprietors, the only proprietors of the soil; and they value this right of property in the land above all earthly treasure.

But in Oudh they have had many enemies who have disturbed them in the enjoyment of this right, and their chief enemy has been the talooqdar.

True he was not the only one. The greedy and

rapacious Government official could and did inflict infinite injury on the villager, by enhancing to an exorbitant amount the demand for Land Revenue; and even where no talooqdar intervened, hundreds of villages have been ruined and desolated by exactions of this nature. Possessed of the most superior natural resources, I have never met with such evidences of general poverty as in Oudh. Miserable and starved cattle, unable to drag the wretched implements of husbandry in use, squalid and deserted villages, ruined wells, and a naked and starved peasantry, sufficiently evidence the wretchedness which prevails.

Much of this misery lies at the door of the native officials of the Kings of Oudh; much more, however, lies at the door of the talooqdar; for he has aimed not only at grinding the peasant by heavy exactions, but has also endeavoured to rob him of his birthright, the property in the soil. The term talooqdar means "holder of a tâlooquah," or "collection of villages;" for the payment of the Land Revenue assessed upon which villages the talooqdar or holder was admitted to engage. The single engagement with one person for a number of villages saved the native Government trouble, and has long obtained; but it used to convey no right of property to the talooqdar in the villages for which he engaged. He paid to the State a lesser sum, and realized from the villages a somewhat larger one, which constituted his remuneration. The size of his talooquah was constantly liable to change. If the central Government was weak and the local official his friend, his talooquah would rapidly expand. If a new official arrived unfriendly to him, he would lose many, or all the villages which he had acquired. It should be observed, that the best native rulers of Oudh were always opposed to the growth of large talooquahs. The Newaub Vizier Saadutalee Khan broke up a number of them, and reduced all to a very moderate size.

These talooqdars varied greatly in their origin. Some, and the greater number, were hereditary heads of rajpoot tribes settled in the neighbourhood. Others again were new families, sprung from some Government official, whose local authority had enabled him to acquire a holding of this description.

Until this system was abused, it no doubt answered well enough; especially where the talooqdar was chief in the tribe for whose villages he engaged. As chief he was the natural medium between his tribe and the Government, and received from the spontaneous regard of his people many perquisites and dues.

But for nearly half a century the talooqdaree system has been greatly abused; and the great aim of the talooqdar has been to supplant the villager in the property of the soil and to constitute himself sole proprietor. Where he succeeded, the owner became a tenant, and was charged with a rent for the land which he occupied without reference to the Government land-tax.

The more usual mode by which this change was effected, was to outbid the owners of a village at the yearly settlement of the land-tax, which generally obtains under native Governments. A talooqdar, possessing a fort and guns, would agree to pay double the tax properly leviable upon a village. He would then draw up an exorbitant rent-roll, which it would be impossible that the cultivators should pay, throw the village into balance; and then seize and confine the villagers, until they signed away their birthright, and executed a deed constituting himself proprietor. These deeds were termed "bye namahs," or deeds of sale and were a by-word of fraud and oppression throughout Oudh.

Sometimes some of the more daring talooqdars would dispense with this somewhat lengthy process for obtaining a bye namah, and would proceed at once to harry a village, burn it, kill the cattle, and drive out the inhabitants, until the required deed was executed.

Against this oppression exercised by the talooqdars little or no redress could ever be obtained. Accordingly the people took the law into their own hands. The dispossessed rajpoot drew his sword, and retired into the jungle, and committed raids upon any one whom the usurping talooqdar endeavoured to settle upon his paternal acres. Driven to this lawless mode of life, he did not confine his attacks to those who trespassed upon his own village, but learnt to prey upon the public generally. He became a dacoit, or professional robber, and a price was set upon his head. There were hundreds of such public offenders in Oudh when we entered the country. And with our rule they ceased. The robber came in and claimed his own, and his own was restored to him. His house arose again on his long-deserted homestead, and the sword and shield were laid aside. Faces that had not been seen for years, and men, at whose names the country side trembled, were seen to enter the crowds, where an English officer presided; and became peaceful citizens.

Now the class against which all this injustice had been committed was precisely that from which our sepoys have been drawn. Under the native Government their complaints were brought to the notice of the Oudh authorities by the intervention of the British Resident. Each family made a point of having some connection in the British army, and through him brought forward their complaints to his commanding officer. The sepoy's petition was countersigned by the English colonel, and forwarded to the Resident, and by him submitted to the King.

Upon this state of things those who link together the annexation of Oudh and the sepoy mutiny, in the relation of cause and effect, build their theory. Under the native rule, say they, the sepoy enjoyed special and preferential privileges, which merged and were lost when Oudh became our own. Before, the English authorities exerted themselves to get justice for him: afterwards, they were bound to render equal justice to all alike; and the sepoy resented the loss of privilege. But for the wide prevalence of this erroneous idea, I should not have thought it necessary to refute an opinion so entirely opposed to fact. The mistake, however, must be corrected.

In effect, the party most benefited by the introduction of our rule in Oudh was the sepoy class. True, their complaints were formerly forwarded through the Resident; but little redress resulted. The British Resident submitted the sepoy's complaint to the King, by whose minister it was forwarded for explanation or redress to the local native officer. This party was probably already long in league with the talooqdar, and if not so before, was easily persuaded, for a valuable consideration, to become his friend. A garbled reply unfavourable to the sepoy applicant, and favourable to the oppressing talooqdar, was in due time prepared, and returned to the minister. The minister sent on this answer with many professions of esteem and regard to the Resident, by whom it was generally forwarded without comment to the Commander, who handed the unsatisfactory document to the complaining sepoy. Some trifling alleviation of the injury complained of might be granted; but this was all. That a sepoy plaintiff ever succeeded in wresting his village from the grasp of the oppressor, by aid of the British Resident, I never heard: if it ever occurred, the cases must have been isolated and extraordinary. What a contrast then, was presented under our rule! Thousands of sepoy families were claimants, and many hundreds of villages at once passed into their hands from those of the talooqdars! Whatever the talooqdar lost the sepoy gained. No one had so great cause for gratulation as he. In the course of my tour through Oudh, I have ridden unattended into many sepoy villages. They all presented one and the same feature; loud complaints of bygone sufferings, mingled with rejoicings at their deliverance. They knew that we brought home money from our regiments cried they, and therefore taxed us the more heavily; but now that has gone by.

I remember, among many, an instance illustrative of the improvement in their condition, which the sepoys derived from the introduction of our rule, which may here be mentioned. It was the case of the village of Akbabad, in the purgunnah of Mugraer, district of Poorwah. It had been included in the extensive talooquah of Doondeea Kheyrah, held by one Baboo Ram-Buksh Singh, a talooqdar belonging to the family which exercised chieftainship in Bysewarrah. He had always been turbulent, and after repeatedly opposing in arms the Government of Oudh, had at length been by them expelled, his fort razed, and himself compelled to fly into the British territories. He has since rendered himself conspicuous by his cruelty to our Cawnpoor fugitives. At the time when the British occupation took place, he was an exile; but soon returned, and laid claim to the proprietary title in all the villages comprised in his late talooquah. The British officers were slow to admit his title, and the summary settlement was made with the villagers, who were rajpoots of the Byse clan, as was Ram-Buksh himself. On the occasion of my riding into this village, where I spent half an hour conversing with the people, they told me that their little village, which did not contain as many houses, furnished upwards of sixty sepoys to our army. They loudly complained of the exorbitant rents imposed upon them formerly by Ram-Buksh, and declared that when these were unpaid he tortured and imprisoned them. If they died in confinement, he threw their bodies into the Ganges, and mocked them by saying that at least they had obtained Hindoo burial! I affected to disbelieve their story, and replied that Ram-Buksh claimed to be proprietor of the village; and, besides, how could a Byse behave so to his own people? They laughed at the idea of his being the real owner; and with loud and bitter asseverations protested that all which they had said was true, and they described the tortures which they themselves had undergone. Their assessment had been greatly reduced. I asked them if they were content with it. They replied in the affirmative, but added that it was heavy still; and finding, on fuller inquiry, that they were right, I caused it to be still further reduced.

It is impossible to reconcile the facts which have been here given with the opinion of the sepoy having suffered from the change of government, which has been so singularly taken up. It is, I am persuaded, simply an error.

That there were many classes in Oudh who were hostile to our government, and who viewed its introduction with displeasure, is true. The principal class of these were they at whose expense the sepoy obtained his advantage, the talooqdars. Under the weak government which we succeeded these men had exercised almost independent authority. They put to death, mutilated, and punished their subject villagers. Never were these acts avenged, rarely were they called to any account for them. Secure in his mud fort, surrounded by a matted wall of live bamboo, and encircled by a wide jungle of from one to two miles in width, in which the thorny corundah tree always abounded, the talooqdar maintained his semi-independent state, and smiled at the weak authority of the capital. How could such a man brook the equal rule of a firm government? how could he brook to surrender the villages which he had long usurped; and to plead on equal terms with the tenant-owner whom he had so long injured and oppressed?

There are those who take the part of the talooqdars, who, misled by appearances, think that they should have been left in undisturbed possession of their blood-stained spoils, and that justice should have been refused to the long-expectant villager.

So, however, did not rule the Government of India, presided over by Lord Dalhousie. And surely if no redress was to be granted, and no wrong to be repaired, to what end was our mission in Oudh? and what business had we in the country? So long as the native government remained redress was not hopeless. No tenure was a fixity; and a talooqdar who possessed himself of a county to-day might be driven from every village to-morrow. Such was not the case, however, under British rule. A title once declared and recognised was as immutable as the Government itself. And the admission of the title of the talooqdar by a British court would have been the consummation of his fraud, would have stereotyped his usurpation! As a rule, the right of the villagers to recover their own was admitted. The fraudulent and extorted "bye namahs" were treated at their proper worth, and generally rejected. Where, indeed, the talooqdar had succeeded in so completely obliterating the village rights that no exercise of proprietary functions by them in any shape could be shown to have taken place within twelve years, then the talooqdar was acknowledged to be the sole proprietor; and the villager remained his tenant, subject to the payment of a moderate rent. And where by the withdrawal of villages the talooqdar's income was too much reduced, or other circumstances of hardship appeared, an allowance of 10 per cent. upon the Government revenue was assigned to him.

No doubt, in some instances, by the indiscretion of local officers, the talooqdars were treated with undue severity. These cases were, however, confined to the single division of Fyzabad, and were all in course of rectification.

The only exception to the Hindoo village system, which was found in Oudh, was in the submontane tract of country north of the Ghogra, included in the Bareytch division. Here few of these original tenures were found to exist. From traces still remaining, it appeared that an ancient and bygone civilization had once existed. This had been swept away; a forest, the growth of centuries, had overspread the country, until in late times the Dehli emperors had made grants of these forest lands to various rajpoot chiefs, on condition of their being cleared; and by them the habitations of man had been restored.

In this tract, therefore, the talooqdar descendants

of these grantees were acknowledged to be the rightful proprietors; and the villages withdrawn from their estates were exceptional and few. Yet it is a fact that many of these very men, who had retained their villages with greatly-diminished assessments, have been most active against us.

There was another class in Oudh who were necessarily hostile to our rule, and who formed a most dangerous element in themselves—I mean the discharged soldiery of the native Government. Of these there were not less than 60,000 when Oudh became British. Service was given to about 15,000 of them in our new local regiments, and a number found employ in the civil departments. For the rest a liberal scale of provision was arranged. Where service had been long, pension was provided: where short, a gratuity was given. Many of these men, however, remained without any permanent provision, and not a few refused employ. Some, because they hoped that the native kingdom would be restored. But the majority could not brook the thought of our stricter discipline. They had been accustomed to a state of licence, which they knew we could not tolerate. Were they dissatisfied with their officers, they confined them. If they wanted fuel, they unroofed the nearest peasant's house; or food, they plundered the nearest grain merchant. These were the characters which were thrown loose upon Oudh; and, no doubt, their numbers swelled the ranks of the mutineers. The only wonder is that they were so quiet before the mutinies broke out, and that for fourteen months Oudh was fully as tranquil as any of our older possessions.

In the city of Lucknow there were many against us. In every Indian city there are a large number of loose and worthless characters: but such was pre-eminently the case at Lucknow. A profligate Court, sunk deep in vice and debauchery, had collected around it thousands whose sole business was to minister to its degrading pleasures. Many of the most striking buildings in the city belonged to men who had risen by their own infamy to be favourites with the King. This whole class of people detested us. Under our government their business was gone. There were many other innocent sufferers by the change of government. Thousands of citizens found employ in providing for the ordinary wants of the Court and nobility. There were several hundreds of manufacturers of hooquah snakes. The embroiderers in gold and silver thread were also reckoned by hundreds. The makers of rich dresses, fine turbans, highly ornamented shoes, and many other subordinate trades, suffered severely from the cessation of the demand for the articles which they manufactured.

But, perhaps, the class most entitled to sympathy was the nobility itself; and the numberless relatives and friends who hung upon it. The nobles had received large pensions from the native Government, the payment of which, never regular, ceased with the introduction of our rule. Government had made liberal provision for their support; but before this could be obtained, it was necessary to prepare careful lists of the grantees, and to investigate their claims. It must be admitted that in effecting this there was undue delay; and that for want of common means of support the gentry and nobility of the city were brought to great straits and suffering. We were informed that families which had never before been outside the zunana, used to go out at night and beg their bread. Every tale of this kind met the readiest sympathy from the kind heart of Sir Henry Lawrence, who, before these troubles began, had applied himself to cause the early despatch of the necessary documents; and had given the sufferers assurance of early payment and kind consideration.

Innumerable taxes, embracing almost every article of consumption, existed in the city under the native rule. The great majority of these were abolished. A new tax was introduced, however, which was highly unpopular, viz. that on the consumption of opium. This drug was very largely consumed in the dissipated capital; and the tax upon it, which obtains in every other part of the British dominions, and than which a more just source of revenue could scarcely be named, was highly obnoxious to the citizens of Lucknow.

With the exception of the important though limited classes which have been mentioned, the mass of the people in Oudh were well affected to our rule. This has been doubted by some, because they made no general effort to assist us. Probably such persons have not duly weighed the characteristic feature of the Indian masses, viz. unconcern as to who may be the ruler. And when it is remembered that the mass of the population was extremely poor, and without organization of any kind; it will readily be understood how impossible it was for them to place themselves in opposition to the disciplined bodies of mutineers who had possessed themselves of the country, and who were in many cases supported from the beginning by the talooqdars.

After the breaking out of the mutinies they sufficiently evidenced their good-will, by assisting and protecting those European refugees who were traversing the country in ones or twos towards Lucknow. Had the villagers not favoured them, not one could have reached the capital. And in most cases these fugitives, as will be hereafter noticed, received from them active aid and assistance. Some of our poor friends were betrayed, but this, with one exception,* was the work of a talooqdar.

One other class of people who are numerous in Oudh demands mention; I mean the "pâsies." These are a race of the lowest caste, feeders of swine, and some of them are found in every village. Their duty is that of village watchmen, and at the same time they are the chief thieves and robbers of the country. But the pâsie never robs that which is committed to his trust, and his fidelity when trusted, is proverbial. By his hand the landholder remits his quota of revenue to the Treasury, and not a rupee is ever missing. To his care the talooqdar entrusts without fear the guard at his fort gate. The pâsies are good hunters, and athletic men, and form an excellent material for soldiers. But hitherto their low caste has excluded them from the high-caste army of Bengal. They have been wiser on the Bombay side; and hundreds of the Oudh pâsies cross the continent of India, and find service in the army of Bombay.

Hereafter we shall be probably wiser in our treatment of them ourselves. During the late disturbances none have taken a greater part than the pâsies. As soon as the civil power became relaxed, they began plundering the roads. When we were beleaguered, and the rebel talooqdars joined the mutineers in besieging us, the greater number of their retainers were pâsies. And good reason have we to remember the repeated war-cry of "Ali," "Ali," "Ali," with which they disturbed our nights. In our future

* Taseen-khan, the infamous zemindar of Sultanpoor, who betrayed Mr. A. Block, C. S.

government of Oudh, the pâsies will need to be repressed with a strong hand.

Reverting to the feeling of the masses, it would indeed be strange if they had not been well affected to us. The worst British Government in India is, in my judgment, preferred by the people generally, to a native rule. But the system introduced into Oudh was of the best. It was modelled on the experience and most approved system of the Punjaub. Our government of the North-Western Provinces has, on the whole, been good. Our revenue system is good, and yet the pressure of the Government demand is in many districts greatly too high. It is too high in Agra, in Alligurh, in Mynpoorie, in Boolundshuhur, and throughout the greater part of Rohilcund. The principle on which that settlement was made, was to claim as the share of Government two-thirds of the net-rental. But the fraud and chicanery opposed to our revenue officers generally caused them unwittingly to fix the demand at more than this share. Still our revenue system was popular with the people,* for it was far more favourable to them than any known to obtain under native Governments. In Oudh, after repeated and most careful examination, I came unhesitatingly to the conclusion, that the Government collector appropriated, if possible, the entire rent, and never professed to relinquish any part of it. Our police system in the North-Western Provinces was only tolerated by the people, for its agents were ill paid and venal. And though crime was kept down, still the honest man was liable to too much annoyance to allow of his liking it. Our civil law was detested. In framing its machinery, the endless

* See Addenda, No. I.

delays, expense, quibbles, and technicalities of English law had been too faithfully copied, and with a too fatal result. The "dewannee," as it was termed, stunk in the nostrils of the people. It was not, however, introduced into Oudh. The simple Punjaub mode of procedure, which is well adapted to the wants of a simple people, took its place, and was generally acceptable. In the police in Oudh, a higher scale of pay was admitted with good effect, and relieved that department of much of the odium of venality. In the revenue, the Government demand was limited to one-half the rent, and the greatest precautions were taken to preserve it moderate. Accustomed to excessive rack-rent, which aimed at engrossing for the State the whole of the rent; the people were at first with difficulty persuaded of the reality of our intention of taking one-half only. When convinced of this, they were loud in their assurances of satisfaction.

Such was the condition of the people in Oudh, when all improvement was suddenly arrested by the military mutiny. The sepoy class were rejoicing in the recovery of their villages, the people everywhere preparing to enjoy in security the fruit of their labours, subject to a fixed moderate taxation; the talooqdars discontented and aggrieved; numbers of discharged soldiers brooding over the recollection of their former licence; and the inhabitants of the cities generally impoverished and depressed. The people of the Province had not been subjected to a general disarmament, as was the case in the Punjaub. It had been objected to this measure, which had commended itself to not a few members of the Commission, that Oudh was not, as the Punjaub, a conquered country. Some attempt had been made to diminish the danger which threatened from the talooqdars, by causing them to dismantle their forts, and surrender their artillery. The first measure was carried out, although incompletely, by the police being charged to cause a roadway to be cut through the battlement of every fort. And this was actually done. A good number of guns were surrendered; but it was known that the talooqdars had concealed many by burying them underground.

CHAPTER VI.

TRUE CAUSES OF THE MUTINY.

What were the true causes of the mutiny in my own opinion; viz. that the native mind had been already alarmed, when the greased cartridge confirmed its suspicion.—That the native army was dangerously organized, ill-disciplined, and discontented; above all, that the North-Western Provinces were denuded of European troops.—Public measures which had tended to alarm the native mind.—Extreme rapidity of recent educational changes.—All public servants, village head men, subject to examinations.—Education in gaols.—The people wondered, and suspected our motives.—The Brahmins fostered their suspicions.—Motives attributed to us.—Recent enactments affecting Hindoo usages. Unwise missionary interference of British officers.—Remarks on Indian missions generally.—General observations on Government education in India.—Grants in aid of missionary education.—Character of native *élèves* of Government seminaries.—Their irreligion.—The alarm excited by the introduction of greased cartridges fostered by designing men.—Instances given of the general native alarm.—Extreme credulity of the natives.—An example instanced.—Reports which were rife at this period in Oudh.—Dangerous organization of the Bengal army.—High-caste system.—Opinion of it given by a pensioned soobahdar of the Bombay army.—A second case illustrative of it.—Consanguinity of the Bengal sepoys.—Loss of discipline of the Bengal army; abolition of flogging; withdrawal of authority from commanders.—General discontent in the native army.—Local nature of the service of the sepoy in Bengal changed by the extension of our frontier.—Addition of pay granted and withdrawn.—Six volunteer regiments only liable for foreign service.—New order of Government directed that all future enlistment should be for general service.—The sepoy could before invalid after fifteen years; a new order put a stop to this.—Sepoys' letters subjected to postage.—Neglect of sepoys by European officers.—Withdrawal of officers for staff employ.—Native officers underpaid.—The North-Western Provinces denuded of European troops.—Sepoys correspond, and then conspire, and lastly mutiny.

The fifth and last reasons enumerated in the fourth chapter are those to which I myself attribute the outbreak of mutiny in India. I conceive that the native mind had been gradually alarmed on the vital subjects of caste and religion, when the spark was applied by the threatened introduction of the greased cartridge; that this spark fell upon a native army most dangerously organized, subject to no sufficient bonds of discipline, and discontented; and above all, that this occurred at a time when Bengal and the North-Western Provinces were so denuded of European troops as to leave the real power in the hands of the natives.

I believe the native Hindoo mind to have been for some time previously alarmed on the subject of caste and religion. Many public measures had tended to this result; but perhaps none more so than the extreme rapidity with which educational measures had of late years been forced on. Local officers, with the approval of Government, solicited contributions from the people for the establishment of schools. These were set up not only in cities, nor yet only in towns; but villages were grouped together into circles or unions to support a school; and every month brought out some new measure to give impetus to the educational mania.

All public servants were required to qualify themselves by literary acquirements, for which examinations were instituted. Not even an ordinary messenger, on the pay of eight shillings a month, could be entertained unless he could read and write. Village accountants, and the head men of village communities, might be required to pass examinations. In respect to the public gaols a perfect mania prevailed. Reading, writing, arithmetic, were required; and sometimes geography, and the planetary system were taught. And murderers and burglars who distinguished themselves as teachers were conveyed from one gaol to another to educate the rest. The people looked on and wondered, not without suspicion. Suspicion ever marks the barbaric mind. Why were we doing all this? Surely not without some hidden purpose of our own. The Brahmins fostered the suspicions. They beheld in the enlightenment of the people, the certain downfall of their faith and their power. And already they perceived themselves to be treated with less consideration than before. It was whispered, and extensively believed, that the object of our Government was to destroy the Hindoo religion, and to convert them to our own.

A striking instance of the working of their suspicions may here be mentioned. The facts were related to me by the late lamented Major Banks. More than a year before Oudh was occupied, while in Calcutta, Major Banks was consulted by the head native officer of the Governor-General's body-guard, who earnestly begged his advice upon a difficulty of importance. The risaldar was a native of Behar, his home being near Arrah. He had a son, who had long been betrothed to the daughter of a Hindoo family of high rank in the neighbourhood. The parties had now attained the age when it is usual with Hindoos to solemnize the marriage; and accordingly the bridegroom's father had made every preparation for the wedding, and had incurred large expense. But at the last hour the bride's family had refused. "Your son," said they, "has been attending an English school: he has become a Christian: he shall not wed our daughter." Those who know how deeply Orientals feel on such matters will understand how keenly the refusal must have been felt. Such affronts are too usually in India settled by the sword.

It may be asked, what object was attributed to our Government by the natives, in the supposed intention to destroy their religion and their caste? This was a question which at an early stage of the mutiny was continually proposed to the natives by ourselves. The regulations of Government prohibited the enlistment of Christians to serve as sepoys in our native regiments. How, then, should we be benefited by the conversion of the soldiery? As the rules stood, a converted Hindoo would be disqualified from employ. Usually no reply could be given. But the only one which I have heard offered by the sepoys themselves was, that once they had become "one of ourselves," they would then be available for general service in any quarter beyond the boundary of Hindostan.

We were believed to entertain views of vast ambition; and these would be aided if we could get rid of the prejudice which restrains the Hindoo soldier to the limits of India, and lead the Brahmin and rajpoot soldier to carry the standards of our unsatisfied conquest over the Hindoo Koosh into Persia, and across the ocean to the rich plains of China.

I apprehend that some of the recent enactments of the Indian Legislature, permitting the Hindoo convert to retain his patrimony; legalizing the re-marriage of Hindoo widows; and threatening the Hindoo institution of polygamy, did much to alarm the Brahmins, and the people generally; and to induce a belief that the Government might intend to interfere yet more radically with the customs and rules held sacred by the Hindoo.

Nor do I think that of late years our missionary zeal in India has been tempered by wisdom. As our empire in the East has extended, we have ever notified to the people that the Government would exercise no interference in matters of religion; and, therefore, the servants of the State were required to abstain from active missionary exertion. This was left to the missionary, who is clothed with no official authority.

His efforts were encouraged by the private countenance and subscriptions of pious servants of the State, who often visited the mission school and chapel, and aided the managing committees with their counsel and advice. Still the active labourer was the missionary; and no one marks more clearly than does the native, the distinction between the duties of his proper vocation, and those of a public servant of the State. Of late years, however, I think that public official influence exercised in aid of missions has been too much felt, and fear that it has assisted in alarming the native mind. Undeniable it is that this alarm was aroused. And in seeking to account for it, it is impossible to shut one's eyes to the fact that the native gentry have been solicited by English civilians to subscribe to the Religious Tract Society; and that British colonels have preached the Gospel to their native soldiers in the public bazaars.

One brief word on the subject of Missions. Encourage the missionary by all means. Send out as many earnest and pious men as possible to proclaim the Gospel to the heathen. The missionary is truly the regenerator of India. Though as yet his labours show little apparent fruit, believe not that they are lost: the land is being leavened, and Hindooism is everywhere being undermined. Great will some day, in God's appointed time, be the fall of it! Hindooism is even now not as bigoted as Hindooism used to be. Nor should disappointment be felt at the small number of converts. A Hindoo proselyte to Christianity incurs a penalty little less than that of martyrdom. He becomes outcast, excommunicate, and loses most of that which is usually accounted to make life valuable. It is not from all that such sacrifice can be expected.

Countenance these, and protect the missionary in his noble enterprise. Speak well of him; employ the deserving among his converts, at least on terms of equality with the deserving Mussulman or Hindoo, and from your private resources aid the good work; but let neither the Government nor its servants take the place of the evangelist. It is not by the arm of force that our pure religion won her way; and with an ignorant, barbaric people, the alliance of the power of Government with missionary labour will but provoke suspicion, and arouse resistance; and thus retard the progress of the faith of Christ.

It must not, from the foregoing observations, either, be imagined that I am a foe to education in India; so far from this being the case, no one would more readily assist its promotion than myself. But I am of opinion that the haste with which this all-powerful engine for moving the minds and opinions of mankind was pushed on, particularly during the last years of Mr. Thomason's administration, and that of Mr. Colvin, was unwise. In my opinion, therefore, this course defeated its own object by creating alarm and dissatisfaction to a considerable extent. Before the period referred to, the progress of public education had been very gradual. It had not, probably, attracted sufficiently the notice and attention of Government. But it was at all events safe. The native mind in India had nowise been aroused in antagonism to it. Greater attention might have been bestowed on this important object, and larger funds devoted to its promotion with advantage, and without exciting public alarm. But the impulse which was given, and which began about the year 1850, was too sudden and too hasty in its action. It also was open to the serious error of laying the people under contribution for its support. The village system of schools was at first supported by the subscriptions of the people. At first one or two district officers induced the landholders and villagers of some portions of their districts to subscribe the funds necessary to establish village schools. Their exertions were much applauded by the Government, and were soon generally imitated by others. The people were everywhere pressed to form themselves into educational circles, and to sign engagements to support one school for each circle.

The general success which attended these exertions was over-estimated. The people, indeed, were supposed to have opened their eyes to the advantages of education with a rapidity equal to that which marked the movements of the Government. Such, however, was far from being really the case. They engaged, indeed, to furnish the necessary funds for the support of the schools; but they did so rather to please the British magistrate who requested them so to do, than from love of the thing itself. Nay, motives of fear of the consequences of refusing sometimes operated. I remember having urged the support of schools upon a very intelligent zemindar of my own district, when he expressed himself well disposed towards the object, and said that he had attempted the establishment of a village school of his own, but found the chief difficulty to arise from the unwillingness of the cultivators to send their boys to school, and thereby deprive themselves of their services. I asked him to influence his neighbours to do the same, and instanced a neighbouring district where general consent had been given. He asked me whether I believed that consent to have been voluntary. I replied in the affirmative. He then assured me that it was not so. He had been over there recently, and had witnessed the refusal of a villager to subscribe. His refusal was reported to the English officer at the head-quarter station, and the recusant was summoned. Sooner than subject himself to the inconvenience of a journey to the station, the villager had subscribed.

It is true that Mr. Colvin had not shut his eyes to the objections to which this system was exposed, and a remedy was in course of application. In all the new settlements of the land revenue which were impending, a special provision of one per cent. upon the Government assessment was to have been provided; which would have formed a suitable and proper fund for the support of village education.

Even then, however, if the Government retains in its hands the management of popular education in India, great caution must be observed. To be sure and free from danger, our progress must be slow. We must not notify, as has been done, that none of the thousands and millions who depend for their livelihood on service, shall obtain it unless they can produce certificates of literary acquirement. Neither should the hereditary head man of a rajpoot village be excluded by a like default from the prized office of representing his brotherhood. It will be just to encourage education, by giving the preference in some branches of the public employ to those who can read and write; but certainly not in all.

I shall, however, be glad to see the connection of Government with schools and colleges for education proportionably relax as the educational efforts of missionary institutions increase. Probably, the funds of the State which are appropriated to this purpose have never been more usefully employed than in grants of aid, to assist the colleges and schools which have been established by missionaries in India. No doubt the Government system of education in India is open to the grave objection, that the opinions of its scholars tend too generally to infidelity; and from this objection the missionary schools are free.

I have not here space for stating the reasons which convince me that the Bible must remain excluded from the Government schools as a class book. And without denying that a heathen must necessarily be benefited by the great enlightenment, as well as by the purer sentiments and morality, derived from the works which are now used in the Government schools; it must be admitted that the standard of excellence which is implanted, is low. Too frequently, the Hindoo scholar leaves the Government school an infidel. Too frequently, he repays the liberal instruction of Government with disloyalty and disaffection. I have seen it stated, that the native scholars of our Government seminaries have, during these mutinies, proved their attachment to our rule. Such, however, has not been the account which has reached me. Young Bengal, by which name this class of native youth is designated in India, is remarkable generally for conceit, disloyalty, and irreligion.

Nor can it be doubted, that it is in India a dangerous thing to educate the native youth, without uniting with that education the strongest restraints of morality. And it may be questioned, whether any rules of morality without the more powerful check of religion will suffice.

We place in a boy's hands the histories of Greece and Rome, and hold up to his admiration the examples of those ancient patriots who have freed their country from domestic tyranny or a foreign yoke. The knowledge which we impart to him, destroys the reverence which he would naturally feel for his own religion, and its precepts. In its stead, we implant no other of a purer and holier kind. Can we wonder, then, at the harvest which we too frequently reap—disloyalty untempered by gratitude; a spurious and selfish patriotism, unchecked by religion; and an overweening conceit of literary attainment, supported by no corresponding dignity of character?

That the proposed introduction of the greased cartridge for use among our native troops did provoke dissatisfaction and alarm, cannot, I think, be denied. By some it is regarded to have been a mere blind; but this opinion I conceive to be founded on the fact that alarm was feigned, long after all real apprehension on the subject had ceased. It is undeniable, that to have used these cartridges, smeared as they were with the fat of the bullock or of the pig, in the ordinary manner, that is, by biting off the end, would actually have involved a breach of caste and loss of privileges to the Hindoo or Mussulman. The report which, on the first beginning of the alarm, became current in India, and was generally credited, is, that while these cartridges were being made up in the Presidency arsenal, a low-caste clashy employed in making them asked water of a high-caste Brahmin sepoy. The latter indignantly refused, for the act would have involved a breach of caste. "Oh!" rejoined the low-caste man, "you need not be so particular, for you will all of you soon have no caste, when you come to put pig and bullock fat into your mouths."

This account may be true or not, but the general alarm on the subject of caste soon became universal. I have little doubt that these were fostered by designing men. Who thus fanned the flame is not positively known, unless, perhaps, by the Government; but the Brahmins generally, and the discontented followers of the ex-King of Oudh, and his minister, Alee Nuckee, lie under general suspicion. The most absurd rumours were circulated and believed. Government, it was said, had sent up cart-loads and boat-loads of bone-dust, which was to be mixed with the flour and sweetmeats sold in the bazaar, whereby the whole population would lose their caste. The public mind became greatly excited. On one day, at Sultanpoor, it was spread over the station that a boat had reached a certain ghaut on the river Goomtee, laden with bone-dust, and the sepoys were hardly restrained from outbreak. A few days later, at the station of Salone, two camels, laden with ammunition, arrived at the house of Captain Thompson, the commandant. It was rumoured that the packages contained bone-dust, and a panic spread through the station. Not only the sepoys in their lines, but the domestic servants about the officers' bungalows, and the villagers and zemindars attending court, hastily flung away, untasted, the food which they had cooked, and fasted for the day. At Lucknow, the rumours which were whispered about were perpetual, and the public mind was never allowed to rest. Now it was at one shop, the next day in another bazaar, that despatches of bone-dust had, it was asserted, been received. It was in vain that facts were opposed to this prevailing panic. I have frequently known parties who asserted the arrival of this dreaded bone-dust receive money, with directions to purchase and bring some of the adulterated flour in proof of their assertion. They always returned with the money in their hands, stating their inability to find the shop where it was sold. Yet was not the public mind undeceived.

Those who, residing in the enlightened countries of Europe, have not witnessed the working of ignorant and barbarous minds, will not readily understand the suspicious credulity by which they are frequently marked. A very extreme example of this, the occurrence of which I witnessed some years ago at the hill station of Simlah, may here be cited.

A report got abroad among the hill men at that sanitarium, that the Governor-General had sent orders to have a certain quantity of human fat prepared and sent down to Calcutta; and that for this purpose the authorities were engaged in entrapping hill men, who were then killed, and boiled down for their fat! It might be thought that it would not be difficult to disabuse them of so absurd a notion. A number of hill men are employed about every household at Simlah in carrying the ladies' litters, and in a variety of domestic duties, which bring them in daily contact with Europeans. But, for long, the attempt to disabuse them was of no avail. The panic increased and spread, until a large number of hill men fled from the station; nor were they, I believe, ever thoroughly convinced of the falsehood of the report.

Rumours not less absurd than this, were in men's mouths at the commencement of the mutinies. There was a Hindoo soobahdar of one of the Oudh local artillery batteries, named Deybee Singh, who had been long in the service of Government, and had been through the whole campaign in Affghanistan. I remember this man being closeted for several hours with Sir Henry Lawrence, recounting to him the wildest stories of plans, which were commonly attributed to our Government, against the religion of the natives. This native officer, who was highly thought of by his commandant, the late Lieutenant D. C. Alexander, did not assert his belief in the truth of these rumours; but neither did he treat them, and laugh at them, as follies. The greater part of the absurdities which he related have passed from my mind; but one, by its extravagance, fixed itself on my memory. It was this. It was, said the soobahdar, believed to be the intention of Government to transport to India the numerous widows whose husbands had perished in the Crimean campaign. The principal zemindars of the country were to be compelled to marry them; and their children, who would of course not be Hindoos, were to be declared the heirs to the estates. Thus the Hindoo proprietors of land were to be supplanted!

I must now advert to the dangerous and faulty organization of the Bengal army at the time when the cartridge question affrighted the minds of men. This consisted in the high-caste system, which prevented the admission of men of low caste into the army. In the armies of Madras and Bombay, the ranks are open to all castes, and high and low do duty together. And not only so: but the same high-caste sepoy who has stickled for his exclusive caste privileges in Bengal, will cross the country and enter the Bombay army, and will there unhesitatingly conform to the different discipline and rules obtaining in that Presidency. Two circumstances illustrating this state of things may here be mentioned. During my official tour in the cold weather of 1856, I visited the Brahmin village of Behta Bozoorg, in the district of Poorwah, and there made the acquaintance of two pensioned soobahdars, Brahmins, the one retired from the Bengal, the other from the Bombay army. I was at the time struck with the difference between these two men. The old Bengali officer was worn out, and seemed to have acquired few ideas and little information during his long period of service. The Bombay soobahdar was a younger man, and had taken his discharge at Aden. He was exceedingly intelligent, and had acquired such a knowledge of men and affairs, that one could converse with him with a certain feeling of equality. While we were expecting the outbreak, I remembered the Bombay soobahdar; and thinking to obtain some useful information from him, I sent for him, and was closeted with him for a long while on his arrival.

He told me that the reports of the intention of Government to destroy their caste and religion had reached his village, and were commonly in the mouths of the Bengal sepoys. He had heard of the medicine-bottle disturbance in the 48th N. I., the cartridge question, and the manifold reports about the bone-dust; but he affected not to believe them. I then inquired, how it was that ill feeling had on several occasions manifested itself in the Bengal army, but never in that of Bombay? He told me plainly, that we had too many men of the same caste and family together, which rendered combination easy. "On the Bombay side," said he, "I stood side by side with men of low caste, and who dared there say a word? Mahratta, Pâsee, Brahmin, Chumar, Rajpoot, and many others, are there found in the same ranks. But here they are all one." Of the justice of his explanation there can be no doubt.

The second fact was mentioned to me by the lamented Captain Fletcher Hayes. He saw, while on board a transport in the harbour of Bombay, a Hindoo sepoy cooking his food with his cross belts on. He inquired from what part of the country he came, and receiving an answer that the soldier was a high-caste man from Oudh, he asked how he came to contravene the rules of caste by acting as he was doing. "Sir," said the sepoy, laughing, "moolk kà dustoor hy," it is the "custom of the country."

But not only were our Bengal sepoys confined to a few of the highest castes, but they were also drawn from the same families. Soldiers, visiting their homes on leave, generally were accompanied on their return by young relations who entered the regiment as recruits, and afterwards were enlisted as sepoys. Thus to the common bond of caste and religion, that of consanguinity was superadded.

But, besides these radical evils of constitution, the army thus dangerously organized had greatly lost its discipline. Perhaps, one of the measures which most affected this, was the abolition of corporal punishment by Lord William Bentinck. Opinion at the time differed greatly respecting the propriety of this measure, and I recollect a conversation on the subject which I had in 1839, with an old pensioned soobahdar, whom I met with in the village of Bahaderpoor, in the district of Etawah. I inquired of him how the measure would work. He replied, that the abolition of the punishment would induce some classes to enter the army who had not done so before. But "sahib," said the old man, "fouj beydurr hogeea," "the army has ceased to fear!"

No doubt, however, the chief cause of the loss of discipline in our army, was the withdrawal of all proper power and authority from the colonels commanding regiments, and from the captains of companies. Gradually all authority had been concentrated at the head-quarters of the army; in consequence of which commanding officers, upon whose exertions and efficiency the discipline of an army really depends, were reduced to ciphers. The commander was powerless to reward or to punish. He could order only the very smallest punishment; and he could not depart from the ordinary course of promotion, in order to reward merit. In all cases in which he desired to do so, it was necessary to obtain permission from head-quarters, and the recommendation was not always attended to. Deprived of all proper, nay necessary authority, regimental officers lost interest in their duty, and discipline suffered proportionately. This state of things had long been viewed with regret and disgust by our best commanders, who would often prophecy that evil would result.

While, however, the Bengal sepoy was thus released from the terror of the lash, and set free from the just control and fear of his commanding officer, other causes were at work, which had produced very general discontent among his own ranks. These must now be mentioned.

The great extension which had of late years taken place in the British frontier, had made a change in the condition and feeling of the native soldier.

By the terms of their enlistment the Bengal soldiery rather resembled a local militia than a regular standing army. The sepoy enlisted to serve in India, and in India only. It was no part of his agreement to bear arms in a foreign land. Nor was this limitation without a sufficient reason in the requirements of his caste. A Brahmin, or a chuttree, is debarred by the tenets of his religion from cooking food on shipboard. He cannot bake the cakes of flour which form his simple food, without clearing for himself a separate plot of ground sacred from the intrusion of others. Should a strange foot be placed within this magic ring, the food which he has cooked is thrown untasted away. These ceremonies cannot be performed on board ship, and therefore there the Hindoo must fast, or subsist on parched corn, which his tenets permit him to eat when so circumstanced. The Brahmin, therefore, naturally abhors the idea of leaving India. He rejoices, as do all the classes from which the Bengal soldiery are drawn, in his home; and delights, if he cannot constantly reside there, still to live so near that he may frequently revisit it. He will generally prefer taking his discharge so soon as he can obtain the smallest pension, in order to return to his ancestral field, before the most certain prospect of promotion. His family, it must be remembered, never accompanies the Bengal sepoy. The women always remain in the privacy of his home. His position in our army in former years met most of these requirements. We had no cantonment more removed than Kurnaul to the westward; and Bengal was our limit on the eastern frontier. These were almost in sight of the sepoys' home, in Oudh, in Behar, and the South-East Dooab. Gradually all this was changed. We moved on to the Sutledge, and placed a cantonment at Loodiana. We crossed the Sutledge. Again we passed the boundary line of India, the river Indus, and placed our Hindoo soldiers in cantonments in Scinde, in the Deyrajat, and at Peyshawur, in countries where the Hindoo was a stranger. Not less was our frontier extended to the eastward, where Bengal sepoys were cantoned at Rangoon, and other stations in Burmah, among a race to whom the Brahmin, and indeed all distinction of caste are alike unknown. At first, a liberal addition of pay reconciled the sepoy to the duty of following his British officer to regions which his ancestors had never known; but this was afterwards stopped. And foreign service batta ceased, when the mandate had gone forth, annexing the new province to the Empire of Hindostan.

A glance at the map of Asia (for Hindostan has ceased to comprise all the British stations in the East) will show how great has been the change. The Bengal sepoy has, no doubt, long felt that change to be a grievance. His services were no longer local. The difficulties in the way of his revisiting his home were greatly increased. The distance of some of our cantonments was so great, as to render it almost impossible within the term of leave allowed. But this was not all. Hitherto the Bengal militiaman had escaped foreign service. Bengal troops had indeed carried the British standards into China, into Burmah, and had assisted in the conquest of the yet more distant islands of Java and the Isle of France. But these were not the regular regiments of the line, but volunteer corps, raised on the especial condition of foreign service. There were six such among the seventy-four regiments which compose the Bengal army. In future, however, this exemption was to cease. The Government declared its intention of altering radically the constitution of its army, and directed that all enlistment for local service should cease. From the year 1856, every sepoy was ordered to be enlisted for general service, wherever the State might require it.

It is not easy for an Englishman, accustomed as his nation is to visit foreign lands, to estimate the magnitude of this change. Certain it is, that it was viewed with great dislike by the Hindoo. The English were then at war with Persia, they were about to invade China. The British frontier was perpetually extending. Where, then, was to be the limit to the sepoy's service? To what unknown distances from his sacred shrines and rivers might not the Hindoo be borne? However politic on other grounds this order may have been, there can be no doubt that the vast change, which it must of necessity make in the position of the Bengal soldier, was not duly estimated; or if weighed, provision was certainly not made to meet the consequences of the dissatisfaction which it would produce.

Still the sepoy possessed, and had long made use of, another remedy which restored him after no long term of service, to his home. Under the old regulations of the native army, he invalided after fifteen years' service, and retired to his home on a monthly pension of four rupees. It was matter of surprise to see young and strong men, in the full enjoyment of health and vigour, relinquishing a service which offered to them certain promotion and increased pay, in order to retire upon this scanty pittance. And yet it was so. Men starved themselves for months, and became weak and emaciated, solely to pass for the invalids. It was attempted to meet the evil by judiciously holding out inducements to longer service. The Government granted an increase of pay for length of service, allowing the sepoy the addition of one rupee after fifteen, and two rupees after twenty years' service. An allowance, also, called hutting money, was granted to them by Lord Hardinge which they had not previously received: and an honourable distinction, accompanied by a valuable increase of pay, was opened to the native officers, by the establishment of the "Order of British India."

Still the love of home proved too strong: the sepoy ranks were too thinned by the early invaliding of men well able to bear arms; and a more stringent remedy was devised. About the same time with the general service order was published another, prohibiting the former practice of transferring men to the invalids. By the new rule it was directed, that a sepoy who was declared unfit for foreign service, should no longer be permitted to retire to his home on invalid pension, but should be retained with the colours, and employed in ordinary cantonment duty. This order, was as usual, read out to each regiment on parade; and I have been informed that in some cases it excited a murmur of general dissatisfaction throughout the ranks. By these two orders the retired sepoy was transformed into a local militiaman, and the former militia became general service soldiers.

When a feeling of discontent has arisen, small matters tending to the injury of the discontented are made much of. An instance of this may be mentioned in the subjection of the letters of native soldiers to postage. They had ever formerly passed free, under the frank of the commanding officer; and there is no doubt that the new law, which, while it greatly diminished the rates of postage by introducing the penny postage of England, abrogated the sepoy's frank, gave rise to very considerable discontent.

The last matter of just complaint by the sepoy which I have to notice, is the diminished interest felt in his condition by the European officer. This will not, perhaps, be so readily admitted by the officers themselves; but of the justice of the charge I have no doubt. I have long noted the improper distance which separates the young British subaltern from the grey-bearded soobahdar, or the young sepoy of his company. I have often remonstrated with my young military friends on the subject. "How can you expect devotion in the field," I have asked, "when you are a stranger to your men in cantonment? Sepoys have been known to carry their wounded captain for miles under the enemy's fire: how can you expect a like devotion to be shown to you, if you do not even know your men?" This defect is not to be charged merely against military men. Ready accessibility and free intercourse with the people, is at least as much required for the proper discharge of civil duties, and almost as much neglected, as in the army. The European in India lives apart from the native. He does not enjoy one of the many means of acquiring correct information on passing events or public feeling, which in European countries is obtained by ordinary social intercourse. Unless he takes pains to make himself readily accessible to the people ; he can but hear with the ears, and see with the eyes, of the native officials by whom he is surrounded. That these, both military and civil, are always venal—that they will endeavour to turn the power, the influence, the opportunity they possess into money—is notorious. There is, therefore, no resource by which the European officer can arrive at the truth, except by making himself easily accessible to all. Then indeed the intriguing pay havildar in a regiment, as well as the rapacious police officer, is held in check by the fear that an account of his misdoings may reach his superior's ear.

The civilian, who is often worn with the arduous duties of the day, has indeed some though no sufficient excuse for not surrendering his few hours of leisure to this necessary intercourse; but the captain of a company has none. And yet too often the native veteran has had reason to complain of neglect and inattention. To what is this attributable? It used not, so old officers tell us, to be so. of yore. The young will plead that the former intimacy between officer and sepoy had its origin in the immoral connections which disgraced our early Indian habits; and that the absence of such bonds of union need not be regretted. Assuredly it need not; such connections could never have tended to generate respect. Intimacy between soldier and officer is not desired ; but confidence and regard are wanted : and ready accessibility and attention to his men's wants and grievances are indispensably required to promote these.

The want of these qualifications may, I think, be mainly attributed to our modern system of withdrawing a large number of officers from each regiment for staff employ. Young men are no longer taught on entering the army to take pride in their regimental duty, and to concern themselves chiefly with the efficiency of their companies. On the contrary, they have been advised by friends, by the Chairman of the Directors at Addiscombe, by their official connections in India, to exert themselves to leave their regiment as early as possible. Staff employ has been held out as the proper object of laudable ambition, and to obtain this the energies of all but the drones were devoted. Is it to be wondered at that regimental duty flagged and has been neglected? That the withdrawal of officers from regimental duty for employment on the staff has been for many years a most serious evil affecting the efficiency of the Bengal army, no one can deny. But the ground of objection generally taken, viz. the paucity of officers left for regimental duty, is not that on which I would insist. The chief injury done to the army no doubt resulted from the want of interest felt in their work by the officers present with the corps, who have seen no prospect of rising into notice, by the most painstaking and successful discharge of regimental duty.

Sir Henry Lawrence was strongly impressed with the opinion that the native officers of our sepoy army were underpaid; and I incline to agree with him. He would compare the status and emoluments which a native gentleman could attain to under native Governments, with those attainable in the British Indian army; and he thought that the disparity was too great. The subject is well deserving of attention: for although the present is certainly not the time when we are likely to be tempted to make large additions either to the number or pay of our native troops; still, we cannot contemplate the permanent maintenance of a system, by which the better classes of the natives of Hindostan would remain alienated from us. When the swell following the recent storm has subsided, it will again be our duty to throw the oil of conciliation upon the troubled waves of the people whom we govern. And even should it be denied that the natives of Hindostan proper are ever again to be treated with consideration, by advancing them to posts of wealth and honour; still it must be remembered that the gentry of the Punjaub and of the other Presidencies have maintained their fidelity and lie under no such ban. In their case, let it be fairly considered, whether the means of honourable employ held out by our Government to the better classes, are sufficient to excite loyalty and to maintain contentment; and if the inquiry result in a negative, let a remedy be applied.

Under native Governments, such as that of Runjeet Singh in the Punjaub, or those of Nagpoor and Oudh, natives, be it remembered, held the highest civil and military offices, and enjoyed emoluments not inferior to those received under our system by Europeans. The father may have received 1000 rupees per mensem, as commandant of cavalry under Runjeet Singh; the son draws a pay of eighty rupees as sub-commander in the service of the British Government. The difference is probably thought by themselves to be too great. "My father used to receive 500 rupees a month in command of a party of Runjeet Singh's horse," said the Seikh Naib Risaldar Sheyre Singh to me, whose good conduct on the occasion of Captain Hayes' murder has been already mentioned; "I receive but fifty!"

No doubt the upper classes of natives, both Hindoo and Mahomedan, on this account viewed with regret the extinction of the dynasties of Lahore, Nagpoor, and Oudh. They were used to repair from our provinces to seek the prizes obtainable at these native Courts. Though these were few, and not easily obtained; nor perhaps often long enjoyed; yet they grieved to see them abolished, and everything reduced to the almost dead level of Anglo-Indian service.

All the causes, however, which have been enumerated, might have been in operation, and yet would have failed to produce the mutiny, but for the capital error which was committed, of denuding our provinces of European troops. Religious alarm might have been excited; the native soldier might have been at the same time discontented and insubordinate; the talooqdars of Oudh, and the royal families of Dehli and Lucknow might have plotted; yet had we possessed a few English regiments in the country, discontent would never have matured into rebellion. As it was, it may almost be said that there were no European troops. From Meerut in the north-west to Dinapoor in the south-east, two weak English regiments only were to be found. These were the 3rd Bengal Fusiliers at Agra, and the 32nd Foot at Lucknow. All our principal cities were without European troops. There were none at Dehli, or at Bareilly; none at Fyzabad, at Mirzapoor, or at Benares. And worst of all, the important fortress of Allahabad, the key of the North-Western Provinces, was equally unprotected! At the important station of Cawnpoor, was only the depôt of the 32nd Foot, and a weak reserve company of artillery. Throughout the entire province of Oudh, we possessed but one English battery of artillery: all the rest were native! This absence of European troops was the one, great, capital error.

No sooner were the religious feelings of our discontented soldiery aroused, than the regiments began to correspond, and to this soon succeeded conspiracy. The sepoys saw their own strength, and our alarm at their proceedings, which it was impossible to conceal. What position, indeed, could be more terrible to the European officer? Himself and his family living in a thatched cottage, surrounded by a multitude of armed men, who might at any moment rise, fire his house, and destroy himself and those dear to him! He had no place of refuge near; he dared take no precaution for his safety, lest by manifesting his mistrust he should provoke an outbreak; but was forced to dissemble, and assume a confidence which he did not feel. Those were indeed fearful days!—There was too much real cause for alarm; and the sepoy readily penetrated the disguise of assumed confidence. Seeing but a handful of Europeans opposed to him, he soon considered himself sure of success, and set on foot one vast conspiracy, which was to extinguish the British rule and race in India in one general massacre.

It was probably most mercifully ordered in our favour by a gracious Providence, that the ill-devised severities at Meerut caused the outbreak to take place there before the plot was ripe. At other stations, and particularly at Lucknow, Europeans took the alarm, and were thus enabled to prepare for their defence; for had the conspiracy been matured, and burst forth, as is believed was the intention, suddenly, upon one appointed day; there is too much reason to fear that it would have been successful.

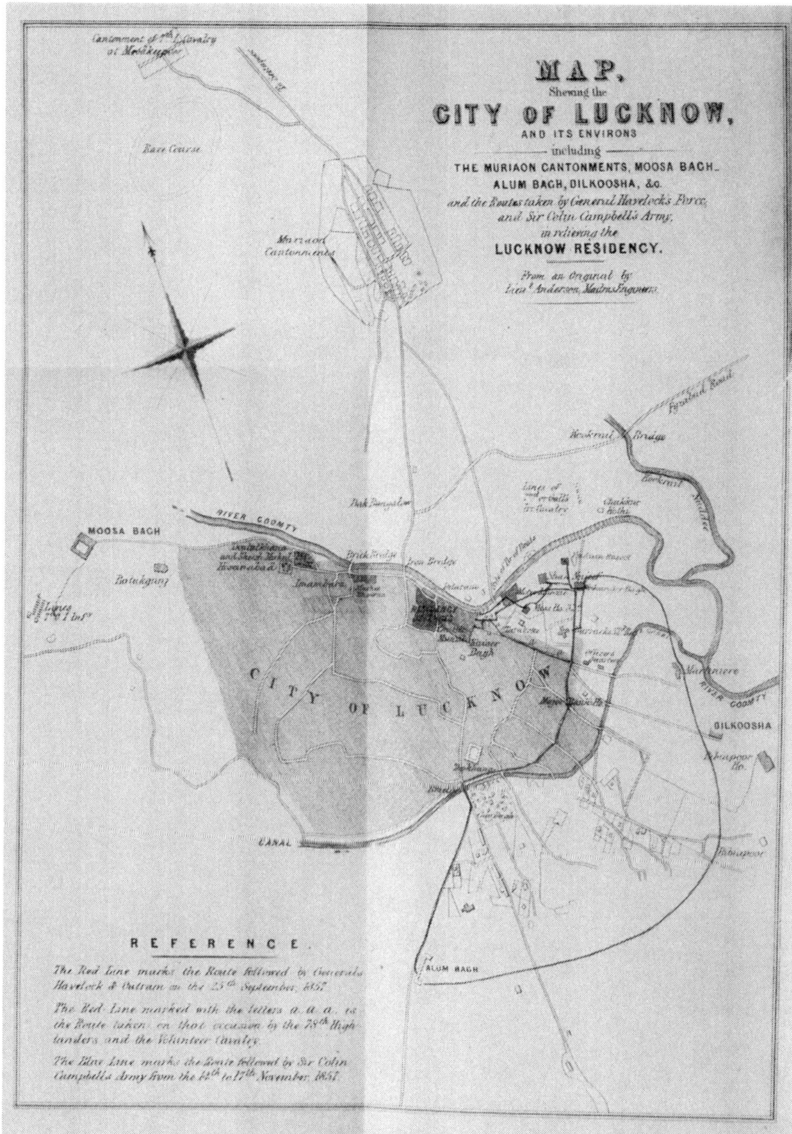
MAP,
Shewing the
CITY OF LUCKNOW,
AND ITS ENVIRONS
including
THE MURIAON CANTONMENTS, MOOSA BACH,
ALUM BACH, DILKOOSHA, &c.
and the Routes taken by General Havelock's Force,
and Sir Colin Campbell's Army,
in relieving the
LUCKNOW RESIDENCY.
From an Original by
Lieut. Anderson, Madras Engineers.
Race Course
Muriaon Cantonments
Dak Bungalow
RIVER GOOMTY
MOOSA BACH
Brick Bridge
Iron Bridge
Imambara
Hosainabad
CITY OF LUCKNOW
Kaiser Bagh
Martiniere
DILKOOSHA
CANAL
ALUM BACH
Bridge
Fyzabad Road
REFERENCE.
The Red Line marks the Route followed by Generals Havelock & Outram on the 25th September, 1857.
The Red Line marked with the letters a. a. a. is the Route taken on that occasion by the 78th Highlanders and the Volunteer Cavalry.
The Blue Line marks the Route followed by Sir Colin Campbell's Army from the 14th to 17th November, 1857.

CHAPTER VII.

MUTINY AT LUCKNOW.

The 30th of May.—Mutiny broke out in cantonments after evening gunfire.—Watched by ourselves from the roof of my house at the Residency.—Mutinous conduct of a Company of the 71st N. I. at the Residency.—Particulars of mutiny in cantonments.—Commenced by the 71st Regt.—Attempt of the men of that regiment to destroy their officers.—Brigadier Handscomb and Lieutenant Grant killed.—Behaviour of the 71st Regt. N. I.; of the 13th Regt. N. I.; of the 48th Regt. N. I.; of the 7th Regt. Light Cavalry.—Sir Henry Lawrence's measures.—Plunder and burning of cantonments.—Escape of Mrs. Bruere.—Operations on the morning of the 31st of May.—Murder of Cornet Raleigh.—Mutineers driven off and pursued by Sir Henry Lawrence.—Mr. Gubbins joins in the pursuit, and makes eight prisoners.—Six brought in.—Conduct of the four troopers who accompanied them.—Three of them join in the mutiny of the corps soon after.—Rising of budmâshes in the city.—They cross the river to join the mutineers.—Mr. Mendes killed.—Ladies abandon Mr. Gubbins' and other houses, and take refuge in the Residency.—Consultation in cantonments, which ended in the formation of a camp of the remnants of mutineer regiments in cantonments.—Sir Henry Lawrence comes up to the City Residency.—Insurrection of the city budmâshes.—They had concerted with the mutineers to join them.—Disappointed in this intention, they commenced an outbreak, which was quelled.

Such was the state of preparations, and such the feeling of the people of Oudh, and of the soldiery, when we reached the 30th of May; the day when we were ourselves to experience the long-apprehended outbreak. Nothing of particular moment had occurred that day. We ourselves had taken our usual drive into cantonments, and had seen and saluted young Grant, Lieutenant in the 71st N. I., who was that evening on duty at the main picket. A sepoy of the 13th N. I. did indeed report at head-quarters that a mutiny would take place on that night, but apparently the information was discredited, for no intimation of it was sent up to us at the Residency. The evening passed away quietly: we had dined, were preparing to retire to rest, when I went up to the roof of the house, and looked over the city towards cantonments. The evening gun fired at nine o'clock, and I was preparing to descend, when a few shots fired from the direction of the cantonments caught my ear. Resuming my place at the parapet, I listened, and soon heard one or more volleys of musketry, followed by dropping shots. Then followed two discharges of cannon. There was now no longer room for doubt. Hurrying down, I alarmed the gentlemen of the house, and the ladies and children were hastened up to the roof. There our arms and ammunition, water and food, had been collected. Presently the lurid glare, which arose from different quarters of the cantonment, announced to us that the bungalows had been fired. Few cannon shots were heard, but the dropping musketry continued for several hours. About 2 A. M. the city magistrate, Captain Carnegie, came up and reported that the Colonel of the 48th N. I. had arrived at the iron bridge with only fifty-seven men around the colours. Shortly after, Captain Germon, of the 13th N. I., arrived, with a message from Sir Henry Lawrence, to the effect that the mutiny had been suppressed, and that there was no cause for alarm. He told us also of the casualties which had occurred.

While this was going on, a company of the 71st N. I., under Lieutenant Sewell, which had been removed from the Muchee Bhowun for suspected disaffection by Sir Henry Lawrence a few days before, and were stationed in the city, were marched down to the Residency near the guns, and were ordered to pile arms. The men would not obey; and as it was thought unadvisable to precipitate an outbreak, they were allowed to retain their muskets. Towards morning the firing in cantonments had ceased; the ladies were therefore persuaded to leave the roof and take some rest; while the men lay down by their arms until the morning.

The particulars of the outbreak in cantonments, as subsequently ascertained, were the following:—Immediately after evening gunfire, the sepoys of the light company of the 71st N. I. turned out and commenced firing; while a party of about forty of the men made straight for the mess-house of the regiment. While they entered at the cantonment gate, a party of the 7th Light Cavalry made their appearance at the opposite one, showing that the destruction of the officers had been deliberately planned. They were fortunately disappointed of their prey. The officers everywhere were on the alert, and left their messes upon the first shot being fired. The 71st mess-house was ransacked and set on fire. Sir Henry Lawrence and staff immediately mounted, and proceeded to the European camp, where were 300 of the 32nd Foot and six guns. The position of the Europeans, as has been already described, was on the right of the Native Infantry parade ground, at the entrance of cantonments. The guns swept the nearest parade, which was that of the 71st. Next to it was the 13th N. I.; and at the further end, and out of reach of grape, were the 48th N. I. Brigadier Handscomb and staff also soon came down to the Europeans. Fearing the mutineers might make for the city, Sir Henry at once removed two guns and a company of the 32nd from the camp, to the road leading to the city, where they were posted. Brigadier Handscomb, approaching too near to the 71st lines, was shot, and fell off his horse dead. The sepoys of the 71st, now becoming bold, advanced out upon their parade ground, and fired upon the 32nd and the guns. These were now ordered to open upon them with grape, and three or four discharges took place, which cleared the parade, and drove the sepoys back into their lines. It was now that Lieutenant Grant was killed. The men of his own regiment rushed by the main picket, and though some attempt to conceal him was made by the sepoys on guard; he was betrayed, and fell pierced with many bayonet wounds and musket-balls.

Retiring from their mess-houses, the officers of the Native Infantry regiments endeavoured to reach their parade ground, where the several regiments were drawn up. Not a few were prevented by the firing, which was going on in the lines; and some were turned back by their own men. A portion of the 71st were got together by Captain Strangways, and after some delay a small number were marched up and took post on the right of the Europeans. They brought, however, neither their colours nor their treasure, of which the mutineers had possessed themselves.

Major Bruere remained with the greater part of the 13th N. I. for some time upon his parade. Many of the men, however, broke away, and forced open the magazine. The Adjutant, Lieutenant Chambers, proceeded thither, in order to prevent the plunder of the ammunition; but was fired upon and severely wounded in the leg. He escaped narrowly with his life, having been repeatedly fired upon, while upon the ground. Finding his men deserting him, Major Bruere at length marched off a remnant of the 13th, with the colours, and took post with about 200 men by the

32nd Foot. The treasure was very gallantly saved by Lieutenant Loughnan, assisted by the Seikhs of the regiment.

Meanwhile, most of the 48th N. I. had assembled on their parade under Colonel Palmer, and had been joined by all their officers. But it soon appeared that the regiment would take no active part against the mutineers. The Colonel proposed to march to the 32nd camp, but the men would not follow. The Interpreter, Lieutenant Ouseley, and the Adjutant, Lieutenant O. Smith, then proposed themselves to go, and ascertain what was going on; but the men would not allow them, saying that they were sure to be killed. The magazine was then opened, and ammunition served out; but while engaged in this duty, Lieutenant Ouseley was struck down by one of his men with a bludgeon, and they then helped themselves. Finding the men deserting in numbers, and yet refusing to face the mutineers, Colonel Palmer proposed to them to march to the Residency in the city; which he accordingly did, making a great *détour* to the left. By the time, however, that he reached the iron bridge, as has been already mentioned, he could only muster fifty-seven men around the colours.

There were but 150 troopers of the 7th Light Cavalry in the lines at Moodkeepoor, when the mutiny broke out. These were immediately turned out by their officers, when about forty of them, before line could be formed, dashed off at full speed towards the cantonments; the rest patrolled during the night, and drew up after daybreak on the right of the 32nd Regt.

While these movements were going on, the bungalows in cantonments presented a general scene of uproar and devastation. The insurgent sepoys and domestic servants of the officers plundered everything that was valuable, and then fired the houses. Lieutenant Hardinge, with his Irregular Cavalry, patrolled along the main street of cantonment; but could not stop this general plunder, which extended to the native Bazaars, and in endeavouring to do so, received a bayonet wound through the arm.

The Residency bungalow and a few others in cantonments only escaped. After placing the guns in position on the city road, and making some other arrangements, Sir Henry Lawrence had retired there and placed guns at the entrance gates.

Mrs. Bruere, the wife of Major Bruere, of the 13th N. I., had a narrow escape. She had returned to cantonments against orders, and was in her house when the mutiny took place. She escaped from it with the aid of a sepoy of her husband's regiment, and fled with her children into the open country, where she passed a miserable night in the greatest alarm. Next day she was able to reach the Residency in safety.

The 32nd did not move from their position, but remained quiet all night. They had been made most judiciously to lie down by order of Colonel Inglis, while the mutineers were firing; and thus escaped injury.

After daybreak the 7th Cavalry were directed to move towards Moodkeepoor, where the officers' houses and the troopers' lines had been seized and fired by the mutineers. They found it occupied by them in force, and drew up to await the advance of the infantry and guns. At this moment, a horseman rode out of the mutineer ranks, and waved his sword towards our men. Upon which about forty troopers broke from the line, galloped off, and joined the enemy.

The body of Cornet Raleigh, a young officer who had lately joined the corps, and who had remained in the lines sick, was found near Moodkeepoor. He had been brutally murdered.

Early on the 31st of May, supposing the mutiny to be at an end, I rode down to cantonments to communicate with Sir Henry Lawrence. I was accompanied by two orderly troopers of the Military Police, whom I armed with rifles. On my way I was surprised to learn that firing continued; and, at the Residency bungalow, that Sir Henry was out with the artillery in pursuit of the mutineers. Hurrying on, I overtook him with a force of four guns and some European and Native Infantry, just beyond cantonments. He had also with him Lieutenant Hardinge and a party of his Irregular Cavalry, and Lieutenant Gibbings with some of the 15th Irregular Horse. In front of us were a body of upwards of 1000 mutineers, chiefly infantry, who were massed about Moodkeepoor. The guns opened upon them at the distance of a mile with round shot; and after a few discharges they broke and fled precipitately. The guns followed slowly with the infantry. I attached myself to the Irregular Cavalry on the left, having first obtained an order from Sir Henry promising a reward of 100 rupees for every mutineer captured or slain. We moved for some distance slowly forward, keeping line with the guns; but seeing little chance of coming up with the enemy at that pace, Mr. F. D. Lucas, an Irish gentleman, who was travelling in India, and had recently come into Oudh, was despatched to obtain permission to move on more rapidly. He soon returned with the desired leave; and the Irregular Cavalry galloped on. We soon came upon a trooper of the 7th Cavalry making off towards the city, and finding escape impossible, he drew up and surrendered. Having no sword, I armed myself with his; but the man, I believe, was allowed to go. Pushing forward at a rapid pace, I got detached from the rest of the Irregular Cavalry, who took more towards the river, and soon found myself followed by four troopers only, one my own orderly, and three of Fisher's Horse. The scene which now presented itself was most extraordinary, the plain being entirely covered with men and women running away and carrying bundles on their heads. At first, I was at a loss to discover who they were; but presently found that they were villagers and camp-followers making off with the plunder gathered in cantonments during the preceding night. An active pony, evidently the property of some gentleman, was being urged along at full speed by its rider, who had one of these bundles under his arm. Overtaken and threatened with a pistol, the man tumbled off, and, abandoning his bundle, took to his heels. We could not stop, but followed fast after one of the enemy, who was urging a cavalry horse at full speed over the plain. Soon getting into broken ground the horse fell, and hurled his rider, who became our prisoner. But what to do with him we knew not, for we had not yet learnt to kill in cold blood. Tying, therefore, the fellow to a tree, we pushed on, and overtook a sepoy of the 71st, carrying his musket, and running with all his might. Finding us gaining on him, he dropped the musket, and strove to reach a village close by. We overtook him; he turned off sharp into a garden. One of the troopers fired his carbine at him so close that I almost thought the shot would have cut him in two. The shot missed him, however, and, reining in my horse, I fired a pistol at him. This also missed, but having a second barrel ready, the man surrendered. We pinioned him tightly, took him into the village, and made him over to the villagers, intending to take him with us when we returned.

Continuing our pursuit beyond this village, we presently caught sight of six sepoys running along, each carrying his musket. They were endeavouring to reach the shelter of a small village which was ahead. As we approached they severally turned and fired at us, continuing their flight after the shot, and loading their muskets as they ran. Coming up with them, they threw down their loaded muskets and drew their swords, of which several had two. Threatening them with our fire-arms, we called upon them to throw down their arms, which presently they did. One of them declared himself to be a havildar, and I made him pinion tightly his five comrades, using their turbans and waistbands for the purpose. One of the troopers then dismounted and tied the havildar's arms. Three of the men belonged to the 48th N. I. and three to the 13th N. I., and one man was a Seikh. One of the prisoners wore three English shirts over his native dress. The arms were collected and laden on a couple of peasants summoned from the village, and the six prisoners were sent back in charge of a single horseman. I rode on a long way without overtaking any more of the enemy, and at last struck upon the road leading to Seetapoor, about ten miles from cantonments. It was now nearly 10 o'clock A.M., the heat was excessive, and, after slaking our thirst at a village well, we commenced our return. On the way we espied two or three sepoys on our right, and gave chase to them. One fellow, who was carrying two muskets, was overtaken, but before he could be secured, we discovered that we ourselves were in danger; for a whole line of mutineers appeared in our front and opened fire upon us. Dismounting, I unslung my rifle, and took a steady aim at one of them, but missed. The shot, however, was too near to be pleasant, and the fellow ran off. It was now our part to retire. Remounting, therefore, I endeavoured to regain the high road, and galloped towards a village close to which it ran. I was aroused by loud cries from my orderly, who was waving his arm and pointing to the village. Looking steadily forward, I discovered a number of sepoy heads behind a low wall at the entrance of the village, and at once turned my horse and made off. No sooner, however, did they see this movement, than they raised themselves above the wall and fired. It was a merciful escape; they all missed! Our only chance was now a rapid flight. Accordingly, putting our horses to their full speed, we rode between the village on our left and the line of mutineers on our right. Many a bullet whistled by us, and struck up the sand about us as we passed, but none of us were hit, and right glad was I to cross a ridge of sand hill, and interpose that protection between us and our foe. Riding back, we carefully avoided every village, and keeping to the open country we safely gained the cantonment, and reached the Residency bungalow there at eleven o'clock. We found that the whole force had returned, preceding us by an hour. The artillery and infantry, moving slowly, had not been able to maintain the pursuit beyond four miles; while one or two of the mutineers had been killed and ten or twelve made prisoners by the 7th Light and Irregular Cavalry. Sad indeed was the aspect of cantonments. Almost every bungalow had been burnt, and presented its charred and smoking walls in melancholy evidence of the night's disaster.

The four troopers who had attended me, behaved, as has been seen, well. Three of them came in with me, and the fourth brought in safely the prisoners entrusted to him. They were duly rewarded, receiving next day 600 rupees from my hands. It is remarkable, indeed, that the three of them who belonged to Fisher's Horse should so soon afterwards have turned against us with the rest of their regiment. I subsequently learned a conversation which they had held with certain of my domestic servants, who were fellow-villagers of theirs, while waiting in my house for their reward. "We like our Colonel," said these men, "and will not allow him to be harmed; but if the whole army turns, we must turn too!" There is great meaning in those words. The feeling of the authority of the "Fouj ki Bheera," or "general will of the army," was, to individual men, or regiments, almost irresistible.

I remained that day until the afternoon in cantonments with Sir Henry Lawrence. It appeared that a number of sepoys and troopers, finding that the outbreak had not proved successful, were slipping back into their lines, which, indeed, they continued to do for several days afterwards. While I was with Sir Henry, tidings of no pleasant character were brought in from the city by repeated messengers. Major Banks reported that the budmâshes of the city were up, and that a body of 5000 or 6000 of them had crossed the Goomtee by a ford, and moved towards cantonments. Some of these men broke into the house of one of the clerks belonging to my office, a Mr. Mendes, who had rashly returned to, and gone to sleep in a residence which he possessed in the city, and cut him to pieces. Major Banks had informed my wife that he did not consider my house to be a safe asylum for the ladies; and she earnestly wrote to me for instructions as to what they should do. In reply I advised that they should all leave my house and go into the Residency. This was accordingly done, and all the ladies from my and the other adjacent houses, took refuge in the Residency.

The question meanwhile at head quarters in cantonments was a grave one. What should be done? I myself recommended the immediate disarmament of the remnants of regiments in cantonments, and the native guards at the Residency; and to this course Sir Henry Lawrence was at first inclined. Much time was, however, lost in discussion, and it was at last thought to be too late to carry out the measure on that day. Sir Henry accordingly decided on placing the native remnants in camp, on the right of the old position of the 32nd and guns. The remaining troopers of the 7th Light Cavalry were brought in from Moodkeepoor, and located in the same position. It was thought that the Europeans and guns would sufficiently overawe the natives. Colonel Halford, of the 71st N. I., was left as senior officer in command, Colonel Case commanding the 32nd. Colonel Inglis was directed to take command of the Residency garrison. Sir Henry Lawrence himself left cantonments, and returned to the Residency; from which he shortly removed to my house on account of its greater coolness. Captain Hardinge with his Irregular Cavalry remained in cantonments, in charge of the Residency bungalow there.

In the afternoon of the same day, a very serious insurrection took place in a quarter of the city called

Hoseynabad, near the Dowlutkhana. It appeared that the city budmashes, who, to the number of about 6000, had crossed the river in the morning, had done so by concert, in order to join the mutineers. Sir Henry Lawrence's prompt attack upon, and dispersion of, the latter had disconcerted the plans of the budmâshes: who, finding the mutineers gone, returned to the city, and commenced an outbreak. For more than an hour heavy firing was kept up, which could be distinctly seen from the roof of my house; but at last the insurgents were completely defeated, and dispersed by the efforts of the city police, assisted by the O. I. Infantry, stationed at the Dowlutkhana; who had been strengthened by the arrival some days before of three companies of the 1st O. I. Infantry from Salone, under Lieutenant C. S. Clarke. Many of the insurgents were killed, and several prisoners taken. Before night all the mutineer prisoners taken in the operations of the day, were lodged in the Muchee Bhowun. They were about forty in number.

Arriving at my home late in the afternoon, I found all the inmates gone. They had sought shelter in the Residency. Six Europeans of the 32nd had been placed in it as a guard; and I was presently joined by Mr. F. D. Lucas. Considering an attack not unlikely, we carefully barricaded all the doors and lower windows with boxes and pieces of furniture, before we retired to the roof for the night.

Thus closed the month of May at Lucknow.

CHAPTER VIII.

THE MONTH OF JUNE—MUTINIES AT THE OUT-STATIONS.

The Lucknow mutineers take the road to Dehli.—Trial and execution of many of the mutineer prisoners.—Mr. Gubbins urges the disarmament of the remnants of the mutineer regiments.—Reason which recommended this measure.—Sir Henry Lawrence could not make up his mind to enforce it.—Account of the events at out-stations.—The Province was quiet till the mutiny at the capital; the troops at out-stations then broke out, and civil government ceased.—The first outbreak at Seetapoor; arrival of refugees from that station.—Good conduct, and subsequent suspicious behaviour, of their sepoy escort.—Other fugitives.—Particulars of the mutiny and massacre at Seetapoor.—Mutiny at Mohumdee; massacre near Aurungabad of the British refugees of the 28th N. I., &c., from Shajehanpoor, and of Mr. Thomason, and others, from Mohumdee.—Escape of Captain P. Orr; joined by other fugitives from Seetapoor; their fate.—Movements of the mutineer regiments; two of them join the rendezvous at Newabgunje Bara Bankee.—Mutiny at Mullaon; escape of Mr. W. Capper, C.S.—Mutiny at Cawnpoor.—Captain Evans at Onao.—Cessation of our communications, both by post and by telegraph.—The Bareytch division; rescue of the ladies from it, by a party under Captain H. Forbes.—Escape of Mr. Wingfield and other officers from Secrora.—Mutiny of the Irregular Horse, of the 2nd Irregular Infantry, and the Artillery.—Lieutenant Bonham, Artillery.—Mr. Wingfield and civil officers retire from Gondah to Bulrampoor.—Faithful conduct of the Rajah of Bulrampoor —Mutiny of the 3rd O. I. Infantry; escape of the officers.—Mutiny at Bareytch; destruction of three British officers at Byram Ghaut.—Mullapoor; abandoned by the officers; their subsequent fate.—Fyzabad division; mutiny at Fyzabad; murder of Colonel Goldney and other officers near Begumgunje; conduct of Rajah Mansingh.—Route of the 17th N. I. mutineer regiment from Azimgurh *viâ* Fyzabad to Cawnpoor.—Fyzabad regiments join the mutineer rendezvous at Newabgunje Bara Bankee.—Mutiny at Sultanpoor; escape of the ladies; murder of Colonel Fisher, Mr. A. Black, and Mr. Stroyan; escape of the other officers.—Good conduct of Roostum Sah of Deyrah.—Mutineers march to Newabgunje.—Mutiny at Salone; escape of the British officers; good conduct of Honwunt Singh of Dharoopoor.—Mutiny at Duriabad; escape of Captain Hawes, and the other Europeans.—The mutineers join the rebel camp at Newabgunje Bara Bankee.

THE mutineers who were driven from Lucknow took, as has been seen, the road to Seetapoor; and apprehension was felt for the safety of that station. Accordingly a camel rider was despatched thither to give warning. Instead of proceeding in that direction, however, the fragments of horse and foot turned to their left, and, passing near the station of Mullaon, reached the Ganges. This they crossed, and proceeded up the Trunk Road towards Dehli. Thus we happily got rid of them. Captain H. Forbes' escape from them, as he was travelling up the same road, when stopped by Sheyre Singh Risaldar, has already been related.

During the next few days a court-martial sat in the Muchee Bhowun for the trial of the mutineer prisoners. Many of them were executed by hanging, and among them the six men whom I had sent in. The sepoy also who had betrayed Lieutenant Grant at the main picket was fortunately recognised, and hanged; but the sentences of death passed by the court were not all confirmed by Sir Henry Lawrence, for he inclined much to clemency. Among those who thus escaped their well-deserved fate were several of the party who had cruelly robbed and ill-treated a European named Yerbury, his wife and family, on the night of the mutiny. Mrs. Yerbury's rings had been torn from her fingers with such violence as to wound them severely, and the party had only saved their lives by flight, while the marauders were engaged in plunder.

These executions took place near the north-west or upper gate of the Muchee Bhowun, at the crossing of four roads, one of which led directly to the stone bridge. The gallows, once erected, was kept standing: and the space around was commanded by the guns of the Muchee Bhowun. More effectually to awe the people, an 18-pounder gun was removed to the road outside, and its wheels sunk into the ground, so that it could not easily be removed. This was kept constantly loaded with grape, and was pointed down the principal thoroughfare.

During the succeeding days I often urged upon Sir Henry the necessity of disarming the remaining soldiers of our native regiments. The reasons which rendered this measure one of extreme urgency appeared to me to be obvious. Out of four regiments, no more than 437 men, viz.—

13th N. I. . .	200
48th do. . .	57
71st do. . .	120
7th Light Cavalry	60
Total	437

had remained faithful to our cause, on the night of the 30th of May; whereas we soon had upwards of 1200 men around the native colours. Many of these had crept quietly back to their lines; but more consisted of the detached guards stationed at the Residency and at different posts about the city. None, indeed, of the latter had actually broken into mutiny, but they had evinced sufficient sympathy with their brethren: and had evidently only been restrained from committing acts of violence by their defenceless position, exposed to the European Infantry and guns.

I have already mentioned the mutinous conduct of a company of the 71st N. I., in refusing to pile their arms. A guard of fifty men over the Court-house of the Tarakotee behaved even worse. They endeavoured to induce a party of Irregular Horse stationed there to join them in plundering a small quantity of treasure that was kept in the Tarakotee; and when these declined, they were with difficulty restrained from pillaging it themselves. All this was reported to us next morning. It seemed, therefore, unwise to retain about us so large a body of men, greatly outnumbering the European force, and many of whom had shown themselves to be disaffected, with arms in their hands. Our small European force would be sufficiently occupied in watching them, whom nobody affected to trust: and would not be available, if required for special service, or to resist the advance of mutineers from the out-stations. These armed remnants were thus a source of weakness, and not of strength. Though most of the commanders professed confidence in their men; that of the officers had been wholly shaken: and the feeling with which they nightly lay down among their sepoys and troopers may be gathered from the graphic account given in the printed letter of Lieutenant Farquhar, of the 7th Light Cavalry, addressed to his mother on the 3rd of September, which is extracted in the Appendix.* There was every reason to believe, in fact it might be looked upon as a certainty, that most of the 1200 sabres and bayonets then nominally on our side, would be turned against us, so soon as those who carried them found us sufficiently engaged against other enemies.

By disarming them, on the other hand, the danger was removed. The well-disposed would remain, and might hereafter, if thought fit, be entrusted with arms. The ill-affected might desert indeed, but that would be a gain. I did not find many to second my proposal: it appeared to me, men shrunk from action, and the *laissez aller* was preferred. I heard, indeed, no valid objection raised to the measure, except the single one, that it would be unjust so to

* Appendix, No. 1.

treat men who had stood by us on the night of the 30th of May. But, though recommending the disarming of all, I was content that these few should be excepted; and if the rest had been disarmed, the native force around us would have been reduced by two-thirds.

Sir Henry Lawrence listened to these arguments; and was often on the point of issuing orders in accordance with my advice. He could not, however, make up his mind to the measure; and disarmament did not take place. Incessant exertion and anxiety, and the bad news which now daily came in from the out-stations, were at this time making sad inroads upon his health.

Of the events which took place at out-stations, it is now time to give account. Up to the end of May, these, and the several districts of Oudh, were quiet; and ordinary business was transacted as before. The Courts remained open, and revenue was paid in, even up to the day on which the troops broke out into mutiny. This, it must be remembered, was the case, although, from the middle of the month, many of the districts of the North-Western Provinces had been in a blaze. The fact appears significant; and certainly does not favour the notion of the movement being one of national revolt.

When, however, the troops at the capital had set the example, all the rest soon followed, and the fabric of civil government fell to pieces like a house made of cards. As the regiments mutinied at each station, the civilians fled, or were destroyed: the offices were burnt; the police and revenue out-stations, and officials left without a head, broke up; the people were left to themselves, and anarchy ensued.

The accompanying map shows the four divisions,

and twelve districts, into which, for purposes of civil administration, Oudh had been divided. In each division was a Commissioner, and every listrict was managed by a Deputy-Commissioner, and one or more assistants. The first outbreak took place at Seetapoor, the head quarters of the Khyrabad division, of which Mr. G. J. Christian was Commissioner. On the 4th of June, a scrap of paper, containing a few lines without any signature, brought in by a police-horseman, stationed on the Seetapoor Road, announced to us that some European refugees from that station required assistance. Captain H. Forbes at once started with a party of mounted volunteers and Seikh horsemen to escort them, and every carriage, buggy, and conveyance available, was sent out to bring them in. Late in the evening they arrived, a party of men, ladies, and children, worn and exhausted, having travelled all that day in the burning sun, and all the preceding night. Some of the ladies had ridden the whole way; others, with the children, had been conveyed in buggies. Many of the ladies had by this time returned from the Residency to my house, and we now gladly received a party of the Seetapoor sufferers—viz. Mrs. Apthorp and three children, and Mrs. and Miss Birch. The other officers and ladies were accommodated at the Residency, at Mr. Ommanney's, and in other houses of the garrison.

This party of fugitives had been escorted in by about thirty sepoys of the 41st Regt. N. I., to which themselves mainly belonged. About half these men had from the first protected them, and had started with them. The second half had followed and joined them on the road, not without suspicion of their having come with evil intention. But there being several well-armed officers of the party, if such ill designs had been harboured, they were not attempted. All the men, therefore, were most cordially received by Sir Henry Lawrence. High praise and promises of reward were given them; and they were placed under their own commander, Major Apthorp, in the Muchee Bhowun. Strange is it, that within one fortnight, even these men could no longer be trusted. A Christian drummer overheard some mutinous discourse, and it was thought best to tender to them the option of retiring to their homes. When this offer was made, it was gladly accepted by all without exception, and not a man remained with the officers whose lives they had before saved.

Some days after, by ones and twos, other fugitives arrived. Mr. Bickers, a clerk, and his family, who had been concealed and kindly treated by the villagers. Lieutenant Lester, Assistant-Commissioner, who spoke highly of the kindness and aid which he had experienced from the people, who had escorted him from village to village. This officer joined my garrison. About three weeks afterwards arrived a native cart, escorted by a few villagers, containing Mr. Dudman, a clerk, and family, and several other East Indians; with them arrived Mrs. Dorin, whose husband, while commanding the 10th Regt. O. I. Infantry, at Seetapoor, had been butchered before her eyes. She was dressed in native clothes: had been hiding in a native village for more than a fortnight, and now found a home in our house. All this party spoke highly of the kindness with which they had been treated; and with Sir Henry Lawrence's sanction, I sent to the zemindar, who had thus protected them, an official document, promising him high reward.

From all these parties we fully learnt the sad particulars of the mutiny at Seetapoor. At that station were quartered the 41st Regt. of N. I., the 9th and 10th Regts. of O. I. Infantry, and the 2nd Regt. of Military Police. The troops rose on the 3rd of June. The outbreak had been long feared, and the Commissioner, Mr. Christian, who had maintained a bold and manly bearing throughout this anxious time, had collected the civilians and their families at his house, which he proposed to defend by aid of a strong guard of the regiment of military police, which he believed to be staunch. He had advised his military friends to send their ladies to him also for safety. But fortunately this had not been done. One lady from cantonments alone came, Mrs. Stewart, and she with extraordinary prudence took a good survey of the position. On two sides of Mr. Christian's compound flowed the small river Sureyan, and there was no means of reaching the high road but through the military cantonment. Considering the position to be unsafe, she returned to her home, and fortunately was one of the first party of refugees. On the morning of the 3rd of June, a cry was raised in the lines of the 41st Regt., that the 10th Irregulars were plundering the Treasury, and as the men were in a state of excitement, the commander, Colonel Birch, who reposed the most entire confidence in his men, called out the two most suspected companies, the Light and the Rifle, and led them to the Treasury. All there was found to be quiet, and the Colonel was about to return, when a sepoy of the guard stepped out of the ranks and shot him in the back. Colonel Birch fell from his horse dead; and Lieutenant Smalley and the Serjeant-Major were then killed. The Adjutant, Lieutenant Graves, escaped, wounded, through a volley of bullets. The mutiny soon spread to the Irregular regiments. In the 9th Regt., the Commandant, Captain Gowan, and his wife, the second in command, Lieutenant Greene, and the Assistant-Surgeon, Mr. Hill, were destroyed. Mrs. Greene escaped. In the 10th Regt., the Commander, Captain Dorin, the second in command, Lieutenant Snell, his wife and child, were murdered. Mrs. Dorin, whose arrival has been mentioned, and the Adjutant, Lieutenant Burnes, escaped.

Captain John Hearsey, commanding the 2nd Regt. Military Police, was protected by some of his men, and escaped. At Mr. Christian's bungalow the scene must have been fearful. At the commencement of the outbreak he proceeded outside to put in readiness the guard of military police in whom he confided. The wretches immediately turned and fired upon him. Flying back into the house, he alarmed the assembled inmates, and the men, ladies, and children, fled out of the bungalow on the opposite side of the house, which faced the river; pursued and fired upon by the miscreants of the military police, and of other regiments, which now joined them. Some were shot down before they reached the stream. Others were killed in it. A few perished on the opposite bank. Two or three only escaped—viz. Sir Mountstuart Jackson and his two sisters, and little Sophy Christian, who was saved by Serjeant-Major Morton. There fell Mr. and Mrs. Christian* and child, Mr. and Mrs. Henry Thornhill and their children, and several others. Those who escaped broke into two parties. Lieutenant Burnes, Sir Mountstuart and Miss Madeline Jackson, Serjeant-Major Morton, and little Sophy Christian, found refuge, though an unwilling one, with Rajah Lonee Singh, at his fort of Mithowlee.

* See Addenda, No. II.

Mrs. Greene, Miss Jackson, and Captain John Hearsey, fled northwards, and, after being joined by other refugees, found shelter at Mutheearee, with the Rajah of Dhoreyrah.

Mohumdee is the second station of the Khyrabad division; and here was stationed the Deputy-Commissioner, Mr. J. G. Thomason, with his assistant, Captain Patrick Orr. A letter was received at Lucknow from the latter officer from Mithowlee, dated the 8th of June, from which the following sad narrative is extracted.

"On the 31st May, Sunday, the 28th N. I. broke into mutiny at Shajehanpoor, and some of the men rushed into the church and murdered the collector, Mr. Ricketts, wounded Lieutenant Spens of the 28th, and killed the doctor. Major James was killed on his parade ground. The following made their escape: Captains Sneyd, Lysaght, and Salmon; Lieutenants Key, Robertson, Scott, Pitt, and Rutherford; Ensigns Spens, Johnston, and Scott; Quartermaster-Serjeant Grant; Bandmaster, and one drummer. Ladies—Mrs. Scott, Miss Scott, Mrs. Lysaght, Mrs. Key, Mrs. Bowling, Mrs. Sheils, Mrs. Grant, Mrs. Pereira, and four children. Lieutenant Sheils, Veteran Establishment, Mr. Jenkins, C. S. They ran away to Powayn; but the Rajah turned them out the next morning, and they came to Mohumdee. Thomason and myself, on hearing of this sad affair at Shajehanpoor, consulted together, and sent away Annie (Mrs. Orr) to Mithowlee, and went ourselves to the fort, to protect the Treasury if possible. On Monday, at about noon, the party from Shajehanpoor arrived, and from that time the most alarming symptoms showed themselves among the men (a company of the 9th O. I. Infantry). I used every means in my power to pacify them, but in vain. By the most strenuous efforts I withheld them, from hour to hour, from breaking into mutiny. Every minute seemed to be our last. The men were civil to me to the last, but each one said he could not answer for what some of the bad characters might do. I succeeded in gaining some influence over them, and kept them quiet till a detachment of fifty men came in on Thursday morning, the 4th, from Seetapoor, sent by poor Christian to escort in the Shajehanpoor ladies. These men brought with them a report that the whole of their Light Company in the Muchee Bhowun had been cut up by the Europeans, and said that they were determined to take their revenge. Seëing the state of things, I sent for all the native officers, and told them to let me know at once, like men, what their intentions were, and, if reasonable, I would give my consent. They came to the resolution of marching at once to Seetapoor, and swore that they would spare our lives, and take Thomason and me into Seetapoor, and allow the others to go away unmolested. I made them take a solemn oath; and they all put their hands on the head of Luchmun Jumadar, and swore.

"Well, we left Mohumdee at about half-past five, P.M., on Thursday, after the men had secured the treasure, about one lac and ten thousand rupees, and released the prisoners. I put as many of the ladies as I could into the buggy, and others on the baggage carts; and we reached Burwur at about half-past ten, P.M. Next morning (Friday, 5th), we marched towards Aurungabad. When we had come about two coss (four miles), the halt was sounded, and a trooper told us to go ahead wherever we liked. We went on for some distance, when we saw a party following us. They soon joined, and followed the buggy, which we were pushing on with all our might. When within a mile of Aurungabad, a sepoy rushed forward and snatched Key's gun from him, and shot down poor old Sheils, who was riding my horse. Then the most infernal carnage ever witnessed by man began. We all collected under a tree close by, and took the ladies down from the buggy. Shots were firing from all directions, amidst the most fearful yells. The poor ladies all joined in prayer, coolly and undauntedly awaiting their fate. I stopped for about three minutes among them, but, thinking of my poor wife and child here, I endeavoured to save my life for their sakes. I rushed out towards the insurgents, and one of my men, Goordhun, of the 6th Company, called out to me to throw down my pistol, and he would save me. I did so, when he put himself between me and the men, and several others followed his example. In about ten minutes more they completed their hellish work. I was 300 yards off at the utmost. Poor Lysaght was kneeling out in the open ground, with his hands folded across his chest, and, though not using his firearms, the cowardly wretches would not go up to the spot until they shot him; and then rushing up, they killed the wounded and children, butchering them in a most cruel way. With the exception of the drummer boy, every one was killed of the above list, and besides, poor good Thomason and one or two clerks. They denuded the bodies of their clothes, for the sake of plunder."

From the scene of this fearful massacre the sepoys removed Captain P. Orr to Aurungabad, and thence sent him under a guard, and made him over to Raja Lonee Singh of Mithowlee. In a postscript dated the 9th, Captain Orr added that he had heard of another party of fugitives from Seetapoor being in the same neighbourhood :—

"I managed," he wrote, "to communicate with the others by letter to-day. Their names are—Sir M. Jackson and sister, little Sophy Christian, Burnes, and Quartermaster-Serjeant of the 10th O. I. The troops are still at Muholee, and cannot make up their minds as to their movements. This morning they went some distance towards Aurungabad, with the intention of going to Dehli, but changed their minds again, and returned to Muholee, *en route* to Lucknow. They are constantly quarrelling about the division of the booty, and a small body of Europeans could snatch the money from them easily."

It is melancholy to think of the sad fate to which, after months of anxiety and suffering, this brave officer was reserved. It is now too well, I fear, ascertained that Captain P. Orr, Sir M. Jackson, Lieutenant Burnes, and Serjeant-Major Morton, fell victims to the savage ferocity of the Lucknow soldiery, upon the withdrawal of the Lucknow garrison.

Eventually the 41st N. I. and the 10th Irregulars secured most of the treasure; and, after plundering the town and station, quitted the province, crossing the Ganges to Futtehgurh. The 9th O. I. Infantry and the military police remained in the province, but removed from Seetapoor to Mohumdabad, the seat of the talooqdar Raja Newabali, who had promised them assistance. Towards the close of the month they marched from Mohumdabad to the general mutineer rendezvous at Newabgunje Bara Bankee.

The third station in this division was Mullaon, where was stationed, as Deputy-Commissioner, Mr. W. C. Capper, C. S., with a guard of a party of the 41st N. I. and 4th O. I. Infantry. The fidelity of these men was soon perceived to be doubtful; nevertheless, Mr. Capper maintained his position for some days after the outbreak at Seetapoor. When mutiny was imminent, he rode away, and reached the capital in safety.

After that of Seetapoor, next followed the mutiny at Cawnpoor, with the fate of which ourselves were so closely connected that it is impossible to omit its mention. On the 3rd of June, Captain Lowe returned from that station with the fifty men of the 32nd who had been lent by Sir Henry Lawrence, and early on the 4th Captain O'Brien arrived with fifty men of H. M. 84th Foot as a reinforcement sent by Sir Hugh Wheeler. On the same morning Captain Edgell and his family, of the 53rd N. I., who had been summoned by Sir Henry, reached Lucknow. On that very day the four regiments at Cawnpoor broke into mutiny.

An express from Captain Evans, the Deputy-Commissioner of Poorwah, stationed at Onao, within twelve miles of Cawnpoor, communicated to us the fact; and he was immediately instructed to secure all the boats he could, and have them securely moored on our side of the river. But the mutineers had been beforehand. The bridge of boats at Cawnpoor was broken up by them, and the boats which had formed it, as well as those at other ferries, were secured under guards on the further side of the stream. On the second day firing began at Cawnpoor, which continued daily afterwards; and it soon became known that the Nana of Bithoor had leagued with the revolted troops, and was besieging Sir Hugh Wheeler in his intrenchment. The country bordering on the Ganges soon became disturbed, but Captain Evans maintained his position in his district till near the end of June, and sent in all the information which he could obtain respecting the state of things across the river. The high road towards Cawnpoor was also patrolled by a native police officer named Munsubali, who rendered good service with a party of police horse. Poor Captain Evans! we all felt for him, for his wife and two fine children were in Cawnpoor when the mutiny broke out, and shared the fate of those who perished there so miserably.

Mr. Arthur Jenkins, of the Civil Service, assistant to Captain Evans in the Poorwah district, was also unhappily at Cawnpoor at the same time, and no tidings of him reached us afterwards. He had left Oudh on a medical certificate, and had intended going to the hills. With the outbreak at Cawnpoor our external communications both with the provinces and Calcutta by post, and by electric telegraph, ceased. The telegraph wire was at once cut, and our post road lay through Cawnpoor. We immediately endeavoured to open new lines direct to Benares and Allahabad; but these efforts were defeated by the mutinies at the several stations, and the disorganization of the districts through which the lines of post must pass. Before, however, our post was thus cut off, Sir Henry had received intelligence from Lord Canning that steamers had been despatched from Calcutta to intercept the China Force, and to bring the regiments, which composed it, to India.

The Bareytch Division, comprising the whole territory north of the river Gograh, was entrusted to Mr. C. J. Wingfield, C. S., as Commissioner. The three civil stations in the division were Bareytch, Gondah, and Mullapoor. There was a fourth military station, Secrora, where Mr. Wingfield himself lived, and where were quartered the 1st, or Daly's, Regt. of Irregular

Horse, the 2nd Regt. of O. I. Infantry under Captain G. Boileau, and an Irregular Light Horse Battery under Lieutenant Bonham.

Daly's Horse were known to be ripe for mutiny, and the native regiments were of very doubtful fidelity: it was, therefore, resolved to bring in the ladies from that division. The anxiety of Captain H. Forbes commanding Daly's Horse, and who was then at Lucknow, for the safety of his family, fortunately hurried this measure. He himself accordingly proceeded to Secrora with a party of Seikh and Volunteer Cavalry, and mounting the ladies on elephants and in doolies, brought them safely into the capital on the 9th. Mr. G. H. Lawrence, C. S., accompanied the party in. It consisted of several ladies and children, including Mrs. Forbes, Mrs. Hale, and Mrs. Boileau from Secrora. Mrs. Forbes and two children were received into my house. Having for some time watched the mutinous feeling of the troops, Mr. Wingfield had made his arrangements for escape. He had reason to place confidence in the friendliness of a neighbouring chief, named Dirg Bijehsingh, Rajah of Bulrampoor, and had arranged that the European officers in his division should seek refuge with the Rajah, on the breaking out of the troops. On the 9th of June, it becoming evident that mutiny was imminent, Mr. Wingfield left the station in the evening on horseback, leaving everything standing in his house, and rode to Gondah. On the next morning, Captain Boileau, Lieutenant Hale, and Dr. Kendall, left Secrora and rode to Bulrampoor; and the 2nd Infantry and the Irregular Horse broke into open mutiny.

The last to leave the station was Lieutenant Bonham. This gallant young officer remained with his battery until noon of the 10th. His men liked him, and he had great influence with them, and he hoped to the last that they would stand by him. At last, however, after the infantry had been some time in mutiny, they bid him go, telling him that his life was no longer safe. They furnished him with some money and a horse, and bade him avoid the main ferry at Byram Ghaut, to which the mutineers had sent a guard. Bonham accordingly left them, taking with him his own serjeant, and the quartermaster serjeant of the infantry, crossed the Gograh at an unfrequented ferry, and arrived in safety on the next day at Lucknow.

Mr. Wingfield did not stay long at Gondah; but perceiving the ill-feeling of the troops, proceeded on, shortly, to Bulrampoor, taking with him the civil officers from Gondah. At this station was an O. I. I. Regt., the 3rd. Captain Miles, the Commandant, and his officers, when Mr. Wingfield, left, were persuaded of the fidelity of their men. Soon, however, they had reason to change their opinion, for symptoms of mutiny having shown themselves, they were obliged to fly, and two days later joined Mr. Wingfield at Bulrampoor. After a stay of a few days at Bulrampoor with the Rajah, the whole party proceeded under the Rajah's escort across the Oudh frontier into the Goruckpoor district, and were kindly received by the Rajah of Bansy. Thence our officers reached the station of Goruckpoor in safety.

Less fortunate, unhappily, were the officers at the station of Bareytch. These were Mr. C. W. Cunliffe, C. S., Deputy-Commissioner, Lieutenant Longueville Clarke, and Mr. Jordan, Assistant. At Bareytch were two companies of the 3rd I. Infantry. When mutiny appeared, the three officers rode off northward to Nanpara, intending to rest there, and proceed on towards the hills. On reaching Nanpara admittance was refused them. This place is the seat of a Rajah of that name, who is a minor. A kinsman of his had managed the estate and dissipated the property. He had accordingly been removed by the civil authorities, and a new agent appointed. The old agent had now forcibly reinstated himself, and had murdered the Government manager. Disappointed in their hope of friendly reception here, the three officers relinquished their intention of taking refuge at Bulrampoor, and resolved to attempt to reach Lucknow. They retraced their steps to Bareytch, and started for the Gograh. Unfortunately they rode to the chief ferry, that of Byram Ghaut, which was guarded by the Secrora mutineers. The fugitives were all disguised as natives, and at first attracted little observation. They were allowed to embark with their horses on a ferry boat, and left the shore. The alarm was then given that Europeans were escaping, and the sepoys crowded into other boats and pursued them, keeping upon them a heavy fire of musketry. The native boatmen upon this jumped overboard, and escaped to land. The fugitives were forced by the fire of the mutineers to crouch down in the boats, and in this position returned their fire with their revolvers. They could not stand up to work the boat. Left to itself, the boat was borne by the current back to the same bank from which they had started. Two of the officers were immediately murdered by the mutineers. The third was reserved for the orders of the native officers at Secrora. Orders were sent by them to destroy him, and, on the next morning, he was taken down to the river bank and shot. This last was believed to have been Mr. Jordan. These facts could only become known by native evidence. They were, however, certified to me at Lucknow by several parties on whose account there was every reason to place credence. One of the young officers was engaged to a young lady at Lucknow, and the marriage was to have been shortly celebrated. The betrothed girl would not credit the story, and clung through the weary days of the siege to the hope that her lover would yet be found alive.

At the last station of the Bareytch division, Mullapoor, no troops remained, and therefore no mutiny took place. Ultimately, however, when civil government ceased in the rest of the country, that district became disorganized also, and the officers there, Mr. Gonne, of the Civil Service, and Captain Hastings, joined by three fugitives from Seetapoor, Captain John Hearsey, Mrs. Greene, and Miss Jackson, and by two gentlemen who had escaped from the sugar factory at Rosa near Shajehanpoor, Messrs. Brand and Carew, were obliged to leave the station, and took refuge in a fort belonging to the minor Rajah of Dhoreyrah, called Mutheearee. From this place we received tidings of them, and Mr. Gonne made more than one unsuccessful attempt to reach Lucknow. The fear of falling into the hands of the intervening bands of mutineers on each occasion compelled him to return. They remained long at Dhoreyrah; but at last the Rajah's people proved faithless, and finding themselves in imminent peril, the party fled. Mrs. Greene, Miss Jackson, and Mr. Carew were seized, and of their subsequent fate I have been unable to obtain any certain information. Captain Hearsey, Mr. Gonne, Captain Hastings, and Mr. Brand, escaped, and were kindly received by Koolrajesingh, talooqdar of Pudnaha, who has a place in the Nipaul Hills. There the refugees found shelter, until one by one they fell victims to the deadly climate of the Turay. John Hearsey alone survived, and when I last received accounts was about to join Jung Buhadoor's camp at Goruckpoor.

The mutinous regiments at Gondah and Secrora first secured the Government treasure, and then, after some delay, moved across the Gograh at Byram Ghaut, and joined the mutineer rendezvous at Newabgunje Bara Bankee.

I pass to the Fyzabad division, which comprised three stations—Fyzabad, Sultanpoor, and Salone. At Fyzabad were posted the 22nd Regt. of N. I., commanded by Colonel Lennox, the 6th O. I. Infantry by Colonel O'Brien, and a Native Regular Light Field Battery under Major Mill. The Commissioner, Colonel Goldney, whose head-quarters and family were at Sultanpoor, had removed to Fyzabad, as the more important position, and exposed to the greatest danger. The 22nd Regt. N. I. was known to have shown signs of disaffection; and the 6th Irregular, the old native "Barlow ki Pultun," was the worst in the old Oudh service. The native battery, though commanded by a noble fellow, Mill, could not be depended on. Much anxiety, therefore, had long prevailed at Fyzabad.

At the beginning of the month Rajah Mansingh, talooqdar of Shahgunje, was in confinement there. He had been arrested by order of the Chief Commissioner, in consequence of information telegraphed from Calcutta, which accorded with what had reached us at Lucknow. At this juncture he sent for the British authorities, warned them that the troops would rise, and offered, if released, to give the Europeans shelter in his fort at Shahgunje. Seeing the critical state of things, Colonel Goldney released him, and Mansingh at once commenced to put his fort in order, and to raise levies. Soon, however, the troops disclosed their intentions. They demanded that the public treasure should be surrendered to them, on the plea of better security. Helpless, the authorities were compelled to comply, and the money was carried off to their lines amidst the shouts of the mutineers. The civilians now prepared for the worst, and sent their families to Shahgunje. But the ladies from cantonments would not accompany them, relying on the faith of the native officers of the 22nd Regt., who had solemnly sworn to Mrs. Lennox that no injury should be done them.

Matters remained in this state until it became known that the 17th Regt. N. I. from Azimgurh were approaching, with a body of Irregular Cavalry and two guns, having mutinied and possessed themselves of a large amount of treasure. When this regiment reached Begumgunje, within one march of Fyzabad, about the 8th or 9th of June, the regiments at Fyzabad threw off further disguise, and openly revolted. The civil officers, Captain J. Reid, Captain Alex. Orr, and Mr. Bradford, thereupon mounted and rode off to Shahgunje. The mutineers bade their officers depart, and told them that they might take the boats then lying at the cantonment ghaut.* These were without the necessary roof of thatch, and almost without a boatman. There was no help for it. All the officers, therefore, except Colonel Lennox, embarked in them, and rowed the boats themselves down the stream, exposed to the burning sun.

Little did they then know the plan laid for their destruction by the mutineers. Begumgunje, where

* Landing-place.

the 17th N. I. lay, is on the banks of the Gograh, and the current of the river sweeps underneath it. A messenger had been despatched by the 22nd Regt. to the 17th, announcing that they had sent off their officers, and inviting the 17th to destroy them. Fearfully was the invitation responded to. As the boats containing the refugees approached, they were met by a fire of grape and musketry, under which many officers fell. Several jumped out into the water, and attempted to swim to the opposite bank. In the attempt Major Mill, Lieutenant R. Currie, Artillery, and Lieutenant Parsons, of the 6th O. I. Infantry, were drowned. Some who reached the other side, fell victims to a party of insurgent villagers. Colonel Goldney was taken from his boat and led up the bank to the mutineer camp. "I am an old man," said he, "will you disgrace yourselves by my murder?" They shot him down. A remnant * of the officers only made their escape down the river, and reached a place of safety. It is but just here to state that Colonel Goldney, from every account which has reached me, maintained a most gallant and manly bearing during these trying scenes at Fyzabad. He had before commanded the 22nd Regt., and long maintained his confidence in them. And this, perhaps, was the reason for his not accompanying the other civil officers to Shahgunje.

Colonel Lennox and his family left the station separately, crossed the river, and reached the station of Goruckpoor in safety.

Mansingh sheltered the fugitives who had taken refuge with him for a few days, and then from real or

* Lieutenants A. Bright, A. F. English, T. E. Lindesay, W. H. Thomas, G. L. Cautley, J. W. Anderson, and T. J. Ritchie, are known to have perished on this sad occasion.

affected fear of the mutineers, desired them to depart. He, however, provided boats for them on the Gograh, to which they were escorted by night; and a party of Mansingh's levies accompanied them some way on their journey. They all reached the station of Dinapoor in safety.

Mrs. Mill, the wife of Major Mill, of the Artillery, made a perilous escape. Unwilling to expose her children to the sun, she had lost the opportunity of leaving the station with Colonel Lennox, and found herself left alone. She succeeded, however, in making her way alone through the country, and at length reached a British station. She had walked the whole way, wandering from village to village. The women in the villages were kind to her, but she lost one of her children, from illness and exposure, on the way.

After the English officers had left, the 17th N. I. entered the station; and before long, a dispute arose between them and the Fyzabad mutineers. The former had brought away a large treasure, but possessed little ammunition. Their tumbrils, it was known, were filled with treasure instead of shot. The Fyzabad mutineers accordingly demanded a share of it, and on this being refused, both parties prepared for action. The dispute was, however, settled by the 17th N. I. paying down a lac and sixty thousand rupees; and they were then allowed to depart. They marched through Oudh by cross roads, making their way towards Cawnpoor, and reached the Ganges opposite that station just in time to take a part in the cruel destruction of the unhappy fugitives from the Cawnpoor massacre. Rajah Mansingh, with whom I was then in almost daily communication, kept me informed of their movements and of their want of ammunition; and wrote me that 500 matchlock men could wrest the treasure from them as they passed not far from Lucknow. I hoped that an attempt might have been made to intercept them. Sir Henry Lawrence, however, decided against the measure.

The Fyzabad mutineers first placed at their head a certain fanatic Molovee, whom they released from our gaol. They proclaimed him to be chief, and fired a salute in honour of him. This man had come from Madras, and was of a good Mahomedan family, and had traversed much of Upper India, exciting the people to sedition. He had been expelled from Agra. In April he appeared with several followers at Fyzabad, where he circulated seditious papers, and openly proclaimed a religious war. The police were ordered to arrest him; but he and his followers resisted with arms. It was found necessary to call in the military, and then he was not captured until several of his followers were slain. He was tried, and recommended for execution; but this had been delayed in consequence of some informality, and he was still in gaol when the mutiny broke out.

The Molovee's reign was, however, not of long duration. After two days he was deposed, and the leadership offered to Rajah Mansingh. This crafty Brahmin temporized, cajoled and flattered the native officers, and despatched his brother, Ramadeen, to Cawnpoor on a mission to the Nana. Meanwhile, through confidential agents, he maintained a correspondence with us. The mutineers loitered some time at Fyzabad, but eventually marched to Duriabad; and towards the end of the month arrived in the general mutineer camp at Newabgunje Bara Bankee.

The station of Sultanpoor was commanded by Colonel S. Fisher, whose regiment, the 15th Irregular Horse, was stationed there. Besides it, there were the 8th O.I.

Infantry, commanded by Captain W. Smith, and the 1st Regt. of Military Police, under Captain Bunbury. Apprehending an outbreak of the troops, Colonel Fisher sent off the ladies and children on the night of the 7th of June towards Allahabad, under care of Dr. Corbyn and Lieutenant Jenkins. The party reached Purtaubgurh safely, but there they were attacked and plundered by the villagers. Three of the ladies, Mrs. Goldney, Mrs. Block, and Mrs. Stroyan, with their children, were separated from the rest, and were taken to the neighbouring fort of Lall Madhosingh, at Gurh-Ameythee, where they were very kindly treated. Madhosingh sent us in their letters to Lucknow, furnished them with such comforts as he could procure himself, and took charge of the articles which we wished to send: and, after sheltering the ladies for some days, forwarded them in safety to Allahabad. The rest of the party, joined by Lieutenant Grant, Assistant-Commissioner, found refuge for some days with a neighbouring zemindar, and were by him afterwards escorted in safety to Allahabad.

The officers who remained at Sultanpoor were less fortunate. The troops rose in mutiny on the morning of the 9th of June, when Colonel Fisher, in returning from the lines of the Military Police, whom he had harangued and endeavoured to reduce to order, was shot in the back by one of that regiment with a musket-ball. The wound was mortal, and Fisher was attended in his last moments by the adjutant of the corps, Lieutenant C. Tucker. The troopers of the regiment would not come near their colonel; but neither did they injure him. They, however, attacked and killed the second in command, Captain Gibbings, who was on horseback near the dooly in which Fisher lay. The men then shouted to Lieutenant Tucker to go; and finding it useless to attempt to stay longer, he rode off, and, crossing the river, found shelter in the fort of Roostum Sah, at Deyrah, on the banks of the Goomtee. There he was joined next day by Captain Bunbury, of the Military Police, and Captain W. Smith, Lieutenant Lewis, and Dr. O'Donel, of the 8th O. I. Infantry. Information was sent in to Benares of their escape, and they were brought in by a native escort, which was immediately sent out by the Commissioner of Benares, Mr. H. Carre Tucker.

Roostum Sah is a fine specimen of the best kind of talooqdars in Oudh. Of old family, and long settled at Deyrah, he resides there in a fort very strongly situated in the ravines of the Goomtee, and surrounded by a thick jungle of large extent. It had never been taken by the troops of the native Government, which had more than once been repulsed from before it. Roostum Sah deserves the more credit for his kind treatment of the refugees, as he had suffered unduly at the settlement, and had lost many villages which he should have been permitted to retain. I had seen him at Fyzabad in January, 1857, and after discussing his case with the Deputy-Commissioner, Mr. W. A. Forbes, it had been settled that fresh inquiries should be made into the title of the villages which he had lost, and orders had been issued accordingly. It is singular that Roostum Sah and Lall Honwunt Singh, in the Salone district, who had both been severe sufferers by the settlement proceedings, should have distinguished themselves by their kindness to British officers.

Thus perished Samuel Fisher, a man well known in India, where he had made many friends and no enemies. A keen sportsman, a splendid rider, he excelled in every sport of the field; while his kind and loving disposition endeared him to all who knew him. Until the day before his death, I had been in daily communication with him, conveying and receiving intelligence. On the 10th of June, no post arrived from Sultanpoor, and we too surely guessed the cause.

Besides Colonel Fisher and Captain Gibbings, two young civilians were unhappily also slain, Mr. A. Block, C. S., and Mr. S. Stroyan. When the mutiny broke out, they crossed the river, and took refuge with one Yaseen Khan, zemindar of the town of Sultanpoor. This man at first welcomed them; but afterwards most basely betrayed them. He turned both officers out of his house, and then caused them to be shot down. This is the only instance of like treachery on the part of a petty zemindar in Oudh which came to our notice.

After getting rid of the European officers, the mutineers sacked and burned their houses. The three regiments then marched for Lucknow. On the way, however, they heard of the discomfiture of the 3rd Regt. of Military Police, which was on its march from Lucknow to meet them; and, turning to the right, took the road to Duriabad. Thence they proceeded on to Newabgunje Bara Bankee, which, by the 27th of June, became the rendezvous of all the mutineers in Oudh.

At Salone, the third station of the Fyzabad division, were quartered six companies of the 1st O. I. Infantry, commanded by Captain R. L. Thompson. These were the last to mutiny. Everything was maintained in tolerable order there by the exertions of the excellent Deputy-Commissioner, Captain L. Barrow, until the 10th of June, and then no blood was shed. The sepoys ceased to obey, and warned our officers to depart. The civil and military officers left together. As they passed through the lines, some of the sepoys saluted, while others were loading their muskets. Captain Thompson was accompanied by a few faithful men, who never deserted him; and a few of his native subordinates attended Captain Barrow. That officer had arranged to be met outside the station by Lall Honwunt Singh, talooqdar of Dharoopoor, with an escort of his men. The chief appeared punctual to his promise, and escorted the whole party to his fort at Dharoopoor. There they remained for nearly a fortnight, and were kindly treated during the whole time. At the end of this, Honwunt Singh, with 500 of his followers, accompanied them to the ferry over the Ganges, opposite Allahabad, and there took leave. He would receive no present for his hospitality. The conduct of this man is the more deserving, as he had lost an undue number of villages, and his case, as well as that of Roostum Sah, of Deyrah, was one that called for reconsideration. Captain Barrow and his whole party reached the Fort of Allahabad in safety.

It only remains to notice the events which occurred at Duriabad, a station and district of the Lucknow division. At this place was a large amount of treasure, about three lacs, which it was desired, if possible, to save. The 5th O. I. Infantry was quartered at the station, commanded by Captain W. H. Hawes. An attempt had been made a fortnight before, to bring in the treasure under escort of this regiment, but it had failed in consequence of the opposition made by some of the men. On the 9th of June, Captain Hawes again attempted its removal. This young officer was enthusiastically devoted to his duty, and was much liked by his men. The treasure was laden, and the men marched off cheering. It had not, however, proceeded more than half a mile, when mutiny broke out. Part of the men wished to go on with the treasure, while the disaffected party detained it. The latter commenced firing, and gained their point. The treasure carts were taken back to the station, and the European residents fled.

The Commandant, Captain Hawes, had a miraculous escape. He was repeatedly fired at, sometimes a volley being directed at him, and at others, single, deliberate shots. He fortunately escaped them all, galloped off across the country, and after being kindly received and treated by Ram Singh, zemindar of Suhee, with other of the Duriabad refugees, he reached Lucknow on the 11th of June. Lieutenants Grant and Fullerton, and their families, who were also kindly entertained by Ram Singh, had previously been put into serious peril. They had placed the ladies and children inside a native covered cart, by the side of which themselves were walking, when they were overtaken by some of the mutineers. Lieutenant Grant carried a double rifle, which he was called upon to surrender. He did so, and the party were made prisoners, and were taken back on the road to Duriabad. On the way they were met by messengers from the regiment, who set them free, saying that it was not the wish of the men to do them harm. The rifle was even returned to Lieutenant Grant, and they were suffered to depart, and reached Lucknow without further accident. The Deputy-Commissioner, Mr. W. Benson, C. S., and his wife, also escaped; first taking refuge with the talooqdar of Hurâha, who treated them kindly, and then riding in the whole way to Lucknow. Captain Hawes, Lieutenant Grant, and his family, took up their abode with us.

After the Europeans had left, the mutineers proclaimed the ex-King of Oudh to be king, and proceeded to search for the extra assistant, a Mussulman gentleman named Abdool Huqueem. Some friends, however, concealed him; and he soon after made his escape, and arrived at Lucknow with a second native extra assistant employed in that district, Alee Ruza Khan, who had been cotwal of Lucknow under the native Government, of whom further mention will be made hereafter.

The 5th I. Infantry did not move from Duriabad for some days, and then marched to the mutineer rendezvous at Newabgunje Bara Bankee.

Thus, in the course of ten days, we had lost every station in the Province. The people had everywhere continued orderly until the troops rose, and then our refugees had, with few exceptions, experienced at their hands kindness and good treatment. After the 10th of June all posts ceased to arrive, and the British authority was confined to the capital, and its immediate neighbourhood.

CHAPTER IX.

JUNE, THE MONTH BEFORE THE SIEGE—PREPARATIONS FOR IT.

The disastrous tidings from out-stations deeply moved Sir Henry Lawrence. —He proposes to remove all the Europeans to the Muchee Bhowun.— Council of War called.—Opinions of Captain Fulton, Lieutenant Anderson, Dr. Fayrer, and Mr. Gubbins.—Removal of stores from the Muchee Bhowun.—Sir Henry Lawrence's intention appeared to be to hold both the Residency and the Muchee Bhowun ; but to make the last stand at the former place.—Sir Henry Lawrence's health gives way.—He appoints a Provisional Council.—The Council refuse to disarm the mutineer remnants, but agree to their being ordered to go to their homes on leave.—The order obeyed : all but 350 men take leave and go.—Major Gall's enterprise and death.—Sir Henry resumes his duties.—Mr. Gubbins' management of the intelligence department.— Native scouts; assistance given by the native gentry; wild and absurd reports.—Full information obtained of the movements of mutineers.— Their concentration at Newabgunje reported to Sir Henry on the 24th of June.—Mutiny of the 3rd Regt. of Military Police.—About the middle of June the engineers begin in earnest to fortify the Residency.—Description of the position, which occupied an elevated plateau.—Water Gate; irregular line of defence from that to the Hospital; Treasury ; Bailey Guard ; Aitken's battery : gateway ; Dr. Fayrer's compound wall ; Financial-office garrison ; Sago's house ; Post-office battery ; Judicial-office garrison ; Anderson's house ; Cawnpoor battery ; Duprat's house ; Martinière school-house ; King's hospital, or brigade mess ; Seikh squares ; Gubbins' post.—Unprotected state of the south and west faces of the position.—New battery commenced on the 22nd of June at the south-west angle.—Unfinished Sheep-house battery, and Malakoff.—Mr. Ommanney's enclosure.—Slaughter-house ; sheep-house ; church ; Evans' battery.—Innes' post.—Redan battery.—Surrounding native buildings —Some of these pulled down, on the west and north-west.—Residency.—Telegraph upon its roof.—Banqueting-hall.—Dr. Fayrer's house.—Post-office.—Mr. Ommanney's house.—Fall in value of public securities.—Cessation of public and private credit.—State prisoners.—Mr. Gubbins' levies.—Abdoolazeez Khan Risaldar ; the artillery darogha Meer Furzundalee ; the overseer Ramadeen ; the architect Pirâna ; the smith Golaub.—Desertion of all the remnants of Irregular Cavalry.—Sir Henry Lawrence's exertions to provision the garrison.—Native pensioners got in.—Measures taken to secure the allegiance of the talooqdars.—Gunpowder and treasure buried.—Vo-

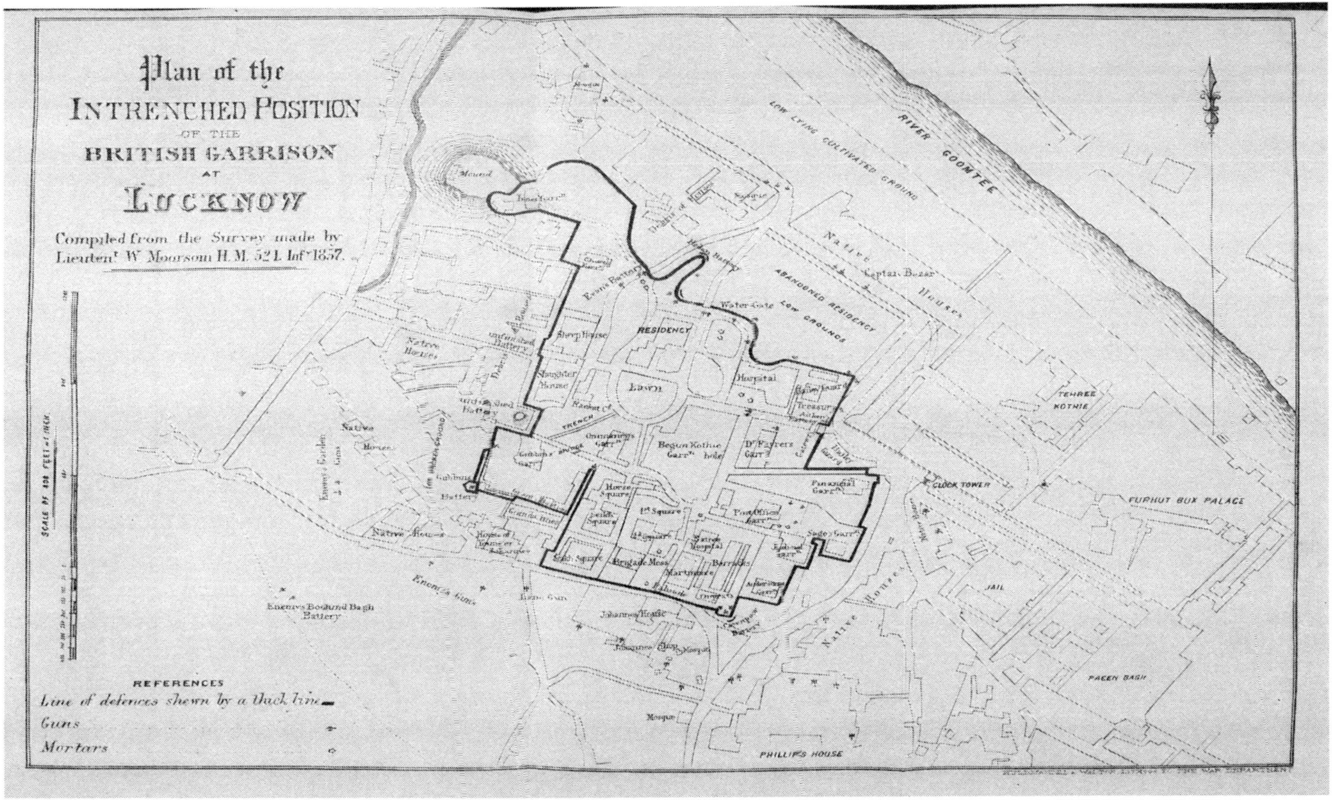

Plan of the
INTRENCHED POSITION
OF THE
BRITISH GARRISON
AT
LUCKNOW
Compiled from the Survey made by
Lieuten.t W. Moorsom H.M. 52 L. Inf.y 1857.
SCALE OF 400 FEET = 1 INCH
REFERENCES
Line of defences shewn by a thick line
Guns
Mortars
RIVER GOOMTEE
LOW LYING CULTIVATED GROUND
Native Houses
Captan Bazar
ABANDONED RESIDENCY
LOW GROUNDS
Water Gate
RESIDENCY
Lawn
Hospital
Treasury
Begum Kothie Garr.n
D.r Fayrers Garr.n
Sheep House
Slaughter House
TRENCH
Mound
Native Houses
Enemy's Garden Guns
Battery
Horse Square
1.st Square
Post Office Garr.n
Brigade Mess
Martiniere
Barracks
Sago Garr.n
Enemy's Guns
Enemy's Boshund Bagh Battery
Johannes House
Mosque
CLOCK TOWER
TEHREE KOTHIE
FURHUT BUX PALACE
JAIL
PAEEN BAGH
PHILLIPS HOUSE

lunteer Cavalry raised by Captain Radcliffe.—Discovery by Captain Fulton of the native guns, and 8-inch howitzer.—Seizure and execution of conspirators.—Communications received from Sir Hugh Wheeler.—News brought by Mr. Gubbins' cossids of the destruction of the Cawnpoor force.—Despatch to Major Rénaud.—Escape of Lieutenants Delafosse and Thompson.—Remarks on the Cawnpoor catastrophe.—Removal of the King's jewels from the Kaiser Bagh.—First fall of rain.

THE recurring tidings of these disasters which daily and hourly reached us, being brought in either by the fugitives themselves, or inferred from the ominous stopping of the post from each successive station, deeply moved Sir Henry Lawrence. Though intending to hold the Residency also, he had all along regarded the Muchee Bhowun as his place of strength. Now, therefore, on the 8th of June, he proposed to remove thither all the Europeans and their families. The measure being much opposed, a council of war was called, comprising most of the civil and military officers. A set of questions was proposed, and written answers were required from each member. The two most important questions were, first, whether both posts, *i. e.* the Muchee Bhowun and the Residency, should be held, or one only; and secondly, whether the ladies should be sent away to Nipaul, or down the Ganges in boats? I did not see all the answers which were given, but certainly among the most valuable opinions given were those recorded by the Executive Engineer, Captain Fulton, and Lieutenant J. C. Anderson, of the Engineers. Both these officers strongly urged the abandonment of the Muchee Bhowun, and the concentration of our force at the Residency. Captain Fulton's opinion was that the Muchee Bhowun was untenable; that its walls would not resist artillery; and that the large masonry drains underneath it would afford the enemy great opportunity of mining the fort. Dr. Fayrer pointed out the existing sickness in the garrison of the Muchee Bhowun, the close and confined accommodation, and gave it as his opinion that, if the number within the fort were much increased, there was great danger of epidemic sickness. I attached my signature to Captain Fulton's opinion. We all, I believe, opposed the removal of the women and children, as no longer practicable.

Sir Henry Lawrence was then extremely weak, and the members of the council separated without any decision being made known. I understood, however, that Sir Henry's faith in the Muchee Bhowun had been much shaken, and though he could not decide on abandoning it, still that he had resolved on making the last stand at the Residency, and abandoning the Muchee Bhowun when it was no longer tenable. Certainly a few days later large quantities of shot, shell, gunpowder, stores of food, beer and porter, and several heavy guns, began to be removed from the Muchee Bhowun into the Residency premises. Still very considerable stores were left in the Muchee Bhowun, and sometimes guns were ordered back there, and the works at the Muchee Bhowun were continued actively; so that Sir Henry evidently clung to the hope of retaining the Muchee Bhowun also.

On the 9th of June, Sir Henry's health entirely gave way. An alarming exhaustion came on; and the medical man pronounced that further application to business would endanger his life. A provisional council was accordingly formed by his authority, at which I presided, comprising the Judicial Commissioner Mr. Ommanney, Major Banks, Colonel Inglis, Major Anderson the Chief Engineer, and myself. Our first business was with a letter from Sir Hugh Wheeler, which was put into our hands by a soobahdar of the 1st N. I., who had been sent with it, by the

General, from his intrenchment. Sir Hugh wrote that the troops joined by the Nana had attacked him on the 6th with heavy guns, and he entreated that aid might be sent. It was too clear that we were in no condition to render it. Not a man could be spared from the Muchee Bhowun, or Residency; and the Europeans in cantonments could not be withdrawn from their guard over their native comrades. Mournfully but unanimously it was decided that aid could not be rendered; and the soobahdar, who wished to go to his home, departed, first receiving from us the reward of 1000 rupees, promised by General Wheeler.

A company of the 9th O. I. Infantry was on duty then in the Muchee Bhowun, under command of Lieutenant Vanrenen. It was their comrades who perpetrated the frightful massacre of the Shajehanpoor fugitives. This company now exhibited signs of disaffection; and it was proposed in the council to disarm it. The measure was strongly opposed by Colonel Inglis and Major Anderson, who were afraid of bringing on a crisis. The majority, however, carried the measure; and the men were disarmed the same day without any opposition; and sent on leave to their homes.

I again urged upon the council the necessity of taking away the arms from the native troops, who so hampered our movements in cantonments: but I could not get them to agree.*

I must freely state that I regarded and still regard our condition at that moment to have been most critical. And if we had not succeeded in depriving the large mass of native troops then around us of their arms; I neither then saw, nor can I now see, what chance we had of successful resistance. Most fortunately the object was effected in another

* See Addenda, No. III.

way. The council agreed that the officer commanding in cantonments should be directed to parade the troops, and inform them that it was our wish that they should take leave, and go to their homes until November. This order was issued on the 10th. On the following day we received Colonel Halford's reply, which was to the effect that the men did not wish to go. The measure was known to be opposed by the commanders, who did not wish their regiments to be obliterated, and still retained some confidence in their men. One of them waited upon us, and said that his sepoys declared that it was the part of good soldiers to stand by their Government in the hour of need, and not to desert them. It was resolved in council that the commanders should be required to enforce the measure by their own advice and authority upon the men; in other words, we would have the men go. The council broke up late on the 11th, but I remained to draft the order, which was despatched by a trooper to cantonments before night; and was communicated to the troops next morning. When the men found that we were in earnest, they all agreed to go; and the work of disarmament proceeded rapidly. All the 7th Light Cavalry went away except the native officers. About 350 sepoys were allowed to remain, of whom 170 men belonged to the 13th N. I., and the rest to the 48th and 71st Regts. Of this number, many were Seikhs. The cavalry horses were brought up and picketed near the Residency; and the arms were brought in in hundreds, and stored in some of the Residency buildings.

Major Gall, commanding the 2nd O. I. Cavalry, had been removed by Sir Henry Lawrence from the command of his corps, over which he was not thought to possess sufficient influence, he being a Madras officer, and the men natives of Hindostan. Sir Henry had appointed him his aide-de-camp; but Gall fretted at his removal, and would not be satisfied unless charged with some service specially his own. He persuaded Colonel Inglis to propose that he should be permitted to carry despatches to Allahabad, and the measure was agreed to by the council. Major Gall selected a party of his own troopers, and left Lucknow on the night of the 11th. The service was a hazardous one, but if executed with judgment was far from impossible. It was necessary to avoid all towns and large thoroughfares, and to go across the country, passing the night in the open. The weather was exceedingly hot, and on nearing the town of Rai Bareilly, Gall was tempted to enter it. He was disguised as a native, but the woman who kept the suray penetrated the disguise, and betrayed him. Some believe that his troopers were the betrayers. There was at the moment a party of sepoy mutineers passing through the place, and information had no sooner been given, than a crowd of them and of the townspeople pressed into the suray. Escape was hopeless. One of the party who escaped informed me that Gall had fired two barrels of his revolver at the insurgents, and then, placing the weapon to his head, had shot himself.

On the 12th of June, Sir Henry Lawrence had sufficiently recovered to enable him to resume his functions, and the authority of the provisional council ceased. By it I had been entrusted with the superintendence of the intelligence department, which I retained at Sir Henry Lawrence's request. This was now organized. We desired information of Sir Hugh Wheeler at Cawnpoor; to forward despatches to Benares, Agra, and Allahabad; and to obtain information of the movements of the mutineers in Oudh.

Until we were ourselves beleaguered, these objects were sufficiently well accomplished. The chief agents were pâsies, a class of men of whom I have before made mention. A tribe of these men live in the neighbourhood of Ramnugger Dhumeyree, about thirty miles north-east of Lucknow, who are reckoned especially daring and trustworthy ; and of these thirty men were at once engaged and located in my compound ; others were afterwards summoned, and some pensioned sepoys were employed. Some of these men went out daily with despatches. They crossed the Ganges at Cawnpoor, though the ferry was strictly guarded by the enemy, and conveyed Sir Henry Lawrence's despatches under the enemy's fire into Sir Hugh Wheeler's camp, and brought us back his replies. Three of these will be found in the Appendix,* and possess a deep and thrilling interest ; particularly the noble and soldierlike letter of Captain Moore, of the 32nd Regt. We also received answers to the despatches forwarded to Allahabad and Benares.

To obtain intelligence of the movements of the mutineers in the interior of the Province, additional agency was employed. Some of the native gentry assisted me. One in particular, Mirza Hydur, a descendant of the Buhoo Begum, who had connections at Fyzabad, furnished me with the most full and circumstantial accounts of what was doing at that station, which were written by an agent there, and despatched to him almost daily by a special messenger. A confidential agent of Rajah Mansingh's also attended, and gave us correct intelligence of the movements of the troops. The agent of Goreeshunkur, zemindar of Morawun, did the same. Several of our native officials, who were lying *perdus* in various parts of the Pro-

* Appendix, No. 2.

vince, managed to send in written accounts of passing events.

We still possessed a few outposts, one at the distance of fifteen miles from Lucknow, from which reports were received. As the mutineers drew nearer, parties of horse used at my motion to be sent out to patrol the main lines of road, sometimes to the distance of twenty miles, in order to test the truth of the reports which reached us. Captain Maclean, of the 71st N. I., had also several native scouts in his employ, and often obtained through them very correct intelligence, which he daily rendered to me. The most wild and absurd reports were at this time abroad. Constant rumours were spread that the enemy was approaching cantonments, when I had good evidence that they were not nearer than thirty miles; but it was no easy matter always to separate the truth from falsehood. I remember, among many other instances, a native groom of Colonel Goldney's coming in from Sultanpoor, and most positively declaring to me that his master's children had been killed. The man protested that he had seen them dead with his own eyes. At the moment I was in possession of recent accounts from Mrs. Goldney, which assured me that the children were safe with herself at Ameythee. I had three assistants in this duty—Captain W. H. Hawes, Captain Weston, and Lieutenant Lester. With their aid the depositions of native informants and translations of native reports used to be taken down. To these I used to attach a memorandum stating whether I considered the information trustworthy or not, and the paper was then forwarded to Sir Henry Lawrence. By aid of these means full information of the movements of the mutineers was obtained. On the 24th of June, I waited on Sir Henry, and told him that it was now clear that all the mutineers were fast concentrating at Newabgunje Bara Bankee, and that there was no doubt that they would come in by the Fyzabad road: if, then, any intention was entertained of giving them battle, perhaps he might think fit to have the line of road examined by the engineers, with a view to select the best battle-field, and preparing, if he thought right, outworks to support our position. I mentioned the Kookrail Bridge as possibly affording a good position. In consequence of this representation, Sir Henry drove out the same evening, and inspected the ground, which he told me afterwards was not sufficiently favourable.

On the 12th June, the 3rd Regt. of Military Police, commanded by Captain Adolphe Orr, which furnished the gaol guard and took most of the civil duties at Lucknow, mutinied, abandoned their several posts, and marched off on the road to Sultanpoor, plundering several houses belonging to Europeans in their way. They were pursued, though somewhat late in the day, by a force commanded by Colonel Inglis, consisting of two companies of Her Majesty's 32nd, two guns from the European battery, about seventy Seikh horse commanded by Captain Forbes, and forty or fifty European volunteer cavalry composed of English officers, civilians, clerks, and others. The mutineers had got well ahead, and though the European infantry pushed on rapidly under a burning sun, it could not overtake them. The guns and cavalry came up with their rear, and did some execution, killing about fifteen of them. As many more were taken prisoners. The mutineers fought well, and killed two of our best native troopers in the charge, wounding several others, including Mr. J. B. Thornhill, C.S. The heat was terrible, and we lost two Europeans from apoplexy. The party returned at night after a harassing duty, and in reporting to Sir Henry Lawrence the capture of the prisoners, the Deputy-Commissioner, Mr. Martin, who had formed one of the volunteer cavalry, expressed a hope that they might be executed, for, said he, they have done their best to kill us. After two days, however, they were all released. It was believed that some of their captors had, at the time, held out their open hand to them in token of quarter. Had such, however, been the case in some instances, it was certainly a misplaced clemency to release the whole.

Before the troops had come up with the mutineers, Captain Weston, Superintendent of the Military Police, had ridden after them alone, and endeavoured to bring back the men to obedience. They treated him civilly, and did not attempt to injure him; but would not listen to his remonstrance. This regiment had been on its way to join the Sultanpoor mutineers. It now, however, left the Sultanpoor road and turned off towards Cawnpoor, which it reached, and joined the Nana in his attack on General Wheeler's intrenchment.

About the middle of the month the engineers began in earnest to fortify the Residency position, and to throw up defences capable of resisting the assault of artillery. On the north side a strong battery for heavy guns, afterwards called the Redan, was begun on the 18th by Captain Fulton, Executive Engineer; and a few days before, the battery on the south side, called the Cawnpoor Battery, from its position commanding the high road from that station, was commenced by Lieutenant J. C. Anderson. I must endeavour briefly to describe the position which we occupied as it stood when the siege began.

It is an elevated plateau of land, irregular in surface, of which the highest point was occupied by the Residency. Towards the river, the ground sunk by rather a steep declivity to the level of the stream. Part of the old Residency grounds were on this low level, but these were abandoned. Beginning at the Water Gate on the north side, the line of defence (marked in the plan *a*, *a*, *a*,) ran along the irregular ridge of the high level, which was protected by a low earth-bank and ditch. Further protection was afforded by sand-bags placed upon the bank, through the openings in which our men, standing in the ditch inside, were able to fire. The work was not more than breast-high, and was insufficient. In the space between the Water Gate and the Hospital, three guns were placed, an 18-pounder, a 24-pound howitzer, and a 9-pounder; and near them were two 8-inch mortars. The line marked *b*, *b*, followed as far as the gateway the exterior wall of the Residency compound, with a fall of several feet down to the road outside. At the Treasury and Bailey Guard, which were on a lower level than the Hospital above, were stationed a party of the 13th N. I., commanded by Lieutenant Aitken. With the aid of his men, this officer constructed, during the siege, a battery for an 18-pounder gun to the left of the Bailey Guard Gate, which was of much service. The gateway was lofty and arched, and the gate in good order. During the siege it was banked up from the inside with earth. The road leading from the Residency through the gateway to the public highway beyond, was throughout a steep descent. Three field-pieces, two 9-pounders, and a 24-pound howitzer were put in position on the road, and completely commanded the ascent from the gateway. South of the gate the wall of Dr. Fayrer's compound was the only defence, which was very weak and low.

It was protected by one and sometimes two guns facing towards the clock-tower. The triangular building forming the external Bailey Guard was abandoned. A barricade was put up to defend the lane which separated Fayrer's from the Financial Garrison. The line of defence then followed the enclosure wall of the latter building. The building itself, which is of two stories, stands on higher ground, and the road outside is low. Beyond this was Sago's house, a smaller lower-roomed building; the enclosing wall and compound of which were abandoned, and the defence confined to the house itself. This house, though situated higher than the road, stood low, and was much exposed. Both it and the Financial Commissioner's office were commanded by the Post-office above, where two 18-pounders and a 9-pounder were placed. Next to Sago's house was the Judicial Commissioner's office, a large double-storied building situated on high ground. Here the external wall and compound which sloped off too much had similarly been abandoned, and a strong line of defence put up of large pointed stakes imbedded in the ground, and protected by a bank of earth. Next came Captain Anderson's house, a smaller one, also on high ground, and of two stories. It formed the south-eastern angle of our position, and was much exposed during the siege. The line of defence was carried close outside it along a deep trench which was dug, with palisades at the bottom.

The Cawnpoor Battery came next; here were placed three guns, an 18-pounder, and two 9-pounders. It was constructed of earth and palisades, and closely abutted on Duprat's house. This last was a single-storied building, with a verandah fronting the outside. The verandah was now protected by a mud wall, which was built along it, and pierced for musketry. The wall, partly protected by a palisade, was continued till it joined the next building, in which were located the boys of the Martinière, under the principal of the college, Mr. G. Schilling.

It had, at first, been intended to defend the Martinière, which is a lofty and strong building, about two and a half miles east from the Residency; and for this purpose arms had been served out to the masters, and for some of the larger boys, and some defences had been added to the building. Its isolated position, however, rendered it untenable under the altered circumstances; and the whole of the inmates had been brought in and located in the building referred to, which was a native one belonging to the native banking firm of Sah Biharee Lall; and which, thereafter, went by the name of the Martinière. It was single-storied; but possessed a good parapet protecting its flat roof. A broad road separated it from the King's Hospital, which was closed by a strong palisade and bank, which extended along the outside front of the Martinière. On the other side of this road was the King's Hospital, a commanding and striking-looking building, particularly on its outside or south front, where the massive outer wall rose to a height overtopping all the neighbouring buildings. In the rear of the main building and outer enclosure were two subordinate ones called the first and second squares. The body of the building was occupied by the officers of the Light Cavalry and N. I. Regts. as a mess, and the building went during the siege by the name of the Brigade Mess. The two inner courts were surrounded by lines of low flat masonry buildings, where many of the families during the siege found tolerably comfortable accommodation: and where, from the high surrounding walls, they were well protected from the enemy's fire. Next to the brigade mess were two square enclosures surrounded by rows of low, flat-roofed buildings, which were termed the Seikh squares, from their having during the siege been occupied by the Seikh Cavalry under Lieutenant Hardinge. Little or nothing had been done for their protection. At the south-west angle the native buildings closely adjoined the line of defence; and to enable the men to fire from the roofs of the buildings enclosing the Seikh squares it was necessary to put up protections of tents, sand-bags, and boards after the siege had begun.

The Seikh squares were separated from the eastern wall of my compound by a broad way which led up to my gate. It was closed near its inner extremity by a very imperfect defence, consisting of a bank of earth and some palisades. Its best defence, however, was a 24-pound howitzer placed so as to sweep the street.

Of the buildings and enclosure which formed my post I have already given some description. No improvement was made in them beyond those already indicated, until eight days before the siege began. At that time, we had no means of mounting artillery along almost the whole west and south faces of the position; that is, from the Church Battery on the N. W. to the Cawnpoor Battery on the S. E. there was not a gun. Captain Fulton had indeed commenced a battery at the Sheep-house, and Lieutenant Hutchinson had begun an elevated battery to the west of Ommanney's house, called the Malakoff. But these, even if finished, would have left the whole south and south-west faces unprotected. At my urgent request, therefore, a battery was commenced by Lieutenant Hutchinson, about the 22nd of June, at the south-western corner of the position, where the outhouses of my compound formed a re-entering angle.

From the Cawnpoor Battery up to this point, the ground outside our position was on the same level as that inside, or was higher. But near the angle where the new battery was begun it fell abruptly about fourteen or fifteen feet. So that the roofs of the outhouses on the west side commanded the neighbouring ground from a considerable elevation. We had to begin the new battery from the lower level, and had therefore much to do to raise it to the required height; but when completed there could not be a finer position for a gun, flanking the two sides of the enclosure, and menacing the whole surrounding area.

On the west face where my outhouses ended, we had scarcely any defence. I obtained from Sir Henry Lawrence a 9-pounder gun, which we placed there in the open, with a low mud bank in front of it; and during the siege we strengthened the earthwork greatly, and put up palisades.

Indeed, at this time it was scarcely anticipated that my post, or other outposts, could be held. And the engineers were more busy in preparing a wooden bridge, by which we might escape into Mr. Ommanney's compound across the narrow lane which separated the two, than in making the outworks of the enclosure defensible against the enemy.

A wall built across this lane connected my enclosure wall with the west face of Mr. Ommanney's, through the centre of whose garden a deep trench was cut diagonally, protected with stakes to serve as an additional defence.

Our defences then followed the outer wall of a range of buildings enclosing an oblong square marked in the plan the Slaughter-house. Here was a guard of Europeans. Here also were the bullocks kept; and close adjoining to them, their fodder; the bhoosa, or chaff-straw, was stored in the racket-court, completely filling it.

The next post across a narrow lane was the sheep-house enclosure, the outer wall of which served as a defence. A small native guard was stationed there.

At the north-west angle of my enclosure the ground rose again to a level with our own position, and continued so to the north-west angle of the sheep-house, where it suddenly again sunk; the church and its whole enclosure, which formed our graveyard during the siege, lying much below the road adjoining it. Originally, therefore, these were excluded from the line of defence, which was carried along the road, marked by a low bank of earth. Near the entrance descent to the church, upon the road, was placed a battery of three guns, viz. one 18-pounder and two 9-pounders, which, from having been commanded during the siege by Captain Evans, the Deputy-Commissioner of Poorwah, was known as Evans' Battery.

These guns protected the church and graveyard below; and at the commencement of the siege, all or most of our supplies of grain and ghee,* &c., were stored inside the former building, where a small guard of Europeans was stationed.

Connected with the main position by a neck of land, and on the same high level with the rest of it, was Innes' post, which formed our extreme outpost on the north-west. From its great distance it had not been originally included in the line of defence, but the importance of the position compelled us to retain it. The house was lower-storied with a flat roof, and

* Clarified butter.

had once been the residence of Lieutenant Macleod Innes, of the Engineers, whence its name. The ground around it, and which was left in the possession of the enemy, lay very low, giving to the building a commanding position. A portion of the front where it was weak was defended by a palisade. On the north the compound was very ill-protected by a low mud wall. The chief security of the post lay in the vicinity of the guns of the Redan Battery, and Evans', by which it was commanded. Beyond it was an elevated natural mound, covered with trees, and with the tombs of an old Mahomedan cemetery, which commanded Innes' post. Precipitous ravines descended from it on three sides. But this, from its distance, was not occupied.

On the north face, not far from Evans' guns, was constructed on a projecting point of high level ground the best battery which we possessed—the Redan. Captain Fulton and Major Anderson devoted their best energies to it, and certainly succeeded. The battery was more than a half-moon, and was mounted with two 18-pounders and a 9-pounder. Their fire swept the Captain Bazar houses, and all the low ground below the battery extending to and beyond the river, and up to the iron bridge.

Between the Redan Battery and Evans' guns was the mortar battery. The low-lying ground north and east of the Redan was abandoned, and a line of earthwork surmounted by sand-bags with a ditch inside connected it with the Water Gate. This line was irregular, following the high level of the ground.

Two guns, 9-pounders, were placed at the Water Gate in battery, thus completing the line of defence.

Viewed as a whole, the defences were very insufficient at the time when we were invested. They were indeed incomplete at the time, and a further delay of a week or ten days would have enabled us to strengthen ourselves greatly. In many places there was nothing really deserving the name of an obstacle to prevent the enemy from coming in, if he had possessed courage to press forward in the face of the heavy fire opposed to him.

The chief weakness in the position consisted in the number of native buildings which surrounded us almost on all sides; and which, as soon as the siege began, became filled with the enemy's sharpshooters, from whose ceaseless fire the garrison suffered more than from any other cause.

Near the Redan Battery on the north and along the west face, Captain Fulton, whose energy, resolution, and ceaseless exertion cannot be too highly praised, having fortunately succeeded in obtaining the necessary authority, demolished a large number of native buildings, and cleared a space which greatly assisted our defence; but there was not an outpost which did not suffer severely from the number of buildings which unhappily were permitted to remain. Under Captain Fulton's instructions, I had a large gang of labourers pulling down the houses, which actually touched and overlooked my premises on the north-west. And thus, at the eleventh hour, a clearance was made of buildings, whose occupation by the enemy would have rendered the maintenance of my post impossible. Still, in that quarter, others remained which commanded the upper and lower windows of my house within 100 yards. And from them during the siege we suffered great annoyance. To the south of my post, although the ground was covered with houses, of which the principal one was that of the younger Johannes, I was not suffered to carry on the work of demolition; but was permitted only to knock off the top parapet of the roofs.

Of the buildings within the line of defence, some few have to be described.

The Residency, which stood upon the highest eminence of the plateau, was an imposing pile of building. It was of three stories. Along the west front extended a wide and lofty colonnaded verandah. The principal entrance was on the east side, under a handsome portico, the outer side of which had been barricaded with chests and boxes. A spiral stairs inside two turrets on the north and south sides led to the roof. From this the view was beautiful, extending over the city and adjoining country. The number and variety of the buildings—the gilded domes and cupolas—the elegant outline of the palaces—the Kaiser Bagh, the Chuttur Munzil and Furhut Bux, all set in the deep green of the surrounding trees and country—together made up a scene of surpassing beauty. But no building could have been less calculated for purposes of defence. Its numberless lofty windows, which had not been walled up, offered an unopposed entrance to bullets and rifle-balls. And the roof, which was protected only by an ornamental balustrade in the Italian style, was wholly exposed. Upon the roof, Captain Fulton had erected, under Sir Henry Lawrence's instructions, a signal post, for telegraphic communication with the Muchee Bhowun, where a corresponding signal was put up. Under the south side of the Residency were excellent tykhanas or underground rooms, in which the women of the 32nd were placed. The ground-floor was occupied by the soldiers. The rest of the building was completely filled with officers, ladies, and children. No sooner had the siege commenced, than its exposed position began to be severely felt, and all the ladies and children abandoned the upper stories. The mess of the 32nd kept possession of a centre room on the first floor, until several casualties had occurred; when they too were obliged to abandon it.

The Residency banqueting-hall was from the commencement converted into a hospital. It was of two stories, with very large and lofty rooms, standing upon almost the same level as the Residency; and being pierced with numerous large doors and windows, it suffered almost equally with the latter in exposure to the enemy's bullets and shot. The openings on the exposed sides were, however, closed and protected with tents and every available material. Still not a few were struck inside it; and among others our excellent chaplain, Mr. Polehampton, was severely wounded by a musket-ball in one of the rooms.

Dr. Fayrer's house was an extensive lower-storied building, and was at first very much exposed to the enemy's fire. The flat roof was protected by sand-bags all round, from behind which the inmates were able to keep up a fire upon the enemy. A large number of lady refugees found a hospitable reception in this house from Dr. and Mrs. Fayrer. There was a large tykhana to this house also; and whenever the fire of the enemy was heavy, the ladies were confined to this portion of the building. In the post-office were the head-quarters of the Engineers and Artillery, commanded until their respective deaths by Majors J. Anderson and Simonds. In the buildings of the Begumkotee, the Commissariat officers and a number of ladies, and of the women and children of the garrison, were located. The capacious and double-storied house of my neighbour Mr. Ommanney, was soon filled with refugees, ladies and gentlemen; and here, after

M 2

Sir Henry Lawrence's death, Brigadier Inglis established his head-quarters. The Judicial and Financial Commissioner's offices were garrisoned by the European clerks, whose families also found shelter in them. In the former the Seikhs of the 13th N.I., and in the latter a party of the 32nd Regt., were also posted. Innes' post was occupied by a party of clerks, with some men of the 32nd, and a few sepoys of the 13th N. I.

Early in the month of June, public securities had fallen exceedingly low at the capital, and I was informed that Government promissory notes of 100 rupees were offered for sale for half that sum. By Sir Henry Lawrence's permission, I then offered to buy as much as two lacs of paper at any rate under sixty per cent., but I could not obtain it. Owners hesitated and wavered, and the only purchase made by me was on Sir Henry's private account, at seventy-five per cent. Two days before the siege began, however, I have been since informed that the same paper was pressed upon our officers at the Dowlutkhana, at twenty-five per cent., that is, at a discount of seventy-five per cent. All credit, however, during the last half of the month was gone. Not a native merchant could negotiate a hoondie or bill; and I was applied to repeatedly to know whether they could not obtain some temporary aid from the Government Treasury. It was of course refused. As there was no longer any prospect of receiving supplies of money from out-stations, it was ordered that the salaries of all Government officials should no longer be paid in full; but that they should only receive such small present allowance as sufficed to meet necessary expenditure.

About this time, several state prisoners were made,

being persons whose previous conduct and present behaviour threw suspicion upon them. The first of these was Moostupha Alee Khan, brother to the ex-King, whom we had found in confinement on our first occupation of the Province. He was reputed and generally believed to be weak-minded, and would have easily been made a handle of by designing men. Mahomed Homayon Khan and Meerza Mahomed Shekoh, were two princes connected with the Dehli family, who were notorious for their intrigues. They also were confined. Newaub Rookunooddowlah, one of the surviving sons of Saadut Alee Khan, a former Newaub Vuzeer of Oudh, who was believed to be in correspondence with the mutineers, was one of the number. Last, was the young Rajah of Toolseepoor, in the submontane Turay, who had been guilty of serious misbehaviour a twelvemonth before, and was already residing at the capital, under surveillance. These native gentlemen were placed in confinement in the Muchee Bhowun.

Large additions were also at this time made to the native police, under orders of Sir Henry Lawrence. Upwards of 2000 of these men were so enlisted; and many of them armed with percussion muskets. They were massed mainly at the Cotwalee or chief police station in the Emambara, beyond the Muchee Bhowun: which was also at this time fortified, and supplied with some small pieces of ordnance. All these men joined the mutineers so soon as the siege had begun. But it must not be forgotten, that they were merely newly-raised mercenaries, without discipline, who were not admitted inside our works, and could have opposed no serious resistance to the enemy.

At the same time I proceeded to raise levies myself of horse, foot, and artillery. A Naib Risaldar, named Abdoolazeez Khan, belonging to the 5th Irregular

Cavalry, stationed at Rohnee, in Bengal, happening to pass through Lucknow on leave to his home, and seeing our preparations, offered his service. During the mutiny and the succeeding nights of alarm, he brought his son and other relatives to sleep upon our roof with their arms. By Sir Henry Lawrence's sanction, I employed him to raise a few trusty horsemen, as all the Irregular Cavalry were now rapidly deserting. He raised about eighteen men, of whom eight or ten, after being dismounted, served in my garrison during the siege, and rendered good service. The 5th Irregular Cavalry had mutinied in the interim, murdering one of their officers, Sir Norman Leslie; and Abdoolazeez Khan, who was promoted at the close of the siege, had reason to rejoice that he had joined the garrison.

The artillerymen had before belonged to the service of the native Government. They had declined our service when proffered in 1856, but had since suffered much from want. Their chief, Meer Furzundalee, had received from us a pension of 100 rupees per mensem. This person now came forward, and offered us the service of some hundreds of artillerymen. By Sir Henry Lawrence's order, a number of his followers were enlisted by me, who rendered good service in transporting and piling shot and shell; but when the intrenchment was formed, a limited number of natives only could be admitted inside, and about sixteen men entered my garrison, and worked the guns under European supervision during the whole siege, in which several of them were killed. The mutineers no sooner learnt that Furzundalee was on our side, than they gutted his house, plundering it of a large amount of valuable property. Unless, therefore, some special compensation has been granted to him, Furzundalee will not have gained much by his loyalty. An old native road overseer who had served under me at Agra, named Ramadeen, a Brahmin, and a native of Oudh, being now driven in from his district employ, also joined me. He brought six of his brethren as foot soldiers; and no men ever behaved better. By night they were my best workmen in constructing the batteries; by day they fought whenever the enemy attacked. Ramadeen and two of his men were killed. The rest survived, and have been pensioned by Government. All the other foot levies whom I entertained went off, either with leave or without it, after the disaster at Chinhut.

I must not omit to mention Pirâna, a native architect, who had also followed me from Agra, and joined me at the beginning of these disturbances. His services were most valuable. He was an excellent workman, and but for his aid and that of Ramadeen, we could never have completed the works which we put up. Pirâna used to work steadily under fire, and I have seen a brick which he was about to lay knocked out of his hand by a bullet. He happily survived the siege, and has no doubt been liberally rewarded.

Captain Fulton similarly retained the services of an excellent native smith, who followed him about everywhere, named Golaub. Before we were shut in, Captain Fulton gave him his option to go or stay, as he pleased. The man remained, and his service was invaluable. Poor fellow! he was found killed by a round shot on the morning of the entry of the relieving force.

By the 25th of June all the remnants of our Irregular Cavalry had deserted us. Some went away by stealth at night, and proceeded either to

Cawnpoor to join the Nana, to the rebel rendezvous at Newabgunje, or to their homes. Some others were paid up, and sent away on leave.

The demand for gold rose at this time greatly in the city. The mutineer sepoys at the out-stations had possessed themselves of large amounts of Government treasure in silver, which was very bulky to carry about, and exchanged it for gold at high rates, wherever they could procure it.

Sir Henry Lawrence's exertions to provision the garrison were unabating. Mr. S. N. Martin, the Deputy-Commissioner, and Lieutenant James, of the Commissariat, were unceasingly at work. Grain was got in from the district, and purchased in the city, and was stored with a large quantity of ghee, or native butter, in the church. The racket-court was filled with fodder for the oxen, and stores of firewood and of charcoal were laid in. In a low piece of ground outside my enclosure, I had in the preceding year got together a fine stack of hay. This we now removed inside the enclosure, and secured in covered buildings. At the suggestion of one of my native visitors, Shurfooddowlah Gholam Ruza, I also now laid in a private store of grain and other articles against the coming siege. There were 500 maunds of wheat, 100 maunds of gram,* thirty maunds of dall,† a large supply of ghee and of rice, five maunds of soft sugar, and last, though, as proved, not least, one maund of tobacco. Besides these, I laid in a store of charcoal and wood. Subsequently, when the Commissariat store of dall (or lentils) was exhausted, twenty-five maunds of that pulse was made over by

* A sort of pea, on which horses are fed in India.

† A kind of pulse, or lentil, split, and much eaten by natives and by Europeans.

me to the Commissariat. The whole of my store of wheat was also at the same time made over to them. But they had more of their own than could be consumed or removed, and the wheat was left in my granary a prey to the enemy.

During this month also a number of pensioned native sepoys were got in, by Sir Henry Lawrence's orders, from the districts. There were about eighty of these men in all, and no suspicion ever attached to any one of them during the siege. They were at first chiefly stationed in the Muchee Bhowun, under command of Major Apthorp, but afterwards came with him into my garrison.

Several attempts were made during the month to secure the fidelity of those talooqdars in the Province whose active hostility was feared, by promises of high reward. Rajah Mansingh, with whom we were in constant correspondence, was addressed, and an offer conveyed to him of a perpetual jagheer, secured on land of 25,000*l.* per annum, if he remained faithful and rendered active aid. A like offer of a grant of 5000*l.* per annum was made to Rajah Nowab Ali, of Mohumdabad, and to Rajah Goorbux Singh, of Ramnugger Dhumeyree, with many others. Their replies were generally evasive, promising, generally, well, but complaining that they now neither possessed followers nor guns with which they could assist us.

Before the end of the month one would scarcely have recognised the Residency enclosure. It had been laid out with extreme taste, and was covered with a profusion of flowering shrubs and trees. Now, these were mostly cut down; the flower-beds were everywhere trodden down, and piles of shot and guns had taken their place.

The gunpowder, brought in from the Muchee Bhowun, was buried underground, as the safest mode of keeping it. During the siege, however, the enemy having approached near, it was removed; and a magazine was constructed in the Begumkotee. We had a large amount of treasure, twenty-three lacs, and this was buried about the middle of the month in front of the Residency. The position was a safe one; and the guard was saved which would otherwise have been necessary for its protection.

A body of Volunteer Cavalry was at this time formed under Captain Radcliffe, of the 7th Cavalry. They consisted of cavalry and infantry officers, and clerks belonging to the public offices. As many as forty sabres were collected in this way, the men being daily drilled and exercised; and this body, when called into action, rendered admirable service.

At the same time instruction in musket and gun exercise was given to the civilians generally; and men who had never used a weapon were thus habituated to the use of arms.

Our European gunners were few; and, to meet this want, a selection was made of fifty men of the 32nd Foot, who were also instructed in gun-drill. On the 21st of June, Captain Fulton, when visiting the old magazine at the Sheesh Muhul, discovered two hundred native guns lying there unmounted. The discovery was fortunately made in time, and they were all brought in, and laid out on the low ground close to the Redan Battery. Many of them were of large calibre, cast for the Oudh Government by General Claude Martine.

At the same time, Captain Fulton made another no less important discovery, having found in the same quarter an iron 8-inch howitzer, which had belonged to the native Government, lying unmounted by the roadside. This discovery was most valuable, for we possessed no artillery for horizontal fire, of larger calibre than 18-pounder guns. Our mortars were 8-inch, and we had a large supply of shells, which, by the discovery of this powerful piece of ordnance, could now be used horizontally. It was immediately brought in; a carriage was constructed for it, and elephant gear prepared for dragging it. Elephants were also trained for the same purpose.

On the 16th or 17th of June, Captain Hughes, commanding the 4th O. I. Infantry at the Dowlut-khana, happily effected an important seizure of conspirators in a house in the city. Emissaries from this secret junta had endeavoured to tamper with Captain Hughes's men, who reported it to him. By his directions the native officers simulated consent, and agreed to visit the conspirators at their residence. They went, however, accompanied by Captain Hughes himself, and the city magistrate, Captain Carnegie, and captured every one found in the house. Upon inquiry, four men, Mahomedans, were found guilty, and were hanged at the Muchee Bhowun. The two principals were, one Rusool Buksh, a native of the neighbouring town of Kakoree, and his son. This man had long been in our civil employ in the North-Western Provinces, and had been dismissed from the service of the Chief Civil Court at Agra for corruption. He had set up after our annexation of Oudh as a legal adviser in the city. His relatives in the town of Kakoree, irritated at his execution, planned an attack on our police station there, which was surprised, and two policemen killed. It was deliberated whether a force should be sent out to punish the town; but it was thought advisable to defer the measure to a season when we had less upon our hands.

On the 26th of June, a letter was received by Sir Henry Lawrence from Major Raikes, of the Gwalior Contingent, at Mynpoorie, announcing the capture of Dehli. A royal salute was thereupon ordered to be fired from the Residency, Muchee Bhowun, and cantonments. This was unfortunate, for soon after we learnt that Major Raikes had been misinformed, and that the intelligence was untrue.

By the 26th of June, many of the mutineer corps were known to have assembled at Newabgunje Bara Bankee, to which place also the rest were rapidly approaching. Great excitement prevailed in consequence, among the wealthier classes in the city. Newaub Ikramooddowlah, the ex-King's uncle-in-law, called on me, and privately offered to receive myself and family. The same proposal was made by the banking firm of Sah Buddree Doss Bunarusee Doss. These offers were civilly declined, with an intimation that we were well able to meet the mutineers. Two days before the siege began, Newaub Mohsunooddowlah sent over to me in great alarm, to say that he should be one of the first objects of the violence of the mutineers. He therefore sought a refuge. I replied, that he might come with his son, and two servants, and pitch a small tent within my compound if he pleased. He, however, hesitated too long, and eventually never came. We heard afterwards that his house had been more than once plundered by the rebels.

On the 25th and 26th of June, we received by cossid despatches from Colonel Neill at Allahabad, dated the the 18th and 23rd respectively. These letters announced the re-establishment of order at Allahabad, and the immediate intended despatch of a force of

400 Europeans, 300 Seikhs, and 2 guns, to Cawnpoor. Intimation of this was immediately despatched to Sir Hugh Wheeler. But it was too late. He had capitulated before it reached. On the 28th, a communication was received from my brother, Mr. Frederick Gubbins, Judge of Benares, conveying to us correct information of what had taken place at Dehli, and giving an account of the number of Europeans which had reached Benares, and of the active exertions made by himself and the magistrate, Mr. Lind, to forward them on.

Since the 18th of June we had received three communications from Sir Hugh Wheeler. Copies of these will be found in the Appendix.* The first, dated the 14th June, was addressed to me, and begged earnestly for "aid, aid, aid." It was hard to refuse such an appeal; but I believe that Sir Henry Lawrence acted wisely in doing so. There were but a very few boats obtainable, which were scattered at different places on the river. There would have been difficulty in collecting them together at one spot, and the enemy was almost sure to be apprised of our so doing, in time to be able to dispute the passage of the Ganges. The idea suggested by some officers was, to make a demonstration opposite Bithoor, and to cross ten miles below Cawnpoor, and thus gain the other side unobserved. But the risk was undeniably too great; and our garrison too weak, to allow of a body of men sufficiently large to be detached to accomplish this movement.

The second letter, written by Captain Moore, H.M. 32nd Foot, by General Wheeler's desire, acknowledges Sir Henry's refusal in manly language, and expresses, in noble and soldierlike terms, the undaunted resolution and devotion of the garrison.

* No. 2.

The third letter received, was written by Major G. V. Vibart, in answer to one from Sir Henry, and vividly describes the piteous condition to which the garrison inside the intrenchment had been reduced. Its burthen was, that "any aid to be effective must be immediate."

It was understood that a private messenger from Sir Hugh had delivered to Sir Henry, a day or two later, a packet containing a memorandum of his last wishes, written when escape seemed hopeless; but this paper did not pass through my hands.

Colonel Halford, of the 71st N. I., received a private letter from the intrenchment, which was kindly shown me; and as such relics are now invaluable, extracts are given in the Appendix.

Early on the 28th of June, Colonel Master, of the 7th Light Cavalry, received a scrap of paper from his son, Lieutenant G. A. Master, 53rd N. I., at Cawnpoor, acquainting him with the capitulation. A copy of this, which has been kindly furnished me, will be found in the proper place. This news was at once communicated to Sir Henry, who thereupon expressed his conviction that the Nana was only designing treachery.

On the same evening two of my cossids returned, who had been sent out with a despatch from Sir Henry Lawrence to Cawnpoor. They brought the despatch back in their hands, and their looks told us that they brought bad news. Captain Hawes and myself took them aside, and they informed us of the catastrophe which had occurred in the destruction of General Wheeler's force, and the imprisonment of a number of ladies and children. They had witnessed it themselves, and they described all the particulars precisely as they have since been related by the survivors. I hastily took down their statement, carried it over to Sir Henry, and placed it in his hands.

Despite the different rumours which continued to arrive, and which discredited this account, by declaring that firing was still going on at Cawnpoor, these mournful tidings were too manifestly true to be disbelieved. Accordingly, Sir Henry at once addressed the officer commanding the reinforcement expected from Allahabad, informing him of the event, and warning him against a too hasty approach, now that the object no longer existed. The letter was taken by one of my cossids, who reached Major Rénaud's camp, but with the loss of his letter. He told his story, which was fortunately believed, and the force halted; while its commander reported the news to Allahabad. At that station the account was disbelieved by Colonel Neill who commanded there, and Major Rénaud eventually received orders to move on, but by slow marches, towards Cawnpoor.

It must be admitted, that in safely conveying these several communications my cossids rendered good service, and that at a time when it was urgently required. There remain yet more important feats accomplished by one of them, the messenger "Ungud," which will hereafter be noticed. This man was a pensioned sepoy, a native of Oudh, who was employed in the intelligence department by my assistant, Captain Hawes. We sent him out late on the 29th, after receipt of this news, to go to Cawnpoor, and bring us word of the intended movements of the Nana.

Lieutenant H. G. Delafosse, of the 53rd N. I., one of the four heroes who escaped from the Cawnpoor massacre, came afterwards to Lucknow with Sir James Outram's force, and recounted to me the whole story of the heroic defence of the Cawnpoor intrenchment, and of the most marvellous escape so gallantly effected by himself and Lieutenant Mowbray Thomson, together with one artilleryman and one private of the 84th Foot. This account I had intended to attach to this work; but as the main facts have already been published, it appears unnecessary to do so. Suffice it to say, that one boat only escaped from that fatal ghaut, and dropped down the river, fired upon by artillery from both banks of the stream. At length it grounded in shallow water on the Oudh side, when it was abandoned by all the men who were capable of fighting, in order to oppose a body of villagers who were firing upon them from the bank. These men proved to be followers of the talooqdar of Doondeea Kheyra, Baboo Ram-Buksh Singh, and were in such numbers that our countrymen were unable to return to the boat; but fought their way through them, and took refuge in a small temple on the river bank. Here they were surrounded, and long maintained a desperate defence. At last, the enemy piled lighted faggots at the door of the building, and, through the flame, threw gun cartridges within. These, exploding, rendered their place of refuge untenable from the flame and smoke. The heroic band stripped, and charged out through the enemy; several were killed, but five succeeded in gaining the river, into which they plunged. One of these five was shot: four only remained—one of these was wounded. After floating down the river for many miles, they were beckoned to the shore by the followers of a friendly Rajah. They landed, naked as they were, and were conducted to his fort. Here they were clothed, fed, their wounds dressed, and themselves hospitably treated for about a month. Afterwards, on Havelock's advance becoming known, they were escorted safely to his camp, and no recompense received. The name of the Rajah who thus hospitably protected them, is Rajah Dirg Bijehsingh, residing at Moriarmow in Bysewarrah. He is the hereditary chief of the most powerful clan in Oudh, the Byse Rajpoots. Long will his name be a pleasing sound in the ears of Englishmen.

The more the frightful catastrophe which befell the Cawnpoor garrison is contemplated, the more it fills one with astonishment. All persons who as myself have since visited Cawnpoor, and sorrowfully gazed upon the miserable earth-bank which formed the only defence around the shot-pierced barracks, have wondered how an officer of Sir Hugh Wheeler's known ability could have trusted to such a place to protect the lives entrusted to his care. The bank was not breast high. The two barracks were commanded on all sides. The treasure, the magazine, the heavy guns were abandoned, without a blow, to the enemy! This seems marvellous! At the other end of the station of Cawnpoor stood the magazine by itself: with ravines on one side of it, and not far from the river's bank on the other. It contained numerous strong buildings, and was surrounded by a high masonry wall. Every muniment of war was contained in it. The Treasury was near. It seems surprising that this place was not selected as that in which the last British stand should have been made. Sir Hugh had, indeed, meant to destroy the magazine, and an artillery sergeant had orders, in the event of mutiny, to blow it up; but the native guard prevented his so doing.

The only explanation which I have been able to find for the extraordinary conduct of Sir Hugh Wheeler, and, I believe, the only one which can be offered, rests on the belief which he firmly entertained, that the native troops would not attack him. An old and deservedly popular sepoy officer, General Wheeler hoped that the native infantry regiments at Cawnpoor would not prove unfaithful; and if they did turn, the most that he expected was, that they would leave Cawnpoor, and march off to join the rebels at Dehli. And there is no doubt but that they would so have acted, had they not been turned from their purpose by the advice of the fiend-like Nana, who brought them back to attack their commander in his defenceless camp.

On the same day on which this dreadful news reached us, I learned from Alee Ruza Khan, formerly cotwal of Lucknow under the native rule, and then enjoying a high-paid office under us, that there was a large number of very valuable jewels in the King's Treasury in the Kaiser Bagh, which, if the mutineers entered the place, were sure to be plundered by them or by their guardians. Having reported this fact to Sir Henry; Major Banks was deputed with a military force to secure them, and bring them in. A large amount of most valuable jewellery was found: comprising a richly-ornamented throne, crowns richly studded with gems, gold pieces from Venice and Spain, and a variety of necklaces, armlets, rings, and native ornaments. These were brought in late on the same day. The cases in which they were found were decayed with age, and fell to pieces when it was attempted to remove them; and the "pearls and barbaric gold" within strewed the place.

They were unfortunately not sufficiently secured; and during the siege the receptacle in which they were placed was more than once broken into, and a large quantity of jewels were stolen. These acts were attributed commonly to the men of the 32nd. Certainly they got hold of a large quantity of the jewels, and sold them freely to the natives of the garrison. Duprat, the merchant, who possessed some stores of wine, received offers of most valuable jewellery in exchange for a dozen of brandy; and I have myself seen diamonds and pearls which had been so bought. During the siege, I had occasion to cause a swimming bath to be emptied, for the purpose of having it cleansed. My servants employed in the duty found at the bottom of the bath, carefully deposited in one corner, a handful of jewels, pearls, emeralds, and gold, which they brought to me. These evidently had been purloined from the royal jewels, and were restored accordingly. A large number of these jewels were preserved, and were taken out of the Residency with ourselves in November.

Major Banks on this occasion discovered a large brass 21-pounder gun complete with carriage and waggon in the Kaiser Bagh. And these, as well as some other small arms which were found, were on the next day brought into our position.

By this time the heat had become intense at Lucknow, and the rains were anxiously looked for. Cholera had shown itself, and several cases of small-pox had occurred, so that the first good fall of rain which took place on the 28th of June, was hailed with general satisfaction.

CHAPTER X.

THE END OF JUNE—DEFEAT AT CHINHUT.

The concentration of the mutineer force at Newaubgunje known to us, and reported to Sir Henry Lawrence.—They march on Lucknow.—Their advance guard reported to be at Chinhut early on the 29th.—Sir Henry Lawrence orders a party of cavalry to reconnoitre, and resolves to attack the enemy in force on the next day.—Mr. Gubbins, and those not actually employed, kept in ignorance of this intention. Hears next morning that the force had started ; news brought in that it was in full retreat.—Account of the engagement ; force employed ; still in column on the causeway when the enemy's guns open on it.—Artillery fire for twenty minutes ; our flanks turned by the enemy ; village of Ismailgunje taken ; retreat.—Loss of the 8-inch howitzer ; death of Colonel Case ; noble conduct of the Volunteer Cavalry under Captain Radcliffe ; loss in the action.—The force of the mutineers precisely stated.—Mutiny of the 4th, 7th, and part of the 1st Regt. of O. I. Infantry at the Dowlutkhana.—Escape of Brigadier Gray and his officers.—Mutiny of the police at the Imambarra.—Investment on the 30th of June of the Residency position and the Muchee Bhowun.—Confusion at the Residency, abandonment of our unfinished batteries.—Desertion of native domestics, and chuprassies.—Effect upon my post of the abandonment of the south-west bastion.—Description of the work.—Mr. Gubbins resolves on attempting to complete it.—The work begun on the night of the 30th of June ; work-people how induced to labour ; night-work continued until the first week in August, when a gun was mounted on the bastion.—Necessity for abandoning the Muchee Bhowun ; order to abandon it telegraphed by Captain Fulton.—The Muchee Bhowun blown up ; its garrison join ours in safety.—Loss of ammunition and guns in the fort.—Sir Henry Lawrence wounded.—His death-bed ; and character.—Succeeded in his civil duties by Major Banks.—Incessant fire of the enemy.—Extract from the diary of a staff officer.—Loose horses.—Desertion of native servants.—My own.—Number of the inmates of my house.—Our household management, and table fare described.—Ladies messing by themselves suffered great hardships.—Noble conduct of ladies.—Want of loaf bread.—Injury sustained from the enemy's musketry from the surrounding houses.—Casualties, Mr. Polehampton, Major Francis, Miss Palmer, Mr. Ommanney.—Sortie on the 7th of July.—Talooqdars who at this time had joined our enemies.—Our information only hearsay : all regular intelligence had ceased.—Mr. Gubbins after the siege had begun employed no messenger but

"Ungud."—Many were sent out by Colonel Inglis, but none brought answers.—Correspondence of the Seikh Cavalry with the enemy.—Enemy's batteries.—And their artillery practice.

We had, as has already been stated, received regular intelligence of the movements of the mutineer troops in Oudh. They had now assembled at Newaubgunje Bara Bankee, twenty miles from Lucknow. These facts were communicated by my daily reports to Sir Henry Lawrence. We knew that the mutineers were in correspondence with the Nana at Cawnpoor. No sooner, then, did they hear that the intrenchment there had fallen, than they moved at once upon Lucknow. My scouts brought word early on the 29th of June, that an advance guard of not less than 500 Infantry and 100 Horse, had actually arrived at Chinhut, a town on the Fyzabad road, within eight miles of the Residency, from Newaubgunje, to collect supplies for the mutineer army which was expected to arrive there on the following day. Sir Henry Lawrence, upon this being reported to him, ordered Captain H. Forbes, with the Seikh Cavalry, to reconnoitre their position. This officer accordingly went out, and soon came upon the enemy's pickets, who fired upon him. He remained observing them during the whole day, and returned at sunset.

Myself as well as some others in the garrison, had expected as well as hoped, that this advance guard would have been attacked and driven back. Sir Henry Lawrence, however, meditated a bolder measure, viz., to attack the enemy in force on the next day, of which myself and those not actually employed were kept in ignorance. In pursuance of this resolve, the force in cantonments was quietly withdrawn at sunset, and moved into the Residency position and the Muchee Bhowun.

I had heard no whisper of an intention to attack, and I learnt the fact with no small surprise early on the following morning from Major Anderson, chief engineer, who brought me a letter from Sir Henry for despatch; and observed that the troops had started too late. The sun was then well up; and the force had been gone only half an hour. The heat was excessive, and on learning the fact I at once arranged to save the wearied soldiers from its effect, by sending out elephants to convey them in after the expected combat. I had made preparation for assisting them in this way, by obtaining a list of the elephants kept by the native gentry of the city some days before, and these had been requested to send them whenever they might be summoned. Sixteen elephants were immediately collected, and sent after Sir Henry's force, under charge of my own horsemen. It was about 9 o'clock A.M., when the risaldar rushed breathless into my room, and announced to me that our troops were in full retreat, and begged that aid might be sent out. I immediately took him to the senior officer present, Colonel Halford, who lost no time in ordering all the officers to their posts. On my way I met a number of Seikh horsemen and native artillery drivers, returning from the field, their horses covered with foam. Not a man of them was wounded. Reproachfully I inquired why they had fled. They replied only, that the enemy had surrounded them. About half an hour later, another of my horsemen came in: he brought in Sir Henry Lawrence's sword-scabbard, which, he told me, he had received from himself with the message that he was unhurt. Not long after, our troops began to come in, and heartrending, indeed, was it to see our wounded and exhausted men extended, covered with dust and blood, under the porch of the Residency.

I found Sir Henry laying a howitzer at the Water-gate, to command the entrance to the Residency, and accompanied him to the Redan battery. A party of the 32nd, under Lieutenant Edmondstoune, had gone out, and occupied the houses on our side of the Iron Bridge, and soon a sharp musketry fire began between them and the mutineers, who had reached the opposite end of the bridge. Our 18-pounder in the Redan was brought to bear upon them, worked by Lieutenant McFarlan, and effectually prevented their crossing. Returning from the Redan, I ascended to the roof of the Residency, and could thence clearly see the enemy putting some guns in position, near Thornhill's House, on the opposite side of the river. Thence I was summoned to the protection of my own post.

An account of this disastrous engagement was afterwards given to me by several officers, Captain H. Forbes, Captain Bassano, Lieutenant Foster Cunliffe, and Lieutenant Bonham. From these I will briefly recount what appears to have taken place. The force employed was composed as follows :—

ARTILLERY.

4 guns of European Artillery, under Lieutenant F. Cunliffe.
4 ditto of Lieutenant Alexander's O. I. Battery.
2 ditto of Ashe's O. I. Battery, under Lieutenant Bryce.
1 eight-inch howitzer, under Lieutenant Bonham.

The whole under Major Simons.

CAVALRY.

Radcliffe's European Volunteers, numbering .	36 sabres.
The Seikh Cavalry, under Captains H. Forbes and G. Hardinge, about	80 sabres.

INFANTRY.

H. M.'s 32nd Foot	300
13th N. I., under Major Bruere	150
48th N. I., under Colonel Palmer	50
71st N. I. Seikhs, under Lieutenant Birch . .	20

The whole under command of Sir Henry Lawrence in person, accompanied by Colonel Inglis.

This force assembled from the Muchee Bhowun and the Residency at the Iron Bridge about sunrise, and marched to the bridge over the Kookrail stream, which is about halfway to Chinhut. So far the road was metalled. But beyond this it was a newly-raised embankment, constructed of loose and sandy soil, in which every now and then gaps occurred, indicating the positions of future bridges. After some halt, during which no refreshment was served out to the men, the force moved on along this heavy causeway. The advance guard was of cavalry with videttes thrown out. After it the 8-inch howitzer led, followed by the European Artillery, and Alexander's guns. The 13th N. I., Bryce's two guns, the 32nd Infantry, and lastly, the 48th N. I. followed. The force moved in the above order. After proceeding about a mile and a half, the videttes were fired upon from the village of Ismailgunje, on our left, and retired, and the 8-inch howitzer was ordered to the front. The troops were still in column upon the causeway, when the enemy made his presence to be felt, by opening upon it with round shot from a distance of 1400 yards. The first shots lobbed into the column, carrying off the head of one of Alexander's Artillery drivers, and killing several dooly-bearers. The enemy then himself became visible, occupying some thick mango-groves on the near side of Chinhut. Our line was at once deployed. The howitzer remained on the road, and Cunliffe's European guns took ground to the right of, and a little in advance of, the howitzer. Next to these was Alexander's Native Battery. Bryce's guns, as I was informed, were not believed to have left the road. The 32nd men were posted on the left, between the village of Ismailgunje and the road, and were ordered to lie down to avoid the enemy's fire. On the right was another small hamlet, which the Native Infantry passed through, and took up a position in front of it.

The howitzer returned the fire of the enemy with effect, its shells being seen to burst among them. The field-pieces also fired with round shot. But the distance, 1300 yards, was too great for them to produce any effect. After about twenty minutes' firing, the centre of the enemy where their artillery had been mainly posted appeared to give way; and hopes were entertained that they were retreating. Our hopes were, however, ill-founded; for presently they were seen advancing in two large separate masses, cavalry, artillery and infantry, on both our flanks, evidently intending to outflank us on both sides. On the right, at the distance of 400 or 500 yards, our field-pieces opened on them with grape, but without much effect; for they continued to move on, parties of their cavalry pushing forward to get into our rear. On the left, their infantry was seen making for the strong village of Ismailgunje beyond where the 32nd were lying. Alexander's guns were ordered over from the right to the left of the road to stop them; but only effected the movement partially and slowly. The banks of the road were steep and very heavy, and the native drivers did not use their best exertions to get their guns over. Some of the waggons were overturned in the ditch. The cavalry were now ordered to charge. The volunteers immediately obeyed the order, and charging under Captain Radcliffe drove back the foremost of the infantry. The Seikhs behaved shamefully. Only two of them charged with the volunteers, the rest turned their horses' heads, and fled.

The enemy's infantry had now gained full possession of the village of Ismailgunje, from which they poured a safe and deadly fire upon our men. The 32nd were ordered to take it. They advanced boldly, led by Colonel Case, but were met by a withering fire—Colonel Case fell badly wounded, Lieutenants Brackenbury and Thomson were soon after mortally wounded; and the men fell back in disorder, towards the road.

A retreat was now ordered. The European artillery limbered up and went to the rear: and Sir Henry Lawrence ordered Lieutenant Bonham to retire with the 8-inch howitzer. Unfortunately, the elephant which was attached to the limber had got frightened when the firing began, and had run off with it. Spare bullocks had been brought out to meet such an accident, but the frightened drivers had let them loose. Lieutenant Bonham seized the limber of a waggon, and mounting on the leading horse, brought it up to the howitzer. Dismounting, however, to attach the limber to the gun, the native riders galloped off with it. At this time Captain Hardinge brought up the proper limber with the elephant; but the animal was so restless under fire, that the utmost exertions of the untrained gunners failed to attach the trail of the howitzer to the limber.

The enemy was pressing on, taking advantage of every break in the ground and of every cover, to pour in a murderous fire of musketry. A bullet struck Lieutenant Bonham, who was carried off, and put upon a limber; and the howitzer was abandoned. At this time many of the artillery-drivers detached their horses from the guns and ammunition waggons, and took to flight.

The retreat had now become general, when Captain

Bassano, 32nd Foot, who had been looking for his commander Colonel Case, discovered that officer lying wounded on the field. The men had passed on: but Captain Bassano desired to bring some back to carry off the Colonel. The enemy were, however, close at hand, and Case would not suffer him. Finding ordinary remonstrance unavailing, the gallant soldier turned to his subordinate: "Leave me, sir," said he, "and rejoin your company." The order was reluctantly obeyed. Soon after, Bassano himself was shot through the foot, but continued to walk with his men despite the wound, and reached the Residency in safety.

Early in the action, the water-carriers had run away: our men were suffering from intense thirst, and were so exhausted that they could scarcely drag themselves along. As many as were able, crowded on the gun-limbers and waggons. The rest kept together as well as they could. Thus they retraced their steps in much confusion, closely pursued by the enemy, who immediately cut off every straggler.

On nearing the Kookrail Bridge a body of the mutineer cavalry was seen who had occupied the road in front. At first some doubt prevailed whether the horse belonged to ourselves or to the enemy; and Cunliffe's guns, which had unlimbered in order to open on them, were prevented from firing. As soon as the doubt was removed, the volunteer cavalry charged them, when they at once broke and fled.

Beyond the bridge the retreat continued, the Europeans being in rear, most gallantly covered by Captain Radcliffe with his handful of volunteer cavalry, who were admitted by all to have been mainly instrumental in saving the force; showing front continually and keeping the enemy's infantry from approaching too near. Some of the Europeans and of the sepoys behaved with much steadiness, loading and firing with deliberate aim on those of the enemy who came near. But more of them hurried on without making resistance. The men of the 32nd, besides their own complete exhaustion, suffered from another grievous disadvantage. Many of their muskets would not go off. They had been kept long loaded without having been discharged, and had become foul. During the retreat one of their officers called upon a private by name, and desired him to turn round and fire upon the enemy. "I will do so, sir, if you wish," said the man, "but it's no use. I have already snapped six caps and the piece won't go off." About this time Captain Stevens, 32nd, was wounded, and was seen to sit down by the road side, where he was soon overtaken by the mutineers and destroyed. The suburbs were now reached, and a short halt was made at a well to allow the men to drink, during which Captain Hardinge rallied some of the Seikh cavalry and brought them back. But he could not get them to face the pursuing enemy: and they soon again abandoned him and fled.

Our mounted officers rendered every aid to the wearied Europeans along the retreat, helping them on by holding them by the hand, or giving them a stirrup: and some taking them up behind. And in this way the suburbs were passed through, the iron bridge recrossed, and the Muchee Bhowun and Residency gained at length.

Some kindness was shown to our men at different places in the suburbs, where women held out to them from their houses small porous vessels full of cool water, which was eagerly swallowed.

Our loss in this sad defeat was very severe. Besides

the officers already named, Captain Maclean, 71st N.I., was killed, and several others wounded, including Captain James of the Commissariat, who received a bullet in the knee.

In artillery we lost the 8-inch howitzer, and three field-pieces, two of Bryce's and one of Alexander's battery, with almost all the ammunition-waggons of our native guns. The loss in European soldiers was very severe, the killed being 112, and the wounded 44, and not a few of the natives had fallen, while more had deserted. The total number killed and missing was nearly 200.

The force of the mutineers, which consisted altogether of regiments stationed in the province, we could estimate with great precision.

They had the two 9-pounder batteries from Secrora and Fyzabad, each of six guns, making twelve pieces of artillery. They possessed besides, three or four small native guns, which could have been of no service in the field, and which they had obtained in the districts.

There were about 700 or 800 cavalry, made up of parties from the 15th Irregulars at Sultanpoor, and the three Oudh local regiments, Daly's, Gall's, and Hardinge's, with some of Weston's police troopers. Of infantry, there were the following corps :—

NATIVE INFANTRY.

The 22nd Regt. from Fyzabad only.

OUDH IRREGULAR INFANTRY.

A few men of the 1st, from Salone.
The 2nd, from Secrora.
The 3rd, from Gondah.
The 5th, from Duriabad.
The 6th, from Fyzabad.
The 8th, from Sultanpoor.
The 9th, from Seetapoor.

MILITARY POLICE.
The 1st Regt., from Sultanpoor.
The 2nd ditto, from Seetapoor.

making in all 9¼ regiments of infantry.

These corps had all lost many men by desertion. Not a few had left, wishing to have no part in the mutiny; many more had departed to their homes laden with treasure. It would be a high estimate to reckon the average strength of a regiment at that time at 600 men. But adopting this, we have a total infantry force of 5550 men, 800 cavalry, and 160 artillery.

When this engagement took place, besides the two main posts at the Residency and Muchee Bhowun, we had a force consisting of two and a half regiments of Irregular Infantry under Brigadier Gray at the Dowlutkhana: viz. four Companies of the 1st, the 4th, and the 7th regiments. None of the men from these regiments had accompanied the force to Chinhut. The position which they held, though some small defences had been put up, was quite untenable against artillery; and the guns which had before been stationed at the Dowlutkhana had been removed. It need not therefore occasion surprise, that soon after receiving the news of our disaster, these regiments mutinied. The first to go was the 7th, the last was the 4th. The men broke out with loud shouts, and commenced plundering the property of their officers; upon which Brigadier Gray and his officers left the place without molestation from the men, and took refuge in the Muchee Bhowun.

The police who filled the large Imambara, situated halfway between the Dowlutkhana and Muchee Bhowun, to which defences had been added, and which was protected by a few small wall-pieces, were not long after the Irregulars in joining the mutiny: and on the next day these wall-pieces opened on the Muchee Bhowun. There is, however, this excuse for them, that their position was incapable of defence against a regular force. The cotwal fled, and concealed himself, but ere long became a prisoner to the enemy;—and was eventually put to death by them.

The pursuing enemy were stopped at the iron bridge by the guns of the Redan battery, and at the stone bridge by the fire of the Muchee Bhowun. They opened fire upon both posts, however, from guns which they put in position across the river: and in no long time, getting the captured 8-inch howitzer into battery, they threw several shells into the Residency post. Numbers of their cavalry soon entered the city by fording the river lower down. Many of the infantry followed; guns were brought over; and by the afternoon we were completely invested. The mutineers got into many of the adjoining houses, which they rapidly loopholed, and opened upon us before night a fire of musketry.

The defeat, the pursuit, and the investment of our posts had been so rapid and unexpected, that for some time all was confusion at the Residency. The three unfinished batteries on my side were covered with crowds of workpeople, men, women, and children, when the guns of our retiring force became louder and louder. So soon as the alarm of the coming foe was spread, all took to flight, and the works were abandoned. Many native servants took the opportunity of escaping; and everything which was at the moment outside the line of works was lost.

We lost at this time all our native "omlah," or writers, who all resided in the city; with very few exceptions all the chuprassies, or civil orderlies, also deserted us. Mine were fortunately an exception; they comprised a jumadar and six men, who stood by me faithfully.

Nor was it wonderful that a panic should have seized the natives ; for the depression among the European soldiers, and also among the upper classes, was great, and sad and anxious looks met one on all sides.

By the abandonment of the unfinished works, the west and south faces of our position had been left almost defenceless, and my outpost in particular, which, as has been seen, formed the south-west angle. Upon the protection which would be derived from the bastion which had been commenced at that corner we had at my post laid great store ; but now this was cut off. The ground from which the bastion had been commenced was about eighteen feet below that of the compound, and, when abandoned, the work was about ten feet high. It had been constructed of great solidity, under Lieutenant Hutchinson's superintendence. The outer enclosing wall, which was ten feet thick, was of masonry, strengthened by very large upright beams, let into the ground at the distance of five feet apart, both on the inside and outside of the wall. These were bound together by cross-pieces of wood, firmly nailed to the uprights. Within the enclosing parapet, earth had been heaped by the labour of women and children, and beaten firmly down by men ; but the parapet had not been completed to the height of ten feet all round. On the east side an opening had been left from the level of the ground, by which the workpeople ascended, carrying their baskets of earth.

Our only chance, as appeared to me, of defending my post, was to complete this bastion, which, as before said, flanked both sides of the enclosure. The labour would be great; but it seemed necessary to attempt it. Before nightfall, therefore, assembling the native servants and levies, I informed them of my intention to attempt the completion of this battery; and offered, to every man who would join me in the work, cash payment at the rate of two rupees for each night's labour. They all agreed to work. Lieutenant Hutchinson, engineer, offered to direct our labours. Lieutenant Charlton, 32nd Regt., who commanded the small detachment of his regiment, then stationed at my post, in aid of our garrison (eight men), volunteered to help; as did several others. As soon as it was dark we set to work. A window in one of the outhouses was opened, and through this we let ourselves down stealthily by a ladder to the unfinished work below. Our first care was to defend the open gap in the work. This could only be done by a retrenchment and palisade, by which a portion of the walls on each side of the chasm was abandoned. The enemy were not on the alert in this quarter; so our men proceeded outside, and, guided by Ramadeen and Pirâna, brought in a large quantity of wood, rafters, doors, planks, &c., which lay about. With these we erected a rough palisade, outside which the earth was scarped as much as possible, to render the ascent difficult. The morning dawned upon us while engaged in this work, the progress of which was sufficiently encouraging. During the whole night my wife, assisted by one of the inmates of our house, Mrs. Brydon, kept us supplied with tea, and brandy-and-water, which they brought down to the work. At daylight we retired, and carefully secured the window. All the workpeople received the promised payment from my hand in cash.

The ordinary day's wages of a native labourer is

one-eighth of a rupee; the high pay punctually paid soon attracted numerous workmen, and falsified the prognostications of those who had declared that none would be obtained. Domestic servants of all kinds, grooms, grasscutters, bearers, sweepers, punkah pullers, and my own levies, formed the motley crew of workmen, and shortly I had as many as seventy-five men at nightly work. Complaint, however, was soon heard, that the high payment attracted private servants from other garrisons, whose services could not be spared. Such were accordingly rejected. Among my best workmen was a syce* of Colonel Inglis', whose horse occupied one of my stables. One of my own, named Sulamut Ali, also became quite an engineer. Another admirable workman was one Konwur Doobey, a naick of the 4th O. I. Infantry, whose services I had obtained to drill my levies. The regiment, as has been before related, mutinied on the 30th of June, and he alone remained. One of the wives, and some of the children of the servants of my garrison, joined the work, and received half payment. For three nights we were little interrupted, and continued to go outside, and bring in a large quantity of wood and batten doors, which were put up around the parapet as protection against musketry. Pits were dug inside my compound which fortunately afforded a good clay, which was made into mud, and with this we continued night after night to raise the parapet of the bastion. Loose earth was filled inside.

On the fourth night the enemy disturbed our proceedings, by establishing posts in the adjoining houses, and keeping up from loopholes, which they made in these, a fire of musketry. Some of these houses were

* Or native groom.

within twenty-five yards of us; and compliments in native abuse used not unfrequently to be interchanged. They killed one of my workmen close to me, and wounded others. Still the work progressed: the men laboured, myself, and the officers of my garrison, assisted and superintended; and Mrs. Gubbins, her sister, and Mrs. Brydon, kept alternate watches during the night to provide refreshment for us, and the bastion steadily rose, in spite of all opposition, to the commanding height required. The window by which we had first descended became a doorway, sufficiently wide to admit of the passage of a gun, and in the first week in August we had the satisfaction of placing a 9-pounder in position. Afterwards, as will be related, this was replaced by an 18-pounder: the parapets were raised to the height of ten feet all round, which effectually excluded musketry fire; and the south-west angle battery became one of the most complete in the place.

No sooner were we invested, than it was discovered that the maintenance of the separate position of the Muchee Bhowun had been a mistake. Our garrison, now further weakened by the losses at Chinhut, was not strong enough to defend the extended Residency position, between which and the former, all communication by letter was now cut off. Sir Henry Lawrence sent me, during the day of the 30th, dispatches to send to the Muchee Bhowun; but I was unable to forward them. My messengers had almost all gone out. A few had deserted, and but a few unacquainted with the city remained. The officer in command at the Muchee Bhowun, Colonel Palmer, managed to convey intelligence that he was ill-supplied with food and with gun ammunition, shot and shell. To remove therefore the garrison from the Muchee Bhowun, and withdraw it to the Residency, became a matter of the most urgent necessity. Fortunately there was a telegraph on the Residency roof, and this was now had resort to. Captain Fulton, Engineers, accompanied by Mr. G. H. Lawrence, C. S., and a third officer, whose name I did not learn, ascended to the roof to convey the message. It was a service of extreme danger. The machine was found out of order, and had to be taken down and restored, under an incessant musketry fire from the enemy. The flight of bullets never ceased while these brave men were performing their arduous duty; for they could be clearly seen upon the roof by the enemy. At last the work was accomplished, and the words, "*Spike the guns well, blow up the Fort, and retire at midnight,*" were transmitted, with certainty of their having been understood, for each letter was signalled in reply from the Muchee Bhowun.

Much anxiety was felt about the success of the movement; for during the day the enemy had been observed to be in force upon the road by which our troops must retire; and had cannonaded the Muchee Bhowun from two guns placed in position upon it.

To assist the movement, and distract the attention of the enemy, Sir Henry directed our several batteries to open fire shortly before midnight. This was done: and a heavy fire in particular was opened upon the iron bridge. The whole arrangements for the evacuation of the Muchee Bhowun were admirably carried into effect by the commanding officer, Colonel Palmer. The officers employed in the duty were furnished with written orders. The force moved out noiselessly at midnight, bringing their treasure, and two or more 9-pounder guns with them; were wholly unobserved by the enemy; and reached the lower Water-gate, without a shot having been fired at them, at a quarter past twelve o'clock. The arrangements for blowing up the Fort were made by Lieutenant Thomas, of the Madras Artillery, who fired the train so as to explode the magazine half an hour after the troops had left. I was at work at my bastion when the explosion took place, between twelve and one o'clock. Suddenly, while we were watching, a blaze of fire shot up to the sky, followed by a loud report; and then a huge mass of black smoke succeeded, which hung mournfully for nearly half an hour over the dismantled fortress.

Thus was destroyed, and most effectually and fortunately destroyed, the fortification of the Muchee Bhowun, upon which so much expense and labour had been expended. No doubt the maintenance of this commanding post in the city must have assisted in overawing the ill-disposed among the citizens; but it may be regretted that all our resources had not been earlier concentrated upon the Residency post. By the destruction of the Muchee Bhowun we lost two large mortars, one 13-inch, the second 10-inch, for which, however, we possessed no shells; two small 5½-inch mortars, three 18-pounder guns, two of which were without carriages, and four or five 9-pounders, with limbers complete. The loss of ammunition was great, viz. 250 barrels of gunpowder, and as many boxes of small arm ammunition, and many lacs of percussion caps. A considerable amount of public stores and much private property was at the same time sacrificed.

But the junction of the two forces at the Residency was an incalculable gain to us. The additional men were actually required to man our defences, and their arrival greatly cheered the spirits of our European garrison, who greeted their comrades with heartfelt pleasure. In consequence of the increase of numbers, the European guard at my garrison was increased from eight to eighteen. The men were located in a large central room on the ground floor of the house, within which they were quite safe from shot and musketry.

Sir Henry Lawrence occupied, at this time, a room on the first story of the north-east angle of the Residency, which was more than any exposed to the enemy's fire. On the 1st of July, an 8-inch shell had entered it, and burst without doing injury to any one. Sir Henry had then been entreated to abandon the room, and, indeed, to remove from the Residency building, which was, from its high position, more than any exposed to the fire of the enemy: but had refused to do so. About 9 A.M. of the 2nd of July, I was summoned by Captain Edgell, then officiating as Military Secretary, to see Sir Henry, who, he said, had been dangerously wounded. I hastened down, and found him laid on a bed in the north verandah of Dr. Fayrer's house. The bed was surrounded by all his staff, his nephew, and the principal persons of the garrison, among whom not a dry eye could be seen.

It has never fallen to my lot to witness such a scene of sorrow. While we were clustered round Sir Henry's bed, the enemy were pouring a heavy musketry fire upon the place; and bullets were striking the outside of the pillars of the verandah in which we were collected. Sir Henry's attenuated frame, and the severe nature of the injury, at once decided the medical men not to attempt amputation; but it was necessary to stay the bleeding by applying the tourniquet, and the agony which this caused was fearful to behold. It was impossible to avoid sobbing like a child. Sir Henry alluded to his having nominated Major Banks to be his successor; and then earnestly pointed out the worthlessness of all human distinction, recommending all to fix their thoughts upon a better world. He referred to his own success in life, and asked what was it worth then? He enjoined on us particularly to be careful of our ammunition, and often repeated—"Save the ladies." He afterwards continued in much suffering, and lingered until the morning of the 4th, when he expired.

Upon his death-bed Sir Henry referred to the disaster at Chinhut, and said that he had acted against his own judgment, from the fear of man. I have often inquired, but I have never learnt the name of any one who had counselled the step, which resulted in so severe a calamity.

Thus passed from among us as noble a spirit as ever animated human clay. Unselfish, kind, frank and affectionate, Sir Henry Lawrence possessed the art of attaching those with whom he came in contact. He was particularly beloved by the natives, and with good reason, for few Europeans treated them with more kindly consideration; and none made more just allowance for those weak points in which they differ from Europeans. On the other hand, from his habit of freely mixing with them, few succeeded better than himself in arriving at just conclusions, and in eliciting the truth. His presence at Lucknow had been of great benefit, and his great talents had been signally displayed in the precautions which he had early taken to lay in provisions, and to concentrate the military stores. To those wise precautions, indeed, our eventual success in defending the Residency position is, under Providence, mainly attributable. He was wounded in the room which he had refused to quit, about an hour before I saw him, by a fragment of an 8-inch shell, which entered the room by the window, and burst, wounding Sir Henry, and slightly injuring Captain T. F. Wilson, Deputy Assistant Adjutant-General, who was standing by his bed. His nephew, Mr. G. H. Lawrence, C. S., who was in the room at the time, escaped uninjured.

Before I had arrived, Sir Henry Lawrence had appointed Major Banks to be his successor in the Civil office of Chief Commissioner; Colonel Inglis to command the troops of the garrison; and Major J. Anderson to command the artillery and direct engineering operations.

On the same day, a meeting of these officers was held at my house, at which Mr. Ommanney and myself attended. On this occasion I gave it as my opinion that the siege was likely to last not less than three months, and recommended that a return of the provisions in store should early be obtained, with a view to their being duly husbanded.

During the first days of the siege, the enemy maintained almost continuously, day and night, a storm of round shot and musketry upon some of our most exposed positions, chiefly the Residency and the buildings along the east face. Many of the bullets were fired from a great distance, and, describing a parabola, fell with fatal effect in places which had before been esteemed safe. Thus the top of my house, despite the high parapet at either end of the roof, was quite unsafe; for frequently musket-balls passing over one parapet, struck with great force the inner side of the opposite defence. When firing from the loopholes on the house-top, it therefore became necessary to put up a screen of boards or boxes close behind the person, to screen the back from bullets.

A staff-officer has well described, in his diary of

the siege, the state of things which obtained in the garrison during the first few days, in the following words :—

"It is difficult to chronicle the proceedings of these few days, for everywhere confusion reigned supreme. That unfortunate day of Chinhut precipitated everything, inasmuch as we were closely shut up several days before anything of the kind was anticipated. People had made no arrangement for provisioning themselves; many, indeed, never dreamt of such a necessity; and the few that had were generally too late. Again, many servants were shut out the first day, and all attempts to approach us were met by a never-ceasing fusilade. But though they could not get in, they succeeded in getting out; and after a few days, those who could boast of servants or attendants of any kind formed a very small and envied minority. The servants, in many instances, eased their masters of any superfluous articles of value easy of carriage. In fact, the confusion can be better imagined than described.

"The head of the Commissariat had, most unfortunately for the garrison, received a severe wound at Chinhut, which effectually deprived them of his valuable aid. His office was all broken up; his gomashtas and baboos were not with us, and the officers appointed to assist him were all new hands. Besides all this, the first stores opened were approachable only by one of the most exposed roads, and very many of the camp-followers preferred going without food to the chance of being shot. Some did not know where to apply, so that for three or four days many went without rations; and this in no small degree added to the number of desertions. Owing to these desertions, the commissariat and battery bullocks had no attendants to look after them, and went wandering all over the place looking for food; they tumbled into wells, were shot down in numbers by the enemy, and added greatly to the labour which fell on the garrison, as fatigue parties of civilians and officers, after being in the defences all day repelling the enemy's attack, were often employed six and seven hours burying cattle killed during the day, and which, from the excessive heat, became offensive in a few hours. The artillery and other horses were everywhere to be seen loose, fighting and tearing at one another, driven mad for want of food and water; the garrison being too busily employed in the trenches to be able to secure them."

It became necessary to take measures to relieve ourselves of these horses, and a party was told off to drive them outside the works, where they were readily appropriated by the enemy. Several lingered close to the works, and four or five died close under my south-west bastion, compelling me to send out men at night, under fire, to throw them into wells, or bury them.

There is no doubt that one great cause of the desertion of the native servants was the insufficient care bestowed upon them. It was difficult to shelter all the Europeans; and the native servants were, therefore, necessarily greatly exposed. Constantly in danger of being struck down by the bullets or shot of the enemy, and ill supplied with food, it is not surprising that many deserted. I myself lost fewer than my neighbours. My baker was shut out; but we retained throughout the siege the services of a khansamah,* khidmotgar,† and cook. The families of the first two resided in my enclosure, which circumstance was a great security for their good be-

* Butler. † Table attendant.

haviour. Moreover, the first had been for twelve years in the service of my elder brother. I retained also a most excellent servant, a sweeper, throughout the siege, until he was killed by a round shot. His wife attended Mrs. Gubbins with equal fidelity. Two bearers and two clashies* also remained by me for long; but being natives of Cawnpoor, and fearful of evil befalling their families there, they dug a hole through the compound wall during the siege, and escaped. The other inmates of my garrison succeeded in retaining more servants generally than our neighbours, which was mainly attributable to the greater shelter afforded by the outhouses of the enclosure, and the greater care taken of them. The private stores which I had laid in always afforded food for these poor people, even when it was not procurable from the Commissariat.

Major Banks, who had commanded my garrison, made over the command, on Sir Henry Lawrence's death, to Captain H. Forbes. We were joined at the same time by Captain and Mrs. Edgell, who abandoned the Residency, as did almost all the other families; for it had now become especially the butt for the enemy's artillery, and was quite unsafe. The number of ladies and gentlemen who were then inmates in our house was nineteen, besides thirteen children, my own family excepted. Up to this date these had all been, in the strictest sense of the word, our guests, entailing, as may be supposed, no slight amount of cheerfully-rendered labour on the lady of the house.

For some time before the siege our supplies had, however, been husbanded. We possessed some

* Tent-pitcher, who also cleans and takes charge of the fowling-pieces.

supply of bottled beer. This, which was esteemed the greatest luxury during the siege, had ceased for many days to be served to the gentlemen, and was reserved for the nursing ladies, of whom there were four among our guests, and for the sick. One glass of sherry and two of champagne or of claret was served to the gentlemen, and less to the ladies, at dinner. One glass of light wine, Sauterne, was provided at luncheon. It must be here remarked that sherry soon came to be of higher value than champagne, or the lighter French wines, which could not be kept after having been once opened. There was a good deal of the latter description of wines in the garrison, and the best never attained a higher price than sixty rupees: the price of sherry rose to above seventy rupees per dozen. Our regular meals had also been diminished from three to two. A cold luncheon only was served, and we made an early dinner at four. By these timely precautions the supplies which we had were husbanded, and the wants of our numerous guests were provided for during the whole siege. Besides, we were often able to render assistance to persons in other garrisons who urgently needed aid, and to the wounded in hospital. After the siege had begun, and the commissariat arrangements got into train, rations were issued of beef or mutton, with flour or rice, and salt, to Europeans, according to a fixed scale. These were made over to my servants and cooked by them, such additions being made to the meal as our store-room afforded. These, however, besides the daily addition of spices, and sugar, were limited to a few canisters of preserved salmon, and a few of carrots, which were produced whenever we invited a friend from any of the other garrisons to dinner. The party invited did not bring his rations, so that the meal demanded some addition. When the sheep were all used up, beef only was served out in rations, which was usually made into stews, in consequence of our rarely getting a piece that could be boiled or roasted.

At dinner, our chief luxury were rice puddings, of which two daily appeared on table. The eggs for these were derived from a few poultry which we had managed to preserve; and the milk from goats and two cows belonging to our guests, which were half starved during the siege. Occasionally a plum pudding or jam pudding was made, and always caused great excitement at the dinner-table. The demand for these delicacies was great; and there was often none left for the lady of the house, who generally helped them. One cup of tea was made for each person at six in the morning, our English maid, Chivers, presiding at the tea-table. Another cup at the ten o'clock breakfast, and another at night. We enjoyed both sugar and milk in our tea, a luxury which few possessed besides our garrison: and this often attracted friends. During the blockade, when our upper story was filled with sick and wounded, it was our regular practice to help them first, both at breakfast and dinner, before any one else. After they had been served, the rest partook.

Altogether, though it was known that there were some families where bottled beer and porter were daily enjoyed, as well as some other rare comforts, our garrison was, perhaps, the best provided during the siege. We and friends owed much to the exertions of our faithful khansamah, Mohumud Aly: who, after escaping the dangers of the siege, and attending me through a dangerous illness which followed it, was himself, to our great grief, taken ill at Benares and died there.

Much wearisome labour and drudgery fell on the ladies in those houses from which the servants had deserted. There they had to perform for themselves and husbands many menial offices, which those of our garrison escaped. But the hardest cases were those where individual ladies messed by themselves. They were at first allowed twelve ounces of meat daily; but this was reduced in August to six ounces, which, poorly cooked, was barely sufficient to afford sustenance: and I have since heard of cases where ladies have had to gather their own sticks, light their own fire, knead and make their own chuppatties, and cook with their own hands any other food which formed their meal. To their honour be it said, that these hardships and privations were always patiently and cheerfully borne. Never probably, indeed, has the noble character of Englishwomen shone with more real brightness than during this memorable siege. Far from being in our way, they were ever a source of comfort and help to us; ready to tend the sick, to soothe and comfort the dying, and to cheer and sustain the living by all those numberless offices of love and affection which woman only understands.

Our greatest want, in the way of food, was that of bread. The bakers had all, without exception, deserted, and we never succeeded in making it during the siege; I do not exactly know why, for yeast could, no doubt, have been procurable: and if no one was before acquainted with it, books could have taught us the art of making bread. But the men were too much engaged in sterner duties, and to have baked for the whole inmates of each garrison would have been too severe labour for the ladies.

In India, the natives do not make loaf-bread with flour, but with a fine granulated preparation of wheat, termed "soojee;" and of this there was but a small supply in the garrison, which was soon exhausted. The flour was therefore kneaded with water, and beaten thin and flat by clapping it between the two hands by our native servants, thus forming what are called "chuppatties." These were baked on iron plates over the fire, and formed our food. They were not, however, wholesome,* producing with many persons, and especially with children, diarrhœa, which proved very difficult to cure.

On the 2nd of July, the enemy advanced in large numbers to the attack on the side of the Bailey Guard Gate; but being met with steady discharges of grape and musketry, were repulsed without difficulty. On the 5th of the month we experienced a heavy fall of rain, and the desired rainy season may be said to have commenced.

No sooner had the siege commenced, than the justice of the warnings of those was acknowledged, who had urged beforehand the demolition of the surrounding houses. The enemy now occupied these on every side, loopholed them, or took post at the windows, and fired on every one who showed himself. Scarcely any traverses had been put up. It was impossible to go outside many of the houses without being seen and fired at; and the casualties which immediately occurred in the case of persons passing on duty from one post to another were numerous. Almost the whole of the enclosure of my post was thus exposed

* Possibly because the flour was insufficiently sifted, and therefore too coarse.

to fire. But the garrison sustained for a long time the greatest injury from the enemy's riflemen posted in a turret which led to the roof of Johannes' house, fronting the Cawnpoor battery. This post used to be occupied by one of the ex-King's African eunuchs, who used his rifle with unerring certainty. The fire from this turret commanded the Cawnpoor battery, which it almost rendered useless, and swept down the main street between the Brigade Mess and the Martinière, the bullets frequently entering the windows of the hospital. By one of these the Rev. Mr. Polehampton, one of our two chaplains, was severely wounded on the 7th of July.

On the same date, an excellent and much-esteemed officer, Major Francis, of the 13th N. I., received his death-wound while sitting in the upper story of the Brigade Mess, by a round shot, which fractured both his legs. Amputation was necessary, and he sunk next day.

Before this we had already had several most melancholy casualties. On the 2nd, Miss Palmer, daughter of Colonel Palmer, of the 48th N. I., while sitting in the lower wing of the Residency, was frightfully injured by a round shot which came in at the window, and nearly carried off her leg. Amputation was immediately had recourse to, but she died on the next day.

On the 3rd, my colleague, the Judicial Commissioner, Mr. M. C. Ommanney, was wounded in the head by a round shot in the Redan battery. The shot grazed his head, and he lingered for two days before he expired.* Several other officers had been wounded, and the hospital began to fill fast.

The first sortie was made on the 7th of July. It

* See Addenda, No. IV.

was directed against Johannes' house, at the Cawnpoor battery, which now swarmed with mutineers: and was intended as a check to them, as well as to enable the engineers to examine the building, and discover whether the enemy were mining from it. The party consisted of fifty Europeans and twenty Seikhs, under command of Captain Mansfield, 32nd Foot. Captain Fulton and Lieutenant Anderson, engineers, accompanied the sortie. It took place at noon, and was perfectly successful. The road outside our works having been crossed, a hole was made in the outer wall of the enclosure, and the door of Johannes' house was blown in. Captain Lawrence, H.M. 32nd, was the first to enter the building, which was found filled with the enemy, a large number of them being pâsies, some of whom were armed with bows and arrows. They did not attempt resistance, but fled immediately, and about twenty of them were killed. Our loss was trifling.

It was afterwards regretted that this opportunity had not been taken to blow up the house.

By this time it had become known that some of the native talooqdars had joined our besiegers, with their followers. These latter were chiefly pâsies, whose predatory habits have been already described, and who were usually armed with sword, and bow and arrows, or matchlock. We learnt the names of two talooqdars who had thus joined our enemies, and who were Rajah Goor Buksh Singh, of Ramnugger Dhumeyree, and Rajah Newaubaly Khan, of Mohumdabad. The Afreedies of Mulheabad had also come in, and were known to have charge of that part of the investing posts which lay to the west of my enclosure. Such information was at first only derived from hearsay report, for at the time all communication on our part with the world outside had ceased. My few remaining messengers, with one or two obtained from other officers, were soon sent out with despatches from Major Banks; but none of these ever returned, nor was an answer ever obtained. Indeed, however trustworthy the messenger might be, it was scarcely possible for him to enter our position, in consequence of the extreme vigilance of the enemy. Posts had been carefully established by them in the houses all round us, from which strict watch and look-out was kept. Beyond these again were other posts and pickets; and all the principal thoroughfares of the city and suburbs were observed, and all passers-by challenged and examined. It was therefore a service of extreme danger and difficulty, either to leave our position with letters or to bring letters in; and the only man who ever effected this was my scout "Ungud." Save by his hand, after the siege had begun, I never attempted to send a letter out.

Later in the siege, Colonel Inglis nominated Captain Hardinge to be Assistant Quartermaster-General to him, and with his assistance endeavoured to effect the transmission of despatches. A number of persons left our intrenchment for this purpose. Once a sepoy of the 48th N. I., fully accoutred, left our works, pretending to desert to the enemy, his despatch being concealed underneath the metal plate of his musket stock. On another occasion an old woman was let out, who promised to deliver the letters entrusted to her to some friend in the city, by whom they were to be forwarded. But none of these, I believe, ever returned; nor had we ever reason to know that they had delivered the despatches. The only messenger besides Ungud who ever succeeded in delivering a despatch, was one Aodhan Singh, a sepoy of the 1st O. I. Infantry, orderly to Brigadier Gray; but he failed to bring in the reply with which he was entrusted.

The enemy used to subject every person who was stopped by any of their pickets, in his passage along the road or through the streets, to the strictest search: so that extraordinary precautions were required to secrete despatches. Those delivered and brought by Ungud were written on small pieces of thin paper, sometimes in the Greek character. They were tightly rolled up, and inserted into a quill, which was then closed at either end with sealing-wax. We were informed that whenever despatches were found upon any person so detained, he was put to death; and many were detained in confinement on mere suspicion of their being "cossids."*

The Seikh troopers posted in the Seikh squares were the channel through which information chiefly reached us. Many of these men deserted us during the siege; and the rest were, during the whole time, a constant source of alarm and anxiety. They were in constant correspondence with the enemy, through their deserters, who used to come up under the walls of the squares, and converse with their brethren inside. Through them also these Seikhs used to obtain supplies of opium, which they largely consumed, and which they retailed at famine prices to the garrison; as well as some other necessaries. From them also they picked up scraps of information as to what was going on in the world outside. The object of these visits of the Seikh deserters was, however, generally the same, *i. e.* to induce their brethren to desert

* Native messengers.

also. We had a party of four of them, more trusty it must be admitted than the rest, under the Risaldar Sheyre Singh, in my garrison. They at night occupied a post on the roof of the outhouses on the south face. Sheyre Singh one night informed us, that, if we chose, we might overhear a conversation which was invited by a deserter outside with the men of his post. Captain Hawes accordingly went down and concealed himself behind the rampart. The deserter approached, and for some time used every endeavour to induce his Seikh brethren to desert. He assured them that our defences could not long keep the enemy off: that no succour could possibly arrive; and that, if the place was taken, they would share our slaughter. On the other hand they were assured of receiving high pay and consideration from the mutineers. After some time passed in converse of this nature, Sheyre Singh informed them that a "sahib" was listening, when the emissary at once took to flight.

Within the first week after the siege began, the enemy had established batteries all round us; but they were chiefly at first erected on the east side, against the Residency, Bailey-Guard Gate, &c., and against the Cawnpoor battery. Fortunately for my garrison, they only brought one field-piece against us at the beginning; which enabled us to carry on our nightly labours with little molestation from artillery. Their batteries were generally well placed, and very near: some guns being put in position within sixty yards of our defences. Where our artillery could fairly reach them, it never failed in soon silencing the enemy's guns; but they were very clever in placing them so that we could bring no gun to bear upon them in reply. Sometimes they kept their gun concealed behind the corner of a building, ran it out, fired, and immediately retired before we could return the shot, pulling back the gun with a drag rope. In other places the gun was kept at the bottom of an inclined plane, to the top of which it was dragged to be fired, when the recoil forced it down the inclined plane again. As soon as the siege began, they commenced making screens along such thoroughfares as were exposed to our fire, made of wooden palisades, placed in a bank of earth; and the roads and passages were everywhere intersected by their ditches and traverses.

Their batteries were usually formed of strong rafters of wood stuck upright, and deeply embedded in the ground, and strengthened and supported by a bank of earth; a square embrasure being left in the centre for the muzzle of the cannon.

Their fire was generally precise, and seldom went very wide of the object aimed at. But they rarely attempted to batter in breach: their object seemed to be rather to drive us from our works where they were preparing to attack: or to destroy life by firing into our buildings when they thought them occupied, and the assault to be unexpected.

Where our cannon could not bear upon the enemy, their batteries were shelled; and three or four shells usually caused a suspension of their firing. Our mortars, 8-inch, were not heavy, and could easily be moved about to the several spots from which it was desired to direct their fire.

The ingenuity of the enemy, however, preserved them in their batteries in a great measure from injury by these missiles; for on several occasions upon which sorties were made, it was discovered that they had dug narrow trenches ten feet deep near their guns, into which they could at once spring and find security when they saw a shell approaching.

The mutineers inflicted, as we had reason to believe, great injury upon the people of the city. At night on the 4th of July, and afterwards on one or two occasions, there was a great uproar in the direction of the bazaars, with occasional shots. The natives in our garrison always explained these disturbances by saying that the rebels were plundering the bazaars; and I believe that they were right.

CHAPTER XI.

CONTINUATION OF THE SIEGE, JULY 9TH TO 31ST.

Improvement in Commissariat arrangements.—Grinding the wheat.—Severe labours of the officers and men of the garrison.—Conduct of the European privates.—M. Duprat, his history, conduct, and death.—Enemy short of ammunition, fire chiefly hammered shot.—Five hundred cannon shot collected within my post.—Prohibition to fire round shot from my post.—Our rifle practice.—Enemy's military music.—Attack on my post on the 14th of July, Lieutenant Lester killed.—Grand general attack on the 20th of July; enemy beaten back at all points.—Lieutenant Grant and Captain Forbes wounded at Mr. Gubbins' post.—Attack on the same post again, on the 21st of July.—Major Banks killed.—Dr. Brydon wounded on the same day inside Mr. Gubbins' house.—Arrival of the messenger "Ungud."—He unfortunately leaves without a despatch from Brigadier Inglis.—The Brigadier objects to Mr. Gubbins undertaking the vacant office of Chief Commissioner.—Mrs. Dorin killed inside Mr. Gubbins' house on the 22nd of July.—Ungud's second arrival; he brings a letter from Colonel B. Fraser Tytler.—Good effect of the news brought by Ungud.—Scene of Ungud recounting his news at midnight.—He goes out again with despatches.—Gunpowder removed inside our works.—Major Apthorp joins my garrison.—List of the several posts.—Sortie on the 22nd of July to burn the Goindah lines.—Enemy's mines, at the Redan, at Sago's house, and at the Cawnpoor battery.—The latter destroyed.—A fourth at the Brigade Mess.—A fifth at the outer Seikh square blown up by Captain Fulton and Lieutenant Hutchinson.—Unceasing exertions of Captain Fulton.—Diminution of the numbers and fire of the enemy.—Movements of the enemy in and from the direction of Cawnpoor.—Enemy establish a Garden battery against my post.—Annoyance from their shells; new missiles used by them.—Danger from our own shells.—Enemy's shells probably obtained from the Cawnpoor magazine.—Rains continued.—Our communications from post to post improved.—Excessive heat; effluvia; sickness; cholera.—Deaths from cholera.—Lieutenant Dashwood and Mr. Polehampton, from small-pox, Mrs. Thomas, and Mrs. Edgar Clarke.—Great suffering, and mortality among the children.—Annoyance from flies.—Casualities by the end of July; 170 in the 32nd Regt. alone.—Mr. Bryson, Lieutenant Arthur, Lieutenant Lewin, and Lieutenant Shepherd, killed.—Also Messrs. Erith and Pigeon, and Mr. Ed. Wittinbaker.—Names of officers who had been wounded.

After the first week the Commissariat arrangements began to work better. The rations were issued from a more protected building, and all were supplied sufficiently well. Little flour was now left, and arrangements were made for grinding our wheat by hand-mills, of which a store had been laid in, in the sheds appropriated to the Commissariat. This was effected by means of our native servants. Some classes of them were excused, and received rations of flour ground by the lower ranks of servants, grooms, grasscutters, &c. These men were paid for their labour, and I lost by their withdrawal for this purpose several of my battery workmen. The better course it seemed to me was that afterwards followed, after we had been joined by Sir James Outram's force, viz. to serve out wheat to the natives, and let them make their own arrangements, which they always can do, to get it ground.

We had by this time got rid of all our loose and valueless horses. Besides those retained for private use, and which depended on private resources for their food, fifty of the best cavalry and artillery horses had been selected, and were made over to the Seikh Cavalry in the Seikh squares.

The labours of the garrison officers and men were at this time very severe. Besides being exposed during most of the day in guarding against, or repelling the attacks of the enemy, there were night duties of every kind. Cattle died and had to be dragged away and buried; there were fatigue parties every evening for the purpose of burying the dead; the sick and wounded had to be carried to the hospital. Traverses and screens to protect the most exposed thoroughfares were commenced, though little progress had at this time been made with them. Then there were embrasures and batteries to be repaired; guns and mortars to be moved and their positions altered. The church had been found to be too exposed a position to contain our stores; besides, fears were entertained that it might be fired by the enemy. Night parties were therefore formed to remove the ghee and grain from it to more central and protected buildings. In all these labours, officers and soldiers, civilians, high and low, worked alike. The privates upon the whole behaved exceedingly well under this ceaseless exertion. Sometimes, however, it was with extreme difficulty that they could be got to work; and at other times, knowing that there was no means of punishment that could be inflicted, they positively refused. On one of these occasions, when a soldier had folded his arms in an attitude of defiance, Captain McCabe, an excellent and most highly deserving officer of the 32nd, adopted a novel mode of compulsion. He called for a sergeant, and ordered him to put the man to bed! The order was obeyed. And McCabe, who knew the men well, declared that the fellow would be so jeered by his comrades, that he would not be likely to misbehave again. The men were very soon deprived of tobacco, of which unfortunately no store had been laid in: this, added to the heavy duties, and many other causes which operated to produce depression, undoubtedly caused much despondency and loss of *morale*. In remonstrating with soldiers for exposing themselves unnecessarily to the enemy's fire, I have more than once received the reply, that it did not matter whether the man was killed then or later. About this time they broke into the stores of wine and spirits belonging to a French merchant, M. Duprat, who, as has been mentioned, occupied a house near the Cawnpoor battery; and laid hands on a large amount of valuable property belonging to him. Measures were taken, under Colonel Inglis' direction, to check such misconduct as far as was then possible; and what remained of the stores was removed.

Duprat himself had joined my garrison on the 6th of July. He was a Frenchman, who had served as a Chasseur d'Afrique in Algeria. He had then left the army, and repaired to the Isle of Bourbon. From this he was persuaded to remove to Calcutta, by D'Orgoni, a foreigner, who held out promises of lucrative employment in Burmah. On arriving in Calcutta, D'Orgoni failed to meet him as promised, and Duprat repaired to Lucknow, where he had succeeded in making a little money by mercantile pursuits. He was known to me, but more particularly to Mr. Lucas, our friend and guest. He proved himself a good and gallant soldier, took regular duty with our other officers, and became a great favourite in my garrison. He possessed a large-bored heavy rifle which he used with skill. Duprat's energy during the night alarms, which the enemy continually practised upon us, often excited our mirth. They used to cluster round our works, and especially the new Bastion which was building, shouting, what appeared to be their war-cry, "Ali, Ali!" oft repeated, and calling upon one another to advance with the words, "Chulo Buhadoor!" "Advance, ye brave!" On these occasions, Duprat, exposing himself more than was prudent, would yell back defiance at them at the top of his voice. "Come on, ye brave! ye rascals, cowards, scoundrels!" he shouted, which generally provoked a discharge of musketry and matchlock balls in return.

Unfortunately, these discharges were not always harmless. Later in the siege, in the month of

August, Duprat, while repelling an attack of the enemy from the roof of the building, which we called Grant's Bastion, was severely wounded in the face by a musket-ball, which came in at the loophole out of which he was looking. He suffered for a long time very severely, and when apparently convalescent, sunk and died, heartily regretted by us all.

The enemy were now closing in upon us on every side. They occupied the nearest houses, and kept up a most galling and dangerous musketry fire. Nothing but a round shot through the house would turn them out of it, and in my garrison the firing of round shot without special leave was strictly prohibited. The enemy were known to be short of ammunition, as shown by their often firing logs of wood, bound with iron, and the military authorities were afraid of giving them shot, for our balls were immediately picked up and returned. Many a shot has in this way been interchanged several times between the combatants. Probably, however, this prohibition was too strictly enjoined, for it rendered the enemy's riflemen round my position exceedingly annoying. Moreover, they soon supplied themselves with hammered shot in abundance, which, at the short distances from which they fired, was almost equally as effective as our own.

During the siege, we at different times collected from our rooms, housetop, and enclosure, as many as five hundred cannon shot, which were sent to our magazine. Of these by far the largest proportion was hammered shot. There was no resource for us, therefore, but to keep them down with our rifles when they became very troublesome: and, as I was myself the most practised marksman in our garrison, I had plenty to do. The enemy were very clever in arranging their loopholes, keeping the inside of the building dark, and allowing no light *through*; so that it was not easy to tell whether the shooter was at the loophole or not. What we found the best practice, and one which we learnt from Captain Fulton, who was himself an excellent shot, was, for one person to watch the opening with a glass, while the marksman kept his rifle laid for the loophole. So soon as the first announced that the enemy had appeared, the latter fired. The fellows showed little pluck; and whenever one of our bullets had fairly entered the loophole, firing would be discontinued from it for several hours. During the first fortnight of the siege, the enemy's fire was almost incessant. It slackened usually towards sunset, and was resumed at intervals during the night. At night, however, they always fired a good deal of blank ammunition.

We were continually insulted by the music of the mutineers. At early dawn their bugles regularly began sounding the assembly, and a variety of regimental calls; while the shrill horns and drums of the Rujwarra (a name used to designate the zemindarree forces) kept up loud and dissonant screams, which were again renewed every evening. Occasionally their bands paraded in our sight and played "God save the Queen," or other tunes which they had learnt in our service.

On the 14th of July, we were roused from dinner at my garrison, by the servants running in to say, that the enemy were forcing their way in on the south side where we were extremely weak. On manning the top of the house, and the parapets on the southern outhouses, we found that they had filled the younger Johannes' house and adjoining buildings. These they loopholed in a moment, and a heavy fire was interchanged for some hours, during which Lieutenant Lester, before Assistant-Commissioner at Seetapoor, was mortally wounded by a matchlock-ball, which injured his spine, and of which he died soon after. It was very difficult to hit the small loopholes of the enemy, and the private soldiers with their muskets rarely succeeded in doing so. But all around the hole, the wall would in a few minutes be covered thick with bullet-marks. It now became necessary to put up some sort of defence on the south side, and we worked all night in erecting a strong palisade of rafters sunk firmly into the soil, and placed upright against the low outer wall; but after unroofing some buildings we could only get wood enough to carry this defence along a little more than half the length required. The canvas walls of tents were therefore stretched along the remaining space. These, though affording no protection against the enemy's assault, were of much service in screening us from their fire, by intercepting their view, and preventing their taking aim at individuals.

The entrance to my house was on the south side by a porch, which it became necessary to secure from fire. This was greatly effected by building up a wall of boxes and tents, leaving access open on one side. Two carriages which we possessed were drawn up outside the porch, and completed the protection. Many a bullet passed through them before the siege was ended.

On the 20th of July, the enemy made their first and most serious general attack. Look-out posts had been established on the top of one of the Residency turrets, and on the Post-office roof, from which the movements of the mutineers were closely watched.

Before nine in the morning it was reported that large bodies of the enemy could be seen on the move in different directions, and we were accordingly on the alert. About ten o'clock, they sprung a mine near the Redan battery, inside the outer Water-gate. This was evidently intended to destroy the Redan, but the enemy had fortunately missed the right direction, and the battery was uninjured. Immediately after, our entire position was assaulted on all sides by a terrible fire of round shot and musketry, under cover of which the enemy in several quarters advanced boldly to the attack. The principal assaults were made at the Redan, and at Innes' post; but the enemy showed boldly in other quarters, and several were shot down close to our defences at Anderson's, and at my post. At the Redan, large masses of them advanced to within twenty-five paces of the battery, but there they were met by the heavy fire of that battery, under the charge of Lieutenants F. Cunliffe, and MacFarlan, and by steady discharges of musketry, and were compelled to retire with great loss.

At Innes' post, Lieutenant Loughman, who commanded a party of the uncovenanted service, and a few men of Her Majesty's 32nd and of the 13th N. I., had to trust chiefly to the musket and bayonet, and made a most gallant defence. The enemy came close under the walls, and brought ladders; but so hot a fire was kept up upon them that they could not plant them against the wall, and after vain but repeated efforts they were forced to relinquish the attempt.

From the roof of Dr. Fayrer's house, that officer and Captain Weston maintained a most effective fire.

At the Judicial and Financial garrisons the storm of round shot and musketry was most severe, and was well replied to.

At Anderson's post, the enemy advanced to the attack, led by a man who carried a green standard. He was shot and fell into the ditch, upon which the rest retired.

At my post, the attack was made chiefly on the south side and around the unfinished south-west bastion. The enemy showed in great numbers, and some ascended the south-east slope of the bastion, where the wall was incomplete, to the crest of the parapet, and were there shot.

Many gathered round the bastion which we called Grant's; and to dislodge them, Lieutenant Grant, of the Bombay army, a refugee from Duriabad, was throwing hand-grenades, when, most unhappily, one of them burst in his hand, shattering it completely, and wounding Captain H. Forbes, who commanded. Grant's hand was amputated, but he died from the effect of the wound a few days later, after first losing his wife and a daughter from cholera in our house. There remained two little orphans, a girl and an infant at the breast, under our charge.

Captain Forbes' injury having placed him on the sick list, he made over the command of my garrison to Captain Hawes.

The result of the day's fight was cheering. The enemy had done their worst, and the engagement had been carried on during the whole day from morning till four o'clock in the afternoon. On the one side our loss had been small, being only four men killed, and about twelve wounded; while the enemy's loss must have been reckoned by hundreds. It was evidently possible to maintain our position against the utmost efforts of which they were capable. The loss which we had inflicted upon them did not, however, deter the enemy from attacking my post in very considerable force upon the following day, the 21st of July. They had discovered our weak side, and crowded in large numbers into the younger Johannes' house and adjacent buildings; and into the Goindah lines. They proceeded to dig a hole in the wall of this latter enclosure, and entered the narrow lane which skirted our compound on that side. A screen of canvas now only separated them from our position, for the enclosing wall was so low that an easy jump would have cleared it. I was on the roof of the outhouses at the south-west angle when Lieutenant Hardinge summoned me to the defence of the lane. I at once comprehended the danger, and hurried to the single loophole by which the lane was commanded. Fortunately the fire from it completely enfiladed the lane, except where two projecting pillars which supported a portico underneath Grant's bastion interrupted its line. No sooner did the enemy see me at this post than some ran back, while a number took shelter behind the portico pillars, from which their muskets protruded. The projecting muzzle of my rifle prevented their leaving their cover, and without doing so they could not reach me, but discharged their muskets at an angle harmlessly. At my right hand was a large loophole which it was necessary to close. A private of the 32nd who joined me, creeping on hands and knees along the roof, brought some boards, with which the opening was quickly barricaded. And only just in time; for the enemy outside fired heavily upon the spot, and more than one bullet fell at our feet hot and flattened from the screen which we had put up. The enemy outside now began to throw over pickaxes and shovels to those beneath the portico, and our position became critical. Had they made a hole into Grant's bastion and poured in through it, our post might have been taken. At this moment I heard the voice of a European behind me, and addressing the party, without turning, begged that the wall in rear of the mutineers might be loopholed, and musketry opened upon them. The person was Major Banks. He approached my post to get a sight of the enemy, and, while looking out incautiously, received a bullet through the temples. I heard the heavy fall, and turned for a second. He was dead; he never moved, and I resumed my guard over the enemy. Long was I kept there, firing on every one who showed himself from two double rifles, which were loaded for me by a faithful chuprassie at my side. After the lapse of two hours assistance came. A mortar was brought down and opened on the enemy. The shells passing close over our heads burst among the crowds below, while we threw ourselves flat along the parapet. The enemy soon fled, those detained beneath the porch springing across the lane with the speed of lamplighters. As they made off, a heavy fire was opened on them from the top of the Brigade Mess. I did not get down from my post till late in the afternoon; and then Major Banks's body was removed. It was buried, as was usual with us, the same night, sewn up in a white sheet. Since the deaths had become numerous, coffins had not been used (we had not indeed the means of making them); but the bodies used to be sewn up in sheets or bedding, and several were committed to the ground in the same grave.

On the same day, later in the evening, as we were seated at dinner, a bullet came in at one of the south windows and wounded Dr. Brydon, who was sitting at table, severely in the back. It was now determined to remove the ladies from the south side of the upper story altogether, and they were all placed below. The rooms on the north side continued to be occupied. A centre suite intervened between the two; in which we dined.

The following night was a memorable one in the siege. Being indisposed, I had retired to rest, when about midnight I was roused by the intelligence that "Ungud" had come in. This was the messenger, it will be remembered, who had been sent out by Captain Hawes, on the 29th of June, to bring tidings of the Nana. He had no letter, but brought tidings, wonderful and strange to our ears, and too good to be readily believed. We had, it will be remembered, received no single iota of intelligence since the siege began: and now Ungud recounted to us the marvellous tale of a handful of men under General Havelock having defeated the Nana in three engagements, and being actually at the moment master of Cawnpoor. The news was astounding. We had all along been expecting that the Nana would cross the river and join the besieging force, if he had not actually done so already. I examined Ungud strictly; and came to the conclusion that the joyful and wondrous news was true. An abstract was made of it, and the messenger sent, together with a note from myself by hand of Lieutenant Hutchinson (Engineers) to Brigadier Inglis, inquiring whether he would send a letter by the scout. His written answer informed me that he would not write. I prepared a despatch immediately: it was addressed to the Governor-General, and enclosed to General Havelock. In it I depicted as faithfully as I could our exact position and circumstances, and detailed our own force, and that which the enemy was believed to have. My despatch was nearly ready when Lieutenant and Aide-de-Camp Birch arrived. He said that the Brigadier could not sleep, and would send a line if the messenger had not started. I promised to detain him. Shortly after my letter was ready, it began to rain heavily. Ungud pressed to be allowed to depart. Heavy rain, he told us, afforded his only chance of passing the sentinels of the enemy. When I attempted to detain him, he declared that if not allowed to go then he would not go at all that night. I gave him my despatch and let him go; sending Captain Hawes over immediately to inform the Brigadier of his departure. Hawes met Lieutenant Birch bringing the Brigadier's note; but the messenger was gone.

These facts have been mentioned to show what actually occurred. The occurrence produced, I fear, some unpleasant feeling between the military commandant and myself. No slight was certainly intended; but I fear my conduct was so interpreted.

On Major Banks' lamented death, the succession to the Chief Commissioner's duties naturally devolved upon myself, who stood next to Sir Henry Lawrence in the Civil Commission. Brigadier Inglis, however, now opposed my undertaking the office, which accordingly remained vacant. Civil authority ceased, and military command remained with the Brigadier: whose correspondence was always, I am bound to say, civil and courteous.*

And it must be admitted that the event showed that there was no occasion for the exercise of civil

* See Addenda, No. V.

power. Martial law prevailed within the garrison, and we had no opportunity during the remainder of the siege of communicating with the native chiefs outside.

On the 22nd of July we experienced another sad casualty in my garrison. Mrs. Dorin, one of the Seetapoor refugees, occupied a room on the north side of the upper story of the house. During the day she was killed by a matchlock ball, which, entering by a window on the south, had traversed two suites of apartments before it reached that in which she was standing. She had rendered herself very useful by her kindness and attention to every one, and was much regretted. After this sad accident, we removed all the large bookcases and wardrobes, and barricaded all the windows on the south side carefully against shot.

Many persons had entertained great doubt of the truth of Ungud's information. But their doubts were happily removed by his reappearance at my post on the night of the 25th of July; and this time he brought a letter. It was a reply by Colonel B. Fraser Tytler, Quartermaster-General of Havelock's force, to the letter which Ungud had carried from me, and confirmed the intelligence which Ungud had previously given us. Colonel Tytler wrote that the General's force was sufficient to defeat the enemy, that the troops were then crossing the river, and that we might hope to meet in five or six days.

This was indeed cheering intelligence; and it was much needed. Not to speak of Europeans, among our native followers great despondency prevailed. We daily lost men, sometimes six or seven in a day; and they had begun to think that relief was impossible.

Many desertions had taken place, and several of the Seikhs, including sixteen men of the 13th N. I., had been of the number. This timely and most welcome news cheered them and raised their hopes. They might not, especially after our mistake about the fall of Dehli, perhaps, have implicitly credited the intelligence which we gave them; but there was no possibility of doubting the particulars with which Ungud furnished them. They crowded round him, putting him a thousand questions, which he as readily answered; and they were at last perfectly satisfied that his tale was true.

It is impossible to overvalue the importance of these visits of Ungud. Again he came, as will presently be related, when hope deferred had made the heart sick; when Europeans doubted; when desertion of natives had become more numerous, and yet more were imminent: and again the certainty of approaching succour revived and refreshed us, and reanimated the languishing fidelity of our native friends.

Nor could any picture more characteristic of the siege be presented, than one which should represent Ungud just after one of his midnight entrances, recounting to our eagerly-listening ears the events which he had witnessed. The low room on the ground-floor, with a single light carefully screened on the outer side, lest it should attract the bullets of the enemy; the anxious faces of the men who crowded round, and listened with breathless attention to question and answer; the exclamation of joy as pieces of good tidings were given out, and laughter at some of Ungud's jeers upon the enemy. More retired, would be shown the indistinct forms of the women in their night attire, who had been attracted from their rooms in hopes of catching early some part of the good news which had come in. The animated and intelligent face of our messenger, as he assured us of the near approach of help, occupies the foreground. All these together form a scene which must live, as long as life remains, in the memory of us all.

From Ungud we learned many pieces of intelligence. Of all these, the most terrible and mournful was the sad account of the massacre of the women and children who were prisoners at Cawnpoor, by that arch-fiend the Nana. We listened to his sad tale of this deed of superhuman wickedness, in hope that more precise intelligence hereafter might assure us that it was not so bad as Ungud represented. But, alas! his words proved all too true. Among other facts, he mentioned that the Risaldar of Fisher's Horse, who had been at first appointed General by the mutineers, had been killed by one of our rifle-balls while reconnoitring, from a loophole; and that a soobahdar of one of the N. I. Regts., named Ghumundee Singh, was then their leader; that a boy of eleven or twelve years of age, a member of the Oudh royal family, had been proclaimed king; his mother, the Begum, being regent; while some authority was still exercised by the Môlovee, who had accompanied the mutineers from Fyzabad.

After a day's rest Ungud again went out, bearing despatches and plans of our position, and of the roads leading to it, from Brigadier Inglis for General Havelock. These were rather bulky, and a reward of 5000 rupees was promised to him if they should be safely delivered.

As has been already related, the gunpowder which was brought in from the Muchee Bhowun, had been buried before the siege in the Low Residency grounds, on the north side, outside our line of defence. This was found to be too exposed a position in which to keep that precious material, which was now far more valuable to us than treasure. The enemy had got near to it, and had set fire to some fodder stacks and tents, which were too close to the subterranean magazine not to cause us considerable alarm. About the middle of the month its removal was commenced, and all the barrels were taken up and safely deposited in the underground story of the Begum Kotee by the 23rd of the month. The removal of the powder was a source of much satisfaction; but it was not effected without severe labour, shared during the night by military and non-military alike, often working in heavy rain, and knee-deep in mud.

Some days later, the roof of the chamber in which the powder was deposited was further secured, by a protection of large beams laid over it, which were then covered with two feet of earth. It was hoped that this would effectually protect it from the shells of the enemy.

After the attack on my post of the 21st, a reinforcement was sent to us of a party of sepoy pensioners, under Major Apthorp, of the 41st N. I., who, being the senior officer, assumed command of my garrison. This now consisted of a party of eighteen Europeans, under Lieutenant Webb, of the 32nd; the sepoy pensioners; a party of the 48th N. I., under Lieutenant R. Ouseley; besides the European gentlemen and my native levies. The pensioners were posted in the lower part of Grant's bastion, and the men of the 48th at the north-west angle of the house.

It will be well to take this opportunity of giving a list of the several posts, and of the officers by whom they were commanded. They were the following:—

No.	Name of Post.	Garrison.	Commandant.
1	Residency	32nd Regt.	Capt. Lowe, 32nd Regt.
2	Redan Battery . .	32nd Regt.	Lieut. Lawrence, 32nd Regt.
3	Innes' House and Church	Uncovenanted clerks and 32nd	Lieut. Loughnan, 13th N. I., succeeded by Capt. Graydon, 7th O. I. I.
4	Sheep and Slaughter Houses . .	Uncovenanted . . .	Capt. Boileau, 7th L. C.
5	Gubbins' House . .	32nd, Sepoy Pensioners, 48th N. I., and Gubbins' Levies . .	Capt. Forbes, 1st L. C., succeeded by Capt. Hawes, 5th O. I. I., and by Major Apthorp, 41st N. I.
6	Seikh Squares	Seikh Cavalry . . .	Capt. Hardinge, 3rd O. I. C.
7	Brigade Mess . . .	Officers of the Brigade	Col. Master, 7th L. C.
8	Martinière School .	32nd, and uncovenanted	Mr. Schilling, Principal of the Martinière.
9	Cawnpoor Battery .	32nd	Daily relief of captains.
10	Anderson's House .	32nd, and uncovenanted	Capt. R. P. Anderson, Assistant-Commissioner.
11	Judicial Commissioner's Office .	Seikhs of the 13th N.I., and uncovenanted	Capt. Germon, 13th N.I.
12	Sago's House . . .	32nd	Lieut. Clery, 32nd Regt.
13	Financial Commissioner's Office .	32nd, and uncovenanted	Capt. Sanders, 41st N.I.
14	Post Office	32nd	Capt. M'Cabe, 32nd.
15	Dr. Fayrer's House .	Sepoy Pensioners . .	Capt. Weston, Superintendent of Military Police.
16	Treasury and Bailey Guard . .	13th N. I.	Lieut. Aitken, 13th N.I.
17	N. E. Line of Defence from Hospital to the Redan	71st N. I. . . . . . 48th N. I.	Capt. Strangways, N. I. Col. Palmer, N. I.

The buildings, which approached closely to my post on the south, had been found to be a source of great danger and annoyance both to my garrison and to that of the Seikh squares. The nearest was that termed the Goindah lines. It consisted of an enclosure surrounded by a high mud wall protected on the top with tiles. It contained a long, low range of building with a tiled roof, in which the Goindahs, or Thug approvers, used to be kept. A narrow lane, which has been already mentioned, separated this enclosure from my compound wall. The Goindah lines had been filled with the enemy on the occasion of the attacks of the 20th and 21st, and the enemy was also suspected of mining. It was, therefore, resolved to destroy these buildings, which afforded them such close and dangerous cover. Accordingly, Brigadier Inglis led out a sortie for this purpose on the 22nd July. The party consisted of some men of the 32nd and Seikhs, and several of the native garrison of my post, and was planned and accompanied by Lieutenant Hutchinson (Engineers). A few shells having been first thrown over to dislodge the enemy, a hole was dug through my compound wall, through which the party passed into the lane, and thence through that already made by the enemy into the Goindah lines. Fire was immediately applied to the roof, and when this had well taken effect the party retired. The enemy made no opposition. But, unfortunately, a private of the 32nd having proceeded in the dark too far in advance, was mistaken for one of the enemy, and was killed by a shot from the top of the Brigade Mess. After the party had retired, the hole was closed with a barrel made fast with earth and mud.

It was now discovered that the enemy were mining around us in all directions. They had been seen working near the Redan, and the officers there were in daily fear of being blown into the air. The engineers, however, were of opinion that only a trench or traverse was being dug by the enemy, and the position was toc completely exposed to the enemy's fire to allow of the work being properly examined. They had another mine near Sago's house, which was being carefully watched; and a third, and more important one, threatened the Cawnpoor battery. This our engineers, under the direction of Captain Fulton, were endeavouring to countermine, when, fortunately, a mistake of the enemy discovered it. They had driven their gallery too near the surface, which caused a portion of it which had become saturated with rain to fall in, thereby discovering it to us. It was forthwith carefully watched, and a rifle fire kept up upon it from the top of the Brigade Mess, in spite of which the enemy contrived to repair it with boards. A mortar was then brought, and some shells thrown over in order to destroy it. At last one fell in the right spot, and bursting inside the gallery, effectually destroyed it. Not long after the enemy began another mine close by.

A fourth mine was being driven by them against the Brigade Mess, where the sound of the workmen could for several days be heard distinctly. A shaft was immediately commenced there, and a sap begun, at which the officers and civilians laboured with great exertion. After awhile the sounds of the enemy's miners ceased to be heard, and their mine, it was believed, was discontinued.

A fifth mine was carried on by the enemy against the outer Seikh square, and, having been discovered, a shaft had been sunk and a gallery begun by Captain Hardinge with the help of his Seikhs. As the enemy continued their work, our sap was carried on as fast as possible by Captain Fulton, who was in the mine on the afternoon of the 28th of July, when our gallery met theirs. When our crowbar broke through the thin partition of earth which separated the mines, the enemy's miners immediately fled, pursued through their gallery by Captain Fulton and Lieutenant

Hutchinson (Engineers). It led across the road to a native house opposite, from one of the chambers of which the shaft had been begun. The enemy commenced filling in earth, but finding our officers close upon them, they abandoned the building. A barrel of powder was then brought and deposited in the shaft, the gallery was tamped, and the house blown up.

It is impossible sufficiently to do justice to the skilful and unceasing exertions made by our engineers, but more particularly by Captain Fulton, in meeting and foiling these numerous and most dangerous attempts of the enemy. It could not be effected without great exertion. Captain Fulton frequently passed many hours in the mines; and what the temperature must have been inside these narrow subterranean passages in the stifling Indian month of July may be imagined. He organized a small body of miners, comprising a few Cornishmen (the 32nd being a Cornwall regiment fortunately contained some miners) and some Seikhs, and there is no doubt that to his untiring perseverance, boldness, and skill, the Lucknow garrison, under Providence, mainly owe their safety.

A few days after Ungud had left us, a sensible diminution in the enemy's fire was noticed. We thought they had removed some guns, and no doubt thought rightly. Fewer of them were seen about, and the fire of musketry was less incessant. It was reported from the look-out, that what was supposed to be a regiment marching in the direction of Cawnpoor had been seen. On the 30th of July a large number of men were seen streaming into the city from the Cawnpoor road, who were, we hoped, some of the mutineers whom Havelock had defeated. Nor was our supposition probably wrong; for subsequent information made known to us that the first engagement which took place between General Havelock and the enemy was on the 29th at Onao.

Before this, however, the enemy had established a new battery of two guns, a 9 and a 6-pounder, in a garden, commanded completely by our new south-west bastion, and 250 yards from it. From this they had begun to cannonade my house, and had made several large holes in the dome which surmounted our pretty octagon drawing-room. This room had, therefore, been abandoned, but we still kept possession of the upper rooms on the north side, which were not exposed to the fire of the battery.

They had also latterly given the whole garrison much annoyance by throwing shells into various parts of our position. These were both 8-inch and shrapnell; fired apparently from 24-pound howitzers placed at a great angle to give a vertical fire. The garrisons at the Post-office and Begum Kotee had several most narrow and providential escapes from the 8-inch shells. They also made up and threw into our works a missile invented by themselves, the object of which was not very apparent. It consisted of one of our shrapnell-shells wrapped up in a strong canvas ("taut") bag filled with gunpowder, and provided with a fuse. It was projected like a shell, vertically. The enclosing powder first ignited, bursting and scattering the burning canvas, and presently, when you thought that the danger was over, the shrapnell itself burst, injuring any one who had approached incautiously. They used also frequently to fire in fragments of the shells thrown by ourselves, tied up in cloth, and logs of wood strengthened with rings of iron.

Much danger was experienced from our own shells. The enemy was so near us that these were thrown to short distances, and the fuses were cut short accordingly. Very frequently fragments of these returned into our position, making in their passage through the air a very peculiar whirring noise most unpleasant to hear, as it was impossible to guess from what quarter the missile was approaching. Very early in the siege our cowherd was killed by a shell fragment while standing in the verandah of the house; and several other accidents occurred from them.

It puzzled us much to know how the enemy obtained so many shells as he evidently possessed, for the supply captured by him in our waggons at Chinhut must have been long before expended. The only and probable solution of the difficulty is to be found in the quantity of ammunition known to have been in the magazine at Cawnpoor, when it fell into the hands of the Nana. The mutineers also possessed some rockets, of which a few were fired into our position.

The rains continued: and though the wet weather often occasioned much discomfort, besides interrupting our earthworks and repairs, yet they were on the whole beneficial to us and injurious to the enemy. Our position, which was high, was well drained, and the repeated washing which it underwent prevented the accumulation of dirt, and diminished malaria; besides keeping the air cool. On the other hand, it filled the enemy's trenches, and damaged his mines, and rendered his communications more difficult.

Our own communications from post to post had by the end of the month been greatly altered and improved. Traverses had been completed in several places where they were urgently required, and short and protected passages had been obtained by knocking holes in the walls of intervening buildings, which were now passed through, instead of being obliged to go round them by the road as before. There was so much to do in my own garrison that I went about little. After being up during the greater part of the night, I felt little inclination to leave the enclosure, particularly as this could not be done without running more risk of being hit, than beset me inside a room at home.

The heat was necessarily excessive, for it is at Lucknow always so in July; but its ill effects were greatly aggravated by the constant effluvia from which we suffered. Conservancy was attended to as much as possible; and everything offensive was thrown into deep pits dug for the purpose and covered with earth. But a great effluvium arose from the bodies of cattle which died in places much exposed to the fire of the enemy, and which there was neither opportunity, nor were there men, to remove and bury. The offal of the slaughtered cattle, which was thrown outside the works over the enclosing wall of the slaughter-house, greatly increased this effluvium; and we suffered from it particularly at my garrison when the wind blew from that quarter. Sickness necessarily resulted from these disposing causes, and we suffered during the month not a little from cholera, fever, small-pox, and diarrhœa, which carried off many of the garrison. The small number of our Engineer and Artillery officers caused the diminution of their numbers by sickness to be severely felt. For some days we had only one engineer fit for duty. Lieutenant Dashwood, of the 48th N. I., fell a victim to cholera on the 9th, and the Rev. Mr. Polehampton on the 19th of July, to the same fell disease. Mr. Polehampton had just recovered from his severe wound when he was taken ill, and was carried off in a few hours. He was much liked and respected in the garrison. Colonel Halford, of the 71st, died on the 29th of a carbuncle; and Mrs. Thomas, wife of Lieutenant Thomas, Madras Artillery, Mrs. Edgar Clarke, wife of Lieutenant Clarke, Assistant-Commissioner at Gondah, of small-pox, on the 16th and 30th respectively.

But the chief sufferers from sickness were the children. Everything was against them. It is difficult at all times for European children to get through the hot weather in the plains of India without injury, even under ordinary circumstances of peace and comfort. But now, when neither fresh air nor suitable food could be given them, the poor little creatures sickened and died in numbers. Some parents who had had two and even three children in good health when the siege began, had not one left when it ended. We suffered also from another very serious though minor nuisance—that of flies. These troublesome insects swarm in all native cities, and particularly at Dehli and Lucknow, and multiplied in countless myriads during the siege. Deprived of our ordinary attendants who usually brush them away at meals, we were sorely pestered and annoyed by them.

By the end of July also our casualties had become very numerous, and the hospital, of which the ground-floor only could be used (the upper story being too much exposed to the fire of the enemy), was full and over-crowded: 170 casualties by death and wounds had taken place in the 32nd Regt. alone. Besides the officers who have been already mentioned, the following were killed: Mr. Bryson, Sergeant of the Volunteer Cavalry, shot dead on the 9th of July.

Lieutenant Arthur, of the 7th Light Cavalry, and Lieutenant Lewin, of the Artillery, shot dead, both at the Cawnpoor battery, the first on the 19th, the second on the 26th of the month. The Cawnpoor battery was terribly exposed, and cost us the lives of many brave men. Latterly, it was thought best to disarm it, and the guns were withdrawn accordingly, while it was maintained as an infantry post by keeping the men constantly under cover. On the 26th of July a very sad accident occurred: Lieutenant Shepherd, of the 2nd O. I. Cavalry, was shot dead in one of the Brigade squares, at night, by the mistake of one of our own garrison posted at the top of the building, who fired unguardedly. Two of our European clerks, Messrs. Erith and Pigeon, had also been killed, and the son of the Superintendent of my office, Mr. Ed. Wittinbaker.

Several of the officers also had been wounded, viz. Lieutenant Bryce, of the Artillery, Lieutenant O'Brien, 84th Regt., Lieutenants Harmer and Edmondstoune, 32nd Regt., and Captain Boileau, 7th Light Cavalry, and Mr. G. H. Lawrence, C. S. Lieutenant D. C. Alexander, of Artillery, and Captain Barlow, Brigade-Major to the Oudh Irregular Brigade, had been severely scorched and injured by an explosion of gunpowder in loading one of the mortars. Mr. Hely, of the 7th Cavalry, had received a wound, from the effect of which he subsequently died. Lieutenant Charlton, of the 32nd Regt., had been struck down by a wound which appeared to all at the time mortal, but from the injury caused by which he was then marvellously recovering, and eventually obtained a complete cure. A musket-ball struck him in the back of the head, and, fracturing the skull, penetrated the brain, in which it lodged, completely hidden from view, until nine months after it showed itself at the aperture, and was taken out on his arrival in England.

Such, as I have endeavoured to describe, was our condition at Lucknow when the month of July came to a close.

CHAPTER XII.

FROM THE 1ST TO THE 15TH OF AUGUST.

The period within which relief had been promised had expired, and expectation was on tiptoe.—Despondency with some succeeded disappointed hope.—But the causes which might have detained General Havelock were numerous and obvious enough.—These mentioned.—Further intelligence brought in by Aodhân Singh, on the 6th of August.—Other persons enter the intrenchment in the daytime.—Monotony of siege life, resembled ship-board.—Sunday, and other religious services.—Sortie made by four privates on the 3rd of August.—Sortie made by Lieutenant Loughnan on the 9th idem; a gun of the enemy spiked.—Lieutenant Sewell's Enfield rifle practice.—Bad muskets with which the men of the 32nd Foot were armed.—The tea and coffee stores for the soldiers exhausted on the 8th of August.—Excellent management by Mr. Schilling of the boys at the Martinière.—Difficulty experienced in getting our linen washed.—Enemy's new 24-pounder gun battery established opposite Innes' post.—Death of Ensign Studdy.—The Residency much shattered.—Accident which occurred, from the falling of part of it.—A new 9-pounder battery erected in a lane south of my house, from which we suffered severely.—The enemy batter our south-west angle houses.—Duprat's house ruined; Anderson's greatly injured.—Second general attack on the 10th of August.—Part of the Martinière house blown down.—The Cawnpoor battery, Sago's house, Innes' post, Anderson's house, Gubbins' bastion, and Financial Garrison attacked.—Enemy everywhere repulsed.—Enemy mining near Sago's post.—Countermined and blown up.—Other mines suspected at Anderson's house; and to the south of my post.—Sortie made in the latter direction by Brigadier Inglis on the 13th of August.

THE period had now expired which had been named by Colonel Fraser Tytler in his despatch which reached us on the 25th of July, and hope and expectation were on tiptoe. During the day and the long watches of the nights, we anxiously listened for the sound of artillery in the direction of Cawnpoor. Some believed at times, and others positively averred, that they had heard distant guns, but day after day nothing came of these sounds and reports. To hope gradually succeeded doubt and disappointment, and with some despondency. An idea was entertained at the Military Head Quarters, that the account given in my despatch of the 22nd of July, which it was known had reached General Havelock, might have been too hopeful, and have represented our condition to be better than it was; but the idea was ill-founded; for the despatch had very faithfully portrayed our circumstances.

Though sufficiently disappointing, the non-arrival of the expected force did not occasion me much anxiety; for the causes which might have operated to detain General Havelock were in themselves numerous and obvious enough. We knew that his troops were few; that the rebel force in Oudh was very numerous, and well provided with artillery; and that the line of road along which our friends would have to advance, was almost throughout the entire distance a raised causeway, flanked by marshes and rice-fields on either side, and intersected by streams at several points. The largest of these was the river Syhee, which crosses the road at the village of Bunnee, seventeen miles distant from Lucknow. Even if diminished numbers, and the sickness necessarily incidental to field operations at that season of the year, had not prevented General Havelock's advance, what more likely than that the enemy should have broken down the bridge of three arches at Bunnee, and that Havelock's force should have been thereby delayed?

This is the explanation which I find set down in my journal as the probable one to account for the absence of the expected relief. We had sufficient and very satisfactory evidence that a relieving force was at no very great distance from us, for it was impossible to

R 2

ignore the diminished numbers of the enemy around us, and their diminished fire. Our native followers frequently noticed the fact, and it served to keep up their spirits. Moreover, more than once bodies of sepoys had been observed marching out in regular order in the Cawnpoor direction: while others disordered and often accompanied by doolies had been seen to return. The enemy did their best to discourage our hopes by calling out to us at night, that they had beaten back our friends, and would soon kill us. In return, we bade them lose no time in tying up their bundles and departing, for that our troops were at hand. They would reply with volleys of abuse, and musketry.

On the night of the 6th of August, we fortunately received some further intelligence. This was brought in by one Aodhân Singh, a sepoy of the 1st O. I. Infantry, orderly to Brigadier Gray, who had been sent out with despatches. He had, he told us, gained Havelock's camp at Mungulwar, had delivered his letter, and received a quill despatch in reply, which he had succeeded in bringing very nearly into our entrenchment. In creeping over the broken and flooded ground, however, to escape the observation of the enemy's posts, it had been unfortunately lost. From Aodhân Singh we received much valuable and cheering intelligence. He was the first who informed us that Havelock had fought two engagements with the enemy at Onao and at Busheergunje; and had defeated him on both occasions with the loss of many pieces of artillery. The General, he said, was constructing a fortified post at Mungulwar; from which, so soon as he had received reinforcements, he meant to resume his advance upon Lucknow. We could not doubt the truth of what he said, for he confirmed it by many interesting details. He had seen his own Commander Captain R. L. Thompson, who, as well as Captain Barrow, both from Salone, and other friends, had charged him to deliver special messages with promises of approaching aid. His arrival, therefore, was a great relief to us, and the intelligence he brought caused us much satisfaction.

During the next few days, a sweeper named Nonnowa, a Seikh trooper named Narayn Singh, who had, or pretended he had, been made prisoner by the enemy on the occasion of the defeat at Chinhut, and a domestic servant formerly in the employ of Mrs. Hayes, who had deserted, found their way severally, during the daytime, back into our works. They could give no precise information upon any point; but told us that our force had defeated the mutineers, who were sending out fresh reinforcements against it. It was not easy to understand how these men had been permitted to pass through the enemy's posts, except by design, either to obtain information of our condition, or to tamper with our native auxiliaries. Brigadier Inglis accordingly very properly caused them to be placed in strict confinement. The khidmotgar,* however, managed after a few days to make his escape.

On the 2nd of August was the Festival of the "Bukra Eed," or "Eed-ool-zohah," much observed by Mahomedans, and it was expected that an attack would take place. But it passed over quietly, without other occurrence than that of a salute of forty guns fired by the enemy in honour of the festival.

The siege by this time had begun to wear an appearance of great monotony, induced by the absence of communication with the external world, and the dull and

* Table servant.

wearying routine of the defence operations. One day followed another so like that which was passed in its events and occupations, that there was little to mark time: and we not unfrequently compared our state of existence to that of ship-board life.

It must be confessed, however, that those ladies who most disliked the confinement of long sea voyages, were now obliged to allow that they had made experience of that which was much more intolerable.

There was little to mark the Sunday from other days. Ordinary labour carried on for amusement, was indeed suspended; but the men and ourselves stood to their arms, or their posts, or laboured night and morning at the works alike on all days. Mr. Polehampton was gone; and our second chaplain, the Rev. Mr. Harris, performed divine service regularly at the Brigade Mess and in the Hospital, also at Dr. Fayrer's house, where he resided, and where daily prayers were offered up, and the Communion also frequently administered.

In my garrison, all joined in morning prayers daily after breakfast, and morning service, with a short sermon, was read on the Sunday at the same hour, by ourselves.

On the 3rd of August, a party of two soldiers of the 32nd and two clerks from Innes' post went out without order, tired of the monotony of the defence, and surprised a picket of the enemy. They crept unobserved up to a wall near which the party of mutineers were reposing off their guard, and suddenly raising themselves above the wall discharged their pieces at them. The enemy's picket fled, pursued by the two soldiers, who made prisoner of a boy, one of the coolies employed upon their works, whom they brought back into our intrenchment. The boy was carefully examined, but no information of any value could be extracted.

On the 9th, Lieutenant Loughnan, of the 13th N. I., made a sortie in the middle of the day from the same post with a few men of his garrison; and succeeded in spiking one of the enemy's guns and returning to his post without his men or himself sustaining any injury. Spiking, however, we found by experience to be of little use, for the enemy possessed many expert workmen; who, by drilling out the spike, or boring a new touch-hole, soon rendered the gun serviceable again.

On the 2nd we sustained a very serious loss of live stock, which now consisted almost solely of gun-bullocks, by the fall of the stack of bhoosa* in the racket-court. One of the side walls of the court had given way and fallen down already. And now a large mass of the fodder fell, burying twelve of the oxen, of which seven were killed. This was a severe loss, as the stock of animals was now daily diminishing, and we could ill afford it. The labour also which was entailed by the accident, in digging out the bodies of animals, and afterwards in burying them, was severe, and was much wanted elsewhere for the improvement of our defences.

About the same time Lieutenant Sewell, of the 71st N. I., who alone in our garrison possessed a double Enfield rifle, gave the enemy considerable annoyance by keeping up a fire from a loophole on the top of the Brigade Mess upon a crowded thoroughfare frequented by the mutineer sepoys. His shots frequently cleared the lane at a distance of 750 yards; and caused so much annoyance to them that they

* Chaff-straw fodder.

shortly afterwards built up a high barricade across it, which completely screened passers-by from our view.

The men of the 32nd Regt. were armed with old and very indifferent percussion muskets; and fired in consequence with little accuracy, rarely hitting a loophole of the enemy. The sepoys on our side as well as the mutineers possessed new percussion muskets, supplied by the East India Company, of much superior make.

By the 8th of August, the few comforts enjoyed by the soldiers were still further diminished by the supply of tea and coffee stored for their use becoming exhausted. A tolerably good substitute was provided by the Commissariat by roasting grain, from which an infusion was prepared, which was sufficiently palatable; and which resembled coffee.

The management of the boys who were crowded in the building which bore the name of the Martinière, both now and throughout the siege, reflected the greatest credit on the principal, Mr. Schilling, and the masters. Besides assisting in the defence of the post occupied by themselves and their masters, the boys were made useful in every way. Some attended other garrisons in the capacity of domestics; and others were employed in fanning and attending upon the sick in hospital. Cleanliness was enforced; and, by measures carefully taken, the health of the boys was preserved tolerably good throughout the siege.

We suffered at this time, and ever since the siege had begun, considerable inconvenience from the difficulty of getting our linen washed. Most of the washermen (dhobies), of whom one or more are entertained in every family in India, had deserted. Still, there remained a very few, who did indifferent washing for the garrison at exorbitant charges. Fortunately, we possessed an abundant supply of excellent water from numerous masonry wells within the intrenchment, and never felt any want of this most precious liquid. Indeed, I was able to keep a large swimming bath full, and to replenish it when required with fresh water, which was both a great luxury and preservative of health. Soap, however, and starch were wanting; so that neither the colour nor the appearance of the clothes after being washed were any of the best. Those who possessed flannel shirts among the gentlemen brought them into use, and white linen shirts were rarely seen in the garrison.

The enemy, meanwhile, continued to establish fresh batteries. A 24-pounder gun had been got in position by them early in the month, on a piece of rising ground facing Innes' post. With this they did great injury to the house at Innes' post, to the church, and frequently fired 24- and 21-lb. shot into the Residency. Later in the siege we at my post suffered severely from the fire of this gun. The outer side of Innes' house was battered in, and the verandah and adjoining room brought down; and so much injury was committed, that it was at last found necessary to construct a battery at Innes' post for an 18-pounder gun, which was put in position there; and soon silenced for the time the fire of the enemy's battery. A shot from this battery, which penetrated about this time to the centre room of the Residency, injured Ensign Studdy, of the 32nd, desperately in the arm. Amputation was resorted to, but the poor young officer survived it but a short time. Several officers were in the room at the time that he was struck. The nature of the injury was singular: the part of the arm and chest which was injured, presented the appearance of a violent contusion. The ball had struck and torn down the fringe of the punkah in its passage; and the body of the poor youth, who was crossing the room at the moment, was swathed round and round with it, so that it took some time to disentangle him.

The Residency itself, which had at the commencement been the chief butt for the fire of the enemy, now showed great marks of dilapidation. It was pierced with shot-holes on every side, and had been abandoned as a residence, all but the ground-floor, which was occupied by the privates of the 32nd Regt. On the 11th of August, on the occasion of a gust of high wind striking the building, a great portion of the north-east wing fell, burying six men of the 32nd Regt. in the ruins. After much labour two were taken out alive, from under the *débris;* but four remained long buried under a mass of ruin, which there were not the means of removing.

The enemy soon discovered that the Residency had been abandoned, and possessing information that my house was full, increased upon it more and more the fire of his artillery. A 9-pounder battery was erected in a lane at the distance of about 120 yards, fronting the south or weakest side of my enclosure, where we had no means of firing a shot in reply. On that side the level of my compound was low, so that it was impossible to raise a gun sufficiently to bear upon the battery of the enemy. He had, therefore, the fire all to himself, and diligently pounded that side of the house, his shot going right through the wall, and falling inside the building. All my parapets on the housetop on that side were in ruins; the walls of the upper-story rooms were knocked into large holes;

large breaches were made below the roof of the entrance-hall; and an occasional shot went through the dome of the drawing-room from this gun also.

My south-west bastion had been sufficiently completed on the 8th of August to allow of a 9-pounder being put in position, but for fear of supplying the enemy with 9-lb. shot, the gun was not allowed to be fought. They accordingly proceeded with their garden battery to knock down all our parapet defences on that side, and on the 15th of August they cannonaded our south-west angle during the whole day, laying in ruins the thick wall of the building in rear of the bastion, which had till then afforded a good shelter for the European soldiers. These had accordingly to be removed; and permission was then given to return the enemy's fire. Next day, accordingly, Captain Thomas, of the Artillery, came down, and with eight well-directed shots silenced for some time the garden battery.

By this time Duprat's house, in rear of the Cawnpoor battery, had been reduced nearly to ruins by the continual fire of the enemy. The verandah first came down: then the outer wall was demolished, bringing down with it all the rafters of the roof.

The house, also, next adjoining to it, Anderson's, had suffered little less severely. Its verandah on the exposed side, and part of an outer room, had been wholly destroyed: and Mr. W. C. Capper, C. S., and another of the garrison, who were buried in the ruins, narrowly escaped destruction.

The Cawnpoor battery itself was a ruin. It was so exposed to the enemy's round shot by night, and to the deadly fire of their riflemen from Johannes' house by day, that it was scarcely tenable.

But the chief event of this fortnight was the

second general attack, which was made by the enemy on the 10th of August. Considerable bodies of them had been seen moving about on the morning of that day in the direction of the Cawnpoor road, and crossing over the river to our side from cantonments. On the south side, they crowded in numbers into Johannes' house. About eleven A.M. a mine was sprung in front of that building, which entirely blew down the verandah and outer room of the house occupied by Mr. Schilling and the Martinière boys, and destroyed upwards of fifty feet of our palisades and defences on that side. The rooms in which were Mr. Schilling and his boys, were thus completely exposed, the doors which connected them with the outer room which had just been blown down, being at the time open. Most providentially that room happened at the moment to be wholly unoccupied. Through these doors the enemy who swarmed in Johannes' house could be plainly seen. For some minutes they neither fired, nor made an attempt to advance; so that Mr. Schilling and his people had time to close the intervening doors securely. The enemy soon after commenced firing, and two privates, who had accompanied Brigadier Inglis to the scene of the disaster, were dangerously wounded by bullets which had passed through the door-panels. The enemy presently occupied in force all the buildings round about, from which they commenced a furious fusilade, and made several attempts to get into the Cawnpoor battery; but all their endeavours were met by such a steady fire of musketry from the defences, that they were forced at length to fall back. About thirty of them got close up to the Cawnpoor battery, sheltering themselves from fire in the ditch. They were soon dislodged by hand-grenades.

A second mine was exploded by the enemy at the same time on the east side, which destroyed some of the outhouses belonging to Sago's house. Two European soldiers who were posted there had a most marvellous escape. They were blown up at their post into the air, and fell upon the road without sustaining any injury; and got safely back, through a sharp fire of the enemy, uninjured, into the defences. The latter then advanced to the attack, but were driven back with heavy loss. Similar attacks, unaccompanied by the explosion of mines, were made at Innes' house, Anderson's, and at my post, where considerable numbers showed themselves, and again attempted to scale the south-west bastion, bringing scaling-ladders close to it. They were dislodged with hand-grenades from the foot of the bastion, and fired upon heavily as they ran back, leaving two bodies, which they were unable to remove, and which in a few days were picked clean by the jackals. It is, as we found, exceedingly difficult to hit a man in rapid motion with a single bullet, firing from a loophole. The number of my own shots that missed astonished me; and where the distance is short, and the enemy numerous, we found a discharge of from eight to ten small pistol bullets, fired from a smooth-barrelled gun, much more effective.

In the afternoon, the enemy made a sudden attack on the Financial Commissioner's Office garrison, commanded by Captain Sanders, coming up close and laying hold of the bayonets protruding from the loopholes; but they were steadily repulsed, and drew off, after keeping up a prolonged fire of musketry. In repelling these several assaults of the enemy, a large number of shells, as many as 150, were thrown by us, and a heavy fire was at times maintained by our batteries, from which it may be presumed that the enemy suffered severely. From their practice of carrying off their dead, however, it was impossible to estimate their number. Our loss was confined to three Europeans and two sepoys killed, and twelve men wounded.

Nor were the enemy's endeavours to destroy our defences relaxed after this defeat. They were soon again heard mining from a house on our side of the street, which they had occupied, near Sago's house. It was desired to examine the work, and destroy the building from which it had been commenced. A sortie was accordingly made into the road by a party of twelve Europeans, commanded by Lieutenant Clery, 32nd Regt., accompanied by Lieutenant Hutchinson, Engineers. On getting out, however, they found a large body of the enemy drawn up, who received them with a volley; and they were fortunate in being able to retire within the works without injury. It was then determined by the engineers to mine and destroy the house, if possible. A countermine, directed at the wall of the building, was therefore commenced, and pushed on as rapidly as possible. The two parties, viz. the enemy outside and our men within, were only separated by a wall and a narrow space of intervening ground, and either could hear the work of the other in progress. During the night of the 13th August, Lieutenant Hutchinson and our engineers and miners worked hard, subject to every kind of obstruction from the enemy, who threw in stones, brickbats, squibs, and rockets; and thrust over bamboos, wrapped at the end with oiled and lighted cloth, with the object of setting fire to the outhouses where our men were working.

By ten A.M. on the next day the garrisons were

warned that the mine was about to be exploded, and it was fired shortly after with great success; the brick building being completely destroyed, and many of the enemy buried in its ruins. Several others were shot down who crossed the road to their rescue; and altogether the whole affair reflected great credit upon the exertions of the engineers. These measures effectually relieved Sago's post from any further attempt at mining for several days. Mines were, however, suspected to be in course of construction against Anderson's post, and the south side of my enclosure. To meet the first a shaft was sunk, from which a gallery was to run to intercept that of the enemy.

On my side, a sortie was made on the 13th of August by a party of Europeans, under Brigadier Inglis, attended by the engineers, into the Goindah lines, where a long, deep trench was found, directed towards the enclosure. This was rendered useless; some of the walls of the enclosure were dug down, and the party retired, unmolested, by the hole in the compound-wall which had been made on a former occasion.

CHAPTER XIII.

FROM THE 15TH TO THE END OF AUGUST.

Ungud returns again on the 15th of August, bringing a letter for me from Colonel Fraser Tytler.—Transcript of its contents.—Account of the delay in its delivery given by Ungud.—News disappointing indeed; yet not a source of any just anxiety.—Colonel Tytler evidently misapprehended our circumstances.—For us to attempt to cut our way out was impossible.—Mr. Gubbins proposes to Brigadier Inglis to consult upon the reply.—The Brigadier shows Mr. Gubbins the answer which he proposed to send.—Transcript of the letter.—Mr. Gubbins proposes some modification, to which Brigadier Inglis would not consent.—Ungud leaves with the despatch.—The serious error in respect to Commissariat supplies contained in this letter noticed.—Ungud's return on the 29th, bringing General Havelock's reply.—Transcript of Havelock's letter.—Account given by Ungud.—Anecdote of Ungud.—Enemy continues his mines.—He explodes one at the outer Seikh square on the 18th of August, which does us serious injury.—Enemy's weak attempt to enter at the breach repulsed.—Breach barricaded, and defended by a 9-pounder gun.—M. Duprat killed.—Sortie to the houses of the younger Johannes and others, which were blown up, on the 18th and 19th of August.—Our engineers mine and blow up Johannes' house.—Sortie.—Enemy's battery spiked by Lieutenant Brown.—Johannes' shop blown up by Captain Fulton and Captain McCabe.—Another mine of the enemy at the Brigade Mess broken into, and blown up on the 29th of August.—Too much praise cannot be bestowed on Captain Fulton.—Ramadeen Jumadar killed.—Attempt to burn the Bailey Guard Gate.—Dilapidation of buildings.—Two new batteries established against my house.—Lieutenant Webb killed in my south-west bastion.—The battery retrenched and altered; and the 9-pounder replaced by an 18-pounder gun.—Excellent practice made by Lieutenant Bonham's artillery with his mortar howitzer, called the "Ship."—Enemy open fire on my house from the 24-pounder battery, opposite Innes'.—All the upper rooms abandoned in consequence.—Native followers greatly alarmed.—Desertion of natives, and of Christian drummers.—Measures adopted to prevent further desertion.—One month's pay issued; declined by the pensioners and N. I. sepoys.—Correspondence of the enemy with the natives inside our intrenchment.—High prices realised at auctions.—Enemy open a 32-pounder gun at the Clock tower.—Lieutenant Aitken constructs a battery against this.—Losses by sickness during the month.—Casualties.—Names of officers wounded.

On the night of the 15th of August, "Ungud," our only successful messenger, came in again at my post, bearing a letter addressed to me by Colonel Fraser Tytler. It was dated the 4th August at Mungulwar; and the following is a transcript of its contents :—

"To M. Gubbins, Esq.

"Dear Sir,

"We march to-morrow morning for Lucknow, having been reinforced. We shall push on as speedily as possible. We hope to reach you in four days at furthest. You must *aid us in every way, even to cutting your way out, if we can't force our way in. We are only a small Force.*"

N.B. The words printed in italics were written in Greek characters.

It appeared from the account given to us by Ungud, that he had received this despatch, as was evident from the date, nearly a fortnight before. He accounted for the lateness of its delivery, by telling us that he had been made prisoner by the enemy, while endeavouring to bring the letter in, and had been long detained in custody. Having been released, however, he had retraced his steps to the General's camp at Mungulwar, which place he had found abandoned. Proceeding on thence to the Ganges, he had found that the whole of General Havelock's camp had recrossed the river to Cawnpoor. Ungud told us that this movement had been caused by the Nana having threatened Havelock's rear, and the Station of Cawnpoor; at which place the General was awaiting reinforcements.

It must be confessed that these tidings were not satisfactory. It was evident that Havelock had made an advance early in the month, intending to relieve our garrison. Colonel Tytler mentioned the intention, and Ungud confirmed the fact. The force, he said, had advanced a second time to Busheergunje, had engaged and defeated the enemy, but had retired, after achieving the victory. It was therefore equally clear, that onward progress had been found impossible, and that Havelock had been obliged to retire without even being able to communicate his intention to us. Why then had he retired? It could not be in consequence of the determined resistance offered by the enemy; for Ungud, who confirmed the first victories at Onao and Busheergunje, which had been reported to us by Aodhân Singh, laughed at and ridiculed their cowardice. They never, he said, stood a charge of our men, and had lost most of the guns which they had taken out.

It was evident, to those who could view the matter calmly, that, finding his rear threatened, and his force too weak, the General had retired to secure his communications. To me, therefore, the intelligence brought by Ungud, though disappointing, was not a source of any great anxiety. We well knew that every available soldier, as he arrived in the country, would be pushed up to reinforce Havelock. Every day, therefore, by which our defence was prolonged, would add to the numbers of the relieving army; and our enemy had of late, certainly, shown no very remarkable or increased boldness.

It was evident, however, that Colonel Tytler's letter, in which he proposed that we should cut our way out, had been written under an entire misapprehension of our circumstances. The thing was simply impossible. Encumbered as we were, with large numbers of women, children, sick, and wounded, guarded by a slender force of Europeans, to have attempted to leave our defences, and lead out this defenceless mass into the streets of the city, crowded with the enemy's marksmen, would have been nothing more than to expose the greater number of them to certain death. Few, indeed, would have been those who would have reached the relieving column. It was of importance that the reply of which Ungud was to be the bearer, should be a clear exposition of our state and circumstances, on which the General at Cawnpoor might build a just plan for our relief. After, therefore, Brigadier Inglis had read the letter, I proposed to him that we should consult upon the reply which should be sent. He courteously came over to my quarters during the day, and showed me the reply which he proposed to send. It was the following:—

"A note from Colonel Tytler to Mr. Gubbins reached last night, dated at Mungulwar the 4th inst., the latter paragraph of which is as follows—'You must aid us in every way, even to cutting your way out, if we can't force our way in,'—has caused me much uneasiness, as it is quite impossible, with my weak and shattered force, that I can leave my defences. You must bear in mind how I am hampered; that I have upwards of 120 sick and wounded, and at least 220 women, and about 230 children, and no carriage of any description, besides sacrificing twenty-three lacs of treasure, and about thirty guns of sorts.

"In consequence of the news received, I shall soon put the force on half rations, unless I hear again from you. Our provisions will last us then till about the 10th of September.

"If you hope to save this force, no time must be lost in pushing forward. We are daily being attacked by the enemy, who are within a few yards of our defences. Their mines have already weakened our post, and I have every reason to believe they are carrying on others. Their 18-pounders are within 150 yards of some of our batteries, and from their position, and our inability to form working parties, we cannot reply to them, and consequently the damage done hourly is very great. My strength now in Europeans is 350, and about 300 natives, and the men are dreadfully harassed; and owing to part of the Residency having been brought down by round shot, many are without shelter. Our native force having been assured, on Colonel Tytler's authority, of your near approach, some twenty-five days ago, are naturally losing confidence, and if they leave us I do not see how the defences are to be manned. Did you receive a letter and plan from me from this man 'Ungud?' Kindly answer this question.

"Yours truly,

"J. Inglis,

"To General Havelock." "Brigadier."

In the general purport of this letter I agreed; but thought that the dangers of our position, especially as regarded the supply of food, were exaggerated; and that General Havelock might be induced, on receipt of it, to attempt our relief with an insufficient force. I accordingly recommended some modification of the despatch, which might represent our prospects of defence in more hopeful terms. But to this the Brigadier would not consent. He informed me that he had consulted the officers of his staff; and that they concurred in the justice of his description. On the following night, accordingly, Ungud started with this despatch.

It is difficult to understand how so serious an error was at the time made by the Commissariat staff, from whom no doubt the Brigadier's information in respect to our supply of food was derived. Much of the grain and provisions had indeed been got in by the civil authorities; and it is probable that the Commissariat had not sufficiently examined their resources. But certainly at the time it was well known in the garrison that we possessed a plentiful abundance of grain and ghee; and a supply of cattle which would afford fresh-meat rations much beyond the period indicated. Rum, indeed, for the soldiers was running short, and fodder had to be used carefully. Facts, however, speak for themselves. We were not put on half-meat rations until the 25th of August, when they were reduced as here shown.

PERSON.	FULL SCALE.	REDUCED SCALE.
Each fighting man . .	1 lb.	12 oz.
„ woman	12 oz.	6 oz.
„ child over 12 years .	12 oz.	6 oz.
„ child under 12 years .	4 oz.	4 oz.
„ child under 6 years .	4 oz.	2 oz.

We were joined on the 25th of September by a force of upwards of 2700 men, under General Outram, which brought in no grain to add to our supplies, but gun-bullocks only. This new force, as well as the old garrison, were fed for eight weeks longer out of the stores of grain which we originally possessed. And when we finally abandoned the place, the granary of wheat laid in by me, which had been put at the disposal of the Commissariat, was left behind, and their own surplus stores required 500 camels to transport.

Ungud did not return for eleven days. But again made his appearance at my post at midnight of the 29th, and brought Havelock's reply; a letter worthy of the noble soldier who wrote it. It was dated at Cawnpoor the 24th of August, and was as follows:—

My dear Colonel,

"I have your letter of the 16th inst. I can only say do not *negotiate*, but rather perish sword in hand. Sir Colin Campbell, who came out at a day's notice to command, upon the news arriving of General Anson's death, promises me *fresh troops*, and you will be my first care. The *reinforcements* may reach me in from *twenty to twenty-five days*, and I will prepare everything for a march on Lucknow.

"Yours very sincerely,

"H. Havelock, Br.-Gen."

"To Col. Inglis, H.M. 32nd Regt."

N.B.—The italics indicate Greek characters.

Ungud had found it impossible to cross the Ganges near Cawnpoor, where one side of the river was held by the mutineers, and the opposite one by the British forces. He had gone by Futtehpoor Chowrâsee, the residence of the talooqdar Jussa Singh, and crossed at the Nana Mhow Ghaut. He told us that the Nana was at Futtehpoor, having been defeated in a fresh engagement by Havelock, at Bithoor, where the mutineers declared that the 42nd Regt. N.I., called by the natives, "Jansen," had greatly distinguished themselves, and boasted that they had crossed bayonets with the British troops. Jussa Singh, he told us, had died of his wounds.

On the occasion of this visit of Ungud, an amusing incident occurred. I had been ill with fever, and was lying down in a room which had been a lady's dressing-room, and which contained a cheval glass. Ungud was seated on the floor by my side, and was replying to the many questions with which I plied him. I presently observed him to put on an anxious look, and direct uneasy glances towards the glass, which was large, and reflected his whole person. Soon he turned round, and facing himself in the mirror, exclaimed with energy "Kia! toom bhee sipahy ho? What! are you also a soldier?" I burst out laughing, the mistake was so absurd. He had taken his own reflection for a strange sepoy, who he thought was listening to his words. Presently, he too discovered his mistake, and joined heartily in my merriment.

There was now, on receipt of this despatch of Havelock's, nothing to be done, but patiently to maintain our position for another month or twenty-five days. We had the satisfaction of thinking that at the end of that time a force would be at hand which would be capable of overbearing all opposition.

Meanwhile, the enemy had continued unceasingly his efforts to mine our position. He was known to be mining at Anderson's post, where a countermine gallery, twenty-five feet in length, had been thrown out to intercept his work. His workmen in a second mine, directed at the Brigade Mess, could be plainly heard, and he was evidently digging in front of the Redan battery, at a work which was believed by many to be a third mine.

Despite the constant vigilance and exertions of Captain Fulton and our other engineers, the mutineers managed at last to do us serious injury by exploding a mine under the outer defences of the left Seikh square, on the 18th of August. The explosion took place between five and six in the morning, and blew down the outhouse at the south-west corner of the square, on the roof of which we had a post, from the loopholes of which Lieutenant Mecham, 7th O. I. Infantry, Captain Adolphe Orr, of the military police, with two sentries, were at the time on the look-out. By the explosion, Mecham and Orr and one drummer were thrown into the air, but descended inside the square amidst the *débris* of the building, and escaped with little injury. The fourth, Band Sergeant Curtain, of the 41st N.I., was unhappily thrown outside the works upon the road, where he was destroyed by the enemy. There were, unfortunately, seven men inside the building, viz., six drummers and one sepoy, and these were all buried beneath its ruins.

As soon as the smoke had cleared away, a breach in the outer wall and buildings was discovered thirty feet in breadth, the houses across the street being thickly filled by the enemy. They, however, hesitated to advance, when one of their leaders mounted to the top of the breach, waving his sword, and calling on the others to follow. He was immediately struck dead by a bullet from one of the officers on the top of the Brigade Mess. A second mutineer leader followed him, but shared the same fate. Their fall seemed sufficiently to intimidate the enemy, who would not thereafter leave the houses, but maintained from their shelter a secure and heavy fire on the breach and exposed square.

The whole garrison was at once under arms, and a party of the 84th Foot were immediately moved down under shelter to keep down the fire of the enemy, while doors, planks, and boxes, were rapidly collected and put up as a barricade at the breach. A house between the two squares was also pulled down, and a 9-pounder gun was got into position, which enfiladed the breach.

At night the barricade was completed. All these measures involved great labour and exertion, and reflected great credit on all the officers engaged, who acted under the personal direction of the Brigadier. They were not effected without loss, and several Europeans were badly wounded. While the younger Johannes' and adjacent buildings were thus filled by the enemy, a heavy fire was kept up between the mutineers and the men posted at Grant's bastion in my post, during which M. Duprat received his death-wound through a loophole from one of the enemy's bullets. Throughout the day, a heavy cannonade was kept up by Brigadier Inglis' orders upon the native buildings opposite the breach, from the 24-pounder howitzer at my entrance-gate, by which they were considerably damaged. It was also now thought necessary to get rid of the younger Johannes' and other adjoining native houses, which afforded so much protection for the enemy, and from which my garrison and that of the Seikh squares had suffered so severely. Accordingly, a sortie was made in the afternoon of the same day by Brigadier Inglis, accompanied by Captain Fulton and other engineers, who went out by the hole in my enclosing wall, and occupied all these houses without opposition from the enemy. Four barrels of powder were then exploded in them, by which they were effectually destroyed, some of the ruined walls being only left standing. Another sortie was made on the next day in the same direction, by which the work of destruction was completed. A large quantity of wood, rafters, doors, laths, &c., dislodged by the explosions, were brought in by the natives of my garrison, and were highly serviceable in repairing our defences. In most of the houses which were examined during these operations, trenches dug as protection against our shells were found. Traces of blood often appeared, however, showing the injury which they at times inflicted. In many of the houses, graves were found, in which the enemy had buried, on the spot, the bodies of their slain.

If the enemy had succeeded in doing us a serious injury by his mine of the 18th, our engineers obtained a much more decided success over the foe in a mine which they exploded three days later, on the 21st of August. Its object was the premises of the elder Johannes, which overlooked the Cawnpoor battery; and from the marksmen stationed in which we had sustained such continual injury. These premises contained two masonry buildings, a nearer one the dwelling-house of Mr. Johannes, and a further one his shop. Close by, the enemy had established a battery of two guns, which gave us great annoyance. On the 17th, a shaft was begun in the Martinière building, in order from it to drive a gallery under Johannes' dwelling-house, which was the nearest. Captain Fulton planned the measure, which was pushed on with unremitting exertion by Lieutenant M. Innes. For sixty-four hours that officer scarcely rested, and the mine was reported ready at daybreak of the 21st. It was fired at 5, P.M., the same afternoon, with complete effect, the dwelling-house and tower, from which the African Rifleman used to fire with such deadly precision, being laid in ruins, and several of the enemy who occupied it at the time, being destroyed.

A sortie was then made by fifty Europeans, who divided into two parties on getting outside, the one under Lieutenant Browne of the 32nd, making for the neighbouring battery: and the main body under Captain McCabe of the same regiment, with Captain Fulton, proceeding to Johannes' shop, to endeavour to blow it up. Browne reached the battery, and found a gunner of the enemy sleeping securely upon one of the guns. After Lieutenant Browne had several times ineffectually snapped his revolver at him, the man awoke and ran away. It was then attempted to spike the guns, but the touchholes were found to be so large and damaged, that it was impossible to do this effectually. Into the touchhole of one of the guns, two large spikes of unusual size were driven: with the other nothing could be done, and it was left. But so useless was this operation of spiking, that ere the party had been four hours within the works, both guns were again battering the Brigade Mess with undiminished effect.

Meanwhile, Fulton and McCabe and their party had reached the shop verandah, and found the doors of the building closed. Captain Fulton, however, placing his back against one of them, and resting his feet against the verandah wall, forced the frame of the door out of the masonry, and fell backwards with it into the interior of the building. The room was full of the enemy, and was intersected by deep trenches dug to protect them from our shells. At the bottom of one of these trenches, Fulton now found himself. After him immediately rushed McCabe and his party, and the enemy quickly disappeared. Two barrels of powder were then placed inside the building, a slow match was lighted, and the shop was completely levelled. Our loss in effecting these operations was three killed and two wounded. The casualties were caused by the enemy, who made no stand against us, taking post behind the adjacent buildings, and firing on any man who happened to be exposed.

The enemy's mine at the Brigade Mess had caused considerable anxiety, the building being so much filled with ladies and children. A countermine gallery, thirty-three feet in length, had been constructed with great labour, from which our men could plainly hear the enemy's miners at work. After much exertion the engineers succeeded in breaking into the enemy's gallery on the 29th of August. Their miners, leaving their tools, fled immediately, followed by ours, who quickly placed a barrel of gunpowder at the end of their sap, next to the shaft, and exploding it, destroyed their work.

Another mine had been again commenced by the enemy, directed against Sago's post. This we had not discovered, when fortunately it became soaked by the heavy rain and fell in.

Thus had been met, and in all but one instance most successfully foiled, all the many endeavours made by the enemy to undermine our works and buildings in August. Too much praise cannot be accorded to the engineers, who, one and all, laboured hard in this arduous duty. But the chief merit, belonged to that much-lamented officer, Captain Fulton. On the 20th of August I experienced a sad loss in my garrison by the death of the Jumadar Ramadeen. We were at the time repairing the parapet-wall on the roof of the out-houses which the enemy's artillery had knocked down. Major Apthorp and myself were sitting near, under the lee of the wall, where the workmen were stooping at their work; when Ramadeen unfortunately stood up erect. He was almost immediately struck by a bullet in the abdomen, and sank upon the roof. The faithful man lingered for twenty-four hours and then died. He never murmured or complained, but expressed himself well content to die in my service. Well did he deserve this poor tribute to his memory. We buried him by himself in the garden, where I hope on some future day a tomb may be erected to mark the resting-place of one who showed so great fidelity.

On the same day an attempt was made to burn the gates at the Bailey Guard by some emissaries of the enemy, who, unnoticed by our sentries, piled up combustibles and wood outside the gate and set fire to it. The flame burnt fiercely, but it was extinguished without injury; and loopholes were then prepared in the side-wall commanding the entrance, through which a man who again attempted to set fire to the gate was, some time afterwards, shot.

On the 21st, a boy who was picking up bullets outside our works was made prisoner; but we could not succeed in obtaining any information from him of the movements of the enemy.

The dilapidation of our buildings under the continual fire of the enemy proceeded rapidly. The Brigade Mess outer wall and upper Guard-houses, and the Cawnpoor battery, formed two of their principal marks. By the 24th of the month the Guard-houses were destroyed, and the Cawnpoor battery had long been, despite constant repair, little better than a ruin. The lower story of the main building of the Brigade Mess was of great strength and solidity, and continued to resist the heavy shot of the enemy, fired at the distance of seventy or eighty yards. The Judicial Garrison house became towards the end of the month so unsafe, that it was found necessary to remove all the women from it, into the Begum Kotee.

The Residency also was so pierced with round shot that it was little better than a sieve. On the 24th the entire length of verandah along two stories on the west side fell to the ground. The whole building became at the same time so unsafe, that it was found necessary to remove from the lower story all the

Commissariat stores which had before been placed there.

Innes' house was at the same time reported to be in a dangerous state, and only a small portion of the building could be occupied by the garrison.

The enemy had now established two new batteries against my house. One mounted a 9-pounder, and was built, with immense labour, of long beams of wood, fixed into the ground, between which earth was then filled in. It was raised to the top of the adjoining houses, and was nearly on a level with my roof, so as to occupy a commanding position. It was placed on our south face, where we had no means of returning the fire, to the right of the battery in the lane. The gun breached the south face of the house and the dome.

On the 26th of August the enemy opened another and more dangerous battery. Facing our south-west angle bastion, at the distance of about 500 yards from it, was a lofty enclosure, known as the Boolund Bagh. Inside this they erected a battery for a 24-pounder, and a 12-pounder gun; and when completed, discharges of heavy shot, fired through two holes cut in the thick enclosing wall, announced the fact to us. The 21- and 18-lb. shot pierced the south-west angle of the house, and, when it struck an outhouse, broke a large hole in the outer wall which formed our defence. Our servants became dreadfully alarmed. Brigadier Inglis came down to examine the new battery from our south-west bastion, into which a number of us crowded. While engaged in reconnoitering it, the enemy, who had probably observed us, opened fire; and one of his heavy shot passing through our earthen parapet, laid two of the party, Lieutenant Webb, of the 32nd, and a faithful sweeper of mine named Lalloo, dead on the ground. The bastion was quickly evacuated, and the Brigadier sent orders to the mortar battery to shell the enemy at a distance of 200 yards beyond my house. Lieutenant Cunliffe passed the order to the sergeant, who, mistaking the proper charge, put an insufficient quantity of powder into the mortar. The first shell, therefore, just cleared the house and burst inside the enclosure, most providentially injuring no one,—but Major Apthorp and Captain Edgell, of my garrison, had a very narrow escape.

The engineer and artillery officers at once pronounced that against such heavy metal as the enemy had now brought against us, the 9-pounder with which the bastion was armed was of no avail. They advised that the bastion should be retrenched, the platform reduced, the thickness of the parapet increased to sixteen feet, and the 9-pounder replaced by an 18-pounder gun. After some days the Brigadier consented to give us a heavy gun, and we at once set to work to alter the battery. By dint of hard work it was soon completed; and on the 31st of the month an 18-pounder gun was dragged into it, and put in position.

Before this could be accomplished, however, we should have been reduced to sad straits, but for the fertility of resource and admirable gunnery of Lieut. Bonham, of the Artillery. This excellent young officer, whose cool and steady demeanour during the mutiny at Secrora, and subsequent share in the engagement at Chinhut, where he was wounded, have already been mentioned, had displayed great accuracy of practice with heavy guns during the siege, and had already been a second time wounded. To replace in some degree our lost 8-inch howitzer, and enable us to throw our shells horizontally as well as vertically, Lieutenant Bonham had contrived an engine which went by the name of the "Ship." It was made by placing an 8-inch mortar upon a strong wooden frame, upon which the piece lay horizontally, the large wedge in front having been withdrawn. Strong lashings secured the mortar to the wooden frame, which was mounted upon cast-iron wheels, by which the Ship was rendered movable. The elevation desired was given by small wedges or coignes placed below the muzzle, and which required careful adjustment. While our south-west bastion was under alteration, the destruction of our house was prevented by the fire of the Ship, which was placed close to the house, and threw a horizontal fire of shells upon the enemy's battery, at an elevation just sufficient to clear the surrounding outhouses. Though much less effective than a heavy howitzer, from the small measure of powder to which the charge was restricted, the fire of the Ship was very effective. Taking great pains in levelling his Ship, Lieutenant Bonham succeeded in striking the wall close to the enemy's embrasure several times; and the shells bursting within the wall, brought down large masses of it. For several days the Ship was thus used with much effect. As soon as its fire began, the enemy ceased firing; but afterwards laboured most assiduously to replace and repair the heavy timbering of which their battery was constructed; and generally opened fire upon us again in the morning. Their fire was particularly dangerous, for this battery overlooked our enclosure, and they were able to strike the lower story of the house.

For some reason they at this time greatly concentrated their fire upon my house, for on the 28th of August they fired a number of 21-lb. shot into the upper rooms on the north, from the 24-pounder battery which they had opposite Innes' post. These heavy shot came right through the outer wall, and compelled us to abandon the upper north rooms, of which we had, till then, retained possession. I have still with me, in England, a trunk which visibly reminds me of this cannonade. We had been unable to find one of these shot, which had pierced the wall of the room, and which used always to be collected, and forwarded at intervals to the magazine. Some days later, our maid having occasion to move a small trunk, complained of its unusual weight; and, unlocking it, discovered the 21-lb. shot reposing on the top of its contents.

The abandonment of these upper rooms rendered it necessary that some of the ladies, for whom there was no longer accommodation in the house, should leave us. Accordingly, Mrs. Banks and her party removed to the Brigade Mess; Dr. and Mrs. Brydon and children, Captain and Mrs. H. Forbes and children, Mrs. Ouseley and children, and Mrs. Aitken, found shelter in Mr. Ommanney's house, and in the Begum Kotee. In the lower story we were, necessarily, much crowded. The rooms occupied by the ladies were low and small; and the gentlemen slept at night either outside under the porch; in the hall, which was not safe from shot; or on the table or on the ground in the room in which we took our meals.

Our native followers, about this time, became greatly disheartened. The increased cannonade around my post, and the absence of tidings of certain and early relief, appeared to them ominous of coming disaster, and the enemy's mines created great dismay. On the 28th, I lost, by desertion at night, one chupprassie (or orderly) and two of my dismounted troopers, being the only men of their number who deserted during the siege.

The chupprassie, a Hindoo youth, was panic-struck, and would, I think, have gone out of his mind if he had remained. On the 29th, one of my native artillerymen deserted in broad day, and, though fired upon by the European sentry who stood near him, escaped.

On the 30th a more serious desertion followed. An East Indian, named Jones, who had been a clerk in one of the offices, had been appointed sergeant; and with ten others, mostly native Christian drummers, who had formerly been in the King of Oudh's service, held charge of the outhouses near the racket-court. Their post adjoined mine on the north, and they looked after the fodder and the oxen. These men were more than half natives, and the families of most of them resided in the city. On the night mentioned they all deserted together, having broken open the door of a small postern on that side, and left their post unprotected.

The Seikh Cavalry troopers in the squares at the same time occasioned us much anxiety. Many of them had deserted; and we were not sure that the rest, who were known to maintain clandestine communication with the enemy, might not at any time follow the example of their brethren. Talking with the other natives, they professed to disbelieve the tidings of approaching succour brought by Ungud; and gave out that we used to conceal him, and then bring him out after intervals, with pretended news.

Under all these discouraging influences, we had much ado to maintain the confidence of the natives who remained with us. We used to talk familiarly with them, point out that the mutineers had failed of success when everything was at the beginning in their favour; and now that the British troops were hurrying to India, as we assured them would be the case, from Bombay, from China, and from the mother country; when the supply of European ammunition, shells, percussion caps, &c., possessed by the rebels must be failing, how could their cause prove successful? Every precautionary measure was taken to support these arguments. Men of doubtful fidelity were placed in posts whence escape would be difficult, and mixed with others who were believed to be more staunch. Several of the Mahomedan domestics of my garrison were made to sleep at night under the eye of the European sentry, and all were watched.

Among my levies were several who had accumulated, by labour at the bastion, sums of money which were large for them. In order to guard against their deserting with their savings, I required them to deliver the money into my custody, and gave them receipts for it. No pay had been issued since the siege began, and several among the natives now desired to receive it. It was resolved accordingly to issue one month's pay for July on the 1st of September. When issued, however, those native soldiers on whom we most relied, the native pensioners and the sepoys of the 13th, 48th, and 71st Regts., declined to receive it. They justly observed that they had no use for it then, and did not know what to do with it, being provided with rations from the State. Their refusal was regarded with much satisfaction, as a proof of their fidelity.

On the 25th, Captain Wilson and Lieutenant Birch came over to me with a message from the Brigadier, requesting my opinion upon a piece of information which had been given by a Mr. Phillips, of the Military Secretary's office. Mr. Phillips would not give up the name of the native who had, he said, informed him that a general conspiracy had been formed by all the natives in the garrison, comprising the Brigade Mess servants, the Native Infantry, all the natives at my post, and the Seikhs, to rise upon the Europeans at the next attack. Their plan was stated to be the following: the Seikhs were to enter my enclosure by twos and threes, on pretence of speaking to me about obtaining an issue of pay. My native artillerymen were then, at a given signal, to turn the guns of my post on the Europeans, when a rising of the natives was to take place everywhere, while an attack from the outside was to be made by the enemy. The information appeared to me to be highly improbable; but I gave my advice that Mr. Phillips should be required to indicate the person from whom he derived his information, and that this latter party should be very carefully examined. Further, that, as a measure of precaution, the Seikh troopers should be prohibited from entering my enclosure; which was accordingly done. Nothing eventually came of the supposed plot.

We used to learn from Ungud that the enemy outside were well informed of all that passed within our intrenchment, and even corresponded with some of the natives inside. We never were able to discover any such correspondent among our Hindostanies; but it was quite impossible to prevent the enemy from obtaining intelligence from the many natives who deserted us, or through the Seikhs.

Towards the close of the month, many auctions were held of the property of deceased officers. The prices realized at these sales sufficiently showed how scarce many articles of ordinary use and consumption had become. Brandy fetched 16*l.* per dozen: it rose, however, before the blockade had terminated, to 2*l*. 10*s*. per bottle. Sherry sold for 7*l*. per dozen. Beer at the same price. A small tin of soup, 2*l*. 5*s*. A canister of sporting gunpowder, 1*l*. 12*s*. Tobacco was in particular demand. Cigars were selling for 2*s*. each, and rose before the blockade was over to 5*s*. apiece. Flannel shirts were in particular demand, and I was offered some as a favour at 3*l*. 12*s*. each.

On the last day of the month, the enemy began firing from a very heavy piece of ordnance, apparently a 32-pounder, which they had got into position at the Clock Tower, about one hundred yards distant from the Bailey Guard Gate. Several round shot from it passed through the gates, destroying two ammunition waggons with which they were barricaded. To oppose this dangerous and close fire, Lieutenant Aitken immediately began to construct, by aid of his own men, sepoys of the 13th N. I. only, under the superintendence of the engineers, a sunken battery, to receive an 18-pounder, between the Treasury and the Bailey Guard Gate. It was very quickly completed; and the men who made the battery afterwards, on several occasions, with the aid of two or three artillerymen, manned and worked the gun which was placed in it with very good effect.

During the month of August, we had continued to suffer severely from the sickness which has been described as prevailing in July; children especially being the sufferers. We had lost, in this month, Dr. MacDonald, of the 41st N. I., by cholera, and, from the same disease, Lieutenant Bryce, of the Artillery, who had recovered from the severe wound before received. The Chief Engineer, Major J. Anderson, was also dead. He had been long an invalid, and died, on the 11th of August, of diarrhœa, fatigue, and exhaustion. He was succeeded in the charge of the Engineer department by Captain Fulton. Among those who died of sickness are also to be reckoned Captain Barlow, Brigade-Major Oudh Irreg. Force, and Mrs. Green, wife of Captain Green, 48th N. I.

We had had, also, many casualties. One hundred and twenty-five privates of the 32nd and 84th Regts. had been killed or died of wounds by the end of the month. And besides those already mentioned, Captain Power, H. M. 32nd, had died of his wound; and one of the clerks, named Wells, had been killed at the battery near Dr. Fayrer's.

Among the wounded were Captain Waterman, 13th N. I., Lieutenant James Alexander, Artillery, Lieutenant Fletcher, 48th N. I., shot through the arm when on look-out duty, Lieutenant F. Cunliffe, Artillery, and Mr. MacRae, of the Engineer department. Captain Hawes, of my garrison, had also received a very ugly wound through the side, while firing at the enemy from the top of the house.

Lieutenant Bonham, Artillery, to whose skill we had been so much indebted, was wounded very severely, and for the third time, by a musket-ball, which struck him in the breast while seated in the verandah of the Post-office. The ball broke the collar bone, and this distinguished young officer was laid up in hospital from the injury he received, during the rest of the siege.

CHAPTER XIV.

FROM THE 1st TO THE 25th OF SEPTEMBER.

Dry weather succeeded by heavy rain.—Distressing accident which caused the death of Lieutenant Birch.—Death of Major Bruere, 13th N. I.—Explosion of a mine by the enemy at Gubbins' bastion on the 5th of September.—A second mine exploded at the Brigade Mess.—The enemy make a general attack; but are beaten back with great loss.—Enemy's battery across the river.—Mines and countermines.—Sortie outside the churchyard.—The enemy's batteries opposed to Gubbins' bastion are not silenced.—Captain Fulton, Engineers, killed in it.—Unrivalled merits of Captain Fulton.—His family left with slender provision.—Lieutenant J. C. Anderson succeeds Captain Fulton.—Raja Man Singh joins the enemy.—Account of Man Singh's antecedents.—His family not long established in Oudh.—He takes the lead in the disturbances between the Hindoos and Mahomedans.—Constant alarms.—Desertion of the cooks of the Artillery, and 32nd Regt.—Dilapidation of the Brigade Mess, Martinière, Innes, &c. posts.—Another mortar howitzer constructed.—Great loss in artillery officers; Major Simons and Lieutenant Cunliffe die.—Clothing of the garrison.—Ordinary colour of it.—Materials for dyeing how obtained.—Eclipse of the sun.—Casualties, and deaths.—Ungud returns on the 22nd of September, the bearer of good news.—Artillery of the relieving force heard on the 23rd of September.—Fears of the natives on the 24th.—Captain Radcliffe, 7th Light Cavalry, mortally wounded on that night.—Entry of the relieving army under Generals Havelock and Outram, on the 25th of September.—Scene at Dr. Fayrer's house upon the entry of the 78th Highlanders.—Excitement within the intrenchment.

The first days of September wer dry. The wind was from the west; the sun beat vehemently by day, but nights and mornings began to be cool. The pools of water were drying up, and we at first believed that the rainy season had closed. Soon, however, the east wind and wet weather returned; and in the third week we experienced deluges of rain, which greatly injured and damaged our own defences;

and added so much to the difficulty and discomfort of Havelock's last advance.

On the evening of the 2nd of this month, a most distressing and melancholy accident occurred. A mine of the enemy being suspected to have been begun in the broken ground and debris on the west side of our position, a party of four officers proceeded out at dusk to examine it. One of the four was Lieutenant Birch, of the 59th Regt. N. I., who was then attached to the Engineer department. The usual warning was sent to the several adjoining posts, including mine, which immediately overlooked the ground which had to be examined. The duty had been satisfactorily accomplished, and the party was returning, when the sentry at the west battery of my post, who most unfortunately had not been warned, seeing objects moving in the dark outside, fired his musket at them. Unhappily the ball took effect upon Lieutenant Birch, wounding him mortally in the abdomen, and he died after much suffering during the night. It appeared, on inquiry, that the sentry who was on duty when the warning was given by Major Apthorp, had been intermediately relieved, and that the warning had not been communicated to the relieving guard. It was altogether a most lamentable and distressing event. Lieutenant Birch had been only married for six months. He had lost his father, who commanded the 41st N. I., at Seetapoor. His poor wife and his sister were residing with us, when the fatal shot was fired.

This was followed by another sad casualty, in the death of Major Bruere, commanding the 13th N. I., who was killed on the 4th of the month by a rifle-ball through the chest. He was an excellent rifleman, and had done good service by his practice from the top of the Brigade Mess. On the date mentioned, while thus engaged, he unfortunately too much exposed himself, and received his death-wound from one of the enemy's marksmen. His remains were carried to the grave by the sepoys of his own regiment, by whom he was much beloved.

With these two sad exceptions, during the first four days nothing of particular importance occurred. The enemy maintained the usual cannonade and fire of musketry all round. This usually began at daylight, and lasted for three hours or more: it then flagged during the middle of the day, and was resumed in the afternoon. The bugling, drumming, and tomtoming, to which we had been so long accustomed, went on as usual at daybreak and at sunset.

The 18-pounder which had been mounted in our south-west battery had been opened, but feebly, upon the enemy's Boolund Bagh battery; for a few shots only were allowed to be fired at a time, and they were not always well directed.

The enemy continued his mines in all directions. One was known to be in progress at the Financial Commissioner's post; a second directed at the Brigade Mess; a third against the Cawnpoor battery; a fourth at the Seikh squares; a fifth pointing at the Church; besides the large mining work which they still carried on against the Redan battery.

Of late, also, we had suspected that they were mining our south-west bastion, on the maintenance of which the defence of our post mainly depended; and some anxiety was felt on the subject. After midnight of the 4th September, I was called away from superintending the repair of our 9-pounder battery, by Captain Edgell, the officer on duty, who told me that the sentry had reported some sounds of mining. We both proceeded to the roof of the out-houses overlooking the south-west bastion, and, screening ourselves behind some of the remaining broken defences, listened long and attentively; but in vain. The native sentry assured us that he had heard the sound of a pick; but we could hear none. Our ears, however, had not been sharp enough, as the events of the next day proved.

It was just 10, A.M., on the 5th September when we were alarmed by the loud explosion of a mine in the direction of our bastion. The report was so close and loud, and the air was at the moment so darkened by smoke, and by the numerous weighty fragments of earth, which were falling and crashing everywhere about, and over the house, that we all believed that the bastion had been blown up. Hastily seizing our arms we rushed down towards it, expecting to find a breach, and great indeed was our delight in finding the bastion to be safe. A mine had indeed been exploded close to it; but the error of distance was sufficiently great to prevent injury to our work.

The mine had been a large one, as was evinced by the size of the crater which it made, as subsequently seen, and the shock which it gave to all the houses throughout the position. The enemy soon came out in force all round, and fixing a huge ladder with double rows of rungs, so as to allow of two or more men mounting abreast, at the mouth of the 18-pounder embrasure, attempted to escalade. But it was an attempt only. They did not show their faces, but thrust the muzzles of their muskets into the embrasure, and fired. They were speedily dislodged by Major Apthorp and the men of the 32nd with hand grenades and musket-shots, while we kept up a heavy fire upon them from the loopholes with which our outhouses were now pierced. After about an hour and a half they fell back into the houses whence they had issued, with heavy loss.

Shortly after the mine at our bastion had been exploded, a smaller one was fired near the Brigade Mess. This last had been discovered: and Captain Fulton had been busy in driving a countermine against it, intending to blow it in. Fortunately our two miners had come up out of the latter to take some refreshment: for otherwise they must have been destroyed with our countermine. This mine of the enemy's also was incomplete, and short, and did no harm. In this quarter also the enemy showed himself well, particularly in the garden outside the Brigade Mess and Seikh square, where a great many of them fell under our musketry. Several other attacks, though less determined, were made in other quarters; and everywhere they were repulsed with heavy loss. During the whole attack, as was always the case, a storm of round shot and musket-balls was kept up; but our men were kept under cover, and we sustained little loss, viz. three men killed, and one wounded. Finally, after maintaining a heavy fusilade upon us from the surrounding houses, the enemy retired: and they were seen many hours after the action, carrying off their killed and wounded in cartloads over the bridges. On this occasion the new battery (18-pounder), erected by Lieutenant Aitken and the 13th N. I. sepoys, rendered good service.

A new work had been established by the enemy across the river, from which they considerably annoyed the hospital and adjoining buildings. An 18-pounder gun was mounted in it; and on the same day on which this attack was made, a shot from it entered and traversed the whole length of the hospital ward, crowded as it was with patients, without, strange to say, wounding any one!

In every direction where the enemy was known to be mining, countermines were dug. Two of these had been constructed out of the Brigade Mess post; and their galleries outside were connected. Another of considerable length extended out beyond Anderson's post, and was used as a whispering gallery. A third had been dug from the Financial Commissioner's post, and by it our engineers were enabled to blow in successfully, on the 2nd of September, a mine of the enemy, which had run into a well, and had, in consequence, been discovered. Their miners were at work when our countermine was fired, and were supposed to have been destroyed. Our countermine outside the Cawnpoor battery had long been ready, and having on the 9th made sure that the enemy were approaching us again by a mine in that direction, it was resolved to explode it. It was a large mine, and our engineers had charged it with two barrels of powder. When fired, the effect was great; the fronts of the houses on the opposite side of the street being blown down. Its explosion, as was usual, greatly alarmed the enemy, who beat to arms and continued long to maintain upon us a fire of cannon and musketry.

Two days later Captain Fulton most successfully destroyed a mine which the enemy was driving against the Seikh square. Our countermine was ready, and from it the enemy's miners could be heard distinctly to be at work quite close. Our mine was accordingly exploded with complete success, burying the enemy's miners, whose groans and cries for aid continued long to be heard.

On the same day a sortie was made under Captain Fulton to examine the shaft and gallery of a mine which had been discovered in the churchyard. The ground was open, and the workmen having been driven away, it was found that a long gallery had been constructed directed against the Church, and of sufficient height to allow of a man walking along it, almost erect. It was destroyed with gunpowder.

It has been mentioned that our south-west battery was opposed to four guns of the enemy, two heavy guns in the high Boolund Bagh battery, and two smaller ones in the nearer garden battery below us. Major Apthorp, who commanded at my post, had frequently represented that these batteries should be well cannonaded and effectually silenced. But the apprehension of supplying the enemy with round-shot prevailed, and our battery was only permitted to reply by a weak and desultory fire. An artillery officer used to visit the battery for two hours every day, and then, after firing one shot every twenty minutes, left it again. These few shots produced little effect on the upper battery; while the lower one was almost wholly neglected. They, however, did not neglect us; but fired repeatedly into our embrasure, occasioning the necessity for constant night repairs, and had knocked the wooden shutters of our embrasure to pieces. This over-economy of shot was destined to cost the life of the most gifted, useful, and energetic officer in the garrison—Captain Fulton. As we continued to suffer from the heavy shot of the upper battery, Major Apthorp had at last obtained permission to try the effect of a continuous cannonade, which Lieutenant James Alexander, of the Artillery, was deputed on the 14th September to carry into effect. He was a good shot, and made excellent practice with the 18-pounder gun. With twenty shots he knocked to pieces the enemy's embrasure and damaged the carriage of the 24-pounder gun, so that it could be clearly seen, muzzle in air, abandoned by the enemy. I may here add that this gun never opened upon us again during the rest of the siege and blockade.

On that afternoon Captain Fulton had dined with us; we had recounted to him with satisfaction the result of the day's cannonade, and I had anxiously begged him to cause the Garden battery to be subjected to a like discipline. As yet not a stick of it had been knocked down: while the enemy were able, at the distance of 240 yards, to fire into our embrasure with the greatest precision. Fulton left us, and went down with some others to examine the effect of Alexander's cannonade. Presently Major Apthorp returned to us with horror in his countenance, and told us that Fulton had been killed!

It appeared that while examining the battered embrasure of the Boolund Bagh with his glass, Captain Fulton had discovered some of the enemy at work there, and had called to Alexander to come with him and resume his fire. Fulton himself proceeded on to the bastion, and entered it before the rest. He approached the embrasure; and at the moment when he reached it, one of the Garden guns unhappily opened fire, and the ball striking Captain Fulton carried off the top of his head. Death must have been instantaneous.

Thus, unhappily, when the siege was drawing to its conclusion, fell George Fulton, the officer whose exertions had mainly contributed to success during the dark days of our defence, of which he was not permitted to see the brighter ending. His untimely end cast a general gloom over the garrison. And well might it do so, for he had been the life and soul of everything that was persevering, chivalrous, and daring. Only eight days before, he had escaped narrowly with his life in a sortie made on the 6th, which has not been mentioned. It was undertaken in order to destroy a house which commanded Innes' shattered post, and which the enemy were loopholing. Descending from the wall, which then formed our defence, by a ladder with some men, Captain Fulton had placed two barrels to blow up the building, and bidden the soldiers to retire: and, supposing that this order had been obeyed, had fired the train, and himself ran back to mount the ladder. On reaching its foot, however, he found that the sepoys had delayed in order to secure some wood outside, and had not themselves gone up. The building within which the gunpowder had been placed was within a few paces, and the explosion was imminent. The men had loitered against orders, and if they had sustained injury, the fault was theirs; but Fulton would not suffer the men to be exposed. The danger was great, but he resolved to meet it. He bid the men mount quickly, and they escaped; but before he could himself do so, the mine exploded. His escape was marvellous, for the wall which was blown down was not ten feet distant from where he stood. A piece of timber only struck him, inflicting a severe contusion.

This is but one instance of the conduct of the man whom we had lost. And it is no wonder that all ranks felt his loss acutely. For my own part, I had lost a personal friend, whose hopeful and cheerful bearing and converse had formed one great solace during the siege. Often has he opened his mind to me in pleasant anticipation of the advantage which might result to himself, and through him to his family, from the prominent part which he had borne in the defence; and which he believed would be acknowledged by Brigadier Inglis, and knew would be born testimony to by me. Little, indeed, did we then believe that these anticipations would be all so soon quenched in death!

The survivors of this memorable siege all lie under great obligation to Brigadier Inglis, for the unceasing vigilance and active perseverance, displayed by him during so many nights and days. He constantly visited the most exposed posts, and ever was to be found where a mine had been sprung, or an attack was being made. The responsibility resting upon him was great, and he acquitted himself of it well. None will, therefore, begrudge him his well-deserved honours. His Staff, Captain T. P. Wilson, and gallant young Aide-de-camp, Lieutenant F. Birch, 71st. N. I., also well deserve the thanks of the survivors. Their labours were unremitting; and in reconnoitring, and conveying orders to the posts and outposts, they were as much or more exposed than others.

But to Captain Fulton, by general consent must pre-eminently be accorded the palm of merit in the conduct of the defence. His highly-gifted and trained mind early detected the error of maintaining the second post of the Muchee Bhowun: and had he been first instead of second in his department, that step never would have been taken. I had it from his own lips, that shortly after the disastrous retreat from Chinhut, Sir Henry Lawrence asked his advice as to what should be done with the Muchee Bhowun. Fulton counselled its immediate abandonment; and on being further questioned, stated that he had recommended this step at the Council of War three weeks before. Sir Henry had forgotten the fact, or had not perhaps noticed it, but he lost no time in then following the advice of Fulton.

Of his skilful and unceasing exertions during the siege, these pages afford an unworthy record; so well devised, so persevering, so constant were they. He did not affect to under-estimate the dangers which surrounded us; but neither was he appalled by them, nor did he lose in contemplating them the calm exercise of his judgment. Above all, by his happy, cheerful confidence and unflinching resolve, he succeeded in inspiring others with the same sentiments. To Fulton all will join in conceding the deserved title of "The Defender of Lucknow."

But he is gone. And has he left none who may justly be the objects of his country's gratitude? Personally unknown to me, there do indeed survive this distinguished officer a widow and a large family of children, who formed during the siege to him an object of intense solicitude. Fulton had I understood been unable to lay by anything; and their means of support, therefore, must be scanty. Perhaps this family, of one of her most worthy sons, may not be thought undeserving of England's care.

But to resume my narrative. Two days after the occurrence of this sad tragedy, the Artillery officers received orders to open the 18-pounder gun effectively upon the Garden battery which had occasioned it. Not very many shots were necessary to reduce it to ruins, for it was not strongly built of rafters stuck upright into the ground. It was effectually silenced; and gave us, although it was afterwards partially repaired and an occasional shot fired from it, no more serious annoyance during the siege or subsequent blockade.

Lieutenant J. C. Anderson of the Madras Engineers, an officer to whose high but unpretending worth this account bears no sufficient testimony, succeeded Captain Fulton as Chief of the Engineer Department.

In the attack of the 5th of September, and about our defences generally during this month, we fancied that more matchlockmen were seen than before, and this we attributed to Rajah Man Singh, talooqdar of Shahgunje, near Fyzabad, having joined the enemy. Of this fact Ungud had apprized us on the occasion of his last visit. From what Ungud had learnt, it appeared that Man Singh had kept away, remaining quiet at his own fort, so long as General Havelock's force was on the Oudh side of the Ganges. During this time he was organizing and increasing his levies, which he maintained by forced contributions from the merchants of Fyzabad and others. When, however, Havelock recrossed the Ganges, Man Singh thought that our cause was hopeless, and leaving Fyzabad marched in, and joined the mutineers at Lucknow. Much importance was attached by the natives inside and without the intrenchment to the defection of this chief; and a salute which we had before heard fired in the direction of cantonments was supposed to have welcomed his arrival. Man Singh was not one of the old hereditary chieftains of Oudh, the settlement of his family in the province having been recent. But more than any of the talooqdars, Roostum Sah of Deyrah perhaps excepted, he was reputed to be a soldier. Recent occurrences which had taken place in Oudh, shortly before its annexation to the British Empire, and which partly gave rise to that measure, had brought Man Singh prominently before the public eye, and had invested him accordingly with unusual importance. A brief account of his antecedents will therefore not be uninteresting.

His family is Brahmin, of the Sagurdeep denomination, and had its origin at Bhojepoor in the district of Arrah, the country of the notorious Konwur Singh. His grandfather Poorundur Pathuk, having relatives in the village of Pulleea near Shahgunje, migrated there with his family. Among his five sons, two, Bukhtawur Singh and Durshun Singh (father of Man Singh), entered the service of the Kings of Oudh, and attained to wealth and distinction. Bukhtawur Singh became "Kuptân" of Cavalry under the Newaub Saadut Ali Khan, and under the reign of Ghazeeooddeen Hydur obtained the "ijara" or farm of the revenue of two large tracts of country; and shortly after the title of Rajah.

Durshun Singh entered the Civil employ, and was made the Chuckladar or Governor of Sultanpoor, and at one time held the government of more than one-half of the Province of Oudh. He also erected the fort at Shahgunje.

Both brothers amassed much wealth, and acquired severally talooquahs, containing many villages, in the usual way. But Bukhtawur Singh having no son, and Durshun Singh possessing three, the landed property became merged into one, and the sons of Durshun Singh succeeded to it. Of these the eldest is Ramadeen Singh, the next Rugburdyal Singh, and the youngest Man Singh. Rugburdyal was for several years Chuckladar of Bareytch, and left it with an ill name for rapacity, cruelty, and oppression, beyond that which usually distinguished Oudh Chuckladars. He acquired by purchase an estate at Fureedabad in the Jounpoor district, where he has since resided. The rightful succession to the talooquah in Oudh lay with Ramadeen Singh. But Man Singh's superior energy and talent led him to be acknowledged as the head of the family, and the fort of Shahgunje was held by him, Ramadeen residing much at Benares. Man Singh intrigued successfully at the Court at Lucknow, where he often resided, and maintained a close connection with the ex-prime-minister, the notorious Newaub Alee Nukee Khan, through whose influence he enjoyed many immunities and privileges. In 1854 and 1855, serious disturbances broke out at Fyzabad between the Hindoos and Mahomedans: in consequence of some unauthorized aggressions which were attempted by the latter sect, who endeavoured to intrude by force into the sacred Hindoo temples at Adjooddea.

This is a place of great antiquity, and reputed to be of the highest sanctity among the Hindoos, and is distant from Fyzabad three miles, on the banks of the Ghogra. The Mahomedan aggression was secretly favoured by the bigoted and imbecile Court at Lucknow. A great convulsion appeared to be imminent; for the Mussulmans, with a fanatic môlovee at their head, were marching on Adjooddea, resolved to enter the Hindoo shrine or die; while the Rajpoots and Hindoos of all the country round were flocking to defend their sanctuary, At this time Man Singh took the lead and placed himself at their head, becoming the acknowledged leader of the Hindoo party. He raised a large body of men, with whom he took post at the Shiwala, or temple which he had built at his private cost, among the numerous convents and temples which crowd the deeply-shaded dells and ravines of Adjooddea. Fortunately the British residents' interposition prevented an encounter between the hostile parties. The king's troops attacked and dispersed the Mussulmans, and the party which was headed by Man Singh remained victorious. It was commonly believed that Man Singh had then declared, that but for the support which the king would be sure to receive from the British, he would have marched to Lucknow, destroyed the Mahomedan dynasty, and established a Hindoo Government in its place. The introduction of British authority into Oudh found Man Singh deeply embarrassed. The large number of followers which he had maintained, had involved him in debt; the special immunities which he had received from the weakness of the Oudh Court, and corruption of its minister, were questioned; the old proprietors of the villages comprised in his talooquah all sued him to recover their lost rights, and the demand for payment of the Government revenue was instant. Under these circumstances, Man Singh fled the province, and remained absent for five months; during which it is believed that he was in Calcutta in attendance upon the ex-minister.

The occurrences which have been mentioned, and the prominent position which he occupied during them, gave him the "great name" with the natives, which this digression has explained.

To return to the siege. We were kept during this month on the *qui vive* at night with constant alarms of the enemy; perhaps not more numerous than during the preceding months; but I find particular mention of them in my journal. They would suddenly begin a heavy fire of cannon and musketry, accompanied with bugling and shouting, which would last for half an hour or an hour, and then die away. We rarely replied by any other fire, than that of a few shells thrown in the direction in which the enemy appeared to be in the greatest number. The men were at the same time kept carefully under cover, to prevent injury from the numerous balls and bullets which would then be flying over and amidst our works. Despite every precaution, casualties too frequently occurred. They also now began to fire several new missiles at us, and among them large logs of wood, projected, no doubt, out of the 13-inch mortar left by us in the Muchee Bhowun.

We lost in this month several natives from desertion, the most important loss being that of the cook-boys of the Artillery and 32nd Regt. These men were believed to have purchased from the soldiers a quantity of gold and jewels stolen from the king's jewellery, and to have decamped with the wealth thus acquired. For a day or two considerable inconvenience resulted. But afterwards the men, judging from what we were told of those of my garrison, were better pleased to cook for themselves: a large portion of their rations having, as they said, been stolen by their cooks.

The dilapidation of our buildings steadily increased. The constant fire kept up on the outer wall of the Brigade Mess at last effected its destruction; and it fell at the beginning of the month, bringing down the buildings on the upper story which it supported. Considerable ruins of the outer wall, as well as other interior walls, still barred the entrance of the enemy.

During this month the enclosing wall of the Martinière school-house was also twice breached, and had as often to be replaced by a stockade. Innes' house had long been pronounced to be unsafe, and now two sides of it fell in, nearly burying the sentries in its ruins. Breaches had been made in the walls of the office houses of the Judicial and Financial Commissioners: and there was not an exterior building along our whole line of defence, which did not exhibit the marks of excessive dilapidation. When we afterwards came to look upon them from the outside, it was singular to behold the countless marks of shot and bullets, which had pierced and peeled its plaster off every wall facing the enemy which had been left standing.

The invention introduced by Lieutenant Bonham, by which a mortar was made to give a horizontal fire, was applied with much benefit to meet the exigencies of those posts, whence we could bring to bear on the enemy no other artillery fire, or an insufficient one. A second "ship" was constructed on the same principle, and was brought into the courts of the Brigade Mess and taken to Innes' post; and was fired at both places with good effect upon the enemy's batteries. We lost on the 8th of September, Major Simons commanding the Artillery, who had never recovered from the effects of the wounds received at Chinhut; and on the 22nd of September, of low fever, Lieutenant Foster Cunliffe of the Artillery, who had long, with much credit to himself, been in charge of the Artillery at the Redan battery. One Artillery officer only, Captain Thomas (Madras Artillery), now remained unwounded. This arm of the service upon which our defence so chiefly depended was originally weak in numbers, had been constantly most severely worked and exposed, and had suffered proportionately. Simons, Lewin, Bryce, and now Cunliffe, were dead. D. C. Alexander, Bonham, MacFarlan, and James Alexander, had all been wounded. Thomas had alone escaped the dangers of the Muchee Bhowun and the siege, but he had suffered severely from illness.

Many of the officers of the garrison were by this time in rags. The refugees from out-stations had brought nothing with them but the clothes upon their backs. At the capital many had lost all their wardrobes when the cantonments were fired and plundered on the 30th of May, and there had been a great destruction of private property and clothes in the Muchee Bhowun. Light clothing was greatly in demand, but the contents of the wardrobes which had been saved having been exhausted, coats now hung in tatters on their wearers. Very wisely, some time before the siege began, the use of white outer clothing had been discontinued, and the light coats and trousers of the officers and men had been dyed of a light brown or dust colour, which came into general use throughout the siege. The privates learnt to make the dye by a mixture of the black and red inks of which our offices contained a large supply. But in consequence of their being put to this use, little of this official necessary was found at the end of the blockade. The superintendent of my office thought to have preserved that under his charge by carefully locking it up in an almirah; but having occasion to open it about this time, discovered that the panels had been removed, and then carefully replaced; but that the ink was gone.

The 18th of September was marked by an eclipse. It lasted for three hours, and almost entirely obscured the light of the sun. The enemy were particularly quiet during the whole time. Major Apthorp and I looked over the parapet of our bastion for some moments, and all appeared deserted around. Not a shot was fired at us.

Besides the casualties which have already been noticed, we had at this time lost three other officers in September. On the 5th, Lieutenant James Graham of the 4th Light Cavalry perished, while labouring under temporary aberration of mind, by his own hand. On the 12th, Captain Mansfield of the 32nd Regt. died of cholera. And on the 15th, Lieutenant Fullerton, who had been Assistant-Commissioner at

Duriabad, died in the hospital. Ensign Hewitt of the 41st N. I. had also been wounded.

Ungud had been sent out again by Brigadier Inglis with despatches for General Havelock on the 16th of the month. He returned on the night of the 22nd, and was the bearer of good news. He brought a letter from General Sir James Outram, which announced to us that an army thoroughly appointed had crossed the Ganges on the 19th, and would, D. V., soon relieve us. The General advised that we should not venture out of our defences; and only attempt anything in aid of the relief force if we could safely do so.

Here, then, at last, were the long-wished-for and expected tidings of coming relief! Havelock had not disappointed us! His letter of the 24th of August had assured us that he expected reinforcements in from twenty to twenty-five days; and on the twenty-sixth day the relieving force had actually crossed the river, and were at that moment advancing to our relief! The spirits of the garrison, European and native, were greatly raised by the intelligence, which spread like wildfire. Nor were we left after this long in suspense. During the morning of the 23rd September, the weather cleared, and the sound of artillery in the direction of Cawnpoor was distinctly heard. By 2, P.M., the reports became quite frequent and loud. We supposed that they could not be further distant than five or six miles, that is, between Alum Bagh and Chillanwa. Later in the afternoon, some field-pieces appeared to have advanced much nearer: for shots were heard which appeared to have been fired at a distance of less than three miles. All now was exultation and joy within the garrison. The natives were at length thoroughly convinced that succour was at hand. And as for Ungud, he literally danced with joy, exclaiming at each shot, "Humara kumpoo âgeea," "Our troops have arrived," and upbraidingly asked the Seikhs whether they were lies which he had been telling?

I find the following entry in my journal on the 24th:—"We heard during the morning the heavy guns of the relief force; but from the wind being from the east, the sound was much less clear than yesterday. The engineers, however, say that the enemy's guns are firing from near the Alum Bagh. The firing continued at intervals during the day; nevertheless, the natives are not so happy as yesterday. Ungud is silent. They doubtless fear that our troops may have met with some check. There is not much firing about us to-day; but the enemy can be seen at work at his embrasures, whether removing guns and timber in order to erect them elsewhere, or what else doing, is not known. During the night there was twice an alarm of firing, &c., by the enemy, but evidently with the object of covering the removal of some guns from near the Cawnpoor battery."

In the course of the following night, Captain Radcliffe, of the 7th Cavalry, was most seriously injured by a round shot while on duty in the Cawnpoor battery. His arm was broken, and the internal injuries were, it was feared, severe. Eventually they proved mortal; and we lost, to the general grief of all, this distinguished officer, whose noble bearing and excellent management of the handful of Volunteer Cavalry which he commanded, had, on the day of Chinhut, done all that could be done by man, to repair our disaster.

The guns of the relieving army were heard again early on the morning of the 25th, and became louder by ten o'clock. While we were joyfully listening to the sound,. a sepoy entered my post, coming in over the works, to the great surprise of the sentry. Before the man could raise his musket, however, the stranger produced a letter, and was recognised to be a messenger from our friends. The letter which he bore was an old one, dated the 16th, from General Outram, and announced his intention shortly to cross the river. He soon went out again with the Brigadier's reply. The messenger could tell us nothing more than we then already knew, viz. that our troops had reached the outskirts of the city.

About half-past eleven the firing ceased; but soon after, numbers of the city people were observed flying over the bridges across the river, carrying bundles of property on their heads. An hour later, the flight became more general, and many sepoys, matchlockmen, and Irregular Cavalry troopers crossed the river in full flight, many by the bridge, but more throwing themselves into the river and swimming across it. The guns of our Redan battery, and every other gun that could be brought to bear upon the flying enemy, as well as our mortars, opened a rapid fire upon them, which was maintained for upwards of an hour. No sooner did this begin, than the enemy assailed us on every side with a perfect hurricane of shot and shell from all their batteries. Fragments of shells were falling everywhere; and the interior of the Residency itself was visited by round shot in places which had never been reached before.

About two o'clock, the smoke of our guns was seen in the suburbs of the city, and presently after the rattle of musketry could be heard. At four o'clock, the officers at the look-out could clearly distinguish European troops and officers in movement in the vicinity of Mr. Martin's house and the Motee Munzil. About five o'clock, we were aroused by a sharp rattle of musketry in the streets, and a few minutes later the column of the 78th Highlanders and Seikhs, accompanied by several mounted officers, were seen from the Financial Garrison house, to turn into the main street leading to the Residency, up which they charged at a rapid pace, loading, shouting, and firing as they passed along; and almost before a cheer could be raised, General Outram rode up, and dismounted at the embrasure of Aitken's battery, near the Bailey Guard Gate. I will here quote the eloquent description of the greeting given to our friends from the account of "a staff officer."

"Once fairly *seen*, all our doubts and fears regarding them were ended: and then the garrison's long-pent-up feelings of anxiety and suspense burst forth in a succession of deafening cheers. From every pit, trench, and battery—from behind the sand-bags piled on shattered houses—from every post still held by a few gallant spirits, rose cheer on cheer—even from the Hospital! Many of the wounded crawled forth to join in that glad shout of welcome to those who had so bravely come to our assistance. It was a moment never to be forgotten."

The Bailey Guard Gate, then riddled with balls and broken, was barricaded, and a bank of earth having been thrown up on the inside, it could not be opened for some minutes, until the earth was cleared away. Generals Outram and Havelock and their staff, and many of the soldiers, entered by the embrasure. Ere long, however, the gates were thrown open, and the stream of soldiers entered, heated, worn, and dusty; yet they looked robust and healthy, contrasted with the forms and faces within.

Nothing could exceed their enthusiasm. The Highlanders stopped every one they met, and with repeated questions and exclamations of "Are you one of them?"—"God bless you!"—"We thought to have found only your bones," bore them back towards Dr. Fayrer's house, into which the General had entered. Here a scene of thrilling interest presented itself. The ladies of that garrison, with their children, had assembled, in the most intense anxiety and excitement, under the porch outside, when the Highlanders approached. Rushing forward, the rough and bearded warriors shook the ladies by the hand, amidst loud and repeated gratulations. They took the children up in their arms, and fondly caressing them, passed them from one to another to be caressed in turn; and then, when the first burst of enthusiasm and excitement was over, they mournfully turned to speak among themselves of the heavy loss which they had suffered, and to inquire the names of the numerous comrades who had fallen on the way.

It is quite impossible to describe the scene within the intrenchment that evening. We had received no post, nor any but the smallest scrap of news for 113 days since the date of the outbreak at Cawnpoor. All had relatives and friends to inquire after, whose fate they were ignorant of, and were eager to learn. Many had brothers, friends, or relatives in the relieving force, whom they were anxiously seeking. Every one wished for news of the outer world, of Dehli, Agra, Calcutta, and of England. Everybody was on foot. All the thoroughfares were thronged; and new faces were every moment appearing of friends which one had least expected to see. Among others, I was rejoiced to meet a most able and promising young officer of Her Majesty's

52nd Foot, Lieutenant Moorsom, who had left us with his regiment in the preceding cold weather, and whom I had believed to be at that moment in the Punjaub. The happy and excited moments passed quickly, until by degrees the excitement moderated. Gradually quarters were found for the officers and soldiers who had come in. Every garrison was glad to welcome in the new comers, who were sufficiently worn and exhausted to require early repose.

CHAPTER XV.

TIDINGS BROUGHT BY THE RELIEVING FORCE.—PARTICULARS OF ITS ENTRY.—EXTENSION OF OUR POSITION.

Re-appearance of some of the former officers of the province, Captain Barrow, Captain R. L. Thompson, &c.—Lieutenant Wm. Moorsom.—Tidings brought by the relieving force; of Dehli; Agra; Cawnpoor.—Order Book of the Nana.—Postal and telegraph communication from Cawnpoor.—Defence of Arrah.—Defeat of the mutineers and Konwur Singh by Major Eyre.—Account given by that officer of the destruction of a body of Oudh marauders.—Sketch given to us of Havelock's operations.—Reinforced by Sir James Outram on the 16th of September.—Outram relinquishes the chief command to Havelock.—The united force crosses the Ganges on the 19th.—Its number and composition.—Marches to Lucknow.—Engagement at the Alum Bagh.—Storming of the Canal Bridge battery.—78th Highlanders left there; while the main body proceed by a circuitous by-road on the right, and reach the Chutter Munzil.—They are here joined by the 78th and Volunteer Cavalry.—Charge up the main street by the 78th Highlanders and Seikhs.—The guns and the second column guided by a sheltered street through the palaces.—Assistance rendered by Lieutenant Aitken, 13th N. I.—Rear-guard, with the wounded and two heavy guns left in the Motee Munzil; reach the palaces after great difficulty on the 27th.—Disaster in bringing in the wounded.—Noble conduct of Dr. Home, 90th Regt., and eight men of the escort.—Account of the affair given by Dr. Home.—Loss sustained by the relieving force.—General Neill, Brigadier Cooper, Colonel Bazeley, &c., killed.—General Outram wounded.—Both generals propose immediate evacuation of the Residency.—After some days decide on remaining.—Reason for this decision.—Position of the Alum Bagh garrison; benefit of that post to us.—Artillery brought in.—The Furhut Buksh, and Chuttur Munzil palaces cleared of the enemy.—Tehree Kotee, and General Sahib's house occupied.—General Sahib's family.—Sortie to the Kuptân bazaar; Captain Hughes killed.—Sortie against Phillips' Garden battery unsuccessful.—Lieutenant D. C. Alexander, Artillery, killed.—Sorties made on the 29th to capture enemy's surrounding batteries.—Major Simmons, Captain McCabe, and Mr. F. D. Lucas, killed.—Grain rations reduced.—Cavalry fail to make their way out.—Plunder found in the palaces.—Prize agents.—China crockery.—Conduct of the city people.—Our letters left at the Alum Bagh.—General remarks on the defence.—Pusillanimity of the

enemy.—General good conduct of all.—Uncovenanted service insufficiently rewarded.—Necessity for our being relieved.—Loss sustained by the garrison.

Several of our old friends who belonged to Oudh, and had fled from our out-stations, now to our great joy re-appeared, having joined Havelock's force. Among these were three of the fugitives from Salone—Captain Barrow, Captain R. L. Thompson, and Lieutenant Swanson. The first of these had exchanged the civil duties, which he had performed so well, as Deputy-Commissioner of Salone, for his more proper profession of a Cavalry soldier,—had raised, and now commanded, the only body of European (volunteer) Cavalry which had accompanied the force. Captain R. L. Thompson, late commandant of the 1st O. I. Infantry at the same station, and Lieutenant Swanson, who had been Assistant-Commissioner there, were Subalterns in Captain Barrow's troop. Several officers served in its ranks as privates, and it was acknowledged by all to have rendered good service, when that service was most valuable.

Captain Alexander Orr, also late Assistant-Commissioner at Fyzabad, was likewise heartily welcomed by us; and from him we first learnt the particulars of the Fyzabad mutiny, and subsequent massacre at Begumgunje. He was employed in the intelligence department under General Outram, and had received some injury in coming in.

These told us of the deaths at Cawnpoor, by cholera, of Lieutenant Grant, one of our Assistant-Commissioners at Sultanpoor, and Captain Beatson, well remembered at Lucknow as the witty correspondent of a local newspaper—since then selected, on account of his high talent, to be his Assistant Adjutant-General, by Havelock.

A young civilian, Mr. H. D. Willock, who had lately been appointed to Cawnpoor, surprised us by his appearance with the force as a volunteer, and detailed all the sad events which had taken place at Allahabad.

I have already mentioned having met Lieutenant William Moorsom, whom we had known at Lucknow when attached to the 52nd Light Infantry. But further notice of this distinguished young officer, of whose lamented and untimely fate recent advices from India have apprised us, is necessary. He had been selected by the Commissioners at Lucknow to conduct a scientific survey of the city in 1856, and had executed an admirable map of a large portion of the city immediately surrounding the Residency, including the palaces of Furhut Buksh, &c., and part of the suburbs in that direction, before he left the station with his regiment. It is from the survey made by him that all the plans had been derived, which were of such essential service throughout the siege, and subsequent military operations. These have been laid before the public in various forms, and convey a perfectly correct representation of our position.

Happening to be in Calcutta, at the time when General Havelock was forming his staff, Lieutenant Moorsom was placed upon it; and having most fortunately preserved private rough copies of his survey, he was able greatly to assist the General's operations by means of them, as well as by his own personal knowledge of the city. It was thus that he was able to guide in through the palaces, the second column of Havelock's army; and afterwards to lead the way when further operations in the palaces were necessary.

Many days elapsed before our eager curiosity could be in any degree satisfied; but the main items of intelligence were soon picked up. The loss of our friends was supposed to be very great. General Neill, a name we had learnt to honour, had fallen in effecting an entrance through the city. The Deputy Quarter-master-General, Lieutenant-Colonel B. Fraser Tytler, was badly wounded; General Havelock's son was known to be also severely wounded, but had not yet come in. Indeed, half the force, with the heavy guns, had not yet entered our works, but were entangled in the Furhut Buksh and Chuttur Munzil, and the yet more distant Motee Munzil Palaces. Dehli had not fallen; but the besiegers hoped that it could not hold out long. Agra was safe, and not besieged. A strong intrenchment had been constructed at Cawnpoor, which had been left under command of Colonel Wilson of the 64th Foot. The fearful massacre of the ladies and children at that station, as related to us by Ungud, was confirmed; and we further learnt, that General Neill had succeeded in getting possession of the Native Order Book of the miscreant Nana, which bore written evidence to his foul treachery. This book contains copy of a "Purwannah," or written order, addressed to the native Soobahdar commanding the 17th Regt. of N. I., then in progress on the Oudh side of the river, from Azimgurh and Fyzabad, towards Cawnpoor. The order begins by stating that it had been agreed that the European garrison at Cawnpoor should be sent in boats to Allahabad, and that boats had been provided for their conveyance. It goes on to say, that it was the Nana's intention, as soon as the Europeans had embarked, to open fire upon them, and to destroy the whole. As, however, (so proceeds the order,) some boats might escape down the stream and be borne by the current under the further bank, the Soobahdar was directed to keep a look-out for them, and to let none escape. This cruel and perfidious order was only too faithfully obeyed.

There had been, we learned, another frightful massacre at Jhansi. The hill stations of Simlah, Mussoorie, and Nynee Taul, were safe. Good news especially this to us, for they were, we knew, crowded with families from the provinces.

Communication with Agra was still carried on by cossid; but the post and telegraph were opened from Cawnpoor to Calcutta. We heard particulars of the outbreak at Allahabad, where Captain Hawes, of my garrison, had lost a brother. My own, I learnt with joy, was safe, and had rendered eminent service to the State at Benares. We heard of the defence of Arrah; and of the marvellous defeat of the mutineer force, and of Konwur Singh, achieved by Major Eyre with three guns and 150 men of the 5th Fusiliers.

On the day following the entrance of the troops, Major Eyre himself, who was sickening with a violent attack of fever, took shelter with us; and when recovering from the illness, dictated to me a particular account of his Arrah and Jugdeespoor campaign, for which I had intended, originally, to have found a place in this Narrative; but the facts connected with this glorious feat of arms being generally known in this country, I have thought best to omit it.

I have, however, given, in the Appendix, Major Eyre's account of a second and most successful brush which he had with a party of marauders, led by two talooqdars from Oudh, who had crossed the Ganges and invaded our older provinces between Allahabad and Cawnpoor. They were overtaken by Major Eyre on the banks of the river, and cut off almost to a man.

We listened eagerly to the protracted history of Havelock's wonderful advance with his small force from Allahabad, chasing before him, at every engagement, the rebel forces of the Nana, at Futtehpoor, at Aong, at the Pandoo Nuddee, until he defeated them in the final stand which they made at Cawnpoor; and drove the hated miscreant and his followers from his own home at Bithoor. We then first comprehended the several movements made by the General in Oudh. His crossing the Ganges with his little force of 1500 men, on the 25th of July, followed by two several actions on the 29th, at Onao and Busheergunje, in which the Oudh mutineers were signally defeated; the heavy loss he had sustained, both in action with the enemy, and from that still more deadly foe, the cholera, necessitating his retreat to Mungulwar on the 31st;—how he had there been reinforced, and had again marched for Lucknow on the 4th of August, as announced to us by Colonel Fraser Tytler, with a force not exceeding 1400 men, and had encountered and a second time defeated the enemy at Busheergunje. We learned how at that place, after the action, despatches from Government had reached the General, announcing to him the mutiny of the Dinapoor Brigade, which was supposed to be moving towards his rear; and that he had been informed by Lord Canning that no reinforcements could be expected early to reach him;—how, with his men dying from cholera, his force weakened and manifestly insufficient, his rear thus threatened by three regiments of mutineers, besides those which the Nana was re-assembling, Havelock, with a heavy heart, turned back from his enterprise;—how, as he left Busheergunje this second time, he himself believed that our rescue was almost hopeless. We heard that the General, with his victorious force, had re-occupied his old position at Mungulwar on the 6th of August, and at once commenced the construction of a bridge of boats across the Ganges to Cawnpoor, for the re-passage of his army; while at the same time he threw up a line of defensive works along the elevated sand-ridge of Mungulwar, amply sufficient to secure him against any attack of the enemy;—how, having completed the bridge, and sent over his sick and wounded, and surplus stores to Cawnpoor, the General had held his force ready to follow: but that at this time tidings reached him that the enemy were re-assembling in force near Busheergunje, and the General deemed it necessary, in order to secure for his army an uninterrupted passage of the river, that the mutineers should be again dispersed;—how, therefore, he again marched out of Mungulwar, on the 11th of August, with a force not exceeding a thousand men, and for the third time took the road towards Lucknow. They told us how the enemy, on this occasion, neither took post at Onao, nor contented themselves with occupying Busheergunje, the scene of two previous defeats; but had taken up a position between the two at Booreaki-Choki;—how they were defeated there, as they had been defeated elsewhere, abandoning their batteries and flying in confusion when the bayonets of the 78th Highlanders were close upon them;—how, having thus dispersed the enemy, Havelock returned with the captured guns to Mungulwar; and finally had recrossed the Ganges to Cawnpoor on the 13th of August, before we had received Colonel Tytler's letter dated the 4th idem, which notified his intended advance.

The causes, therefore, which had operated to make Havelock fall back, were thus shown to have been actually those to which they had been attributed by thinking minds in our garrison; with the additional consideration, of which we were ignorant, of the danger which threatened from the Dinapoor mutineers. We further learned, that Ungud had correctly reported to us the fact of a second engagement having been fought between Havelock and the Nana at Bithoor, after he had thus returned to Cawnpoor; showing the necessity on that account, had no other existed, of his retirement from Oudh. That action, as we now learnt, took place on the 16th of August, in difficult ground, for the enemy were strongly posted; and though they did not, as Ungud had heard, cross bayonets with our troops, yet all who were present declared that the "Jansèn," or 42nd Regt. N. I., had made a stout defence, and resisted our attack better than the enemy had been known to do before.

"With this action," (I here interpose a quotation which is given in "A Biographical Sketch of Sir Henry Havelock,") "terminated Havelock's first grand campaign for the relief of Lucknow. Strictly speaking, perhaps, it was concluded on the day on which he re-crossed the Ganges. In this great effort he had fought five pitched battles against an enemy vastly superior in numbers; he had been compelled to leave open his communications, to carry with him his sick and wounded; to dare the rays of a scorching, often a deadly, sun; to march without tents; to carry with him every article of supply. With these difficulties to encounter, he had advanced three times, and three times had struck so great a terror into the enemy, that his retreat had been invariably unmolested. He found, indeed, that he could gain victories, but that for want of cavalry he could not follow them up; that the enormous numbers of the enemy enabled them to recruit, and more than recruit, their losses as he advanced; that another large body under the Nana Saheb, and Jussa Singh, was always ready to interpose between him and the Ganges. He fought, in fact, more conscious that victory would secure his retreat, than facilitate an advance, which, with his numbers, was impossible."

And now the wearied and exhausted troops enjoyed a month's rest at Cawnpoor:—a rest from active service in the field, which was most diligently and usefully employed by the General, in preparing his resources for the next move upon Lucknow. A battery of heavy guns was, by great exertions, organized; the Volunteer Cavalry increased and improved; and every measure taken by which the efficiency of the force could be increased. This rest did much to recruit the soldiers, broken by fatigue, sickness, and exposure. Many came out of hospital and joined the ranks, which assumed a more healthy and vigorous appearance.

At length the long-expected reinforcements arrived, commanded in person by Major-General Sir James Outram, G.C.B. This distinguished officer, after bringing to a satisfactory close the Persian expedition entrusted to his command, and receiving the honorary distinction of the Red Riband of the Bath, had hurried round to Calcutta. There he had been immediately appointed to the military command of the Dinapoor and Cawnpoor Divisions. The Government had also wisely reappointed him to the post of Chief Commissioner for the affairs of Oudh, which he had held before he started on the expedition to Persia. General Outram steamed up the Ganges, hastening on the reinforcements, and collecting as he proceeded every available soldier. He was joined at Buxar by Major Eyre of the Artillery, who had just completed the discomfiture of Konwur Singh, and the destruction of his fort at Jugdeespoor. From Allahabad the General moved on by rapid marches, and joined General Havelock with the desired reinforcements on the 16th of September. On that day the letter was despatched to us, which came to hand only on the 25th. The united forces amounted to no large number, barely, indeed, sufficient to attempt the dangerous enterprise before them. But it was decided to advance immediately.

With rare, but characteristic generosity, General Outram, whose superior military rank placed him at once in command of the army, declined to take it. "He felt," he said, in the divisional order which he issued on the occasion, "that it was due to General Havelock, and to the strenuous and noble exertions which he had made to relieve Lucknow, that to him should accrue the honour of the achievement."

"The Major-General, therefore," the order proceeded, "in gratitude for, and admiration of, the brilliant deeds in arms achieved by General Havelock and his gallant troops, will cheerfully waive his rank on the occasion, and will accompany the force to Lucknow in his civil capacity as Chief Commissioner of Oudh, tendering his military services to General Havelock as a volunteer. On the relief of Lucknow the Major-General will resume his position at the head of the forces."

Preparations were now immediately made for crossing the river. The head-quarters, and the greater part of 64th Regt. of Foot, were left under Lieutenant Colonel Wilson at Cawnpoor, to garrison the strong intrenchment which had been thrown up at that station upon the bank of the river; and on the morning of the 19th the rest of the army crossed the Ganges by a bridge of boats, constructed with admirable skill and celerity by Major Crommelin, of the Engineers, and encamped by 10, A.M., in two brigades on the left bank of the river.

The force numbered 3179 men, and was composed as follows :—

European Infantry	2388
Ditto Volunteer Cavalry	109
Ditto Artillery	282
Seikh Infantry	341
Native Irregular Cavalry	59
Total	3179

Subjoined is the detail of the regiments employed.

GENERAL HAVELOCK'S ORIGINAL FORCE.

Corps.	Whence come.	Remarks.
H. M.'s 64th Foot, two companies	Bombay . .	Head-quarters at Cawnpoor.
„ 78th Highlanders .	Ditto.	
„ 84th Foot . . .	Burmah.	
1st Madras Fusiliers . .	Madras.	
Capt. Maude's Battery of Royal Artillery . .	Ceylon.	
Capt. Barrow's Volunteer Cavalry	Allahabad.	

JOINED GENERAL HAVELOCK AT CAWNPOOR.

Corps.	Whence come.	Remarks.
H. M.'s 5th Fusiliers . .	Mauritius.	
„ 90th Light Infantry .	Part of the China Force from England.	
Major Vincent Eyre's Heavy Battery of four 24-pounders and two 8-inch howitzers .	Burmah. The heavy guns were taken up at Cawnpoor to replace the ordinary 9-prs.	
Capt. Olpherts' Battery, Bengal Artillery . . .	Benares.	
Capt. Dawson's 12th Native Irregular Cavalry . .	Ditto.	

These were divided into the following two Brigades :—

FIRST BRIGADE.

UNDER GENERAL NEILL.

H. M.'s 5th Fusiliers.
H. M.'s 64th and 84th.
1st Madras Fusiliers.
Captain Maude's Battery.
Major Eyre's Battery.
Captain Barrow's Volunteer Cavalry.
Captain Dawson's 12th Native Irregular Cavalry.

SECOND BRIGADE.

UNDER COLONEL HAMILTON, 78TH.

H. M.'s 78th Highlanders.
Captain Brazyer's Seikh Regt. of Ferozepoor.
H. M.'s 90th Light Infantry.
Captain Olpherts' Bengal Battery.

The enemy offered but slight opposition to the passage of the river, opening fire from one gun only, with which they retired as soon as Olpherts' battery advanced to the front. During the remainder of the 19th and 20th the heavy guns and the Commissariat stores were brought across.

On the 21st September the force advanced towards Mungulwar, where the enemy were found in position, with six guns. From this they were speedily driven by the Infantry and Olpherts' battery, and being pushed from the thick cover of gardens and standing crops, were soon in rapid flight. They were pursued for several miles by General Outram in person, with the Volunteer Cavalry under Captain Barrow, who followed the enemy through Onao, and came up with their main body between that town and Busheergunje. Here two guns were abandoned by the large retreating force to this handful of horsemen, with which, and a third gun before taken, a standard of the 1st N. I., and several camel-loads of ammunition, they rejoined Havelock and the main body. The army encamped (or rather bivouacked) at Busheergunje.

On the 22nd they marched fifteen miles in a deluge of rain, and halted on the Lucknow side of the bridge which crosses the river Seye, at Bunnee. The enemy had retreated so rapidly that some stragglers only were overtaken at the end of this march. On the 23rd, after a march of ten miles, the enemy was found posted strongly at Alum Bagh, with a large body of Infantry and Cavalry, and six guns. The latter were well served for a short time, but were soon silenced by our artillery. The Volunteer Cavalry and Olpherts' Horse battery then advanced to within range of the Alum Bagh, the Infantry coming on in line. On nearing the Alum Bagh, the enemy opened fire from two guns. One of these, a 9-pounder, was posted on the high road, about 400 yards from the enclosed garden. There was a race between our Artillery and Cavalry which should take it. Captain Olpherts' artillery came up to the gun first, from which the enemy, upon seeing our charge, had at once fled, notwithstanding their large masses of Infantry and Cavalry on the right and left. A short stand was made by them about the Alum Bagh garden; but they were soon driven out by our Infantry, and were pursued nearly to the canal. Our troops were then withdrawn, and occupied for the night the Alum Bagh position, under a heavy cannonade from the enemy.

On the 24th the force was halted, to give the men a rest, and prepare for assaulting the city; the heavy guns being, however, engaged during the whole day in replying to an incessant cannonade, which was kept up by the enemy.

On the 25th the force marched at 8, A.M., for Lucknow, after depositing the baggage and tents in the Alum Bagh under an escort of infantry and guns, the latter, including two heavy ones, viz. one 24-pounder and an 8-inch howitzer. The 1st Brigade, led by Sir James Outram, encountered a terrible fire of musketry from some houses and walled enclosures which flanked the road. From these the enemy were gallantly driven, not, however, without sustaining heavy loss, by Her Majesty's 5th Fusiliers, the 1st Madras Fusiliers, and Her Majesty's 64th and 84th Regts., supported by Maude's battery. Both brigades met at the Char Bagh upon the canal. Here the entrance to the city lay over a bridge across the canal, which had been injured, though not cut through, by the enemy. The bridge was defended by a battery of four guns, including one or more heavy ones; and the houses close behind it were loopholed, and full of riflemen and musketeers. It must be confessed that an uglier position to assault, it would not be easy to devise. For awhile Maude's Light Field battery, posted on the road, endeavoured to silence the enemy's guns; but after a number of his gunners had fallen, it was found necessary that the Infantry should advance. While, therefore, a portion of the 1st Brigade, lining the bank of the Char Bagh, which skirts the right side of the canal, poured a heavy fire of Enfields on the enemy's gunners, the battery itself was most gallantly stormed and taken by the 1st Madras Fusiliers, supported by the 5th Fusiliers, led on by Captain H. M. Havelock and Colonel B. Fraser Tytler.

From this point the direct road to the Residency passes through a thickly-populated part of the city, the distance being somewhat less than two miles. It was believed that this road had been cut through, and strongly barricaded in several places by the enemy;

who would also be able to pour in a deadly fire of musketry from the loopholed houses on either side. It was therefore resolved not to attempt to force an entrance through it; and General Outram accordingly led the force by a circuitous by-road which skirted the city on the right and the canal on the left. The guns taken at the canal bridge were upset into the canal, the sides of which are there not less than fifty feet deep; and the 78th Highlanders were ordered to hold the entrance of the main street while the baggage passed. The main body of the force, with Generals Outram and Havelock, followed the by-road, until it debouched on the Dilkoosha road, near the 32nd hospital. Thence leaving the 32nd barracks on their left, they took the road to Sikunder Bagh; and thence, still following the road, which there makes a sharp angle to the left, they entered a walled passage in front of the Motee Munzil Palace. From the canal bridge their progress was comparatively unmolested until they approached this position, when they became exposed to a heavy fire of grape from four guns posted at the gate of the Kaiser Bagh, as well as of musketry from the "Khoorsheyd Munzil," or 32nd mess-house, which was strongly occupied by the enemy. Two of the heavy guns, under Major Eyre, opened on the Kaiser Bagh battery and twice silenced it for a time. But the enemy's gunners were so screened by buildings that they suffered little damage, and soon opened fire again.

Messages having here reached the Generals from the 78th Highlanders, reporting that they were hard pressed, the column halted for some time, and then moved on, by a circuit, to avoid the enemy's fire, through the garden of Mr. Martin's house, under the walls of the Hirun Khana, into a narrow passage leading to the Chuttur Munzil and Furhut Buksh palaces, where they found shelter from the storm of musketry which poured on them from every side. The 90th Regt., with two of the heavy guns, were left at the Motee Munzil to assist the 78th Regt. Meanwhile that gallant corps had been hard pressed, in maintaining itself at the head of the main entrance street. They first carried and occupied the houses on both sides, bayoneting and throwing out of the windows on their bayonet points the enemy found inside. But before the baggage had all crossed the bridge, which occupied more than two hours, a large column of the enemy with two guns attacked them from the city side. Our Artillery having long passed on, there was nothing for it but to leave the houses into which a heavy and close fire of artillery was now being poured, and to charge the guns. This was done accordingly, and both guns were taken, but not without heavy loss. One gun was dragged to the bridge and hurled into the canal; the second was spiked.

The baggage having all crossed, the regiment now followed the main body after replenishing the pouches of the men, their full supply of sixty rounds having been expended. Proceeding along the by-road which had been traversed by the Generals, the 78th were joined by Barrow's Volunteer Cavalry, which formed in their rear to protect it; but the narrowness of the lane did not admit of a charge, and, advancing at a slow pace, the Cavalry suffered considerably. On reaching the cross-roads at the 32nd Regt. hospital, the 78th and Cavalry, instead of following the road to the Sikunder Bagh, turned up to the left by the road leading direct to the Kaiser Bagh, which will readily be recognised on consulting the plan. This led them by the gate of the Kaiser Bagh itself, where they took the battery which was playing on the main column of the army in the Motee Munzil. Spiking the largest gun, they proceeded on, and soon came up with, and joined, the Generals at the Palace lane, where we left them.

The two Generals, after spending some time in seeking, without success, for a route by which the Residency position might more safely be reached, resolved, as the evening was now closing in, to force their way through the streets. Accordingly, leaving the shelter of the palaces they emerged, accompanied by the 78th Highlanders and Brazier's Seikhs, into the small square, subsequently called "Doolie Square," from being the scene of the abandonment of our wounded and doolies; through the gate where General Neill fell; into the main street, which led them, under a murderous fire, aimed at the distance of a few paces from the houses on either side of the street, to the Bailey Guard Gate. This street was intersected by numerous deep trenches, so that the Artillery could not pass by that way; accordingly, the remainder of the main column, comprising two of Eyre's heavy guns, Olpherts' battery, &c., &c., were guided by Captain Moorsom, Quartermaster-General's Department, by a sheltered street through the Chuttur Munzil and Furhut Buksh palaces leading by the Paeen Bagh, and taking the enemy's battery at the Clock Tower in reverse, reached the Residency in comparative safety.

As this second column was approaching, Lieutenant Aitken, of the 13th N. I., hearing from his battery at the Bailey Guard Gate the shouts of our men, and thinking that they might get entangled in the lanes, and suffer from the gun under the

Clock Tower, took twelve men of his regiment armed, but carrying also pickaxes and shovels, for the purpose of clearing away, if possible, the enemy's battery there. Aitken's men met our advancing column near the battery, which was taken in reverse by the latter, who seeing our sepoys mistook them for enemies, and severely wounded three of them with their bayonets before the mistake could be explained. Lieutenant Aitken then proceeded on with his men and occupied a portion of the Tehree Kotee, making several prisoners. Communication was thus completed through the Tehree Kotee with the Furhut Buksh and Chuttur Munzil palaces.

The party of the 90th, under Colonel Campbell, who had been left in the walled passage of the Motee Munzil, were not fortunate enough to get in on that night. With them were almost all the doolies containing the wounded; Brigadier Cooper, of the Artillery, with two heavy guns, under Lieutenant Fraser, and a large number of ammunition waggons. A considerable interval, irregular and difficult to pass, and completely exposed to the fire of the enemy from the Kaiser Bagh and Cheena Bazaar, separated the Motee Munzil buildings from those of the Chuttur Munzil; and the enemy, taking advantage of every neighbouring wall and enclosure, had closely invested this party, and kept up upon them during the whole of the 26th an incessant fire of grape and musketry. Reinforcements were sent by the Generals, which, under the able guidance of Colonel Napier, Engineers, and Captain Moorsom, reached the Motee Munzil with little loss. Nothing, however, could be done to remove the guns during the day. For the 24-pounder had been left upon the road outside the walled passage occupied by our troops, and was exposed to so heavy a fire of musketry that no one could approach it. It was withdrawn after dark by the skilful exertions of Captain Olpherts. Under his directions, Private Duffy crept out unobserved by the enemy, and succeeded in attaching two drag-ropes to the trail of the gun. These were fastened to the limber, the bullocks were yoked on, and the gun was fortunately drawn in. In assisting this operation a very distinguished officer of the Madras Artillery, Captain Crump, was unfortunately killed. The whole column, guns, waggons, and infantry, remained in the same position until three o'clock of the following morning; when, taking advantage of the darkness, they moved out in silence, and, most fortunately, passed the enemy's posts unobserved. Had the enemy been watchful, the line of heavy guns and waggons passing close under their fire, though in the dark, must have suffered most severely. As it was, however, they were fortunately not aroused until the column reached the entrance to the palaces, and their fire then did little damage. Altogether, the position of our two heavy guns in the Motee Munzil enclosure was very critical; and at one time it was almost judged necessary to abandon them. Their extrication, therefore, was highly creditable to Captain Olpherts and all concerned. We lost there two valuable officers: Brigadier Cooper and Major Crump of the Artillery; besides many men wounded.

Not so successful—indeed, grievously calamitous—was the removal of the doolies containing the wounded from the Motee Munzil. General Outram had directed that they should be escorted to the Residency, under the guidance of some person from our garrison who was well acquainted with the *locale*. Mr. J. B. Thornhill, a young civilian of great gallantry, and whose wife was cousin to Lieutenant H. M. Havelock, who was then among the wounded, undertook to be their guide. There was a way through the palaces skirting the river, wholly screened in all but two places from the enemy's fire, along which it was intended that the wounded should be brought. Unhappily, Mr. Thornhill missed his way, and led the doolie bearers and their escort into the square, since termed "Doolie Square," and through the very gate where General Neill fell, into the streets of the city. Here a murderous fire arrested their progress. A few of the doolies were forced on under the fire, and reached the Residency; and among these was that which contained Lieutenant H. M. Havelock, who had been badly wounded in the arm. Others which were just entering the square were turned back, and regained the right path along the river. But not a few, it is sad to think, were cut off: the doolies having been abandoned by the bearers in that fatal square, where many of our poor wounded officers and men afterwards perished miserably.

Nine unwounded men of the escort, including Dr. A. C. Home,* of the 90th Regt., with five wounded officers and men, being cut off from advance or retreat by the enemy, took refuge in a small building which formed one side of the gateway where General Neill had fallen on the previous evening, and there defended themselves with heroic and marvellous fortitude and courage, during the whole of the day of the 26th and the succeeding night, though surrounded by hordes of the enemy, and almost hopeless of relief. They were providentially rescued early on the following morning by the force which, as just described, escorted in the heavy guns from the Motee Munzil.

* This officer has also received the Victoria Cross.

PLAN OF THE LOCALE.

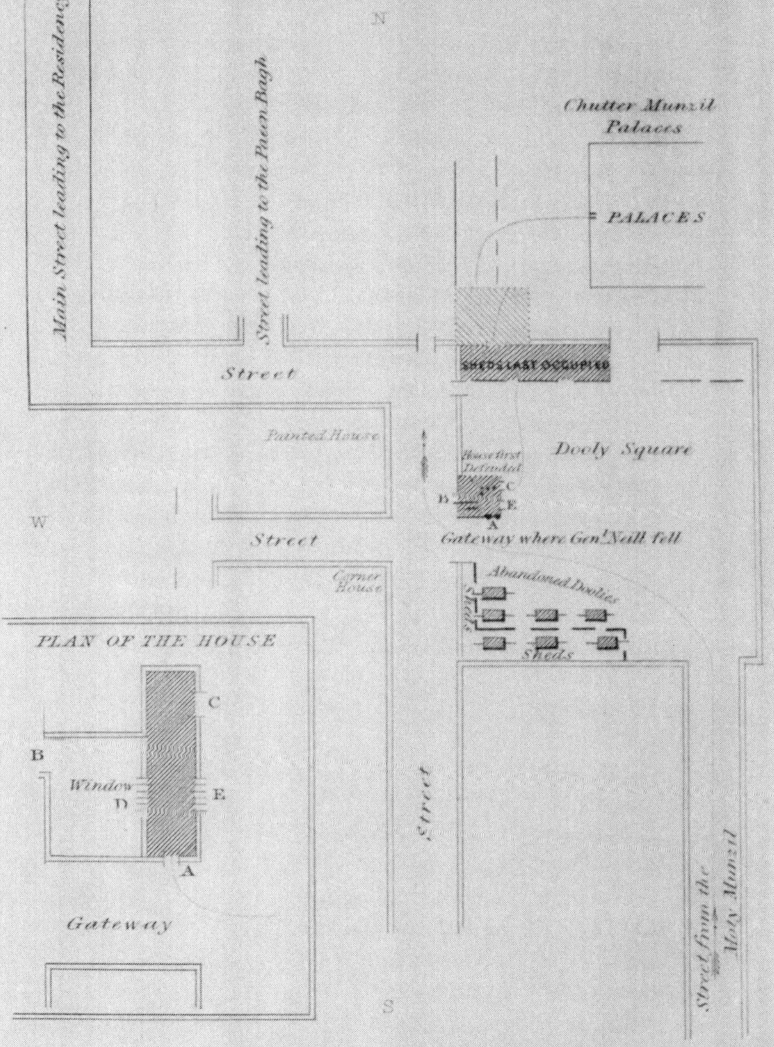

A. *Door by which the Refugees Entered.*

B. *Door into the Street.*

C. *Door into the Square.*

D. *Plastered Venetian Window.*

E. *Venetian Window into Square.*

N.B. The shaded part is that occupied by our Men.

I think it will be allowed that history records few nobler instances of intrepidity than was afforded by this little garrison. To my mind, Privates McManus, Ryan, and Hollowell deserve as well to have their names inscribed in the annals of heroic fame, as any which have found a place in them. All three were presented with the Victoria Cross by General Outram. I feel sure that the following more full account of the glorious conduct of these brave men, with which I have been favoured by Dr. Home, will be read with the deepest interest. The doolies, sad record of the destruction of our wounded, remained in the square, and often did they meet our gaze from the loopholes of our new position on the surrounding walls; and as often as they were beheld, were the hearts of the beholders steeled to wreak a fearful retribution on the murderous foe.

Poor young Thornhill did not survive. He reached, indeed, the Residency early on the 26th, but the injuries he had received were so severe that he died shortly from their effect.*

Account given by Dr. A. C. Home, of Her Majesty's 90th Regt., of the defence made by a party belonging to the escort which accompanied the doolies and wounded on the 26th September :—

"While the leading column of the force, with Generals Outram and Havelock, had pushed on to the Residency, the rear-guard of Her Majesty's 90th Regt., with the doolies containing all the wounded, remained during the night of the 25th of September in the passage in front of the Motee Munzil palace. Here, on the morning of the 26th, Colonel Campbell, Her Majesty's 90th, came and told me that he had made arrangements for sending the wounded to the

* See Addenda, No. VI.

Residency. Supposing me to be the senior medical officer present, he directed me to take charge of them thither. He said that Mr. J. B. Thornhill, C. S., would guide us, and told me that we should have to cross about forty yards of dangerous ground just after we left the gate of the passage, and about 300 yards more of like exposure farther on, after leaving the shelter of a masonry house then in front of us (Mr. Martin's house); but that, when these were got over, we should be in perfect safety. Major Simmonds, of the 5th Fusiliers, with about 150 men, he said, would escort us. We accordingly collected the doolies, and made a rush for Martin's house. From the instant that we left the gate, we were exposed to a heavy fire from a battery of the enemy's across the river; and while waiting there, their round shot tore through the walls of the house in every direction. After half an hour, when we had re-formed the doolies into some order, we again moved on, Major Simmonds' party keeping ahead to clear the road. We ran on as quickly as we could across a nullah, about three feet deep in water, through which we waded, and there a number of the doolie-bearers and of the wounded were killed by the enemy's grape. We thence continued our course along a high wall, which afforded us shelter.

"After this I fancy that Thornhill lost his way, for he led us into an oblong square lined on each side with sheds. On entering this square, a heavy musketry fire was poured upon us by the enemy, who were posted behind walls and upon the roofs of the sheds, on the right or river side, and within a short distance of us. We rushed on through the square as quickly as we could, and sheltering ourselves as much as possible under the arched sheds, passed through an arched gateway on the left side, exposed to a dreadful fire in front and rear. The enemy were crowded in a corner house, forming the angle of a street running opposite to this archway, and fired upon us within a few paces, so that their bullets would tear through several men. Here our men fell thickly; and all the doolies were deserted. A number of doolie-bearers had been killed, and the rest were dispersed and hiding in every direction. One or two of the doolies ran the gauntlet, and got through.

"Mr. Thornhill having now discovered his mistake, had become greatly excited, and begged me to turn the doolies back; but this was no longer possible. Dr. Bradshaw and my apothecary went back, and got the rear bearers to take their doolies up, and then returned and went along the river bank, and got safe into the Residency. These rear doolies were mostly those which had not yet been brought into the square. In rushing back through the archway, to try and turn the doolies back, Thornhill was shot through the arm, and almost immediately after a second shot grazed his temple. Our position at this time was the following:—Between thirty and forty doolies were scattered in the street, in the square, and in the sheds on either side: the bearers who remained unwounded were dispersed and hiding everywhere. Dismounted troopers of the enemy were entering the square, armed with swords, and three sides of it were surrounded by the enemy's musketeers and riflemen, pouring into us a deadly fire. I did not like to leave the doolies, and remained, though the case appeared desperate.

"Seeing presently some stragglers of the escort, I joined myself to them, and we entered an open doorway, in a house which formed the right side of the archway. There were present, including myself, nine sound men, two wounded officers, Captain Andrew Becher,* of the 40th N. I., and Swanson, 78th, and three wounded men: total, fourteen. At this time we were completely cut off. This was about ten o'clock. The mutineers having discovered where we were, were flocking round, and kept up a constant fire upon the doorway. The only thing which checked them was the intrepidity of Private McManus, of the 5th Fusiliers, who kept outside the doorway, sheltering himself behind a pillar, and managing to screen himself under that slight cover, from which he kept up, for half an hour, a constant fire on the assailants. He killed numbers of them; and the fear of his intrepidity was so great, that he had at last often only to raise his piece to cause all the enemy to stoop, and leave their loopholes. They now got a great accession to their numbers, and the noise they made was fearful. They kept reviling us; and, indeed, we were so close, that continually words passed between them and Captain Becher. The assailants kept pressing continually closer, and were then not more than twenty yards from us. They kept on saying, "Why do you not come out into the street?" and their leader called on his men to rush on us, saying that there were but three of us in the house. To undeceive them, we gave a loud cheer, wounded and all joining. We barricaded the doorway partly with lumber, which we found in the house, partly with sand bags, to obtain which we stripped the dead natives close about the door of their waistcloths. The bodies of these natives about the doorway also offered an impediment to their

* This excellent, and highly-valued officer, who was Assistant Adjutant-General to Sir James Outram, died of lock-jaw, soon after his arrival.

making a rush upon us. From their position at this time, the mutineers could fire freely on our doolies in the square.

"One of our number, Private Ryan, Madras Fusiliers, was in a sad way about the fate of Captain Arnold, of his regiment, who was lying wounded in one of the doolies near. He called for a volunteer to assist him in removing the wounded officer. Private McManus, 5th Fusiliers, instantly came forward, though wounded in the foot. We removed our barricade, and the two rushed across the gateway, through the terrible musketry fire, and into the square, when they tried to lift the doolie, but found it beyond their strength. They then took Captain Arnold out of the doolie, and carried him through the same heavy fire into the house. The ground was torn by musket-balls about them, but they effected their return in safety, though Captain Arnold * received a second wound through the thigh, while in their arms. A wounded soldier was also brought in, in this way, and he also, poor fellow, received two mortal wounds while being carried in; the men who carried them miraculously escaping.

"Our situation at this time seemed to ourselves far from desperate: we thought that, by holding out for an hour or two, we were sure to be relieved by the rear-guard when it marched up to the Residency. In fact we were expecting them every moment. We therefore, kept up a very steady fire from the doorway, and from the window that looked into the square. An hour passed away, and three of our men had received wounds which disabled them from firing.

"The conduct of Private Hollowell, of the 78th,

* This distinguished officer underwent amputation and died soon after in hospital.

was most splendid: cheering the men, keeping up their courage, and doing everything to prevent them giving way, himself all the time firing most steadily, and constantly with effect. At length he killed their leader. The assailants, it must be explained, showed themselves only at intervals, when they would come forward as if resolved to make a rush; but Hollowell always managed to kill one at this critical moment, which stopped them. At length he, as above said, killed their leader. He was quite an old man, dressed in white, with a red "cummurbund,"* and armed with sword and shield. Soon after this, the noise in the street quite ceased. An occasional shot was fired at us, but the street seemed to have been deserted. Just before the leader fell, the assailants stealthily pushed the door open at B,† and fired into us through the plastered Venetian window at D; but, most providentially, without effect. Stationing myself at that window, and looking through the hole blown through it by the musket-shot, I was enabled to shoot with my revolver, through the body, a man who came to repeat the fire. He staggered, and fell dead in the doorway. At the same time, Hollowell shot another man endeavouring to drag this one away.

"We now broke through this plaster which closed up the window, and got into the outer room. From the door we could see that the streets were quite deserted, and there was no noise whatever. The bodies of several of our soldiers were lying without their heads in the street. About a quarter of an hour elapsed, during which not a shot was fired on either side; when suddenly, one of the men called our attention to a dull rolling noise in the street, which

* Waistband.

† See accompanying plan.

seemed to indicate that the enemy were bringing down a gun against us. I soon after saw some persons pushing a screen on wheels towards us, against which at the distance of a few yards a minié rifle had no effect. This screen they pushed up against the door B. We now retreated into the original room. The enemy now mounted on the roof, scraped through the plaster, and threw quantities of lighted straw down into the room. Soon the smoke became intolerable, and the building itself got on fire.

"Thus situated, we knew not what to do. Numerous plans were suggested and abandoned. At last we raised the three most helpless among the wounded, and dragging them after us, rushed from the back-door C, which led into the square. We had only about ten yards to run, when we got into the shed on the north side of the square. Here we found some dead and dying sepoys. In making this passage, Lieutenant Swanson of the 78th, received a second wound, of which he died; and one of the wounded men was again wounded. We were now, including myself, six men capable of using arms, and four more of the wounded men capable of standing sentry. One end of this arched shed had a passage broken into it; and we were suddenly roused by two shots fired at us through this. After this, we put one man to guard this entrance; and his presence there was enough to keep the assailants off. The fire of the enemy at this moment recommenced upon us through the doorways and numerous loopholes in the walls. From our first position in the house at the archway, we had in a great measure protected the doolies; but now the enemy were able to come through the archway, and reaching the doolies, commenced massacring the wounded. We were powerless to prevent this. The enemy crept up to them along the sheds, keeping the curtains of the doolies between us and them, and thus we did not see them actually doing this deed of butchery. They used swords. Had we seen them, however, we could have done nothing. One wounded officer, Lieutenant Knight of the 90th Regt., was lying in a doolie. A sowar came up and was about to kill him. Knight sprung out of the other side of the doolie, and had instantly fifty shots fired at him, two of which struck him in the leg, making three wounds; but despite of his wounds, he succeeded in distancing his pursuers who followed after him, and he joined the rear-guard, shot through the legs in three places. The enemy now dug holes in the roof of the shed, and fired down on us. To avoid this, we broke through a mud wall, into a court-yard, on the north side of the shed, where we providentially found two pots of water.

"At this time, hope was gone. We saw plainly that we should not be succoured, and despaired; but broke through into the court-yard, just to escape the imminent death which threatened us by the fire from the roof. The wounded with us were calling out to us to shoot them, for we heard the cries of the poor wretches across the square, who were being inhumanly butchered. About thirty yards from the court-yard was the rear of a large building. Myself and another man crept forward cautiously and noiselessly to this wall. We found about eight feet from the ground an arched opening. Climbing on his shoulders, I managed to get inside this building, and found a spacious court-yard looking into a garden, and as I thought a place to which we had been directed by Providence for our defence and preservation. The walls were thick, the doorways few. I advanced a few feet into this building, but dared go no further. I beckoned to the rest to come, but there being some hesitation, we were discovered by the sepoys on the roof, and fired upon. We now retreated back again into the first shed where the enemy had pierced the roof, carrying with us the water.

"It was now nearly dark, and we made our preparations for relief of sentries. Nine men were told off in three reliefs, giving three sentries, and we clustered close round the doorway. It soon became dark, and the scene baffles description. Here we were in the shed. Lying near us were dead men of the enemy, a dead horse shot that morning,—dead and living huddled together; and our own wounded, some of them delirious. The enemy on the roof over our heads, pacing backwards and forwards, their footfall being distinctly audible, and enemies all round us. All hope of relief had long left us, and we were merely, as we thought, clinging together in desperation. The intolerable thirst and the overstrained excitement of the whole day began about this time to overpower me, and I should not have cared at some moments to have been put out of suspense by death. Again the hope of life would return. The enemy now set fire to several of the doolies. We heard the moans of the unhappy dying men within them, but dared not communicate to one another that the horrid sounds had reached us.

"After our return to the shed, the enemy altogether ceased to fire at us. Our own ammunition would hardly afford more than seven rounds to six men, and we wholly abstained from firing. In this condition, we passed the night; frequently jumping up, in alarm that the enemy was approaching, and then sinking to sleep from exhaustion. About 2, A.M., we heard a heavy firing close to us, and a great rush of the enemy over our heads. We now felt certain that our situation was known, and that the firing proceeded from a party sent to our relief. To describe the revulsion of feeling is impossible. We raised a cry of 'Europeans!' 'Europeans!' and then united to give one loud cheer, and shouted with all our might, 'Charge them!' 'Charge them!' 'Keep on your right!'

"The firing suddenly ceased. After waiting a few minutes, we gave ourselves up to despair. A little after, rousing ourselves, we consulted as to what we should do. I proposed to the men, either to force our way back to the rear-guard, or forward to the Residency. They agreed. But on creeping forward under shadow of the building, I found a large fire burning in the archway, and great numbers of men clustered about it. Escape that way was utterly impossible. Whilst by the way by which we had come, we had to rush through the men who had just successfully repelled our own soldiers. To escape, and carry away the wounded was hopeless. We resigned ourselves completely to our fate. A little after daybreak, we were roused by distant firing. This time it had no effect upon us. It, however, approached nearer and nearer, when Ryan, suddenly jumping up, shouted, 'Oh boys! them's our own chaps!' We then all jumped up, and united in a cheer, and kept shouting to keep on their right. At the same time we fired at the loopholes, from which the enemy were firing. In about three minutes we saw Captain Moorsom appear at the entrance-hole of the shed, and beckoning to him he entered, and then by his admirable arrangements we were all brought off safely, and soon after reached the palace with the rear-guard of the 90th Regt."

The loss sustained by the relieving force in the

actions fought on the march to Lucknow, and in forcing its way to the Residency, was extremely severe, amounting to no less than 535 killed, wounded, and missing. Two officers of high rank, viz. General Neill, and Colonel Bazely of the Bengal Artillery, had been killed. The fate of the latter officer was for some days doubtful, but his body was at last discovered in the main street, not 300 yards from the Bailey Guard Gateway. The severest loss had fallen on the 78th Highlanders, the heroes of so many previous fights. They had lost two officers killed, and six wounded; forty-three men killed and missing, and seventy-five men wounded; making a total of 126: a fearful loss for one regiment to sustain, if its weak state from earlier casualties be considered.

The following statement will furnish the further melancholy particulars of the loss which had been sustained:—

LIST OF CASUALTIES IN GENERAL HAVELOCK'S ARMY, FROM THE DATE OF CROSSING THE GANGES, ON THE 19TH SEPTEMBER, TO THE 26TH SEPTEMBER.

Regiment.	Killed and Missing.				Wounded.			Grand Total of Loss.
	Killed.							
	Officers.	Men.	Missing.	Total.	Officers.	Men.	Total.	
Staff	2	0	0	2	8	0	8	10
Madras Fusiliers	0	13	11	24	2	35	37	61
H. M.'s 5th Fusiliers	0	7	16	23	2	29	31	54
H. M.'s 64th Foot	1	0	0	1	0	10	10	11
H. M.'s 84th Foot	2	9	9	20	4	24	28	48
78th Highlanders	2	37	6	45	6	75	81	126
H. M.'s 90th Light Infantry	0	11	26	37	3	46	49	86
Seikh Regt. of Ferozepoor	0	6	1	7	0	37	37	44
Volunteer Cavalry	0	3	1	4	3	11	14	18
12th Native Irr. Cavalry	1	3	0	4	0	8	8	12
Artillery	2	15	7	24	2	22	24	48
Native ditto	0	5	0	5	0	12	12	17
Total	10	109	77	196	30	309	339	535

In the passage through the city, the force had been compelled to abandon several ammunition waggons, which could not be dragged along. The carriage of one of our small howitzers also having been broken, it was abandoned, but another, taken from the enemy, was substituted by Captain Maude. Several field-pieces captured from the mutineers were also brought in, spare cattle and limbers having been specially provided by Captain Olpherts for this purpose.

I found General Outram, on the evening of the 25th, wounded through the arm by a musket-ball, which had struck him early in the day, before the Canal Bridge had been carried. He had tied the wound round, and, though faint and exhausted, had suffered little inconvenience from it during the whole day's exertion. Both he and General Havelock were under the impression that the garrison was on the point of starvation, and that we had been reduced to our last ration. They congratulated themselves, therefore, greatly, on having relieved us before it was too late. Gradually, and not until much inquiry had been made, was their mistake, and the actual condition of the garrison in respect of food, discovered. With this impression on their minds, both Generals spoke to me severally and decidedly, as if their minds were made up as to the necessity of an immediate evacuation of the place. General Outram desired me to open communication with the city people, with a view to obtain the necessary carriage in order to abandon the intrenchment; nor could it be immediately understood how entirely we had been cut off from all communication with every one outside our works. With the intention of immediately retiring, carrying with them the long-beleaguered garrison, our friends had brought nothing in with them, but what they carried on their backs. All their baggage had been left in the Alum Bagh; and they were in consequence soon put to great straits for want of the ordinary necessaries of life, when it had been decided that they should remain in the intrenchment.

This decision was not come to for several days. But when the real state of things had become known; when the impossibility of obtaining a single bullock or cart from outside had been learnt; when the extreme difficulty of conducting out by the way by which they had entered a large crowd of women and children, and the impossibility of finding conveyance for the sick and wounded, had been considered; and when, lastly, it was reported that the stores of grain inside our works were very extensive, and would be sufficient to feed the entire force for upwards of two months, if used with proper economy; General Outram decided on adopting the only course which was then, indeed, open, viz. to remain with us, and to share our blockade.

For some days, the position of the detachment left in the Alum Bagh in charge of the baggage and wounded caused General Outram some anxiety. They had there, indeed, a force of 530 men, including wounded, two heavy pieces of ordnance, and some lighter guns. The post was not quite unprotected, being surrounded by a masonry wall: but it had never been contemplated that it should be held for any length of time; and the arrangements necessary for doing so were consequently defective. In the place were a large number of native camp-followers, for whom there was no supply of food; and a large number of cattle of every description, for which no fodder remained. The supply of provisions for the European force there was limited. Fortunately all these difficulties were eventually overcome; though at one time the General contemplated the retirement of the force upon Cawnpoor. Some supply of food for the camp-followers was obtained by forays in the neighbourhood, and more was brought under escort from Cawnpoor; not, however, before a number of them had deserted. The cattle were subsisted upon the standing crops and trees which surrounded the position, and eventually were escorted to Cawnpoor, where they were much wanted for forwarding supplies. After no long time, abundant supplies and stores were received from Cawnpoor for the Europeans at the Alum Bagh, who fared far better there, than any of the old or new garrison inside the city.

The maintenance of this external post at the Alum Bagh proved eventually of essential benefit to us in securing our communications with Cawnpoor, and facilitating our sending and obtaining intelligence. Correspondence was carried on between Cawnpoor and Alum Bagh by one set of cossids; and between the latter place and the Residency by another set. Along the first line, our messengers were rarely interrupted; but the passage of the cossids through the city was at all times hazardous, and many letters were lost; being intercepted by the enemy.

During the night of the 25th September, the artillery waggons, and many of the second column of the relieving force, remained outside the intrenchment. They extended in a long line, filling the street which intersected the Furhut Buksh and Chuttur Munzil, almost from one end to the other. Deep trenches dug by the enemy had to be filled up, and obstacles to be dug away, which occupied two days, at the end of which the guns and waggons were safely parked within the intrenchment. Several 9-pounder guns were, indeed, retained about the new extended position, including the palaces of Furhut Buksh and Chuttur Munzil, which the enemy had fortunately evacuated, and which it was now resolved to retain. For this purpose, during the next three days such portions of the palaces as were required to secure our new position were cleared of the enemy, who had not altogether abandoned them.

The Tehree Kotee, which next adjoined our intrenchment, was occupied, and some sepoys and other armed men who were found in it were bayoneted or shot. Between this and the Furhut Buksh palace intervened a building known as the General's house, from its being the residence of the "General Saheb," the ex-King's brother, then with the Queen-Mother in England. This was occupied, and a large number of females, with two sons of the "General Saheb," were made prisoners. The inferior females were set at liberty: and difficulty being experienced in locating the others, they were glad to be domiciled with the females of my khansamah's * family in my garrison. They lived there quietly until the Residency was evacuated, behaved well, and made no attempt to escape. They then accompanied our force in its retreat to Cawnpoor. One of the boys, a very handsome and fair child, though placed in one of the most secure buildings in my enclosure, was wounded during the blockade. A musket-ball struck him, and fractured the collar-bone; but he recovered from the injury.

I must now detail the operations by which our new and extended position was secured, as well as our old one improved.

On the morning following the arrival of the relief force, a sortie was made from the north side of the

* Native butler.

Z

intrenchment to clear the Kuptân Bazaar and adjoining buildings, and to destroy the enemy's batteries in that quarter. It consisted of 150 men of the 32nd Regt., under Captain E. Lowe, accompanied by Captain Bassano and Lieutenant Lawrence, of the 32nd, and Captain Hughes of the 57th N. I. It was completely successful. The whole of that quarter was cleared of the enemy, many of whom were bayoneted or shot down in trying to escape by the river. Captain Lowe was joined in the Tehree Kotee by Lieutenant Aitken and his sepoys of the 13th N. I., and with their assistance completely cleared that range of houses of the enemy, of whom a number were destroyed. No less than seven guns were brought in by this party, viz. an 18-pounder, a 9-pounder, a 6-pounder, and four small pieces. Unfortunately, Captain Hughes, after making his way for some distance towards the iron bridge, spiking two large mortars, and destroying a magazine of the enemy, received a very severe wound from a musket-ball in the shoulder while trying to force a door. He had been attached to my garrison since Lieutenant Webb's death, and much interest was felt in him. The bullet lodged in the shoulder, and a deep incision had to be made before it could be extracted. Captain Hughes never rallied after the operation, and died two days after he had been struck.

The morning of the 27th saw the rear-guard, with the remaining heavy guns, ammunition waggons, &c., which had been left in the Motee Munzil, safely brought within the palaces, which operation has been already described. Several other buildings connected with the Furhut Buksh and Chuttur Munzil palaces were also taken possession of on the same day, with considerable loss to the enemy. Barricades were also thrown up in several quarters to strengthen our new position.

The enemy's batteries by which we had before been surrounded had now been on two sides taken and destroyed; that is, northward up to the bank of the river, and on the east side. His other batteries which extended from the north-west to the south-east angle all along the west and south faces of our works, remained in his possession. Nor were these idle or silent, but kept up a heavy fire of round shot upon our position, which was the more dangerous as we had received into our intrenchment so large an addition of men and cattle. Before, therefore, a decision had been come to upon the ultimate course of action, that is, whether the force should remain at Lucknow, or attempt a retreat; Sir James Outram had resolved that the enemies "moorchas," or batteries should be taken and their guns destroyed.

In the afternoon of the 27th, accordingly, a sortie was made from the Bailey Guard Gate to the buildings which afterwards formed part of Lockhart's Post (78th Highlanders), directed against a battery of the enemy known as Phillips' Garden Battery opposed to our south-eastern angle, and intended to capture their guns. In consequence, however, of the large number of troops required for the operations in the palaces, an insufficient force, not exceeding 120 men, was sent. The party was in consequence unable to accomplish their object; and were obliged to retire after spiking two guns.

It had been intended to send out other sorties on the 28th against the batteries of the enemy; but at the suggestion of Lieutenant J. C. Anderson, Engineers, of the old garrison, who was well acquainted with their several positions, it was resolved to defer the operations for a day, in order to give time for forming a proper plan of operations.

On that day unfortunately, we lost, by one of the enemy's round shot, one of the few surviving Artillery officers of the old garrison, Lieutenant D. C. Alexander, who, while walking on the road outside the Bailey Guard Gate, was struck in the thigh by a 6-lb. shot. The thigh bone was smashed, and before any operation could be performed, this gallant officer, who had only recently recovered from his former injuries, sank and died. I saw him in the hospital just after he had been brought in; when he addressed me, saying, "You can at all events bear witness that I have done my duty." Poor fellow! most heartily do I fulfil his last wish. He had never shrunk from peril or exposure: and when during the engagement of Chinhut, his native drivers were slack in bringing forward his guns, he jumped upon one of the leading horses himself, and dashed forward with the gun.

It was reported on this day (the 28th) in the garrison that the intrenchment was to be repaired and provisioned for three months, and a new garrison from the relieving force placed in it; the 32nd, and the rest of the old garrison, being withdrawn with the generals. The fact was, that General Outram had not then made up his mind as to the course which he would pursue.

On the following day, the 29th, three sorties were made at dawn against the surrounding batteries of the enemy: one from the left square of the Brigade Mess; another simultaneously with it from the Seikh square, made in two parties, led severally by Captain Hardinge, and Major Apthorp. The object of the first was to capture the enemy's 18-pounder at the left front of the Brigade Mess; that in front of the Cawnpoor battery; any other guns at intermediate points, and, if possible, the guns to the left of the Cawnpoor road. This sortie was only partially successful. The 18-pounder gun, which had the very night before done serious mischief to the walls of the square, was captured, and burst; and the houses lying between it and the second 18-pounder in front of the Cawnpoor battery were taken possession of, and destroyed; but in the operation Captain McCabe, a most distinguished officer of Her Majesty's 32nd Regiment, and Major Simmons of equal or more distinction in the 5th Fusiliers, were mortally wounded. Further considerable loss appearing inevitable, if the objects of the sortie were persevered in, the party was, under the orders of General Outram, withdrawn. The second sortie was very successful. One party under Captain Hardinge took and destroyed a heavy gun of the enemy on the right front of the Brigade Mess, and advancing, met the second party commanded by Major Apthorp, who was accompanied by two other officers from my post, Captain H. Forbes and Lieutenant R. Ouseley. Both parties meeting assailed in front and rear a second gun, known by us as the "Lane Gun," which was taken and brought in, and all the artillerymen bayoneted inside the adjacent houses. The destruction of this battery was matter of much rejoicing to my garrison, for it had battered for weeks and completely knocked in the upper story of the house on the south side without our being able to fire a shot in reply. Captain Forbes and Lieutenant Ouseley proceeded against a third gun and the raised battery on the same side; which had also given us great annoyance. Lieutenant Ouseley very gallantly climbed up the battery, and this gun also was taken and destroyed.

While this party was thus engaged, they were covered by myself and a party of the 32nd, posted on the top of Grant's bastion. We kept ourselves under cover, and maintained a steady fire upon every loophole of the enemy from which they attempted to annoy the party engaged in the sortie. One poor fellow incautiously leaned over the parapet, and was at once struck senseless by a ball in the head. We could see the enemy in one spot firing heavily from the ground-floor of a mosque, where they were protected by intervening buildings from our fire. Lieutenant Maitland of the Royal Artillery was near at hand, and I suggested to him to bring down the minarets of the mosque on top of the enemy. The suggestion was executed with beautiful precision. A 9-pounder was placed in position, and in three shots both minarets were struck down at the distance of 400 yards, and fell in ruins on the heads of the enemy.

In retiring, however, from this last battery, Mr. F. D. Lucas, whom I have already mentioned, as being an Irish gentleman and a traveller, who had joined our garrison from the commencement of the siege, and was universally liked and esteemed by us, received his death-wound from a musket-ball. In addition to the destruction of the guns, this party also demolished various musketry posts of the enemy, and discovered the shafts of two mines, which had been commenced against the Gubbins bastion, and blew down the house from which they had been sunk.

The third sortie, commanded by Captain Graydon 7th O. I. Infantry, advanced from the Redan battery along the road to the iron bridge, and destroyed the 24-pounder of the enemy, posted opposite Innes' house, which had so long battered that building, the Residency, the Church, and my house; spiking at the same time several smaller guns. The houses surrounding the enemy's batteries, however, not having been occupied, a very heavy fire of musketry was opened upon our party, which compelled them to withdraw, after sustaining very heavy loss.

Lieutenant J. C. Anderson, Engineers, who had to draw up the plan of these operations, which were on the whole most successfully carried out, did not think it advisable to advance against more distant batteries, which were accordingly allowed to remain unattacked. In course of the execution of these operations, Lieutenant J. C. Anderson sustained a severe injury from springing down from too great a height, which confined him to his quarters.

The active part of the engineer operations within the old intrenchments accordingly devolved on Lieutenant Hutchinson, Engineers, as Directing Engineer: who displayed in the discharge of this duty, as untiring perseverance as his predecessors.

General Outram having found it wholly impossible to procure carriage; and having moreover at length made sure that there was in the stores of our garrison a sufficient supply of grain; while the gun-bullocks which accompanied the relief force would supply plenty of fresh meat, resolved on the 30th to remain blockaded with ourselves, until additional troops should arrive to co-operate with us. Grain rations were accordingly reduced; while the issue of rations of meat was continued on the same scale as before. No other course, indeed, was any longer possible without running extreme risk, and hazarding a fearful loss of life. On the same day on which this resolution was come to, Lieutenant Innes, Engineers, after careful examination of the enemy's mine at the Redan battery, which had for so long a time been a source of anxiety to us, blew it up. The result proved that those who had all along declared that a mine was in progress had been right; while our engineers, who had discredited it, had been for once mistaken. A gallery of great length was discovered, being no less than 158 feet in length. Despite which, there were still fifty feet wanting before it would have reached the most advanced point of the Redan. Moreover, the direction of the mine was 30° too much to the right; so that little injury could have resulted from its explosion, even if it had been completed.

An unsuccessful attempt was made on the following night by Captains Barrow and Hardinge commanding severally the Volunteer and the Seikh Cavalry to slip out from our position, in order to join the detachment at the Alum Bagh. This measure had been directed by the General in consequence of the extreme scarcity of fodder and the large number of animals, horses, and bullocks, which required food. The only grass procurable was on the low cultivated land along the river, and such as had sprung up during the rainy season, in the very confined extent of broken ground, and among the *débris* of buildings by which we were surrounded on other sides. Even this was not to be obtained without loss of life. For the enemy kept a sharp look-out, and shot down all our grasscutters whom they could reach. The only time during which it was possible to go outside for this purpose, without running the greatest risk, was at night. The cavalry proceeded out in silence for some distance, when they were stopped by a heavy fire of musketry, which compelled them to retire. It was afterwards believed that the fire had proceeded from one of our own outposts.

Disappointed in the attempt to get out, the cavalry could only do their best to feed their horses, which were put upon the smallest possible grain rations. All the grass that was found close around was cut. And occasional expeditions were made at night across the river, when the standing crops on the further side were cut, and brought in. Thus, and by eking out the fodder in every possible way, it was made to last throughout the blockade. On more than one occasion Sir James Outram was nearly giving orders that all the horses should be turned out. But eventually this was not done, and the horses were preserved, though in bad condition, until our final relief by Sir Colin Campbell.

During the first few days a good deal of plunder of various descriptions, which had been found in the newly-occupied palaces and buildings, was brought in. Not very much that was valuable, however, was found, and much of that was destroyed. The palaces contained many mirrors, and much gilded furniture of antique pattern, which, beyond that actually required for accommodation, was useful only to make barricades. A good deal of native clothing, a few jewels, and many native arms, some rich and of great value, were brought in and sold by the finders for very low prices. A few stores were found, but they were very limited, having evidently been no more than what was intended for the use of the mutineer troops who had occupied the buildings. There was a little tea, a small store of grain, and one or two bales of the much-prized article, tobacco.

Very soon, however, all such property was declared to be prize, and prize-agents were appointed to collect it. What they got, however, was little, and of a very nondescript and inferior description, and could have brought little gain to the army. I have seen strings of doolie-bearers coming in, carrying copper and brass boilers, and large dishes of the same material, which must, I presume, have been abandoned afterwards with the Residency. Still, it was quite necessary that promiscuous plunder should be stopped. For this purpose the guard at the Bailey Gate received orders to detain all property suspected to be plunder. The only exception made was crockery. Of this, both the old garrison and the new comers stood greatly in need. In my own house more than one round shot had fallen into the pantry, causing an indescribable destruction of cups and saucers, plates and dishes, which were therefore in great demand. The newly-occupied palaces afforded great means of replacing these, for several rooms were found to be full of boxes, which contained nothing but crockery. These were speedily ransacked, emptied out on the floors, part removed, and the rest trodden under foot. The floors were soon covered foot deep with broken crockery and china. Some of the sets were exceedingly handsome, of English and French manufacture, embellished with the sort of armorial devices which had been adopted by the several Kings of Oudh. There was a great quantity of crockery, of China manufacture, mostly of coarse quality; and the prevailing pieces were bowls innumerable, from the size of a small slop-basin to that of a large punch-bowl. When I visited the room everything of elegance had been removed; but I saw, with several of my friends, many exceedingly elegant and highly ornamental hand-basins, which would be prized in this country.

A good deal of disappointment was expressed by many after the entry of the relief force, that the inhabitants of the city had shown no token of sympathy or good-will. The example of Cawnpoor was referred to, where, after the last defeat of the Nana at the entrance of the Station, our troops were welcomed in by the citizens, who brought out to them presents of milk, butter, food, and sweetmeats. Nothing of the kind, it was objected, had taken place at Lucknow; and the inference was drawn that our rule on the Oudh side of the Ganges was unpopular; and that the people sympathized with the mutineers more than with ourselves. Such persons overlooked the essential difference between the positions of our force at Cawnpoor and at Lucknow. At the first place the enemy had been wholly defeated and driven away. In Lucknow his position had been turned, and our force had indeed entered by efforts of gallantry and resolution, which have rarely been equalled, and never surpassed; but the foe had not been vanquished, and had at once closed in upon our rear. Communication with such of the citizens as were friendly remained, therefore, little less difficult than before.

General Outram had brought with the army an ammunition waggon laden with the letters and newspapers which had been for so many months lying in the post-offices, addressed to parties who were shut up in Lucknow. This cart had remained with the rest of the baggage at Alum Bagh; so that, with a few individual exceptions, we none of us received any of our letters until the place was finally relieved.

Before closing this chapter, a few remarks on the result of the siege generally are required. And first it must be observed, that, with the weak and unfinished defences which we had to protect us, it would have been quite impossible for us to maintain the defence for a single week, if we had been surrounded by a courageous enemy. Next to God's good Providence, whose almighty Hand all should humbly recognise in our wonderful deliverance; we owe it to the pusillanimity of our foe. The points at which a dozen men abreast might have entered our position, without making so much effort as you have to do in crossing an ordinary fence in England, were numerous. It is surprising that the enemy did not direct his assault at them. At these places ladders were not required to effect an entrance; yet the mutineers generally selected those points to attack, where ladders were necessary. It was thought that they feared we had mined those places where access was more easy. And this belief may have deterred them. When they attacked, moreover, they lacked that determined courage, which faces danger with resolution. Brave men among them there were, no doubt; and these were sacrificed in their attacks. But the brave were not many; the mass were poltroons. In the plan of the intrenchment, which has been given, will be observed two unfinished batteries on the west side. The one nearest to, indeed just outside, my post, had been raised to a commanding height upon the *débris* of houses destroyed by Fulton, and which completely overlooked my compound and that of Mr. Ommanney. Had the engineer who was constructing it, Lieutenant Hutchinson, been able to complete the work, it had been intended to have called it the Malakoff. As it was, it was never finished; but remained a large undefended mound, separate from, and outside our works. There was nothing to prevent the enemy from occupying it, except a musketry fire from the roof of my house, which commanded it in turn; but the artillery of the enemy swept this roof, so that we had been compelled to abandon it. An adventurous foe would soon have occupied and strengthened it, and half-a-dozen riflemen placed there would have been, almost if not quite, enough to render my post untenable. No one could have moved outside the house without a certainty of being shot. As it was, they never made the attempt; and the Malakoff remained neutral ground throughout the siege.

Great praise has been bestowed upon those who took part in this defence; and no doubt deservedly so. All behaved well. During the whole siege I never heard of a man among the Europeans who displayed cowardice before the enemy. There were not a few who croaked, whose dispositions were less hopeful than others; who were prone to exaggerate danger, and to under-estimate the resources at our disposal, and for many weeks the prospect was alarming enough. The months of June and July were the worst;—while the anticipated danger was threatening us; and when first in its worst-expected form it had actually come to the door. At the commencement of the latter month several of the men contemplated the destruction of their females, if the enemy should overpower us. I was, during those terrible days, one evening taken aside by a military man, who was one of my garrison. He had, he told me, agreed with his wife, that if the enemy should force his way in, he should destroy her. She had expressed herself content to die by a pistol-ball from his hand. He was, he told me, prepared, if I should fall, to do the same deed of despair in respect to my own wife; and he required of me a pledge, that if he should first perish, I would act the same part by his. I declined to give it. The necessity, I told him, had not arisen; there was, therefore, then, no need to provide for it. And besides I could not do it.

All behaved well. Engineers, artillery, staff, civil servants, uncovenanted, clerks, merchants,—all did their duty to themselves and to their country; and remembered that the honour of England was then in their hands. In one respect we certainly deserve much less credit than is due to the brave army of Havelock and the illustrious conquerors of Dehli. Every man felt that he was fighting for his own life, and for the life and honour of his own family, or of those of his companions. There was no choice; it was a necessity to fight to the last; for after the example of Cawnpoor, who could trust the enemy? Many, doubtless, were actuated by yet nobler motives. The political importance of holding Lucknow against the wave of mutiny, everywhere surging over the land, could not be exaggerated. As yet the rebels had met with no check. If Lucknow, the most important city in Upper India next to Dehli, could be held, and the British flag still made to float over the battered seat of British authority in Oudh, the effect would be immense. It would dishearten the mutineers; it would cheer our friends among the people; it would check the spirit of mutiny elsewhere. And such, doubtless, was its effect. We often heard through Ungud, that the mutineers when demanding money or aid from men who were disposed to be our friends, had been met by the taunt, "Come to us when you have taken the Bailey Guard!"

Our mainstay in conducting the defence, it need scarcely be told, was the 32nd Regt. of Foot. Long may "Lucknow" grace the regimental colours! The mortality among the officers was fearful. I believe that only two of the number escaped unwounded. And though at times the men lost heart, were careless, or insubordinate: yet, balanced against their general conduct, their sufferings, and privations, their constant fightings and ceaseless labours; it may well be confessed that they right nobly maintained the high character of the British soldier.

Nor should the constancy and fidelity of the native soldiers of all arms be forgotten; nor the extraordinary, and, to us, unappreciable temptations by which that fidelity was tried. It is almost marvellous that they continued faithful.

I must not forget to do justice to my own service. There were nine of us in the intrenchment, viz. M. Ommanney, G. Couper, S. Martin, G. Benson, W. C. Capper, J. B. Thornhill, G. H. Lawrence,* A. Boulderson, and myself. Two were killed, two were wounded, and five have escaped. They all took their turn of duty with the military: and shared their labours, dangers, and difficulties. In short, they all did their duty well.

Sufficient justice has, I think, scarcely been done to the clerks and uncovenanted service. The admirable conduct displayed by this class, which contained such men as Kavanagh and Williams, during the siege, surprised us all; particularly because in times of peace this body is too often noticeable for want of energy and character. Several of them rendered excellent service in the Volunteer Cavalry. All behaved well during the siege, and were often very conspicuous in repelling the fiercest attacks of the enemy. They deserved, I think, better at the hands of Government than they have received, or had at least received, when I left India.

General Outram bestowed upon them a donation of three months' pay; and the Government have granted

* This young officer's name has not yet been mentioned. He possessed a good rifle, was an excellent shot, and killed many of the enemy, but suffered much from sickness, and was afterwards wounded by the explosion of a shell.

them six months' batta. But these sums united will not make up to them the ordinary salaries which they would have continued to enjoy if the public peace had not been disturbed. The uncovenanted and clerks deserved better of the State than this.

Besides this numerous class, and those who have been specially mentioned in this narrative, there were others in the garrison, not belonging to any of the services, but who had been attracted to Lucknow by trade and other pursuits. Among these were Mr. Parry, Secretary to the Branch Dehli Bank; Mr. Rees, formerly a Master in the Martinière College, then connected in business with M. Duprat; Signor Barsotelli, an Italian who had just imported and disposed of an invoice of alabasters from Florence; Mr. Kight, Editor, and Mr. Chick the sub-editor of the "Central Star," local newspaper; Mr. Ereth, railway contractor; Mr. Cameron, Mr. James Hill, M. Geoffroy, and Mr. Johannes, merchants; and some others, who all, I believe, behaved well. Mr. Cameron in particular, a merchant from Calcutta, deserves especial mention. He acquired, by the instruction which he received from our Artillery officers, a good knowledge of gunnery and mortar practice; and rendered excellent service in superintending the mortar batteries, when Artillery officers were not available.

In this review of services, of which England may well be proud, I must not omit the most valuable exertions of the medical men, who were, like others, greatly overworked during the siege. To Dr. Scott, the old and highly-esteemed surgeon of the 32nd Regt.; to Assistant-Surgeon William Boyd, of the same regiment; Dr. J. Fayrer, the able and well-known Residency Surgeon; to Dr. J. Campbell, of the 7th Light Cavalry; to the talented Assistant-

Surgeon of the 2nd O. I. Cavalry, S. B. Partridge; to Dr. Bird, doing duty with the Artillery; and to several more, I bear my hearty tribute of praise. Everything was against them; bad air, bad food, and an insufficient supply of medicines; yet they, at the cost of no small personal exertion and daily risk, struggled manfully, with unwearying perseverance, through their many difficulties.

Nor would it be right, in what professes to be a faithful record of facts, to omit adverting to those ladies who undertook the trying duty of ministering to the sick and wounded. There were several of these devoted women, these excellent Sisters of Charity. Probably, if asked, they would name, as the best representative of their order of mercy, the bereaved widow of our chaplain, Mrs. Polehampton.

During all these prolonged operations, and despite the utmost efforts of the enemy, we had never lost a single foot of our original position; nor did they ever acquire an inch of ground. Most fortunate, however, for us was it that our relief was not longer deferred. I entertain myself no manner of doubt as to the impossibility of our having maintained our position unassisted, until the time when the final relief under Sir Colin Campbell arrived. It was not that we should have starved; for, as has been seen, we possessed, thanks to Sir Henry Lawrence's wise precautions, abundance of grain. It was not that we were in immediate danger of being blown up; for, as has been observed by Lieutenant Innes in his "Rough Notes," "our subsequent sorties made us acquainted with four mines, all of them innocuous" on account of the error in their direction. That able young officer further goes on most justly to say, "Our real dangers consisted in the probable determination of all the natives still with us to abandon us soon; the fearful exhaustion that would consequently have ensued; the necessity of abandoning our outposts; the losses by musketry and mining that would have followed. Opposition to an assault would, with our then diminished numbers, have been next to impossible: and thus most assuredly does the Lucknow garrison owe its lives to the timely arrival of Generals Outram and Havelock and their brave troops."

The garrison of Lucknow originally was 1692 strong. Of these 927 were Europeans, and 765 natives. We lost, in killed, of Europeans 350, and 133 natives, and of the latter 230 deserted, making a total loss of 713. There remained of the original garrison, when relieved on the 25th of September by General Havelock, a total number of 979, in which both sick and wounded are included, of whom 577 were Europeans and 402 natives. We had lost during the siege forty-one military, and two civil officers; and one Assistant-Chaplain.

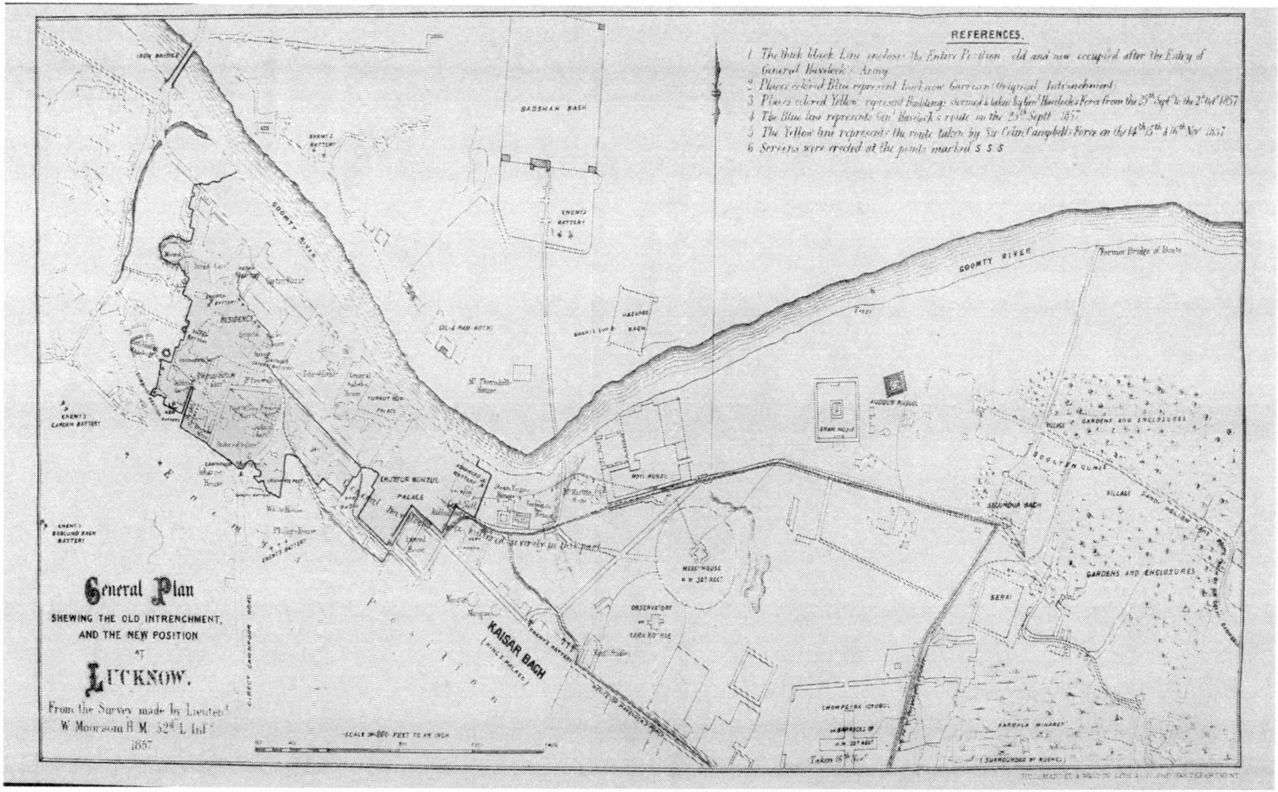

General Plan
SHEWING THE OLD INTRENCHMENT,
AND THE NEW POSITION
at
LUCKNOW.
From the Survey made by Lieutent
W. Moorsom H.M. 52d L. Infy
1857
REFERENCES.
1 The thick black Line encloses the Entire Position old and now occupied after the Entry of General Havelock's Army
2 Places colored Blue represent Lucknow Garrison (Original Intrenchment)
3 Places colored Yellow represent Buildings stormed & taken by Genl Havelock's Force from the 25th Sept to the 2d Oct 1857
4 The Blue line represents Genl Havelock's route on the 25th Septr 1857
5 The Yellow line represents the route taken by Sir Colin Campbell's Force on the 14th 15th & 16th Novr 1857
6 Screens were erected at the points marked S S S
IRON BRIDGE
BADSHAH BAGH
GOOMTY RIVER
RESIDENCY
CHUTTUR MUNZUL
PALACE
FURRUT BUX PALACE
KAISAR BAGH
(KING'S PALACE)
MOTI MUNZUL
MESS HOUSE
OBSERVATORY
SECUNDRA BAGH
SERAI
SOOLTAN GUNGE
GARDENS AND ENCLOSURES
SCALE 800 FEET TO AN INCH
Former Bridge of Boats

CHAPTER XVI.

THE BLOCKADE.

The remaining period of investment should properly be called the Blockade.—Sir James Outram assumes command.—Brigadier Inglis retained charge of the old intrenchment; General Havelock of the palaces, and the Oudh Field Force.—Daily rounds of General Havelock.—The changes in our position described.—New buildings and position occupied.—Additions made to the old intrenchment.—Chief attempts of the enemy during the blockade directed against the new position.—Their mines, and our very extensive countermines.—Communication with the provinces.—Desirableness that some part of our position should abut upon the open country.—Our force insufficient to effect this.—Impossibility of native merchants rendering us assistance. —Vengeance taken by the mutineers upon the villagers who had aided Havelock. — Manufactory of Enfield rifle cartridges established.—Musket preferred to the Enfield rifles in *mêlées.*—Native soldiers rewarded.—Our food during the blockade.—Substitute for tobacco.—Diminished strength and physique of the garrison.—Bad condition of the hospitals; want of room, proper food, and medicines.—Assistance which Mr. Gubbins was able to render; names of officers received into his house.—Enemy's management of their guns.—Projectiles fired by the enemy, cylinders of wood, stone and brass shells.—Advice given by Furzund Ali and Runjeet Singh respecting the obtaining of supplies. —Account of Runjeet Singh.—Attack of the enemy's battery in Phillips' garden; successful; but the 8-inch howitzer not taken.—Measures taken to extend our position along the Cawnpoor road.—Major Haliburton, and Major Stophenson mortally wounded. — Attempt abandoned.—On our retirement the enemy press on and attack Gubbins' post.—Escape from a musket-ball which penetrated a loophole.—Remarks on the construction of loopholes.—Repulse of the enemy in an attack on the palaces.—Good news of the capture of Dehli.—Captain Bruce's low-caste police.—Extracts from Journal.—Overtures from Rajah Man Singh.—Lockhart's post.—Advanced garden post.—Communications from Man Singh.—Letter received from Captain P. Orr, and other refugees from Mithowlee at Lucknow.—Semaphore telegraph established between the Residency and Alum Bagh.

With the arrival of Havelock's relieving force, the siege of the Lucknow Residency, properly so called, terminates. Many of the surrounding batteries of the enemy were soon, as has been seen, captured; they refrained from any general assaults, and the remaining period, during which the force commanded by Generals Outram and Havelock shared the investment of the whole garrison, may be best designated by the term suggested by Havelock, that of "blockade."

From the time when this glorious feat of arms had been accomplished, Sir James Outram assumed the command.

The entire position occupied by our troops was divided into two commands; that of the old Residency intrenchment, and the newly-acquired palaces. Of the first, Brigadier Inglis retained charge, having under him the survivors of the old garrison, military and civil; with the addition of Barrow's Volunteer Cavalry, and detachments of the Artillery, 1st Madras Fusiliers, and 78th Highlanders, furnished from the relieving force.

The rest of the newly-arrived troops, forming what was then called the Oudh Field Force, was commanded by General Havelock, and occupied the palaces and the Tehree Kotee.

Sir James Outram, with his staff, fixed his head-quarters in Dr. Fayrer's house.

General Havelock, and such of his staff as were unwounded, took up their abode in Mr. Ommanney's house. From this a walk round all the posts of the palaces embraced a distance exceeding two miles, which was traversed by Havelock soon after daybreak every morning. Having accomplished this inspection, he called in, on his return, to make his accustomed report to General Outram.

The changes which had been effected in our position I will now describe.

On the north and east, the old Residency position was completely relieved by the extension of the new line of defence; on the north as far as the river Goomtee, and eastward so as to include the Tehree Kotee, Furhut Buksh, and Chuttur Munzil Palaces. Thus, instead of the hospital, Fayrer's house, Sago's house, and the Financial Commissioner's office on these sides being exposed to close assaults by the enemy, the positions of the mutineers were thrown back at least 1000 yards. The Bailey Guard Gateway, up to the very entrance of which the enemy had before sometimes advanced, became a central locale in the extended position which was now occupied. The attention of the old garrison was now only required to be directed to the west and south faces of the old position, viz. from Innes' post at the north-west angle to my post; and then along the south front to Anderson's house. Here the new line of occupation again began, with the post termed Lockhart's, or the 78th Highlanders, which extended from a barricade thrown across the direct Cawnpoor road, close to Anderson's house, eastward to the gaol, which was occupied by the 84th Foot. A succession of posts followed, terminating on the east side with the advanced garden post on the Goomtee, held by the 90th Regt. From this extreme position the river formed our boundary to near the north-west angle of the old defences at Innes' post.

Very fortunately this large addition made to our defences on the east side comprised lofty and extensive ranges of palaces, built of solid masonry, rising nearly from the river's edge, which afforded much more than sufficient accommodation to our troops. The enemy, it is true, placed a few guns across the river, and occasionally fired round shot into these buildings; but by abandoning and barricading the river-face rooms, it was not difficult to protect completely the lower stories of such buildings as were exposed. So that the enemy's artillery could do little more than make butts of the upper stories unoccupied by us, and the gilded domes, which they knocked about a good deal. From the extended position also, and solid construction of these palaces, little damage was sustained from the enemy's shells, which were not unfrequently thrown in from the Kaiser Bagh and city side.

The south side, however, of the new position was less favourable; for it there followed a broken line of buildings closely contiguous to those still occupied by the enemy. In some places a narrow lane separated our troops from the mutineers; in others, a small space was by tacit accord, left neutral between them. Nowhere was our position on this side bounded by a clear open space, which would have afforded to our sentries a good view of the enemy's movements.

On the west and south sides, the old line of defence of the original Residency position was maintained, with the exception of two additions made, the one to Innes', the second to my post. At the former, a commanding mound, at a small distance in advance of Innes' house, was taken possession of, and fortified by Lieutenant Hutchinson, Engineers, and a very useful line of defensive trenches connected it with both Innes' house, and outward with a small mosque in the direction of the iron bridge, which had also been occupied. At my post we seized the opportunity afforded by the destruction of the enemy's batteries, to improve our defences on the south side, where we had been, in fact, all through the siege wholly unprotected. For this purpose, the lane outside the low south compound wall was seized, and the enclosure beyond it, known as the "Goindah lines," occupied; and inside the latter a new raised-battery was constructed, and armed with a 9-pounder gun.

During the period of the blockade, the Cawnpoor battery was also greatly improved, indeed completely renovated, by the active exertions of Captain Thomas, of the Madras Artillery. From being little better than a heap of ruins, and exceedingly unsafe, it became the show battery of the garrison, and was armed with 18-pounders, so as completely to defy any attempt of the enemy on that side. One of the two unfinished batteries on the west front (the Sheep House battery) was also completed and armed. But the enemy having made no attack afterwards on that side, there was not, I believe, much occasion to use it.

Although during the blockade the enemy did not much relax their musketry fire on the exposed fronts of our old position, which they also cannonaded from a distance; yet their chief attempts were directed against our new positions, in the palaces, and at Lockhart's post, where the close contiguity of the buildings occupied by themselves afforded great facilities for mining, and approaching our troops unobserved. Our engineers accordingly were, during this period, chiefly engaged in counteracting the enemy's attempts; and executed, under the superintendence of Captain Crommelin and Colonel Napier, of the Engineers, a series of countermine shafts and galleries, which is said to be unsurpassed in modern warfare. At first the enemy succeeded in exploding successfully two mines, by which we lost a few men. Latterly, however, our position became so protected by these subterranean defensive galleries, that their efforts to injure us always proved abortive; and on several occasions their works were broken into, and their miners destroyed.

Our communication with the provinces and the rest of India was much improved after the entry of the relieving force, but still was far from being in a satisfactory state. In fact, we were still closely blockaded, and though the greater distance at which we kept the enemy, and our more extended position rendered it less easy for him to intercept all our messengers; yet this was too frequently the case, and the cossids, or letter-bearers whom we employed, had to use every precaution in order to reach the British post at Alum Bagh. The distance between our outposts and Alum Bagh is about four miles, the road for the first two miles running through the city, and after leaving it being closely bordered by gardens and detached buildings, in which the enemy had established pickets. Once there, the road to Cawnpoor was generally clear. Occasionally a messenger despatched thence with a packet of letters, newspapers, and cigars, would arrive safely, but more frequently the approaches were found to be too closely guarded, and the attempt failed.

In one way or another the enemy managed to capture a large number of our native camp-followers and servants; and upwards of 1200 of these were understood to be prisoners in the Kaiser Bagh, at the time of Sir Colin Campbell's arrival. This inconvenience, and the far greater evil, the absence of supplies of food and fodder, would no doubt have been greatly diminished had any part of our position abutted on the open country. But though few disconnected buildings and enclosures interposed between our extreme advanced post in the Chuttur Munzil Garden, and the open country, they were sufficient to enable the enemy to complete his blockade.

Our position was already sufficiently extended, indeed more so than the limited forces at the General's disposal could properly guard; so that it was impossible to spare men to occupy the steam-engine house, the 32nd mess-house, Martin's house, and Motee Munzil, which would have opened our communications with the country. I was not unfrequently asked, during the blockade, why the native merchants, many of whom I believed to be well affected to us, never attempted to throw in supplies. The reason was obvious enough—the thing was impossible. We were closely invested on all sides, and since an armed force would have found much difficulty in forcing its way in, how could a defenceless merchant have brought in supplies? Moreover, at this juncture no one in Oudh dared openly to avow himself to be our friend. To do so would have exposed the party to certain plunder and destruction; and those who wished us well found little inducement to run such risks in the uncertainty of our continuance in the province. It was reported by several persons that Oudh would be given up, while many thought that it would be temporarily abandoned. Yet these parties wondered that assistance was not rendered to us by the people! To such it is a sufficient reply to recount the actual experience made by General Havelock's army on its first and second entry into Oudh. Upon the first occasion, the villagers in the vicinity of Havelock's position of Mungulwar readily came forward, bringing whatever supplies their villages afforded; but after the army had retreated across the Ganges, when they returned a second time into Oudh and reoccupied Mungulwar, no supplies were brought. On inquiry it was discovered that the villagers who had on the first occasion evinced a friendly disposition had been most severely punished by the mutineers, who did not hesitate to kill, mutilate, and plunder those who had aided our force. Without, therefore, denying the unfriendly feeling, too prevalent among many classes of the citizens of Lucknow, it must yet be admitted, that it was wholly unreasonable to expect that those friendly to us should have attempted to force their way through the blockading force of the enemy, to render us assistance.

The regiments which formed Havelock and Outram's force were all armed with the Enfield rifle. Unfortunately but little of that description of ammunition had come in with the force; and the musket-ball cartridge, of which we had large quantities in store, was useless for the Enfield rifle. Some little anxiety was at first felt on this account; and to husband the rifle ammunition, muskets, of which we possessed a large store, were served out to many of the men. Soon, however, the manufacture of rifle cartridges was established, under the superintendence of Major North of the 60th Rifles, who had himself been well instructed at a school of musketry.

Lieutenant Sewell of the 71st N.I., fortunately possessed a mould, and a second was found in the garrison, and these two officers organized a manufactory, which was established at the Treasury. Entire skill in the making was soon acquired by about a dozen natives whom they employed; and the cartridges which they turned out, were as neat and good as those which are usually served out to the army. Many of the newly-arrived privates were excellent shots, their bullets striking, or falling near the mark, at very long distances. For this sort of practice, these weapons were much approved by the men of the 32nd Regt., who, as has already been said, were armed with old muskets of inferior description. But I have heard the men, in discussing the respective merits of the old and new weapons in a *mêlée*, where rapid firing was required, give the preference to the musket. The reason assigned was, of course, the greater rapidity with which it could be loaded: and such being, I believe, undoubtedly the case, the fact appears not wholly undeserving of consideration.

A few days after General Outram had assumed command, he called for returns of all the native soldiers, and fighting men of every denomination, who had behaved well. These were accordingly all paraded before him, and, after having been publicly thanked, received at the General's hands substantial proofs of the satisfaction of the Government. Every man who had been recommended received, at least, one step in military promotion; some of the native officers gained more than one step in army rank, and to several the Order of British India was awarded. Runjeet Singh, who had acted as leader among the old pensioners, was rewarded with the full pay of a soobahdar, and received the Order of Merit. To Ungud, our trusty messenger, was assigned the full-pay pension of a soobahdar. Sir James Outram, from some scruples connected with the denomination assigned to him in the list, viz. that of "Scout," did not grant him the Order of Merit, which, I think, he had well deserved; and the reason for his deprivation of which Ungud could not understand. He was, however, not ill off. Brigadier Inglis had promised him a reward of 500*l*. for the safe delivery of each despatch entrusted to him, and the promise was faithfully fulfilled. Ungud had conveyed three despatches, and brought back acknowledgments of all. He, therefore, received 1500*l*. in cash after the withdrawal of our garrison.

A man of his class who in India is possessed of this sum of money, is accounted rich.

The pensions of all the other old pensioners were doubled. That of Furzund Ali, my Artillery Commandant, was raised from 10*l.* per mensem to 20*l.*; and his native artillerymen were assured of stipends for life; and my foot levies, who were not in regular military service, were similarly recompensed. The only native soldiers who were made exceptions, were the Seikh Cavalry, who had caused us so much anxiety during the siege.

These rewards were judicious and well-timed, and all returned from the General's presence with joyful countenances. The European soldiers, however, the assignment of whose recompense was left to the future orders of the Government of India, grumbled not a little at the prior notice taken of the natives; and though unjustly, perhaps not unnaturally. "—— those black fellows!" they were overheard to say; "there they go—as usual, petted and rewarded, while we gets nothing."

Of food, meaning wheat, and beef obtained by slaughtering gun bullocks, we had indeed a sufficiency to have lasted for some time after the period at which we were actually relieved; but in converting it into wholesome food, we lay under the same difficulties as before. No bakers had accompanied Havelock. Bread was still a thing unseen, and only remembered; chuppatties constituted our staple fare. As with us, so with our newly-arrived friends, this preparation of flour was found unwholesome, producing with many persons diarrhœa and dysentery. Indeed, I attribute the illness which deprived us and the country of so valuable a life as that of General Havelock, to his inability to procure food properly prepared. The want of green food and vegetables was also much felt; and scorbutic affections increased, and became common during the blockade. The relieving force had brought a large supply of all those necessaries of which our garrison stood so much in need, viz. rum, spirits, wine, tea, coffee, sugar, and though last, not least, tobacco; but all these had been left at the Alum Bagh, and it was impossible to get them in. From plenty the relieving force, therefore, suddenly found itself reduced to almost absolute want; not only of the above necessaries, but also of clothing, which, as the weather during the blockade became daily colder, was severely felt. This was the more vexatious, because abundance of everything wanted was in store within four miles of us. How well and unmurmuringly all this was borne by our friends will be in the remembrance of us all.

The soldiers, who felt the loss of tobacco more severely than anything else, were put to a variety of shifts. They dried the tea-leaves left after infusion, and smoked them. The guava trees, and other garden shrubs, were stripped of their leaves, which, after having been dried in the sun, were used as a substitute for tobacco.

The want of proper change of food, and air, and the usual comforts and stimulants, had imperceptibly reduced the strength and physique of every one of the old garrison, even where the health had not, to appearance, been much impaired—as was soon felt upon attempting any vigorous exertion after leaving the place. A similar enfeeblement, though less in degree, became soon observable in the men of Outram's force.

By far, however, the most distressing feature of our

condition during the blockade was the state of the hospitals, and the sufferings of the sick and wounded. The hospital accommodation was limited, and the patients were much crowded. And though a large room in the Begum Kotee was appropriated to the use of the wounded officers, who were removed from the large hospital and placed in it, they gained little by the change; for this room was soon filled to excess, and the air became heavy, stifling, and poisonous. Some of the privates who were located in the hot but open sheds in the Horse Square, perhaps, suffered less than the rest. Others, again, were placed under canvas in tents, which were pitched for the purpose, near the large hospital. It was only by great exertion, and after delay of several days, that anything like the required quantity of room and bedding could be procured. Medicines were short: chloroform was wholly exhausted; there was no sago, arrow-root, or tapioca; milk was extremely scarce; so that it was hardly possible to prepare the rations in any form in which they would be acceptable to the weak stomachs of the wounded. The necessary consequence was, that the mortality among our wounded countrymen was great. Gangrene appeared, and every wound sloughed; so that slight ones not unfrequently proved fatal. Nothing could exceed the attention and exertions of the medical men, and both Generals frequently visited the sick beds, and did what they could to cheer and comfort the suffering. But sad it was to see so many gallant fellows succumb, and to be able to do so little for their assistance!

I was fortunately able, at this juncture, to render some assistance, by receiving several of the wounded into the upper story of our house. The capture of most of the surrounding guns had rendered it possible once more to occupy the upper story. The drawing-room, with its shattered dome, was still dangerous, and remained empty. The centre room on the south side, was still occasionally pierced by round shot. But a strong barricade, composed of boxes filled with earth, put up at the inner doorway, prevented the shot from entering the other rooms of the house. We were thus able to place in airy and well-ventilated apartments, and to supply with food better prepared than was obtainable in hospital, Colonel B. Fraser Tytler, and Lieutenant H. M. Havelock, who had been wounded in forcing the entrance of the city, and Major Eyre of the Bengal Artillery, who sickened immediately after it. Lieutenant Bonham of the Artillery, and Lieutenant Charlton of the 32nd, and Mr. Macrae and Mr. Cameron of the old garrison, who were making little progress in hospital, also joined us. Mr. Cameron unfortunately died: and was succeeded in the vacant room by an officer whose case was one of very general interest, and whose very appearance and manner were sufficient to excite sympathy and regard, Captain Denison of the 90th Light Infantry. He had been unfortunately struck by two bullets in the right arm, in securing one of the outposts at the palaces. He was in the act of extending his arm while pointing with his finger in a particular direction, when two balls struck it, fired by the hidden enemy. Amputation was necessary; but, unhappily, at that time, amputation was generally followed by fatal results. He was removed from the hospital to our house, when it was too late. He improved slightly on the first day, but afterwards relapsed, and never rallied. His place was filled by Captain Phipps of the same regiment; who, though wounded only by a slug in the thigh, was, from the bad condition of the wound, at one time in great danger.

We lost another officer in our house also, whose fate was much lamented, Captain L'Estrange of the 5th Fusiliers. He had received a very painful flesh wound at the storming of the enemy's battery, at the Canal Bridge. He was one of Major V. Eyre's companions in arms at the relief of Arrah; and had greatly distinguished himself in that glorious little campaign the success of which alone prevented a revolt throughout the whole Province of Behar. Unfortunately this gallant officer was also removed from hospital when it was too late. His case was already hopeless.

Sad is it to think that among the heroic little band of officers who accompanied Major Eyre from Buxar to the relief of Arrah, several have already perished. Among them none were more conspicuous than Captain L'Estrange and Captain the Hon. Robin Hood Hastings, whose untimely death at Ghazeepoor we afterwards learnt.

Captain L'Estrange's place was taken by Captain Adair of the 5th Fusiliers, who happily survived.

I have already referred to the great relief which the old garrison experienced from the capture and destruction of the enemy's batteries. During the blockade, they did not attempt to advance these so close as they had done before. They generally placed their guns at a greater distance, and not unfrequently their shot did more damage than when the guns were nearer, by falling inside the intrenchment, instead of passing over it. The extent of the relief thus obtained may be estimated from the instance of my post, where, in lieu of seven guns bearing upon the house, we never during the blockade had more than three; one of these, a loud ringing brass gun, which they used to discharge four or five times at early dawn, was indeed placed within 240 yards, but it was fired in such a position that the shot always flew over our heads. Their most damaging battery was a new one placed at the south-east corner of the old intrenchment behind Phillips' house, which could not be reached by our guns, and which did considerable damage to the Judicial Commissioners' post, held by Captain Germon, 13th N. I.

The ingenuity of the enemy, but at the same time the poverty of his military resources, was evinced by the projectiles which were thrown from his mortars into our works during the blockade. The mutineers had two large mortars, but possessed no shells for them; and instead of shells fired huge cylinders of wood, which not unfrequently occasioned loss of life. Some of these were eighteen inches long by twelve diameter, and such was their weight that they must have pierced any but a very strong roof, if struck by them. They also threw in shells made of hollowed stone, of large size, which generally burst well, breaking into several fragments. They also made and fired vertically a number of brass shells of small size: but these generally failed to burst, from some defect in the arrangement of the fuse. I had a collection of these missiles, which would have been hereafter interesting; but they were abandoned with the rest of my property when the place was evacuated.

Having thus endeavoured to convey a general idea of the state of things inside cur works during the blockade, I proceed to note the several occurrences which appear to be of interest.

Sir James Outram was very anxious that measures should be taken to afford us the means of communicating with the native grain merchants, and through them the means of introducing supplies. I therefore frequently consulted with Meer Furzund Ali, the Artillery Darogah, and Runjeet Singh, and other natives who formed my garrison, on the subject. They all recommended the course which also approved itself to me, viz. the seizure of the iron bridge and the occupation of the grain suburb of Aleegunje, beyond it. Aleegunje abuts upon the open country, and by holding it our communications would have been greatly improved. Mention has already been made of Meer Furzund Ali, and I must say something more of Runjeet Singh, who also rendered good service during the siege.

Runjeet Singh is an old pensioned native officer of our sepoy army: a native of Duriabad, in Oudh, where he was found by Captain Hawes, when he formed there the cantonment of the 5th O. I. Infantry. Runjeet Singh had been dispossessed of two villages belonging to him by a neighbouring talooqdar, which he now re-claimed, and which were restored to him by the British district officer. On the occurrence of the mutinies, and the disorganization of our Government, Runjeet Singh thought it best to leave the neighbourhood, fearing the vengeance of the talooqdar. He came therefore to Lucknow and offered his service, and was enrolled among the pensioner force, which aided in the defence of the Residency, and was stationed at my post. Before the siege, he brought in a number of other pensioners, all of whom behaved well; and it was he who recommended to us the messenger "Ungud," also a pensioned sepoy, who rendered such signal service in conveying our communications. Runjeet Singh was always cheerful, and bore himself admirably during the siege, and has been liberally rewarded.

During the day of the 1st of October, orders were

issued for the attack of the iron bridge, but they were subsequently countermanded, and an attack in force on the enemy's Cawnpoor battery ordered instead. The firing of the force of between 500 and 600 men, composed of detachments of different regiments under Colonel Napier, ordered to attack the enemy's Cawnpoor road battery, began at 3, P.M. In this battery, known also as Phillips' Garden Battery, the enemy were believed to have the 8-inch howitzer taken from us at Chinhut, which the General was very anxious to recover. It appeared, on subsequent inquiry, that our party had gone steadily to work, and had possessed themselves by nightfall of certain houses commanding the enemy's battery. Some of the buildings, however, remaining in the hands of the rebels, it was thought advisable to await the morning before the attack was made. Early next day, the battery was taken and three guns, viz. two 9-pounders and one 6-pounder captured, with small loss to ourselves. But the 8-inch howitzer was not found. It was reported that this piece had been removed by the enemy during the night. Singularly enough this party discovered, and rescued from death a private of the 1st Madras Fusiliers, who three days before had fallen down a well, and had remained in it all that time undiscovered.

On the 2nd of October, a heavy cannonade was kept up from the 18-pounders of the Redan battery, upon the buildings at the entrance to the iron bridge, leading to the belief that an attack in that quarter was intended.

On the 3rd of October, the 78th Highlanders, under Major Haliburton, began to extend our position along the direct Cawnpoor road, working from house to house. On the 4th he was reported to have been mortally wounded, and died on the 5th. Major Stephenson,* also, of the Madras Fusiliers, and several other officers having been severely wounded on the same service, the attempt to extend our position in that direction was abandoned, and the troops were retired early on the 6th. Our extreme position in that direction accordingly extended up to the barricade thrown across the Cawnpoor road opposite Anderson's house. Probably in consequence of the withdrawal of our advanced posts, the enemy pressed on, and assembled in large numbers in the forenoon, in the buildings around the centre bastion of my post, from which they kept up a very severe fire of musketry. We replied sharply from our loopholes; but they were so close that their shot repeatedly struck the loopholes, and one of my levies was shot dead by a ball which entered by a loophole through which he and myself were looking at the same time. My head being a little withdrawn at the moment, I was mercifully preserved, and only received some brickdust in the face.

On the subject of loopholes it may be as well to mention the result of our experience in respect to their construction. Those which we first made were found to be much too large. They were usually, that is at first, made in the form of a perpendicular slit in the parapet-wall, about four inches wide externally, and widening inside to four or five times that width; much in appearance resembling what are seen surmounting the turrets of European castellated buildings. These, however, were found to admit the enemy's bullets too easily, and in their subsequent construction we took a lesson from themselves, by merely piercing a hole through the wall large enough externally to permit of the muzzle of a musket or

* This gallant officer afterwards died of the wound he received.

double barrel to protrude. On the inside the loophole was made considerably wider, so as to allow of aim being taken to the right or left. Our original defective construction of this description of defence cost us many valuable lives; and in the new fortifications which I have since had the opportunity of observing elsewhere, I have noticed the same defect. Similarly, our first embrasures for artillery were often made too wide in the interior opening. Two feet afford a space amply sufficient to work a long 18-pounder, widening, of course, to five feet or more externally.

The enemy suffered on the same day a severe check, with a loss of, some say thirty, and some 150 men, at the Furhut Buksh Palace, where they attacked and followed inside our lines a party of our work-people. The Seikhs and Europeans closed in behind them, and killed a large number.

Fodder continuing to get daily scarcer, the General was still anxious that the Irregular and Volunteer Cavalry should make their way out to Alum Bagh, failing which, he declared that all the horses must probably be turned out, not excepting his own chargers. One of our pensioned sepoys assured me, at the close of the first week, that if we could extend our position to the Dilkoosha road, he should be able to summon a number of zemindars, through whom arrangements for supplies could be made. I mentioned this to the General, but the extension of our position was considered impossible. We lost during this week Lieutenant G. W. Greene, of the 13th N. I. of dysentery.

We were roused at my garrison on the night of the 9th of October by General Outram's Private Secretary, Mr. W. J. Money, coming over with the good tidings of the capture of Dehli, the king and his begum having been made prisoners: and the march of Brigadier Greathed towards Oudh commenced. This, though not wholly unexpected, was great news, and gave much encouragement to the native portion of our garrison, who now began to think that they did not after all choose their side so badly. The General's despatch in reply to this news urged the rapid advance of Greathed's brigade upon Lucknow. He, however, then expected a further six weeks' blockade; and the event proved that he was not wrong in his expectations.

News was received on the 10th of October through Captain Bruce, the Military Magistrate at Cawnpoor, of the action fought at Boolundshuhur by Brigadier Greathed's column. Anticipating its early arrival, Captain Bruce proposed to join it with a hundred of his "low-caste police." He had raised at Cawnpoor a police force, consisting solely of men of the lowest caste, viz. "mehturs," or sweepers; and I understood that they had been found exceedingly useful. Whether, however, it would be desirable to extend further this principle of enlisting the lowest caste men *only*, into our new police, certainly admits of a doubt. Most assuredly I would include this class in every description of native force which may hereafter be raised; but to enlist these men *only*, to the exclusion of others, would, I think, answer no good purpose, and would give great general offence.

I will now make a few extracts from my daily journal.

October 14*th*.—The rascally Seikh, Jowahir Singh, who deserted from my post a few days before the arrival of the relief force, returned into the intrenchment this day. He had the assurance to be the bearer of a message from Rajah Man Singh (of Shagunje) offering to us an escort of 10,000 men, if we will evacuate the place, and retire to Cawnpoor! He deserves to be hanged. He also brought overtures, I understood, from the Seikhs who before deserted us; and who now think of deserting back again. These rascals were referred to the General commanding at Cawnpoor, and told to present themselves to him. There is, I think, some disposition to exaggerate the influence and importance of Rajah Man Singh, as well as to palliate his misconduct. Of his position in the province I have already elsewhere given an account. His conduct has simply been that of a time-server. He wished to stand sufficiently well with both parties, ourselves and our enemies, to enable him to join whichever proved victorious. With this view he protected our officers and their families, while coquetting with the mutineer leaders, and sending his brother on a mission to the Nana at Cawnpoor. He long wavered about joining the rebels with his rabble troops; but when General Havelock retired for the second time from his advance on Lucknow, and recrossed the river, he thought that fortune had declared against us, and joined the mutineer force at Lucknow. At present the prospects of the mutineers are gloomy, and Man Singh would, no doubt, be glad to feel his way towards the abandonment of their cause, if necessary. I really regard it to be of little importance to ourselves what part he takes.

October 15*th.* — Accounts from Captain Sibley, commanding at Alum Bagh, this day received, mention the desertion of a great number of camp followers from that post, from want of food. Also the great increase of the sick there, which now amount to 135!

October 16th.—This night, and not unfrequently during the blockade, the enemy opened a heavy fire upon our works during the night, causing us to turn out and prepare for attack. But they never attacked or showed themselves in the open ground.

October 17th.—The enemy exploded two mines this day, blowing down by the first a portion of the enclosing wall of the advanced Garden Battery beyond the Chutturmunzil Palace, where they made a bold show of entering, bringing their colours into the breach. The leading men being shot down, however, they retired, leaving twelve dead bodies on the ground. The second mine, which exploded in the afternoon, destroyed one of our outposts in the Furhut Buksh Palace, killing three men.

October 19th. — Visited this morning the 78th Highlanders, or Lockhart's post, and barricade across the main street, leading from the Kaiser Bagh towards the Bailey Guard Gate. This barricade is about 300 or 400 yards from the gate. It was through this street that Generals Outram and Havelock, with the 78th and the Ferozepoor Regt. Seikhs, charged in, on the memorable 25th of September. Our poor fellows must have fallen at every fourth or fifth step; and now their bodies are lying where they fell, covered with a little earth. The body of Colonel Bazely, of the Artillery, whose fate was for some time uncertain, was found in this street a short distance beyond the barricade, and was recognised by the ring he wore. The effluvium here is still very bad. In the evening, visited the advanced Garden post beyond the Chutturmunzil Palace, held by the 90th Regt. From the loopholes of a building on the south side of this garden, you look out upon the open place or square, where still are seen the doolies which contained those of our unfortunate wounded, who were cut off on the 26th of September.

October 20th.—A cossid brought in to the General despatches from Captain Bruce at Cawnpoor, from which it appears that Rajah Man Singh's agent sent into Cawnpoor a letter for Sir James Outram, containing a defence of his conduct. He explains his having joined the mutineers, by stating that they had made prisoner of his aunt at Lucknow, which compelled him to come in; that he was preparing to leave the city again with his levies, when he learnt that our troops had forced their way in, and were about to attack the Kaiser Bagh; and that fearing the dishonour of the King's begums by us, he had hurried back to their defence. He hoped General Outram would not think the worse of him for thus acting; but did not wish to have his name associated with the rebels, and promised that on receipt of a safe conduct his agent should attend. Captain Bruce's answer was a good one. "That Man Singh might well have known that we did not war with women, and that the humblest female was secure, much more the family of the King; that if a friend, Man Singh must separate himself from the rebels, and might then send in his agent to General Outram at Lucknow." Sir James replied much to the same effect, and Man Singh professed compliance, and his agent was more than once expected; but he, nevertheless, never came, neither did his master dissociate himself from the rebels.

October 21st.—Our compound, meaning the enclosure surrounding our house, continues, indeed it continued to the end of the blockade, exposed to the enemy's musketry from two high square buildings known as the Black and Gray Towers; and to go across it was always dangerous. To enable the ladies and other inmates of our garrison to get some fresh air, the porch of the house had been barricaded, by enclosing two sides, and leaving one side open. This morning, while the ladies were seated there, one of our native servants was shot dead within a few steps of them; and as they kept up a heavy musketry fire from the towers, a 9-pounder was opened upon them, which soon cleared them out. Next day, however, Captain Thomas's (Artillery) orderly, entering our compound after him, was shot through the body by a musket-ball from the same quarter.

October 22nd.—The enemy made an attack on Alum Bagh this day, and, hearing the cannonade, we were a little anxious. Subsequently, however, we heard that they had been beaten off, without ever coming to a close attack.

October 26th.—The good news of the defeat of the Mhow mutineers, by Brigadier Greathed's column, at Agra, reached us to-day.

October 28th.—We lost to-day an excellent officer, Captain Graydon, of the 44th N. I., in command of Innes' post, who was struck by a musket-ball in superintending the new works beyond that post.

October 30th.—In the account already given of the mutinies at Seetapoor and Mohumdee, mention was made of the escape from the former place of Lieutenant Burns, 10th O. I. Infantry, and of a young civil officer, Sir Mounstuart Jackson and his two sisters, and from the massacre near Aurungabad of Captain Patrick Orr; and of their having together found a refuge with Raja Lonee Singh talooqdar of Mithowlee. Before the siege commenced, communications had been received from all three gentlemen. So long as the mutineer regiments remained in the neighbourhood of Seetapoor, it was vain to attempt their rescue; but when the 41st N. I. and 10th O. I. Infantry had crossed the Ganges to Futtehgurh, and the two other regiments had removed to Mohumdabad, the road by Seetapoor to Mithowlee was left open: and I had then proposed that a party of Volunteer and Seikh Cavalry should be sent to bring in the refugees. The measure, however, was thought too hazardous, and was not attempted; though great interest was felt by all at Lucknow in the sufferers, and especially in the two Misses Jackson, who had but recently come out from England, and had resided for some months at the capital, before they removed to Seetapoor. After the siege had commenced, we received no further tidings of these refugees, until General Outram's arrival. From him we learnt that he had heard from Captain Patrick Orr, who was very anxious that his party should leave Mithowlee and join the General's army. This could not be effected; and reports had got about, after the arrival of the relief force, that the mutineers had got possession of them; and had brought them prisoners to Lucknow. On this day a letter from Captain Patrick Orr was received by his brother, Captain Alexander Orr, which confirmed these sad reports. The letter was dated the 29th, and bore the signatures of the six refugees, viz. Captain Patrick Orr and Mrs. Orr, Sir Mounstuart and Miss Madeleine Jackson, Lieutenant G. Burns, and Serjeant-Major Morton. It mentioned that there were two children with the party, viz. little Sophy Christian, and a daughter of Captain Orr's; that they had been sent in by Raja Lonee Singh, the men being put in chains; and that since their arrival at Lucknow they had been relieved from their fetters, and had been well treated in the Kaiser Bagh.

Sad news was this; and it is to be hoped that a severe retribution will some day fall on Lonee Singh, for thus basely surrendering our friends. Under existing circumstances, there was no possibility of rendering aid, and the best that could be hoped was, that their lives might not be taken. Of this, however, no assurance could be felt, considering the character of the bloodthirsty wretches in whose hands they were. When Sir Colin Campbell's army left Lucknow, nothing had been effected for the relief of the prisoners. Subsequent accounts have mentioned the death from sickness of little Sophy Christian; the murder of the men; and the final escape of the two ladies, and of Mrs. Orr's daughter. These ladies were rescued, after the capture of the city of Lucknow, by Captain McNeill and Lieutenant Bogle, of the Bengal Artillery. From the account given by them it appeared that they had been protected and well treated by one Darogah Wajid Alee.

Certain intelligence having now been received of the early approach of a relieving force, under the Commander-in-Chief in person, the General despatched to-night to Alum Bagh, plans of the city and its approaches, together with his advice as to the best means of effecting a junction of the forces. The plan recommended by Sir James Outram was that eventually followed by Sir Colin Campbell, viz. to make a *détour* from Alum Bagh to the right to the Dilkoosha, and thence advance by the Martinière, Sekundur Bagh &c. Some anxiety was felt respecting the safe receipt of this despatch, and the authorities at Alum Bagh were instructed to notify the arrival of the messenger by hoisting a flag. It was satisfactory, therefore, to see next day the ensign flying from the top of the Alum Bagh Garden House. This success suggested the idea of communicating by semaphore telegraph, although the distance was great; and from the haze which often overhung the city, it was uncertain whether our glasses could distinguish the movements of the machine. All necessary particulars being fortunately found under the head "Telegraph," in the "Penny Cyclopædia," in my library, the General ordered the immediate erection of a semaphore on the top of the Residency, and copies of the necessary instructions were sent to Alum Bagh.

CHAPTER XVII.

THE LONG-LOOKED-FOR-RELIEF—NOVEMBER.

General Havelock looks ill.—Casualties on the 4th of November.—Ensign Dashwood mortally wounded.—News received of General Hope Grant's approach.—Captain R. P. Anderson's post.—Mr. Kavanagh's enterprise.—He reaches the Commander-in-Chief's camp in safety.—His account of the appearance of the city.—The arrival of the Commander-in-Chief at Alum Bagh telegraphed on the 13th.—On the 14th of November, his force seen advancing towards the Dilkoosha.—Lieutenant Havelock and Mr. Gubbins repair on the 15th to the top of the Chutturmunzil.—Description of the beautiful and extensive view.—Sir Colin's force did not advance on that day.—Its advance on the 16th of November as seen from the top of the Chutturmunzil, described.—The force reaches the Sekundur Bagh; then the Shah Nujeef, and the Kudum Rusool.—Appearance of the groups of the opposing enemy.—Co-operation of our own batteries.—Mines under the wall concealing our advanced battery, sprung.—The battery opens.—The storming party issues and carry the steam-engine house, king's stables and Hirun Khana.—The serjeant's bungalow fired.—Account of the storming of the Sekundur Bagh, and Shah Nujeef.—Leave certificate men among the slain.—Operations of the 17th of November.—Bombardment of the 32nd Mess-house.—Storming party. —Mess-house occupied ; Tara Kotee taken ; Motee Munzil taken.—Communication betweeen the armies effected.—The Generals meet.—Orders made known for the immediate abandonment of the Residency. —Disappointment of the garrison.—General Havelock hears of the honours bestowed upon him.—It is impossible to over-estimate his services.—The Kaiser Bagh breached on the 18th of November.—Preparations for evacuating the position.—Native guns burst.—Further operations of Sir Colin's army.—Brigadier Russell disabled.—Colonel Biddulph killed.—Sir Colin's head-quarters.—He visits the intrenchment once.—The ladies, and sick, and wounded leave the intrenchment on the 19th, and proceed to the Dilkoosha.—Mr. Gubbins visits Sir Colin's head-quarters.—Anecdote of Sir Colin Campbell.—Sandy lane leading to the Dilkoosha.—General order of Commander-in-Chief.—Supplementary order.—The garrison retires on the night of the 22nd of November.—Captain Waterman's escape.—Camp at Dilkoosha on the 23rd.—Letters and papers received.—Sir Henry Havelock expires at Dilkoosha.—His remains interred at Alum Bagh.—Camp moves to Alum Bagh.—Description of Alum Bagh.—

Halt there on the 25th and 26th.—March to Cawnpoor.—Troops composing Sir Colin's army.—Its number and loss.—Remarks on the relief.—The Commander-in-Chief's order of the 23rd of November.

We now entered the fifth, and happily the last month of the siege. The only entry worth notice on this date, which I find in my Journal, is, that General Havelock was not looking well, but pale and thin; no doubt from want of proper stimulant and food, and from the confinement and bad air, and the effect of former long exposure.

November 2nd and *3rd.*—The enemy's musketry continuing to be very annoying from the south side, and having lost another of my native levies, shot through the head, while walking across the compound on the 2nd, I had a quantity of sun-dried bricks made, with which, during the night, the wall was raised four feet, so as to screen our west portico and part of the compound from the fire of the enemy's towers. Our Generals seem to contemplate that the Kaiser Bagh shall be assaulted as soon as Sir Colin's army arrives, on two sides, viz. by his force from the side of the Dilkoosha, and by ours from our present position.

November 4th.—This day exemplified a feature of our siege life, which we had often before noticed, viz. that upon many of the days which appeared to be the quietest, when neither the enemy attacked, nor we had made a sortie, several casualties would occur. In the forenoon, Ensign Dashwood, 48th N. I., while sitting sketching in the Residency grounds, was struck by a round shot, and lost both his legs. The shot was fired from across the river from a 6-pounder gun, which the enemy used to move about, firing first from one quarter, and then from another. In this case poor young Dashwood had warning from a first shot fired by the enemy, which passed near him. Still he did not move, and received his death-wound from a second discharge. Two men of the 5th were mortally wounded, by exposing themselves in the advanced garden post; and two more, a man of the 32nd, and an artilleryman, were badly hurt at my post, making five casualties.

November 6th.—News was received this day that the Dehli column, under General Hope Grant, had reached a position on this side of the Bunnee Bridge, and were halted there. Also that the Commander-in-Chief had arrived at Cawnpoor, and was expected at Alum Bagh by the 10th. This glad news has put us all on the *qui vive.*

The General has ordered the construction of a battery for heavy guns, to be erected in the extreme advanced garden, in order to co-operate with the relieving force. This garden is surrounded by a very high wall, which it is intended to mine and blow down, so as to unmask our heavy battery when ready.

All along during the blockade some anxiety had been felt respecting the movements of the mutineer Gwalior Contingent, which, with a large park of artillery, including a number of heavy guns, were approaching the Jumna. Despatches this day received, mentioned that they were marching on Jaloun, which is on the direct road from Gwalior towards Calpee and Cawnpoor. Doubtless the Nana has been at work there.

November 10th.—Went over Anderson's house, today, the outpost at the south-east angle of our original position, held by Captain R. P. Anderson, and Mr. Capper, C. S. It has been terribly battered, and the exposed side is a ruin. It is extraordinary how the garrison, cooped up in so small a space, did not suffer more from the enemy's 8-inch shells, of which several burst inside the building. It became known this day, that on the previous night, Mr. T. H. Kavanagh, belonging to the uncovenanted service, had gone out of the position, having volunteered to reach the Commander-in-Chief's camp, in order to make himself useful as a guide. The undertaking was most hazardous, from the number of the enemy's posts and pickets which must necessarily be passed; besides which, the road followed by Mr. Kavanagh led through the heart of the city. We were therefore much relieved by seeing the signal hoisted at the Alum Bagh which was to announce his safe arrival. Mr. Kavanagh disguised himself as a native budmâsh, or irregular mutineer soldier of the city, "with sword and shield, native shoes, tight trousers, a yellow silk koortah (or jacket) over a tight-fitting white muslin shirt; a coloured chintz sheet thrown round the shoulders, a cream-coloured turban, and a white waistband or cummurbund. His face down to the shoulders, and hands to the wrist, were coloured with lamp-black, the cork used being dipped in oil to cause the colour to adhere." Thus attired, he placed himself under the guidance of a native scout, named Kunnoujeelall, who had before been employed to convey correspondence. After nightfall they forded the Goomtee, the depth of water being about four and a half feet, and the river's breadth 200 feet, re-dressed on the further side, and went up its left bank, passing by several of the enemy's pickets, until they reached the iron bridge; which they crossed, and threaded their way through the heart of the city to the open country on the further side. Before reaching it they lost their way, and finding it dangerous to make for

Alum Bagh, proceeded on beyond it, until they reached in safety the Commander-in-Chief's camp.

Respecting the appearance of the city, Mr. Kavanagh remarks that the chouk, or principal street, was not lighted as much as it used to be before the mutinies, nor was it so crowded; and that the part of the city through which he passed seemed to have been deserted by at least a third of its inhabitants. His account thus confirms those which had frequently been given to us by the natives, of the oppressive practices of the mutineers, and of large numbers of the native merchants and other citizens having abandoned the city and removed elsewhere. Mr. Kavanagh's enterprise was most daring, and deserves the highest commendation; and it is gratifying to know that he has been highly rewarded by Government with a present of 2000*l.* in money, and admission into the regular Civil Service of India.

November 11*th.*—The enemy have repaired their former battery in the lane south of my post, and opened a gun upon us this morning. Our new battery in the Goindah lines, however, having been completed and armed, we were able to silence their fire with a few discharges.

November 12*th.*—At noon to-day, communication by semaphore was effected between the Residency and Alum Bagh. The arrival of the chief at Alum Bagh, and his intended advance to Dilkoosha on the 14th, was announced by telegraph. The enemy do not seem to know the meaning of the working of the long arms of the machine, but observing the figures occasionally on the roof, have opened a smart fire of musketry upon it. Sandbag defences have, however, been piled on the roof, so that their fire is harmless.

November 13*th.*—The chief telegraphed from Alum Bagh his positive intention of moving on the Dilkoosha to-morrow at 7, A.M. Colonel Campbell, C.B., of the 90th Foot, sunk last night. He was wounded in the leg on the 26th September, but, like so many others, the wound became unhealthy, and amputation was necessary, which he had not strength to bear. The mines intended to bring down the wall, which conceals our new advanced heavy battery, were charged this night.

November 14*th.*—During the forenoon, the advance of the relieving force towards the Dilkoosha was clearly visible from the top of the Residency, the smoke of the guns being plainly seen; and by the evening, we could distinguish that the Dilkoosha was in possession of our troops. After dusk, beacon signals lighted on the Dilkoosha and Martinière, which were answered from the Residency top, announced that both buildings were in the possession of our friends. The enemy around our post appear nowise disheartened, if we may judge by the continued musketry fire which they kept up during the night.

November 15*th.*—The Commander-in-Chief being expected to advance from the Dilkoosha and Martinière to-day, it had been intended to unmask our new battery by exploding the mines under the surrounding wall about 10, A.M. Accordingly, after an early breakfast, Lieutenant H. M. Havelock and myself repaired to the top of the Chutturmunzil Palace, from which all the operations could be watched. The illustration* of this lofty and elegant building, by the pencil of Colonel Vincent Eyre, Artillery, which is given, will convey a good idea of our position. But I must

* Lost in the Ava.

endeavour to give some description of the extended and beautiful view which it commands. Standing on this elevated position and facing eastward towards the Dilkoosha Park, you look perpendicularly down upon the Goomtee which skirts the building on your left. Beyond this extends a level plain, covered with green sward, broken and bounded by various royal residences and gardens. The nearest of these is the "Dilaram" or "Heartsease" House, which stands near the river bank, and is now unoccupied. Further on, but thrown back at the distance of a mile, is the Badshah Bagh, or King's Garden, comprising buildings of some size and elegance, embosomed in a thicket of orange and other fruit trees. This is occupied by the enemy, of whom one or two can be distinguished upon the roof looking out. Here they have also a battery of two heavy guns, from which a shot is occasionally fired: the building where ourselves are seated being generally the mark.

Further on and near the river lies the Hâzuree Bagh, or Breakfast Garden, lately occupied as a residence by one of our officers, but now abandoned. Only two days ago the enemy had a heavy gun there in position in the gateway; but our glasses tell us that it is no longer there. It has been removed, no doubt, to be used in repelling the advance of our countrymen. The eye then glances down a long reach of the river, till it rests upon the Chukker Kotee, before the residence of Major Gall, of the Irregular Cavalry, now occupied by the enemy, who have established below it a bridge of boats, which is generally taken to pieces at night, and reconstructed in the morning. They are now restoring it as we look. The enemy is, however, manifestly not quite at ease, for we see numbers of irregular zemindaree foot soldiers wading across the river to the other side, carrying on their heads matchlocks and bundles. The left guns of our new masked battery would, but for the intervening wall, sweep this long reach of the river and command the bridge of boats. All that would be required, in order to bring them to bear upon it, would be a hole in the wall a couple of yards square, which could be easily made. On the right bank of the Goomtee the country is thickly wooded as far as we can see, with mango groves and fruit gardens; the eye resting in the distance on the double-storied mansion of the Dilkoosha, which looks like an old French château.

Nearer, and a little to the left, are seen the lofty and fantastic stories of the Martinière; and we can with our glasses distinguish the figures of our men passing along the open galleries. Nearer still, but yet distant, we distinguish the walls and gateway of the Sekundur Bagh, marked by its gilt-topped turrets, and here we can see that numbers of the enemy are clustering. Some irregular horsemen are moving about outside. A few of them wear the red uniform which distinguished the 15th Regt., which mutinied last June at Sultanpoor, and looked on at the death of their brave commander Fisher.

Still nearer, and to the left, stands that old renovated tomb, high on a mound overlooking the river; that is the Kuddum Rusool, first used by us as a powder-magazine, now occupied by the enemy. And closely adjoining it, that flat white dome marks the site of the Shah Nujeef, which is the name given to the tomb of one of the former kings of Oudh, Ghazeeooddeen Hydur. It is a strong massive building, standing among a number of low mud huts, and surrounded by trees. Its strength is not discovered till you approach near this building, and here it was that our advancing troops received their only short check.

As the eye withdraws to the nearer vicinity, it now catches a conspicuous and solid-looking building of two stories, distinguished by four towers at the corners. This is known as the Mess-House of the 32nd Regt., but was named under the native rule Khoorsheyd Munzil, or Happy Palace. We must scrutinize this building with the glass. Its structure is massive; all the windows on the ground-floor are furnished with strong iron gratings, and it is surrounded by a moat all round, passable only at the two entrances, of which the principal one immediately faces us. But see! the enemy has not been idle; all those windows are bricked up inside the iron-grating, for three parts of their height, and the masonry is most carefully loopholed. It may cost many lives to take that house unless it is carefully approached. A garden of low trees and bushes surrounds it, which is itself enclosed by a mud wall, separating it from the high road. It was this enclosing mud wall which was lined by the enemy's musketeers on the 26th of September, and on the open space near the road stood the 24-pounder gun, which it was impossible to approach from the leaden tempest which was poured upon it. The mess-house itself bears testimony that our heavy guns did not traverse the road in front of it in vain, on the 25th. Those large holes, one so conspicuous in the nearest tower on the left side, is the mark of one of our 8-inch shells, directed by Lieutenant Fraser.

But crossing the road to the nearer side, what is that extensive range of building abutting upon the river, and distinguished by a pavilion with four richly-gilded domes? This is the Motee Munzil, or Pearl Palace, and that pavilion is the Shah Munzil, or Royal

Hall. It is the prettiest building of the kind at Lucknow, spacious and airy. Here European guests used to be invited to banquets, and to view the fights of animals on the opposite side of the stream. It was in a lane formed by two walls on the south face of this enclosure that our wounded, under escort of the 90th, spent the night of the memorable 25th September, and there also Colonel Campbell received his wound.

Close on the near side of the Motee Munzil stands a European-looking building in an extensive orange garden. This is called Martin's House, but was the royal library in the king's time. The enclosure of Martin's house is separated from our advanced garden post by a small open space, exposed to the fire of the Kaiser Bagh; on the near side of which stand the steam-engine house and its dependent buildings. These it is intended to assail from our advanced battery, and to capture, so soon as Sir Colin's force shall have approached sufficiently near. The buildings which have been severally described must be taken before the forces can unite.

To the right of the 32nd mess-house, and separated from it by a narrow lane, stands the Tara Kotee, or Observatory, a handsome and classically-designed building, erected by the late astronomer, Colonel Wilcox. This place, from the sandbags upon the roof, we see that the enemy intend to defend.

And now the eye falls upon the gilded domes, and cupolas, and archways of the Kaiser Bagh palace, which forms a picture of itself. Its numerous buildings and squares cover a very large area, and it is chiefly the creation of the present ex-King. Those two large mausoleums, however, belong to a former age. The larger is the tomb of Saadut Alee Khan, the most sagacious ruler that Oudh has had, and the smaller one of his mother. Their substantial masonry contrasts strongly with the less solid modern edifices: and they are destined, unless they are destroyed by the hand of war, long to survive them.

But what is that dark superstructure which fringes the palace gateway and curtain wall? It is a mud-wall parapet closely loopholed, and from those loopholes a fierce fire of musketry was kept up on our troops advancing towards their present position under General Havelock.

In rear of the Kaiser Bagh, and to our right, extends the city, and under that large yellow house on the direct Cawnpoor road the enemy have an 18-pounder, from which ever and anon they send a heavy shot into one of the umbrella-topped buildings near us, where they may espy figures to be moving. To avoid attracting the attention of the gunners at this battery, and of those who are watching us from the Badshah Bagh across the river, we show ourselves as little as possible at the windows of our airy room. In our rear are the battered fronts of the buildings of the old Residency post, and the scarcely-less battered Clock Tower, formerly held by the enemy. In front again, and at our feet, so near that we can hail the officers, is the new battery of six mortars, which are intended ere long to open on the Kaiser Bagh. And directly beyond them lies the garden containing our advanced battery, the unmasking of which we came to witness. It is, indeed, a lovely view which is obtained from the top of the Chutturmunzil. But the city of Lucknow is beyond doubt very beautiful and surpasses every city in India that I have seen. On this occasion, however, beauty was not the main recommendation to the Chutturmunzil top, but the command which it gave us, so far as the wooded nature of the country would permit, of the line along which the Commander-in-Chief must advance.

We were, however, doomed to disappointment on the 15th of November, for Sir Colin Campbell did not advance. Towards noon the enemy reconstructed their bridge of boats, and we distinguished a number of irregular troops, cavalry and infantry, who crossed to our side of the river, formed, and advanced towards the Martinière, where the wood soon concealed them. Soon another similar party, but accompanied by guns, advanced from the Kaiser Bagh to join the first, and was lost to our sight. Presently our guns were seen to open on the right face of the Martinière, and soon we saw the enemy's horse, foot, and guns return much faster than they had gone. In the evening the Commander-in-Chief erected a telegraph on top of the Martinière, and the communication "advance to-morrow" was made out just before dark.

November 16*th.*—Accordingly Havelock and I again repaired by 9, A.M., this day to the upper story of the Chutturmunzil. But the enemy at the Badshah Bagh across the river were not disposed to let us view this day's proceedings in quiet, and twice dislodged us with round shot from their battery. However we as often returned. About 10, A.M., the firing of artillery on *our* left, *i.e.* the river side of the Martinière, clearly showed that the chief was advancing. The advance presently reached nearly to the Sekundur Bagh, where a very heavy rattle of musketry began, and was kept up for some time. We could, by aid of our glasses, distinguish our guns opening on the place, and see many of the shot strike. Presently the tide of war appeared to reach the building itself, and we could plainly see the gleaming bayonets of our men pouring into it. After awhile they emerge again, and presently appear to be engaged with the enemy about the Shah Nujeef Tomb and the Kudum Rusool. Our vision is sadly impeded by buildings and the thick wood with which the environs are covered. Here and there we obtain a glimpse. One opening in the trees we steadily watch, and see heavy guns moving towards the Shah Nujeef and horse artillery pass, and repass. And now we clearly distinguish the costume of a Highland regiment. Oh! that must be the 93rd.

But do you see yon low range of mud building, with tiled roof? mark the number of sepoys hiding behind it, and peering out towards the Shah Nujeef, and occasionally one fires; but see! the further end of the range has been fired, and the enemy is flying from his covert as fast as his heels will take him. Mark again that party of irregular foot soldiers carrying matchlocks, who are advancing from the direction of the Kaiser Bagh. They enter the shrubbery of the 32nd mess-house, and make their way through the trees and bushes towards the scene of action. Another group of matchlock men have collected at a gap in the mud enclosing wall of the mess-house facing the Shah Nujeef. But they do not fire: one man only looks through the opening, the rest are safely sheltered behind the wall. Now watch again the opening in the trees to see what is doing at the Shah Nujeef. The firing continues, and all that we can distinguish are a few sepoys carrying muskets, running for their lives. This much, however, is no bad symptom: the place must have been carried.

And now it is our time to assist; and the order is given to unmask our battery, and commence the attack of the steam-engine house and dependent buildings. First begin the mortars at our feet, which throw a flight of shells into the buildings to clear them and an adjacent stockade of the enemy. They are worked by Captain Maude, R.A., and burst well. And now the General is impatient that the battery should open; but there is some delay about springing the mines which are to level the surrounding wall. At length fire is applied, and they explode; but weakly. Two breaches are made to the right, with a long piece of wall intervening: and on the left the wall is only split and shaken. This is disappointing; as all the guns cannot be worked, but it could not have been helped: the engineers had laid abundance of powder, but in the interval of the chief's unexpected halt the powder got damp. So soon as the dust clears away and discloses the breach, a heavy fire of musketry and shot is directed towards it by the enemy from the Kaiser Bagh—and as the room from which we are gazing is directly in the line of fire, it soon dislodges me. General Outram remains, and narrowly escapes being struck by a 6-lb. shot. And now our heavy guns open a deafening reply, pounding the steam-engine buildings and the Hirun Khana; and the enemy's fire so far relaxes as to enable me to resume my forward post. But that long piece of wall which interposes in front of our battery sadly impedes the fire of our artillery. The guns are turned upon it, and round shot after round shot passes through it as it would through a sheet of paper, leaving only a round hole behind. At last, however, large masses crumble and break away, affording on the right at least a clear space for the artillery. And now two mines driven under the Hirun Khana explode, throwing up bricks and timber high into the air; and knowing that the time for making the assault has come, we are on the tiptoe of expectation. And so are the brave fellows of the

5th, 64th, 84th, 87th, and 90th, who, after so many weeks of confinement and patient endurance, are awaiting the signal to advance.

It is half-past three, and the bugle sounds, loudly responded to by cheers from the palaces; and see! the storming party are already at the breach fronting our battery. They scramble up the broken ground, the officer leading a few paces ahead, the men cheering, pass over the breach and disappear. Meanwhile musket-shots are coming thick from the Kaiser Bagh, and puffs of smoke seen issuing from the domes of Saadut Alee and his mother's tombs, show that the enemy have placed their riflemen in these commanding positions. They are not left there, however, undisturbed; for shell after shell fired from Captain Maude's battery, bursts about the buildings, from which the riflemen are soon dislodged. See! the steam-engine house is occupied, and our men are pushing on towards the serjeant's bungalow. Only look at the enemy flying from the further side of it, and disappearing in the shrubbery of Martin's house. To the right our men are seen traversing the "King's stables," and Generals Outram and Havelock can be distinguished giving orders for the occupation of the place. The Hirun Khana we cannot see, but soon hear that it also is in our possession. The Kaiser Bagh guns are, however, firing into the serjeant's bungalow, the most advanced building of our new post; and it evidently is not intended to keep it, for our men are firing it, and as soon as it is in flames retire to the steam-engine buildings. Night is now coming on, but before it falls dark, the Commander-in-Chief's force seems to have drawn a little nearer towards the 32nd mess-house. This building we had noticed during the day to be held by matchlock men. Now, however, some heavy shells fired from the chief's artillery fall on it, and we see the matchlock men abandon it before the day closes, and wonder if they will venture to reoccupy it during the night; for now the mess-house and the Motee Munzil only interpose between us and our advancing friends.

We did not on that evening know how terrible a retribution had been wrought by Sir Colin's force upon the mutineers at Sekundur Bagh; or of the temporary check and severe resistance which they had met with at the Shah Nujeef. These are so memorable, however, as to deserve separate mention here. The Sekundur Bagh is a garden of 120 yards square, surrounded by a high enclosing wall of solid masonry. Its gateway faces south, and had been protected by the enemy with new defences, while the top of the wall had been very carefully loopholed. From these a fearful fire of musketry was opened on our advancing troops. Our infantry laid down until the guns, which were brought up within forty yards, had breached a hole in the east face of the wall sufficiently large to allow of three or four men entering abreast, when it was most gallantly stormed by the 93rd Highlanders, who, discharging their rifles once at the enemy's loop-holes, rushed in with the bayonet. The front entrance being opened, the 53rd Foot, 4th Punjaub Infantry, and the detachments of the 90th and other regiments under Major Barnston entered on that side. Once an entrance had been effected the enemy made little resistance, but in most cases threw away their arms and clasping their hands begged for mercy; but none was shown them, and steel and bullet did their work, until two thousand men had been slain, and lay in weltering heaps inside that fatal square. The revolving pistol here displayed its destructive power, and one officer alone who carried two revolvers destroyed no less than ten of the enemy. About thirty of them eluding their pursuers within, endeavoured to escape by a postern on the north side, but here they were intercepted by a party of the 90th, who let only two or three escape.

The slain were all sepoys, of different mutineer regiments, many belonging to the 71st N.I. On examining their bodies many leave certificates, above forty in number, were found upon them, a fact of much significance; as it fully shows that men who had been on leave at the time of their corps mutinying, and who, therefore, are by some esteemed guiltless, had actually joined the mutineers and been in arms against us. This fact was probably not known to the Government, or these men would not have been permitted afterwards to receive their arrears of pay on the faith of these abused certificates.

Had not the bayonet done here its work so effectually, I doubt not that all the owners of these "tickets of leave" would have presented themselves as so many honest men at Cawnpoor or Benares, and would have received from our unsuspecting paymasters wages for the very days during which they had been fighting against ourselves!

From the Sekundur Bagh, Sir Colin led Major Barnston's regiment of detachments against the Shah Nujeef. Behind a parapet, raised on the massive terrace of this tomb, the enemy were clustered, and poured a frightful fire on a company of the 90th, which got up within fifteen yards of the main building. They could discover, however, no entrance; and both subalterns * who commanded it having been wounded, the men fell back behind some neighbouring

* Lieutenant E. C. Wynne, Ensign H. Powell.

huts. As Major Barnston was bringing up the rest of his regiment, some of our guns were got into position, and opened on the Shah Nujeef; and one of the first shots fired, which was a shell, wounded Major Barnston desperately. This distinguished officer died of this wound subsequently at Cawnpoor. The guns were now allowed to batter the place for two hours; after which Brigadier Hope was ordered to take it with the 93rd Highlanders. Finding that no breach had been effected, Brigadier Hope was obliged to send for a heavy gun, which was brought up by Captain Peel, of the Shannon, and was dragged by the sailors and men of the 93rd, under a fearful fire of musketry, close up to the wall of the Shah Nujeef. Here, with the muzzle almost touching the building, the 24-pounder was worked. The dust and smoke were so great, that it was almost impossible to see what was the effect of this cannonade, unexampled except in naval warfare. A breach was made in the outer wall, but there was yet an inner wall, which seemed to present a serious obstacle; and the enemy from the elevated terrace still maintained a fire of musketry, which could not be effectually kept down by the rifles of the 93rd. There was a tree standing at the corner of the Shah Nujeef, close to the building, and at this juncture Captain Peel offered the Victoria Cross to any of his men who would climb it. Three men immediately ascended the tree up to the level of the terrace, and from this position fired on the enemy. Their names are—Harrison, leading seaman, Lieutenant N. Salmon, and Lieutenant Southwell. The last named fell killed, and both the others were wounded. By this time, however, the enemy, alarmed by the progress of the attack, began to desert the place. Their fire slackened: the Highlanders rushed in at the breach, and the Shah Nujeef was taken.

November 17th.—During the night of the 16th, a new battery was constructed in front of the steam-engine buildings, in which an 8-inch howitzer and two heavy guns were placed. By nine o'clock, A.M., Havelock and myself were again at our look-out on the Chutturmunzil, scrutinizing the 32nd mess-house, and the Motee Munzil, to discover what might be the intentions of the enemy regarding their defence. We soon came to the conclusion that the former building was abandoned. The enemy could nowhere be seen about the premises; but, early in the forenoon, a single man approached the chief entrance, and, after cautiously looking in at the venetians, entered, and presently retired again. About half-past nine, the fire of heavy guns in the direction of the Shah Nujeef showed us that the chief's force was on the move. Gradually it drew nearer; and now the bombardment of the 32nd mess-house has begun on both sides, and the 8-inch shells, fired from opposite directions, meet and burst on the devoted house. It must be confessed that our shell practice is the best; for many of the shells from the chief's side burst in the air. The ground around the building is light and sandy. See those shells exploding in it, and throwing up a volume of sand and dust, as from the crater of a mine. No part of the enclosure escapes: now a shell pierces the building, and then others plough up the ground beneath the trees and bushes, here, there, and everywhere; while rockets, the most fearful looking missile of destruction, leaving a long, white, meteor-like wake behind them, fling themselves upon the place. Nothing can live under such a fire; if there lurks a single enemy in the place, we shall now see him fly.

But no one issues from the building: it must be, it is unoccupied.

Now, through an opening to our right of the 32nd mess, we distinguish a heavy gun placed in position, with five or six men around it. Their dress arrests our attention. Who are they? Not long are we in doubt: they are the brave sailors of the Shannon; that straw hat forms no part of any military attire. But see! they withdraw from the gun, and enter that low hut near it. It is to avoid the heavy musketry fire kept up by the enemy from the Tehree Kotee roof. Again they leave their cover, and, rapidly discharging their gun, add its fire to the storm which envelopes the ill-fated mess-house. The day is now waning, when one of our Artillery officers, hot from his battery, comes up to view from the height the effect of the bombardment. We assure him that the building is abandoned. "It is not, sir," is his reply. Again we assure him that we have kept steady watch from an early hour, and that it is empty indeed. "No, sir! it is not," he again declares. "But how do you know?" we inquire. "The art of war teaches me that the enemy must be in it," he replies; and the gallant fellow, who knew not what fear was, again descends to his battery. It is now three, and if the enemy have any men concealed in that massive pile, we shall soon know; for, see! the red coats are approaching: they are moving down in regular order along the road leading from the Shah Nujeef, and now are lost to view. Presently a party of them are seen advancing in skirmishing order. They have reached the enclosing wall; they are over it, through the shrubbery, and now the leading officer enters at the door which we have been watching; and while a larger body follow, rushing at a double up to the building, he re-appears upon the roof, and presently a British ensign floats on the right hand tower of the Khoorsheyd Munzil. It is Captain Wolseley, of the 90th, who has placed it there.

The building was indeed, as we supposed, abandoned, but the fire is so heavy from the Tehree Kotee and adjacent buildings, that it is no easy work that our noble fellows have to do. See! the ensign is struck down; and now it is again raised, and fixed more firmly than before. But again a shot strikes it down, and probably the staff is damaged, for they have taken it down through the garden to that group of officers, probably Sir Colin himself and staff, whose caps are visible inside the enclosing compound wall. To the right, this wall is lined by the captors of the mess-house, and a heavy fire of musketry, with occasional shot and shell, is directed from the Kaiser Bagh upon them. And now they cross the wall, enter the Tehree Kotee enclosure, charge up its main avenue, and are hid from us by the trees. But the Tehree Kotee has been fired, for volumes of smoke are seen issuing from its lofty windows. Again let us turn our eyes to the group of officers and men on the left of the mess enclosure. They are standing directly opposite to the entrance of the Motee Munzil, from which they are separated by a broad highway. But down this road, sweeping the line that leads to the Motee Munzil, fly thickly the bullets from the Kaiser Bagh, which is distant about 450 yards. There is a pause. Presently the passage is attempted, and European and Seikh, the one in red, the other with swarthy visage and a dress of corresponding colour, stooping, dart across the road.

There they go, by twos and threes, racing across the passage, and are lost from sight at the entrance of the building. Thank God! not one has been left on the road: the fire has, we hope, been harmless. But is the Motee Munzil unoccupied? That we cannot tell. It has been closely watched during the day, and no hostile figure has been detected there; but some shots fired from its neighbourhood have aroused suspicion that those extensive courts may not be wholly empty. Some shots are now fired inside. Ah! there is some work doing! Ten minutes elapse, when see! the enemy is flying from a postern close by the river bank. There are about seventy-five of them; and as they issue, they run for their lives down the right river-bank. Our men have not discovered them. Ah! now they see them, and five or six rifles are discharged after the fugitives. One only falls; but he is motionless, and will rise no more. The rest take to the river, hastily stripping themselves of some of their clothes. They wade across; but as the water rises about them, the fire of our rifles increases, and showers of bullets strike the water all along the single file of men. They have reached mid stream, and now their heads alone are visible. Sometimes some struggling and confusion may be seen, doubtless where a bullet did its errand; but at last, almost all succeed in reaching the opposite bank, and are lost in the orangery of the Hâzuree Bagh.

The work is now accomplished: the Motee Munzil, the last post of the enemy which separated the two armies, is now our own: Martin's house, which intervenes, has clearly been abandoned. And now a young officer advances from the steam-engine post to communicate with our friends in the Motee Munzil. It is Lieutenant Moorsom, Her Majesty's 52nd Foot, who is so valuable in the Quartermaster-General's

Department, to which he belongs. He advances cautiously, and caution is necessary, for that road and open space which lie between Martin's house and the steam-engine is exposed to the musketry of the Kaiser Bagh. The enemy is also cannonading from the Badshah Bagh, across the river, in the same direction. But of their round shot he must take his chance. He stoops, and crosses the dangerous interval in safety, and runs up to Martin's house. Presently two officers approach our outpost by the same way, bearers, no doubt, of communications from Sir Colin. And now our general, Sir James Outram, and staff, followed by General Havelock with his, are going over; and my companion, Lieutenant Havelock, weak as he is from the severe wound in his left arm, has gone to join his father. The fire from the Kaiser Bagh is heavy, and must be twice crossed before Sir Colin can be reached. Both generals narrowly escaped from a shell which exploded close to them, and each had one of his staff wounded; Lieutenant Havelock having unfortunately been dropped upon the road, with a second bullet in his wounded arm.

And now all is gratulation throughout our garrison, and speculations are hazarded whether the enemy will make a stand in the Kaiser Bagh, and how far its broad courts and detached palaces may be defensible. In no long time, however, it was rumoured from the Commander-in-Chief's camp that Lucknow was to be abandoned, and that we were to retire upon Cawnpoor immediately. At night I was informed by Sir James Outram that the ladies were to quit the garrison within twenty-four hours. No property was to be removed; and though it was not avowed, it was pretty generally understood that the men were to go along with the women. Great was the revulsion of feeling produced by this intelligence. A handful of men, we had defended the Residency post for nearly six months; and now that our force was strong in numbers, and stronger still in guns, we were to go, and to go in all the hurry and confusion attending a move on the brief notice of twenty-four hours! One feeling of disappointment and gloom succeeded the previous satisfaction produced by the events of the day; and the orders to abandon everything being peremptory, the ladies began sewing pockets, in order to convey about their persons any valuables which they might be able to save. With these sad feelings, common, I believe, to every one of the garrison, and certainly shared in by both our generals, the day of our relief closed.

November 18th.—We learnt this morning, to our great satisfaction, that General Havelock had been informed by the Commander-in-Chief that the honour of Knight Commander had been conferred upon him. He is now, therefore, Sir Henry. Never was this distinction more nobly earned. It is impossible to over-estimate the value of the services rendered by that gallant officer, and the army of heroes which he commanded, at that most critical period of the mutinies, the months of July and August. In braving the inclemency of the season, they, as well as the army of Dehli, achieved what it was till then believed that no Englishmen or other Europeans could do: and in putting to flight with their small numbers the masses of disciplined troops opposed to them, supported by so powerful an artillery, they taught all British soldiers to despise the foe; and thereafter, whatever the disparity of numbers, they always advanced to assured victory. A corresponding terror was struck into the ranks of the mutineers. As for our garrison, we owe our safety, under Providence, I feel assured, to the exploits performed by Havelock's army; for it was the knowledge of what they had effected, viz. the repeated defeats of the Nana, and the occupation of Cawnpoor, that kept up the heart of our native troops, and prevented their deserting us. Long, therefore, will the recollection of the name of Havelock, and of the 78th Highlanders, the 1st Madras Fusiliers, and the 84th and 64th Regts., be cherished by all who formed part of the garrison of Lucknow. Little did we then think how soon our congratulations upon this well-earned honour would be turned to mourning for the General's untimely death.

This day heavy batteries were opened upon the Kaiser Bagh by Captain Peel on the side of the Commander-in-Chief, and from our advanced post under Colonel Eyre. The palace gate was effectually breached, and our Artillery officers were of opinion that the palace could then have been taken by assault without difficulty. After reaching Cawnpoor, we learnt from the native prisoners released by the enemy, that on that occasion they had packed their valuables, and had made every preparation for abandoning the whole of that position. Both generals waited again to-day on Sir Colin Campbell, to urge him to reconsider his orders for the abandonment of Lucknow, to which measure both are evidently opposed. All that can be obtained, however, is promise of some delay beyond the twenty-four hours. But it is manifest enough, that if the move be so hurried as was at first proposed, much of the twenty-four lacs of treasure, and many of our guns, must be abandoned.

This was a busy day in the garrison, every one

being engaged in preparing or procuring carriages or conveyances of some sort for the removal of the ladies. The best of the carriages presented a miserable appearance, being most of them pierced with bullet-holes, and the seats and cloth rotted by exposure. Announcement was also made that any property which could be saved might be brought away, and that some carriage would be furnished from the chief's camp for the transport of the baggage of individuals. All our artillerymen that can be spared are hard at work destroying the numerous guns of native manufacture, which have lain without carriages from the commencement of the siege on the open ground near the Redan battery. There are upwards of 200 of these, of various calibres, some of them very heavy, and bursting them is an operation of great labour and difficulty. These guns having, moreover, been all previously spiked, the spikes have to be first drilled out before the pieces can be burst. Captain Evans, Bombay army, formerly one of our district officers, who has had charge of the Church battery during the whole siege, superintends this operation, and a number of explosions took place to-day.

Both on the 17th and on this day there was some severe fighting, which could not be seen by us, on the left of Sir Colin's army. Several important posts were taken from the enemy by the left brigade. Its commander, Brigadier Russell, of the 84th, was disabled, and was succeeded by Colonel Biddulph, 45th N. I., who was most unfortunately killed. The command of the brigade finally devolved on Brigadier Hale, of the 82nd. In the afternoon, it became known that the departure of the ladies had been postponed until next day.

Sir Colin Campbell fixed his head-quarters at the Sekundur Bagh, from the precincts of which the bodies of the two thousand slain had been removed and buried. Here we used to be visited daily in the morning by General Outram, who was sometimes accompanied by Havelock.

From the Sekundur Bagh to the Residency the distance is not less than two miles; and the Commander-in-Chief being necessarily greatly occupied in perfecting his own position, and superintending the operations of his own army, was unable to visit the intrenchment for four days. On the afternoon of the 20th November, His Excellency rode over to the old position, and after communicating with the Generals, again returned to his camp. This was the only visit I believe, which he paid to the Residency. He had not, as will afterwards appear, leisure to examine the works; nor did he enter my house or compound.

19*th of November*.—At noon this day, the ladies and women of the garrison left the intrenchment. Most of them were conveyed in carriages, closely packed, every description of vehicle being pressed into service on the occasion. Many were seated on native carts, and not a few walked. They were conducted through the Bailey Guard Gate, the Furhut Buksh and Chutturmunzil palaces, and emerging near our advanced battery, crossed the line of fire from the Kaiser Bagh to Martin's house. Thence they entered and passed through the court of the Motee Munzil, on the further side of which they gained the high-road leading to the Sekundur Bagh. Here, and near Martin's house, they were exposed to the fire of the enemy's guns placed on the further side of the river. Screens, formed of the canvas walls of tents, or doors placed on each side of the way they traversed, as far as the Motee Munzil, concealed the march of the fugitives from the enemy, and on one side of this a ditch or traverse had been dug, along which, dismounting from their carriages, they walked past all the exposed places. All, most fortunately, reached the Sekundur Bagh in safety, and received a most kind welcome from the Commander-in-Chief and those around him.

Up to Sekundur Bagh the road was good, but here the made road terminated, and it was necessary to follow a narrow lane (that by which the army had advanced) deep in sand. During the forenoon the enemy had been seen in its vicinity, and an officer passing along it had been wounded. The Chief, therefore, wisely resolved on detaining the ladies till nightfall, and to send them on in doolies, to avoid the accident of the horses being unable to drag the vehicles through the heavy sand. The poor animals were indeed in miserable condition. Mine had been fed during the siege on two pounds of grain per diem, besides hay; but they had had no grooming, and had almost lost the use of their limbs by standing in the stall, or outside exposed to the rain so long without exercise. My grooms, of whom two only had remained with us, were too useful to be spared from other duties—the first being one of my best battery architects, the second supplying the garrison with water from the excellent wells which we fortunately possessed. At nightfall, accordingly, the ladies were all put into doolies, and passing through lines of pickets, reached the camp at Dilkoosha before morning in safety. Wearied and exhausted as they were, they were glad to partake of refreshments, thoughtfully and kindly provided by H.M. 9th Lancer Mess.

On the evening of the same day, the whole of the sick and wounded were removed by the same route to the Dilkoosha, so that by nightfall the fighting men alone remained in the garrison. Thus had been accomplished, and well accomplished, the chief mission of Sir Colin's army.

November 20th.—I rode out this morning to the Sekundur Bagh, where Sir Colin Campbell had established his head-quarters, to pay my respects to him; for till then, I had not seen him. The route, as will probably be understood, lay through the Furhut Buksh and Chutturmunzil palaces to the advanced Garden battery, and so far it was safe. It then emerged from the extremity of the position which we had occupied, and led by Martin's house, and the court of the Motee Munzil to the high metalled road, leading to the Sekundur Bagh. Approaching the Sekundur Bagh, I met a European soldier dragging a goat away by the horns—a native was following, imploring its release. As I neared, I discovered the latter to be a servant of my own, and accordingly addressed the soldier, and asked him if he could not let my goat go. "It's yours, sir, is it, then?" said the man, and unwillingly restored the goat to freedom. Three, so my servant said, had been taken before.

I reached the Sekundur Bagh without accident, and was most kindly received by Sir Colin Campbell. He and General Mansfield had their beds in the open ground on the south of the Sekundur Bagh enclosure, which screened them from the fire of the enemy. A small piece of table stood by, covered with letters and newspapers just received at head-quarters from England. Sir Colin kindly took the trouble to explain to me the reasons which induced him to decide on abandoning the Residency post. It was, he said, a false position. It could not be reached without incurring severe loss by a relieving army. I assured him that we all deferred to his better judgment in the matter. He spoke on the subject of the annexation of Oudh, and gave it as his opinion that the measure was impolitic, and unpopular with all classes. Here I could not agree with him.

The carriages which had conveyed the ladies on the previous day to Sekundur Bagh were still on the ground, and Sir Colin led me to a spot at the south-west angle of the enclosure, to which he wished to have one of the carriages removed, which had been left standing not far from where his own couch was laid. This latter position the Commander-in-Chief said was exposed to fire, and he wished the carriage removed to a spot which he believed to be safe.

I mention the following anecdote as characteristic and therefore not unworthy of record. The spot where we both stood, be it remembered, was actually under the enemy's fire. A soldier of the 93rd Highlanders approached Sir Colin at this time. "Please sir," said he, "there is a lady in that further carriage with a child, and she wants me to help her, sir." His Excellency turned towards the man and somewhat amused me by replying, "Is she pretty, man?" "Oh, Sir Colin," said the soldier, "I told you, that she wanted me to help her." "Is she pretty, man?" was again Sir Colin's reply, "for I thought that if she was pretty, you would be all the better pleased to help her." "There you are, Sir Colin," rejoined the Highlander, "at your old nonsense." "Oh, yes, help her, man," was the answer.

I turned with the man, and found that the carriage referred to was Dr. Fayrer's, to which a pair of my horses were attached. The lady referred to was an English wet-nurse, who had been engaged by my wife to take care of the infant of Lieutenant Grant and Mrs. Grant, who had died in my garrison. With the help of some Europeans and a number of natives, we started the carriage out of the heavy sand, and moved it to the position indicated by Sir Colin. We had scarcely got it there, when a young officer of Artillery came up and told me that in its new position the carriage was yet more exposed than before. While endeavouring to move the vehicle, according to his advice, the enemy's gun fired, and the crashing of the shot through the trees told that it was approaching us. Directly in front stood a horse artillery gun, with six horses, removed only a few paces off, which fortunately saved us, the shot having passed through two of the horses and spent itself. The horses were now urged forward into the sandy lane, where they soon stuck, being unable to drag the carriages through the heavy sand. Leaving two vehicles there, I removed the infant and her nurse into one which was drawn by a pair of powerful English horses, and lightening it by taking off the boxes, I urged the animals forward, and succeeded by great exertion in driving the carriage to the Dilkoosha. That is indeed a nasty lane!—narrow, and deep with the heaviest sand,—shut in completely on either side by high grass and thick orchards, sufficient to conceal hundreds of the enemy. I thought myself fortunate to get through it without a shot; and had the enemy here attacked our advancing troops, while entangled in the lane, they would, I conceive, have done so to great advantage. I could not remain at the Dilkoosha, for all capable of bearing arms were expected to remain at their posts until the place was finally evacuated, and I returned accordingly, after staying a few minutes to partake of what was to me the greatest possible luxury, bread-and-butter, which was afforded to me by the kind hospitality of Lieutenant Walker, of the Artillery, and his mess. It was the first that I had tasted for five months, and was the greatest treat imaginable. Sir Colin's camp was at the time well supplied. In the native bazaar, attached to it, bread, butter, and other provisions could be bought; though the price of everything was, as might have been expected, high.

During this, and the two following days, the preparations for evacuating the position were carried on and completed. All our artillery was gradually withdrawn, until by the evening of the 22nd a few pieces, which were not worth removing, only remained mounted within the position. A large quantity of shot was thrown down wells, the rest removed. The greater part of the unmounted native guns were destroyed. Still, a considerable number, which there was not time to burst, were left behind.

The treasure, amounting to more than twenty-three lacs of rupees, or 230,000*l.*, which had been buried under ground during the siege, was exhumed, and removed in safety to the Dilkoosha. With it were sent the remainder of the ex-King's jewels, which had been removed from the Kaiser Bagh two days before the Residency was invested. During the confusion attendant on the siege, many of these had been purloined. Still a quantity of valuable jewellery was preserved.

On the 21st, just four days after he had received the tidings of the honours bestowed upon him, Sir Henry Havelock was seized with dysentery; and so dangerous were the symptoms, that he was removed in the afternoon of that day to the Dilkoosha, in hopes that the change of air might check the progress of the disease.

On the same day Sir Colin Campbell issued a general order commending the conduct of the garrison, and congratulating Generals Outram and Havelock on having been the first to bring relief. Hearty and soldier-like as was the order, which will be found in the Appendix, it was thought by those who had neither formed part of "the remnant of a British regiment," nor belonged to the "company of British artillery," therein commended, to be not a little defective. The Commander-in-Chief had not visited the several posts of the garrison, and a wish was felt that this might be done. Nothing was so likely to leave a correct impression of the actual events of the siege, and of the labours of the several garrisons, as a personal examination of the posts themselves. With this view I addressed the chief of the staff, requesting that Sir Colin would, if he could spare time, examine the defences of my post before the place was abandoned. In reply, General Mansfield stated that there was not time to do so; but added, "an order will appear this evening correcting the Commander-in-Chief's omission in yesterday's order, with regard to the civil functionaries who have aided in the defence of Lucknow." The following order accordingly appeared on the 22nd:—

"Head-quarters, Shah Nujeef, 22nd November, 1857.

"When the Commander-in-Chief issued his order of yesterday, with regard to the old garrison of Lucknow, His Excellency was unaware of the important part taken in aid of the soldiers by the civil functionaries who happened to be at the Residency when it was shut in by the enemy. 2. His Excellency congratulates them very heartily on the honour they have won in conjunction with their military comrades. This is only another instance that, in danger and difficulty, all Englishmen behave alike, whatever their profession."

On the afternoon of Sunday, 22nd of November, it became known that we should evacuate the place at midnight. It would have been a melancholy satisfaction to have blown up our houses and property as we retired, and at all events to have prevented our barbarous and cowardly enemy from polluting with his presence the scenes of so much constancy and suffering; but it was rightly judged that this might compromise the safety of the retiring garrison.

Everything, therefore, was done to maintain until the last moment the usual ordinary appearance of things. At midnight we silently marched out; the outposts first retiring, and being joined by the others as they passed along. I was attended by six chupprassies or native orderlies, who had faithfully stood by me during the siege, fought by my side, and behaved throughout with unvarying fidelity.

The secret of our departure was withheld from the natives till the last moment, to prevent its being disclosed to the enemy. But it was impossible that they could witness the preparations which were going on, and not guess at the result which was coming. The old pensioners of my garrison were sadly disheartened; they are all Oudh men, and hoped to have returned with flying colours to their villages; whereas, in lieu, they are required to leave their country, and feel doubtful as to our intentions of returning. Besides, they are old and decrepit; and though they have kept faithful watch behind our defences, they tell us that they can no longer perform the same marches as robust men. And now it is midnight, and we move along. As we pass the gate of the General's quarters, we see him seated on his horse; but it is no use waiting with him, for he means to be the last man to leave the Bailey Guard Gate, while we are anxious to join our friends at the Dilkoosha. Forward, therefore, we pass the gate, and the Clock Tower, turn sharp to the left, and enter the Tehree Kotee enclosure, and pass in succession the Furhut Buksh and Chutturmunzil. All along we see files of ranks ready to join us; and here the Artillery staff, there the Engineers, fall in. We have now left our defences, and glance up to the right towards the Kaiser Bagh, to see if the enemy is visible. No, all is still, and not a shot is fired. The high-road is reached—now the Sekundur Bagh is passed, and we are halted for some time in the sandy lane. Again we move on, and emerge into the open country. It is bitterly cold, as we are again halted for half an hour, without being able to discover why. And now we are in the Martinière Park, and halt again; we know our way, why longer tarry with the military, who seem to be taking up their positions for to-morrow? Come along—we strike off to the left, and soon hit the direct road to the Dilkoosha, and turn down it. Who comes there? Friends! Has the garrison left? It has, and we are part of it. Good night! We pass on, and in a few minutes reach the camp.

One officer of the garrison had a narrow escape from falling into the hands of the enemy. The hour fixed for our departure was midnight, and before this arrived many of the garrison laid down to take some rest, making sure of being awoke when the movement began. Among these was Captain Waterman, of the 13th N. I. He fell fast asleep, and his friends failed to awake him. The troops had marched out of the Residency, and had cleared the palaces altogether before he awoke. His consternation on awaking may well be imagined. He was alone in the abandoned position, and could discover no traces of his friends. Appalled by the horror of his position, he followed in the track of the retiring force as fast as he could, but not until he had left the old position far behind him did he overtake the rear-guard. The shock he had undergone was too great for him, and he long suffered from its effects.

I found my way early on the 23rd of November to General Havelock's tent, to inquire what benefit he had derived from his removal to the Dilkoosha. I was directed to a common soldier's tent, which was pitched near the one in which we had found shelter. Entering it, I found the General's aide-de-camp, Captain Hargood, and his medical attendant Dr. Collinson, lying down. They whispered to me in mournful accents the grievous news that Sir Henry's case was worse, and pointed to where he lay. It was in a doolie, which had been brought inside the tent, and served as a bed. The curtain on my side was down. I approached, and found young Havelock seated on the further side upon the ground by his dying father. His wounded arm still hung in a sling, but with his other he supplied all his father's wants. They told me that the General would allow no one to render him any attendance but his son. I saw that to speak was impossible, and sorrowfully withdrew.

During that day the camp halted at the Dilkoosha. The ladies and children, and the wounded, were provided with such accommodation as was available in tents and in the buildings of the palace. General

Outram, with the troops of the late garrison, held the rear of the position occupied by the army, viz. those posts which faced the enemy, who, however, during the day, only maintained a desultory cannonade. They remained for many hours in entire ignorance of our having abandoned the Residency, nor did they, I believe, attempt to enter it till near noon in the day.

And now the long-accumulating letters and papers pour in upon us. Since the outbreak at Cawnpoor, our communications by post had been closed, a period of nearly six months. Letters of June, August, and November tumble in together. Mournful, and full of sad fears and alarms, are the English letters, mixed with complaints of our silence. Others had been heard of: why not we? It was, indeed, impossible to have written. The only messenger who during the siege conveyed our despatches, and brought us replies, it will be remembered, was "Ungud," and it was not safe to charge him with more than a minute scrap of paper. It was impossible to have transmitted private letters. Some about the military head-quarters no doubt did send tidings of a personal nature; but we were not among the number. Nor was private communication opened by the arrival of Havelock's force. Cossids, obtained with difficulty, still carried General Outram's despatches in sealed quills. But not a single private letter was despatched during the whole seven weeks of the blockade by General Havelock himself.

On opening the papers, what most touches and affects us is the earnest and hearty sympathy of which the Lucknow garrison has been the object at home. The heart of Old England has indeed overflowed towards us. And to obtain such overflowings of English sympathy, what would not Englishmen do? Shall I say what is strictly fact, that I never doubted that it would be so: that in the darkest hour of our beleaguerment, I always was assured that thousands of our countrymen would hasten to our relief; and felt that the only chance of success possessed by our treacherous enemies was to overpower us at the beginning, before one of our soldiers could reach Cawnpoor. How fully have those expectations been fulfilled! How promptly was succour provided! How large and sufficient the force sent, and how amply has British, and indeed foreign, sympathy provided to relieve the distress and desolation which the late sad events have caused! Truly, with these facts before one, well may one feel proud to be an Englishman!

November 24th.—In the forenoon of this day Sir Henry Havelock, who had been gradually sinking since his arrival at Dilkoosha, expired. He lived just long enough to see the accomplishment of that for which he had so nobly fought, and to hear that his exertions had been appreciated by his Queen and country. He had the satisfaction of being tended during his last moments by a beloved son. But higher consolations far than these, the warrior had. He had lived a Christian, and now his end was peace! His remains were conveyed to Alum Bagh, and there interred.

About 11 o'clock General Hope Grant's Division, accompanied by the Commander-in-Chief, all the ladies and wounded, moved to Alum Bagh, leaving General Outram's Division on the ground.—No opposition was offered by the enemy. Avoiding the cloud of dust which marked the line of carts, camels, carriages and vehicles of all kinds, mixed with troops, European and Seikh, I, with other camp-followers, made our way through the fields, which contrasted pleasantly with the scene of our long confinement. Cultivation had not been neglected during the disturbances, and the crops looked well. The fields of sugar-cane especially drew the attention of our camp-followers, and were being rapidly cleared. The small villages near which we passed were deserted. In one only were a few peasants to be seen. About 3, P. M., we approach Alum Bagh, and a line of Lancer Pickets ranged in front arrests the further progress of the living stream, which, constantly fed from the rear, swells into a lake. Mounting an adjacent eminence we look down upon the singular spectacle presented by this confused mass of men, cattle, carriages, doolies, and engines of war. But why are we stopped? has the enemy shown himself? No, but yonder is Alum Bagh, and we are going to take up a position on the Cawnpoor side of it. Pickets of cavalry and horse artillery now advance over the plain in front of Alum Bagh, and take up their position; and presently the stream of troops and refugees flows on again, and settles for the night within the assigned boundaries. Half a mile of clear ground separates the camp from Alum Bagh, beyond which again are seen the suburbs of Lucknow.

November 25th.—The camp halted to-day to allow Outram's Division to come up. I went over to see the Alum Bagh.—It was one of the royal gardens, being a square of 500 yards, enclosed by a wall about 9 feet high, and entered through a handsome gateway. The interior had been full of large fruit trees, and the centre is occupied by a double-storied summer-house of masonry. All traces of the garden have now disappeared, the fruit-trees having all been cut down. The wall, on the city side, has been strengthened by a strong ramp of earth; and an interior

On Stone by W. L. Walton. E. C. Wynne, delt. Printed by Hullmandel & Walton

GATEWAY OF THE ALUMBAUGH.

London: Richard Bentley, New Burlington Street, 1858.

earthen ramp or traverse has been thrown up all round the centre building to stop the enemy's round shot. Well-formed earthwork bastions have been erected at each corner, and the face of the enclosure next to the high road has been protected by a ditch. Major Sibley, 64th Regt., commanding the post, took us to the look-out upon the roof, whence we could with glasses distinguish the enemy crowding the top of the Residency. The garrison at Alum Bagh suffered little inconvenience from the enemy during our blockade. At first high grass and groves of trees surrounded the position on all sides, affording cover to the enemy's riflemen, who did some damage; but these were burnt and cut down, when the annoyance ceased. The enemy have occasionally succeeded in throwing 12-lb. shot inside the enclosure, but have rarely done any damage. During the afternoon Outram's Division joined the camp, without molestation. They passed, however, several carts, and bodies of camp-followers, stragglers of yesterday's march, who had been surprised by the enemy, and destroyed.

The united camp halted at Alum Bagh, on the 26th of November, during which arrangements were made for leaving there General Outram's Division, to watch the rebels in Lucknow; and on the 27th, the Commander-in-Chief marched towards Cawnpoor, escorting, with General Hope Grant's Division, the wounded, the refugees, and treasure. A march of seventeen miles brought us to Bunnee, where, during the night, the sound of a heavy cannonade in the Cawnpoor direction having been heard; the tents were struck early on the next day, the 28th, and after a weary and fatiguing march which continued all day, we reached after nightfall the camp pitched within two miles of the Ganges. Sir Colin had crossed the river during the afternoon, into the intrenchment at Cawnpoor, where his presence was much needed to assist and re-assure the force commanded by General Windham, which was beleaguered by the mutineers of the Gwalior Contingent

We had hoped that we had done with the alarms of war for some time to come; so that the booming of heavy guns, the smoke of which we could see across the river, was nowise a welcome sound. The mutineers having possessed themselves of the town of Cawnpoor, and of the whole military station, and advanced their posts near to the bridge of boats, it was not an easy operation to take the army, and its immense convoy across. This was, however, happily effected without loss, and after passing the night in making a weary march of four miles, and pricking on the tired cattle over the sands of the river, we found ourselves before daylight of the 30th located in rear of the Commander-in-Chief's army, and close to the melancholy and battered memorials of Sir Hugh Wheeler's disaster at Cawnpoor.

Here, then, this account terminates: not without rendering earnest thanksgivings to that merciful Providence who preserved us through those fearful perils, by which we were so long encompassed,—and caused our lot to differ from the sad fate of our countrymen and countrywomen who perished in that fatal place.

The force under Sir Colin Campbell, by which the relief of the Lucknow garrison, and its withdrawal in safety to Cawnpoor, had been thus so gloriously and successfully achieved, numbered about 4550 men, and thirty-two guns.

Among the latter were eight heavy guns, 24-pounders, and 8-inch howitzers, which were manned by the naval brigade. The 68-pounders which were brought from the Shannon frigate by Captain Peel, had been left at Allahabad in consequence of its having been found impossible to procure the necessary cattle for their transport. The other guns were all field-pieces, forming the usual complement of one heavy field-battery of Royal Artillery, one Bengal horse field-battery, and two troops of Bengal and of Madras Horse Artillery.

The cavalry consisted of H. M. 9th Lancers from Dehli; a detachment of the military train just arrived from Calcutta; and detachments of the 1st, 2nd, and 5th Punjaub-Seikh Cavalry and of Hodson's Horse.

The infantry comprised H. M. 8th, 53rd, and 75th Regts. from Dehli, and the 93rd Highlanders who had recently arrived, also detachments of the 5th Fusiliers, 23rd Welsh Fusiliers, 64th Regt., 82nd Foot, 90th Light Infantry, and of the 1st Madras Fusiliers. There were two regiments of Seikh Infantry, the 2nd and the 4th, and detachments of Bengal and Punjaub Sappers and Miners.

The loss sustained by the force in accomplishing our relief was severe, amounting to 122 killed, and 414 wounded. Among the former, ten were officers; and there were thirty-five officers wounded.

The following detail affords the particulars of the loss, showing the brunt to have fallen on the Artillery and Naval Brigade, and on the 93rd Highlanders. We had to mourn several officers of distinction, killed: Colonel G. Biddulph, Quartermaster-General's Department; Captain Hardy, Royal Artillery; Captain Wheatcroft, 6th Dragoon Guards; Captain I. Dalzell, 93rd Highlanders, and others. The list of wounded included a large number of the staff, and Sir Colin Campbell himself was in the number.

Regiment.	Killed.			Wounded.			Grand Total.
	Officers.	Men.	Total.	Officers.	Men.	Total.	
Staff	2	0	2	6	0	6	8
Engineers	0	3	3	0	17	17	20
Artillery and Naval Brigade	2	18	20	9	76	85	105
Cavalry—9th Lancers	0	0	0	0	0	0	0
Military Train	1	0	1	0	0	0	1
Seikh Cavalry	0	3	3	1	5	6	9
Infantry—							
5th Fusiliers	0	5	5	0	3	3	8
8th	0	0	0	0	1	1	1
23rd Fusiliers	0	3	3	1	18	19	22
53rd	0	10	10	3	63	66	76
64th	0	4	4	0	7	7	11
82nd	1	1	2	1	13	14	16
84th	0	1	1	0	8	8	9
90th	0	6	6	3	22	25	31
93rd	2	37	39	7	62	69	108
1st Madras	1	3	4	0	12	12	16
Punjaub Infantry	1	18	19	4	72	76	95
	10	112	122	35	379	414	536

It has been said that the withdrawal of our forces from, and the abandonment of the Lucknow Residency, occasioned much disappointment to those who were relieved by Sir Colin Campbell. I must guard against the supposition that it is intended to condemn that measure. So far as can be judged from subsequent events, the course decided upon by the Commander-in-Chief, disheartening as it was to us, was yet by far the wisest one. True, the enemy were ready to abandon the Kaiser Bagh; and when they had abandoned it, the capture of the rest of the city might not have been found difficult. True, that at the time our prestige suffered injury from the relinquishment of Lucknow to the mutineers; yet the reasons which recommend the policy which was actually followed are far more cogent.

It would have been useless to expel the mutineers

from Lucknow unless we could have maintained our possession of that capital. For this purpose, there was not at the time assembled at Lucknow a force sufficient, without neglecting military operations of more vital importance. The enemy then held Futtehghur, and the whole of Rohilcund: and a large and well-appointed force threatened Cawnpoor. To provide for the safety of our older provinces, and of the line of the Trunk Road; and to expel the enemy from the Dooab was the first consideration. Nor did we lose much in actual prestige. For the mutineers occupying the city of Lucknow were more effectually threatened, and kept in check by the force left at Alum Bagh, under command of Sir James Outram; than they would have been if the same force had garrisoned the Bailey Guard or Kaiser Bagh. In the former case the troops maintained an offensive attitude; in the latter they would soon have been reduced to a state of defence. We have, therefore, good grounds for applauding the decision of withdrawing the garrison and abandoning the city altogether, which was come to by Sir Colin.

Nor have we less reason to admire the skill and eminent success with which these measures were carried out. Excepting, perhaps, the slight check at the Shah Nujeef, where, as is generally admitted, some sacrifice of life would have been prevented by a more free use of heavy artillery, the whole course of operations was indeed most admirable. Every member of the garrison, European and native, was withdrawn, without the loss of one life. The whole of the treasure, and all the European guns, were brought away. And little else was left to the foiled enemy, but the bare walls of the Residency buildings.

Subsequent accounts tell us that they have done

their best to destroy these monuments of our defence. Most of the houses have been levelled. Of some, not a trace remains. One turret alone marks the site of the Residency: and a few pillars only indicate the position of Gubbins' house.

I annex the order conveying merited praise to his army for this glorious achievement, which was issued by Sir Colin Campbell on the 23rd of November.

"The Commander-in-Chief has reason to be thankful to the force he conducted for the relief of the garrison of Lucknow.

"2. Hastily assembled, fatigued by long marches, but animated by a common feeling of determination to accomplish the duty before them, all ranks of this force have compensated for their small number, in the execution of a most difficult duty, by unceasing exertions.

"3. From the morning of the 16th till last night, the whole force has been one outlying picket never out of fire, and covering an immense extent of ground, to permit the garrison to retire scathless and in safety, covered by the whole of the relieving force.

"4. That ground was won by fighting as hard as it ever fell to the lot of the Commander-in-Chief to witness, it being necessary to bring up the same men over and over again to fresh attacks; and it is with the greatest gratification that his Excellency declares he never saw men behave better.

"5. The storming of the Sekundur Bagh and the Shah Nujeef has never been surpassed in daring, and the success of it was most brilliant and complete.

"6. The movement of last night, by which the final rescue of the garrison was effected, was a model of discipline and exactness. The consequence was, that the enemy was completely deceived, and the force retired by a narrow tortuous lane, the only line of retreat open, in the face of 50,000 enemies, without molestation.

"7. The Commander-in-Chief offers his sincere thanks to Major-General Sir James Outram, G.C.B., for the happy manner in which he planned and carried out his arrangements for the evacuation of the Residency of Lucknow."

CHAPTER XVIII.

CONCLUDING OBSERVATIONS.

Effect of the brief British rule in Oudh has been for good.—Future brighter prospects of the province.—Its superior natural resources.—System of administration.—Moderation of assessment.—Importance of the Land Revenue settlement.—Ill effects of high assessment.—Two examples given.—Dacoits of Oudh.—Desolation of many parts of the province when first occupied.—Improvement after thirteen months.—Example in illustration.—The term "martial" properly inapplicable in the sense of "turbulent" to the population.—Habits of the people.—The talooqdars under a strong Government will cease to be turbulent.—Talooqdars who have shown fidelity should be rewarded.—Their names stated.—General conduct of talooqdars in other parts of the country.—Konwur Singh; Amor Singh.—Rajah of Pachete.—Landed aristocracy of Bengal.—Cessation of dacoity in Oudh.—Future power of the British Government in India.—Its greater independence of Indian prejudices.—Danger which may thence result.—Under the East India Company, during the rule of a century, there was no national revolt.

In quitting for a season the fine province, which has been the scene of so much useful and successful exertion, as well as of so much and such lengthened suffering and sorrow, it is gratifying to know that the effect of our brief rule in Oudh has been for good. It is pleasing, also, to look forward to brighter prospects; and to anticipate the yet far greater improvements which a continuance of enlightened government may effect. Superior in natural resources to the rest of the North-Western Provinces generally, and inhabited by an industrious population, this noble province, properly administered, should be the brightest gem in the Indian diadem. The system of administration laid down by the Government of Lord Dalhousie, on the model of the Punjaub, promises the avoidance of many evils by which that of our older provinces has been disfigured. A simple code and procedure for civil and criminal law have been bestowed. A moderate, a very moderate, assessment of the land revenue for thirty years, and a settlement of the titles to land, are now the main desiderata. Hitherto, in the case of every province which has come under our rule, by cession or by conquest, we have at first fallen into the dangerous error of fixing our land revenue demand too high. Nor is the Punjaub exempt from injury arising from the same grave mistake. Let Oudh reap the benefit of our matured experience, and let us hope that this evil may be avoided there.

The revenue has been now settled for three years: and an assessment completed, respecting the moderation of which no doubt can be entertained. Before it expires, a better one will, it is hoped, be concluded for a longer period: and under a fixed and moderate demand, the province will no doubt attain that prosperity, which will afford the best justification for its having been brought under the British rule.

I speak of the settlement of the land revenue first, because it is unquestionably the most important measure: and that upon which the welfare of the province, and indeed of every other province in India, most essentially depends. This may not be always, indeed, understood in England; where some have been found so ill-informed, as to attribute to selfish motives of finance alone, the great efforts which have of late years been made by the Government of the East India Company, to effect an equable adjustment of the land tax. Yet even in England it should not be difficult to understand, how an exorbitant, or unequal, and ill-adjusted land tax necessarily saps the foundation of all public prosperity. Nine-tenths of the population, be it remembered, are agricultural. If, then, the burthen of land tax imposed upon the country be excessive, nine-tenths of the people suffer. All improvement is checked; a general squalor and low state of living and comfort, never in India too high, prevails; and crime is multiplied. The people are in want; and steal and rob they will, however active may be our exertions to prevent them. Numberless illustrations could be given of this state of things. I was once collector of a district, where the native revenue officials were known to request that payment of revenue might not be pressed, saying "that it would soon be collected when the dark nights returned;" that is, the people would acquire then, by theft, the means of paying it!

In another, I remember some villages where the assessment pressed heavily, the head men of which were constantly getting into trouble from the thievish habits of their people. One of these men happening to visit Agra some years later, came to see me. "Mobarick," I inquired of him, "how are the thieves of your village?" "Sir," replied the head man, with an offended air, "we do not steal now; our revenue payment has been made easy." He proceeded to tell me of the large reduction that had been made, and assured me that the neighbouring villages to his had, for a like reason, given up their malpractices.

But to return to my subject. When we entered Oudh, its dacoits, or professional robbers, were reckoned by hundreds; and many of the richest and most fertile tracts lay waste for miles. Our officers reported that they had ridden for twenty miles, in some directions, over the richest soil, without seeing a field or a village. Where were those by whom the land had before been tilled? Where were the teeming thousands of Oudh?

They were to be found in all the adjacent British districts, whither they had fled to escape the grinding exactions and unrelenting tyranny of their own land. In those new districts they had cleared the forest, raised new villages, and acquired valuable properties. Before these military mutinies began, after a brief tenure of thirteen months, how changed was the scene! All those numerous dacoits had become peaceable and quiet subjects, residing in the ancestral homes from which violence had driven them. Thousands of the cultivators had returned to re-claim their long-deserted lands; and everywhere new dwellings were rising; new villages re-appearing; and new wells were being dug. Old fields everywhere were yielding again to the plough; and soon the face of the country would have so changed, that those who first entered it would scarce have known it again.

In a part of Oudh where the people had suffered generally less than in other quarters, I recollect an example illustrative of the change which had begun, which may deserve mention. It was in the district of Sultanpoor that, riding in January, 1857, through a well-cultivated neighbourhood, I drew up in a field where a peasant was ploughing, to inquire the rent which he had engaged to pay for the land. He named a very low one; and on my expressing doubt as to the correctness of his reply, "Sir," cried the man, "who would give much for a field which has not been tilled for twenty years?" I found, on inquiry, that the peasant had said no more than was true. The field belonged to a neighbouring village, the inhabitants of which had long resisted the endeavours of a powerful talooqdar to take possession of their property. At last he had prevailed; had fired the village, and slain many of the proprietors. I rode through the village, which had been a large one, but now exhibited little more than bare mud walls, which the action of the rains was fast reducing into heaps of earth. A few of the old proprietors met me. They pointed to their desolate abode; but they told me, with brightened aspect, that they had now recovered possession of their own; and that all would be well.

It is usual to speak of the population of Oudh as being martial; that term being generally used to convey the idea of a proud and turbulent people, whom it would be difficult to keep in obedience.

This, however, would be a very incorrect description of their character; for I am persuaded that in no part of North-Western India are the habits of the natives more industrious and peaceful; and nowhere will the British Government be more readily obeyed than in Oudh. The people of Oudh have been called martial, first on account of the large proportion of our sepoys which have been drawn from the province; secondly, because of the turbulence of the talooqdars, who are known frequently to have been in arms against the native Government; and, lastly, from the number of robbers and dacoits who have long infested the country. As regards the first fact, it is no doubt true that the brahmins and chuttrees (*i. e.* rajpoots) of Oudh are greatly habituated to seek service. Though clinging with the utmost tenacity to their ancestral fields, they disdain agriculture, and will not consent unless pinched by severe want to handle the plough. But, doubtless, the poverty to which these classes have been reduced by the rapacity of the Government and talooqdars, and the injustice from which they have suffered, have led many to abandon their houses and seek foreign service, who, under a happier state of things, would have been glad to remain at home. Nor do these habits necessarily consist with turbulence. The Goojurs of Dehli and Meerut are turbulent; the mountain tribes that inhabit the hills beyond Peyshawur and the Soleymânee range are turbulent. The Bhutties of the Cis Sutledge country, the Mewatties of Ulwur and Bhurtpoor, are turbulent. If these men cannot wage war, they will plunder. If they are restrained from plundering, they will steal.

Not so the people of Oudh. Their habits are orderly and peaceable: and they are driven to draw the sword only by the provocation of sudden insult, or the intolerable burthen of extreme oppression. The talooqdars of Oudh have indeed been turbulent. But when turbulence was so well rewarded, who would not have practised it who could? The obedient was ground to the dust: while the bold man who built a fort and armed it, and defied his sovereign, paid little, or got off scot free! This state of things, however, will entirely pass away. All forts will, no doubt, now be dismantled; all cannon be taken away; and a Government stronger than India ever knew before will succeed one that did not deserve the name. We shall hear, then, no more of the turbulence of Oudh talooqdars. It is not unlikely that the number of this class in Oudh may be reduced in our re-settlement of the province after these mutinies have been finally quelled. Some of them have no doubt justly incurred the forfeiture of their estates; though under circumstances so peculiar and extraordinary, as to demand the largest exercise of clemency.

Those, of course, who have distinguished themselves by fidelity, will be most liberally rewarded. Especially it is to be hoped that Rajah Dirgbijeh Singh, of Bulrampoor, will have no cause to regret that he sheltered and escorted to a place of safety, the British Commissioner of Bareytch, and the large party of refugees who accompanied Mr. Wingfield. And that the Rajah of the same name who resides at Moriarmow, and is the head of the Byse clan, will never repent having sheltered, fed, and nursed the naked and bleeding heroes who alone survived the massacre of Cawnpoor.*

There are those who represent the talooqdars as a class of men politically necessary; and who think that the conduct of the people, in those parts of the country where they had maintained their position, contrasts favourably with other quarters where little

* Besides the Rajahs of Bulrampoor and Moriarmow, here mentioned; the services of Lall Honwunt Singh, talooqdar of Dharoopoor, and owner of the strong fort of Kaleekankur, on the Ganges, and of Rajah Madho Singh of Gurh Ameytee, have been mentioned in an earlier part of this work. Should these have maintained their fidelity during the later period of the mutinies, they should not fail of their reward. The conduct of the first, especially, Lall Honwunt Singh, in escorting Captain L. Barrow and the whole of the European residents of the station of Salone to his fort, maintaining them there for a fortnight, and then forwarding them, under protection of a strong guard, in safety, at a very critical time, to Allahabad, deserved the highest praise. Nor should the good service of Roostum Sah, Chief of Deyrah, in the Fyzabad District, and of Ram Singh, Zemindar of Suhee, in Duriabad, and of that other zemindar, whose name has escaped me, but who sheltered Mrs. Dorin and her companions, fugitives from Seetapoor, be forgotten.

The name of Hurdeo Buksh, Chief of Kuteearee, in the Mullaon District, who sheltered Mr. Probyn of the civil service, and other refugees from Futtehghur, has long since been brought to notice in the local despatches, and his eminent services will no doubt be duly recognised.

On the other hand, punishment would not unjustly befall the following talooqdars, who distinguished themselves by the most active and unprovoked hostility, viz.—

1. *Munsubalee,* talooqdar of Rusoolabad, district of Poorwah.

2. The heirs of *Jussa Singh,* talooqdar of Futtehpoor Chowrassee, in the same district.

Both these men joined the mutineers, and aided them to the utmost. Jussa Singh was killed in an action with General Havelock, but his policy was taken up by his heirs.

3. *Rajah Dirg Bijeh Singh,* talooqdar of Muhônah, district of Lucknow

trace of them remains. I do not think that facts bear out this opinion.

What were Konwur Singh, the rebel chief of Jugdeespoor, in Arrah, and his brother, Amur Singh, but talooqdars? who had under our former system been favoured to the utmost; retaining undisturbed their numerous villages, and their extensive revenues. Yet it is well known that their influence over the sepoy inhabitants of the villages comprised in their talooquahs was one main cause of the mutiny of the Dinapoor Brigade. And that they compelled, by summonses notified by beat of drum, those sepoys who were at their homes on leave, to arm, and join their standard. What has been the behaviour of many of the talooqdars of Jounpoor and Azimgurh? What were the Rajah of Pachete, and other titled

This man was the first talooqdar to throw off our authority. He has always borne a bad character, both as a landlord and a subject.

4. *Rajah Newaubaleekhan*, talooqdar of Muhomdabad, district of Seetapoor, and

5. Rajah Goor Buksh Singh, talooqdar of Ram Nugger-Dhumeyree, district of Lucknow.

Both these zemindars raised an armed rabble, and were the first to join the mutineers in the siege of the Residency, taking a very active part in all their measures.

6. Rajah Lonee Singh, of Mithowlee, in the Seetapoor District, whose surrender of the Seetapoor refugees has been noticed fully in another place.

7. Rajah Ruzzak Buksh, of Juhangeerabad, in the district of Lucknow. No sooner was the weakness of our Government felt, than this talooqdar proceeded to eject those villagers who had recovered their ancient properties by order of the British Courts. Upon many of these the most frightful atrocities were perpetrated. Several were slain, and some were buried alive!

8. But though last mentioned, none have more deserved condign chastisement than the Zemindars of Mulheabad, in the Lucknow District. They are Afreedee Mussulmans, whose ancestors settled at Mulheabad and the adjacent villages. The descendants retain all the characteristic vice and treachery, with none of the virtue, of the parent stock. They were among the very first to give trouble, and took a conspicuous part in the siege.

rebels in Bengal, but talooqdars? And what has the wealthy and artificially-created landed aristocracy of Bengal done in aid of the State, during the late momentous crisis? Nothing, I believe, but present addresses, which might well have been dispensed with. Yet they owed their wealth and the titles to their estates solely to the British Government. And they might justly have been expected at such a crisis, to have come forward heartily and liberally, in aid of the rulers to whom they owed their all.

The third example of the turbulence of Oudh, found in the dacoits, formerly abounding in the province, has ceased with the dacoits themselves. They were the offspring of tyranny and oppression. These ceased; and so did they. The Chutree remains; but he is a dacoit no longer.

I have said that the British Government which will rule India after these mutinies are suppressed, will be the strongest that India ever knew. Of this result it is difficult, I think, to entertain a doubt. The British Indian Empire was before essentially founded on opinion. It will hereafter have the securer basis of physical power. We relied before upon the support of an army raised from our native subjects. Hereafter we shall trust more to the bayonets of our own countrymen. The Government will in future be more free to act, and be less fettered by the fear of offending the prejudices of India. Much good may be expected to result from this greater freedom of policy and legislation. Nor can it be doubted that the baneful system of *caste* will receive a heavy blow in our altered policy. There is, however, I think, some fear that the new principle may be pushed too far. Possessed of extraordinary power, and urged by popular opinion from home, the Indian Government may be led to forget that principle which has been the safeguard of the empire for a hundred years—I mean our respect for the feelings and religion of the people. The system which has been so long pursued, has at least conciliated them: and when our Government sustained the severest shock recorded in the annals of any ruling race, though our assailants were their own brethren, the people looked coldly on. Rarely did they espouse the rebel cause. They felt in the main, content: and looked for little benefit from a change. Greater loyalty the conqueror may not look for from the conquered; the ruling from the subject race. Far different might have been the result had our rule been less moderate. A military mutiny would have brought about a national revolt, the consequences of which it were difficult to foresee. Let it then ever be remembered, to the honour of the East India Company, whose imperial functions are now, it is believed, soon to pass away; that no such fearful catastrophe did occur during the century of their rule. And let English rulers never forget the principle which has always been impressed upon their servants—to conciliate the feelings; and to do no violence to the honest scruples of the subject race.

ADDENDA.

No. I. Page 73.

Our revenue system had in native estimation many faults. These chiefly consisted in the severity and lasting nature of the punishment with which we visited default. The landed property of a defaulter was liable to sale by public auction: and when thus sold, he lost for ever what had perhaps been the inheritance of many generations. A milder process was that of "*transfer*," by which a landholder lost possession of his estate, for periods varying from five to fifteen years. Both of these processes were disliked; but the former is viewed by the land proprietors of Upper India, with a hatred and disgust almost equal to that which they feel towards our Civil Law Courts. The former penalty I have never enforced in my capacity as a revenue officer. And I hold it in almost equal detestation as the native landholder himself. That of transfer ought very rarely, indeed scarcely ever, to be used. But to avoid using it, the British revenue officer must be watchful, and must understand his duty. The native villager has as little forethought, or self-denial, generally, as a child: and will squander upon expensive marriage ceremonies, and other charges, which redound to his repute, any ready money which may come into his possession. As themselves express it—"They eat, they drink, they enjoy themselves;" and when the Government Collector comes, there is nothing to pay. To prevent this, the tax-gatherer must watch the ripening of the crops; and must present his demand before the money has been dissipated in marriage festivals and other follies. But to do this the collector must not be asleep; but must ever be wakeful. With these exceptions our revenue system and laws generally gave satisfaction. The processes were quick and simple. And business was transacted without the intervention of native lawyers and pleaders; directly by the villagers themselves with the British revenue officers.

No. II. Page 122.

In the death of Mr. G. J. Christian, the service lost an officer of high and distinguished ability; and great revenue knowledge. He had served with distinction as Secretary to the Board of Revenue at Agra; but was more valuable to us in Oudh, for the admirable settlement of the land revenue of his division, which had been effected under his superintendence. He had maintained a manly bearing throughout these disturbances; and his loss was a source of deep and general regret.

No. III. Page 147.

The only officer from whom I received support, in my proposal to disarm the remnants of the mutineer regiments, was Captain R. Edgell, officiating then as Military Secretary. He agreed with me in the necessity of the measure, and drew up at my request a written memorandum recommending it. In it he sufficiently showed that the European force outside the Residency ought to be a *movable* one: and that it at the time failed to possess this character, in consequence of the necessity which existed, for its watching the native troops. He showed that if the latter were disarmed, the European force would at once assume its proper character, and become available for action wherever its services were required. This paper was read before the Provisional Committee, but without moving their opinion.

No. IV. Page 208.

Mr. M. C. Ommanney had been for twenty-three years in the Civil Service of the East India Company, and by his ability and assiduity had earned himself a deservedly high name. He had served long in the Saugor territory; and had distinguished himself by his admirable investigation into, and settlement of, the difficult and involved land tenures in the Jounpoor district.

No. V. Page 227.

In Major Banks we sustained a severe loss. Naturally possessing great intellectual ability, he united to it untiring industry, and had made himself one of the best Hindee scholars in India. He was much valued in the Military Secretary's office in Calcutta, and had reluctantly quitted that post to accept civil duty at Lucknow, with which he was quite unacquainted. His ability and ceaseless industry, however, had overcome the main difficulties which opposed him; and, had he survived, he would have excelled in civil, as he had done in military office. From the time that he had been charged with the chief civil authority, he had made it a point of duty to visit daily all the chief posts in our position. In so doing he had unnecessarily exposed himself; and this he particularly used to do on the outer defences of my post. The parapet was little more than breast high; and in passing along the roofs of the outhouses, we were compelled to stoop, in order to screen ourselves from the fire of the enemy. Major Banks was short, yet, walking erect, his head was exposed; and he would rarely, if ever, stoop. Often have I remonstrated with him upon this practice, before the day on which it probably cost him his life. Having had, at the moment when he was struck, my back turned to him, I cannot tell whether the bullet entered by a loophole, or whether his head was exposed above the parapet.

No. VI. Page 323.

Mr. John B. Thornhill, C. S.—He was a gallant, noble young fellow, ever ready to place himself in the front in danger, and anxious to render service. He had received a severe bayonet wound in the pursuit of the mutineers, on the 12th of June, as has been mentioned already; and displayed much gallantry in that action. He had volunteered his assistance on this occasion, with the especial object of rendering aid to his relative, young Havelock; and succeeded in accompanying his doolie on foot, although thus severely wounded: and entered the Bailey Guard Gate along with it. His fate excited general and deserved regret.

APPENDIX, No. 1.

EXTRACT FROM A PRINTED LETTER ADDRESSED BY LIEUTENANT FARQUHAR, OF THE 7TH LIGHT CAVALRY, TO HIS MOTHER, DATED THE 3RD SEPTEMBER, 1857.

"WHEN we got to cantonments, we were ordered to go to the Artillery parade ground, where a camp was going to be formed. Here we went, and here we remained for a fortnight, encamped with the eighty men that remained of our regiment, being informed almost daily, by means of spies, that during the night these eighty swells intended to cut our throats. The 48th N. I. was encamped next to us. Fifty of them stuck to their officers on the night of the mutiny; but on the following day some 150 men who returned, and merely expressed their sorrow for deserting their officers, were taken back. These were pleasant fellows to have close to you!

"The consequence was that the officers of each regiment had to sleep together, armed to the teeth, and two officers of each regiment had to remain awake, taking two hours at a watch, to watch their own men. We kept these watches strictly; and, I believe, by that means saved our throats. I used to sleep every night (every officer here has slept in his clothes since the mutiny began) with my revolver under my pillow, a drawn sword on my bed, and a loaded double-barrelled gun just under the bed. We remained in this jolly state a fortnight; and I can tell you I was not sorry when an order came down from Sir Henry Lawrence * that we were to pay up our men, and send them home on leave till the 15th of October, and then come down to the Residency."

* N.B. It will be seen that this order emanated from the Provisional Council appointed on the 9th of June.

APPENDIX, No. 2.

COPIES OF LETTERS WHICH WERE RECEIVED AT LUCKNOW FROM SIR HUGH WHEELER'S INTRENCHMENT AT CAWNPOOR, IN JUNE, 1857.

From Sir H. M. Wheeler, K.C.B., to Martin Gubbins, Esq.

MY DEAR GUBBINS,

We have been besieged since the 6th by the Nana Saheb, joined by the whole of the native troops who broke out on the morning of the 4th. The enemy have two 24-pounders, and several other guns. We have only eight 9-pounders. The whole Christian population is with us in a temporary intrenchment, and our defence has been noble and wonderful, our loss heavy and cruel. We want aid, aid, aid! Regards to Lawrence.

Yours, &c.,

(Signed) H. M. WHEELER.

14th June,
Quarter-past 8, P.M.

P.S.—If we had 200 men, we could punish the scoundrels and aid you.

From Captain Moore, H. M. 32nd Foot, dated 18th June, 10, P.M.

SIR,

By desire of Sir Hugh Wheeler, I have the honour to acknowledge your letter of the 16th.

Sir Hugh regrets you cannot send him the 200 men, as he believes with their assistance we could drive the insurgents from Cawnpoor, and capture their guns.

Our troops, officers, and volunteers have acted most nobly; and on several occasions a handful of men have driven hundreds before them. Our loss has been chiefly from the sun, and their heavy guns. Our rations will last a fortnight, and we are still well supplied with ammunition. Our guns are serviceable. Report says that troops are advancing from Allahabad; and any assistance might save our garrison. We, of course, are prepared to hold out to the last. It is needless to mention the names of those who have been killed, or died. We trust in God; and if our exertions here assist your safety, it will be a consolation to know that our friends appreciate our devotion. Any news of relief will cheer us.

Yours, &c.,

(Signed) J. MOORE, Captain,

By order. 32nd Regt.

From Major G. V. Vibart, dated Cawnpoor, Sunday night, 12, P.M., 21*st June.*

MY DEAR SIR,

We have been cannonaded for six hours a-day by twelve guns. This evening, in three hours, upwards of thirty shells [mortars] were thrown into the intrenchment. This has occurred daily for the last eight days: *an idea may be formed of our casualties,* and how little protection the barracks afford to the women. Any aid to be effective must be immediate. In event of rain falling, our position would be untenable.

According to telegraphic despatches received previous to the outbreak, 1000 Europeans were to have been here on the 14th instant. This force may be on its way up. Any assistance you can send might co-operate with it. Nine-pounder ammunition, chiefly cartridges, is required. Should the above force arrive, we can in return insure the safety of Lucknow. Being simply a military man, General Wheeler has no power to offer bribes in land and money to the insurgents, *nor any means whatever* of communicating with them. You can ascertain the best means of crossing the river. Nujuffgurh Ghaut is suggested. It is earnestly requested that whatever is done may be effected without a moment's delay. We have lost about a third of our original number. The enemy are strongest in artillery. They appear not to have more than 400 or 500 infantry. They move their guns with difficulty, by means of unbroken bullocks. The infantry are great cowards, and easily repulsed.

By order,

(Signed) G. V. VIBART, Major.

EXTRACT FROM A PRIVATE LETTER FROM MAJOR L. M. WIGGENS, DEPUTY JUDGE-ADVOCATE-GENERAL, TO COLONEL HALFORD, 71ST N. I., DATED CAWNPOOR, 24TH JUNE, 1857.

"I WAS agreeably surprised to receive your most welcome letter of the 21st, the messenger of which managed cleverly to find his way here; but that surprise was exceeded by the astonishment felt by us all, at the total want of knowledge you seem to be in regarding our position and prospects; while we have been, since the 6th of the month, equally in the dark respecting the doings of the world around us. Your loss at Lucknow is frightful, in common with that of us all; for since the date referred to, every one here has been reduced to ruin. On that date they commenced their attack, and fearfully have they continued now for eighteen days and nights; while the condition of misery experienced by all is utterly beyond description in this place. Death and mutilation, in all their forms of horror, have been daily before us. The numerical amount of casualties has been frightful, caused both by sickness and the implements of war, the latter having been fully employed against our devoted garrison by the villanous insurgents, who have, unluckily, been enabled to furnish themselves therewith from the repository which contained them. We await the arrival of succour with the most anxious expectation, after all our endurance and sufferings; for that, Sir Henry Lawrence has been applied to by Sir Hugh, and we hope earnestly it will be afforded, and that *immediately*, to avert further evil. If he will answer that appeal with 'deux cents soldats Britanniques,' we shall be doubtless at once enabled to improve our position in a vital manner: and *we deserve* that the appeal should be so answered forthwith. You will be grieved to learn that among our casualties from sickness, my poor dear wife and infant have been numbered. The former sank on the 12th, and the latter on the 19th. I am writing this on the floor, and in the midst of the greatest dirt, noise, and confusion. Pray urge our reinforcement to the Chief Commissioner.

"Yours, &c.,

(Signed) "L. M. WIGGENS."

From Lieutenant G. A. Master, 53rd N. I., to his father, Lieutenant-Colonel Master, 7th Light Cavalry, dated Cawnpoor, June 25th, 8½ P.M.

We have held out now for twenty-one days, under a tremendous fire. The Raja of Bithoor has offered to forward us in safety to Allahabad, and the general has accepted his terms. I am all right, though twice wounded. Charlotte Newnham and Bella Blair are dead. I'll write from Allahabad. God bless you!

Your affectionate son,

(Signed) G. A. MASTER.

APPENDIX, No. 3.

MEMORANDUM SHOWING THE ORIGINAL STRENGTH OF THE LUCKNOW GARRISON, AND ITS REDUCTION BY DEATHS, DESERTIONS, ETC., DURING THE SIEGE.

Strength of the Garrison on the 1st July.	Reduction during the Siege.	Remaining strength of the Garrison, when relieved by General Havelock, on the 25th Sept., including sick and wounded.	Number of Officers killed and died in Garrison, from the 29th June to the Relief by Sir Colin Campbell.
Europeans . 927	Europeans. Killed . 350	Europeans. 577	Military . . 41
			Civil . . . 2
Natives . . 765	Natives. Killed . 133	Natives . 402	Assistant-Chaplain . 1
	Deserted 230		Warrant . . 5
Total . 1692	Total . 713	Total . 979	Total . . 49

MEMORANDUM SHOWING THE STRENGTH AND LOSSES OF THE RELIEVING FORCE UNDER GENERALS OUTRAM AND HAVELOCK.

Numerical strength of the Force which crossed the Ganges under General Havelock for the Relief of Lucknow.		Left at the Alum Bagh Post including wounded.	Number of Killed and Missing in General Havelock's Army, from the Crossing of the Ganges to its reaching the Lucknow Residency.	Strength of General Outram's Force inside Lucknow on the 26th September, including wounded.	Strength of the same when finally relieved in November, including sick and wounded.	Total killed and wounded of the Relieving Force.	Number of Officers killed and wounded.
European Infantry . .	2388	400	138	1850	1674	Up to the 26th Sept. inclusive.	Killed, including died of Wounds.
Ditto Volunteer Cavalry .	109	19	4	86	74	535	29
Ditto Artillery . . .	282	42	46	194	190	During the Blockade, up to the 25th Nov.	
Seikh Infantry . . .	341	57	12	272	229		Wounded.
Native Irregular Cavalry .	59	13	7	39	39	431	47
Total . . .	3179	531	207	2441	2206	966	76

APPENDIX, No. 4.

General Order by His Excellency the Commander-in-Chief.

Head-Quarters, Shah Nujeef, Lucknow,
21st November, 1857.

Although the Commander-in-Chief has not yet had time to peruse the detailed report of Brigadier Inglis respecting the defence made by the slender garrison under his command, His Excellency desires to lose no time in recording his opinion of the magnificent defence made by the remnant of a British regiment, Her Majesty's 32nd, a company of British Artillery, and a few hundred sepoys, whose very presence was a subject of distrust, against all the force of Oudh; until the arrival of the reinforcement under Major-General Sir J. Outram, G.C.B., and Sir Henry Havelock, K.C.B.

2. The persevering constancy of this small garrison, under the watchful command of the Brigadier, has, under Providence, been the means of adding to the prestige of the British army, and of preserving the honour and lives of our countrywomen. There can be no greater reward than such a reflection; and the Commander-in-Chief heartily congratulates Brigadier Inglis and his devoted garrison on that reflection belonging to them.

3. The position occupied by the garrison was an open intrenchment; the numbers were not sufficient to man the defences, and the supply of artillerymen for the guns was most inadequate. In spite of these difficult circumstances, the Brigadier and his garrison held on; and it will be a great pleasure to the Commander-in-Chief to bring to the notice of the Government of India the names of all the officers and soldiers who have distinguished themselves during the great trial to which they have been exposed.

4. The Commander-in-Chief congratulates Sir James Outram and Sir Henry Havelock on having been the first to aid Brigadier Inglis.

The Governor-General in Council has already expressed his opinion on the splendid feat of arms by which that aid was accomplished.

APPENDIX, No. 5.

Account dictated by Major Vincent Eyre of the Destruction by him of a Marauding Force from Oudh, on the 11th of September, 1857.

On the 11th of September General Outram's Force was encamped at Aŏng, one march on the Allahabad side of Futtehpoor, when tidings were brought that certain talooqdars * of Oudh had crossed the Ganges into the Dooab with two guns and 300 men, and had surrounded the town of Koondun Puttee and plundered the house of one Cheyda Lall. It was further stated, that they intended to destroy the towns of Hutgaon and Khaga; their ultimate design being to intercept our communications between Cawnpoor and Allahabad, and to intimidate the native officials and compel them to join them. It was reported, that this was but the advance party to be followed by a still stronger force. General Outram accordingly directed an expedition to proceed at once to Koondun Puttee to repel the invaders. The force consisted of 100 of Her Majesty's 5th Fusiliers, fifty of Her Majesty's 64th Foot, and two guns; to be joined at Hutgaon by forty troopers of the 12th Irregular Cavalry under Captain Johnson, the whole under the command of Major Eyre of the Artillery. Two days' cooked provisions were served out, and the force left camp at 2, P.M., on the 10th of September, and reached Hutgaon at nightfall, where it was punctually joined by Captain Johnson's Irregular Cavalry, who had marched twenty-four miles for that purpose. The night being dark, and there being no distinguishable carriage road, the force halted until after midnight for the moon to rise, and reached Koondun Puttee by a very circuitous route across fields and swamps a little before daybreak. The villagers reported the Oudh rebels to be near at hand, if not actually within the walls of the place: their boats being moored about a mile off. Major Eyre, therefore, ordered the cavalry to proceed in two parties under Captain Johnson and Lieutenant C. Havelock to guard the gates of the town. And should the rebels have fled, to pursue them to their boats, and hold them in check until the body of the force could come up. The rebels hearing of our approach had retired, and the cavalry pursuing, reached the river bank just in time to prevent their boats leaving the shore.

* Their names were ascertained to be Bhugwân Singh (Kunpoorea) and Sirdar Singh (Byse).

A brisk fire was maintained on both sides by the cavalry from the high bank, and the enemy from their boats, until the arrival of the main body, the enemy defending themselves with vigour. On the arrival of the force, the detachment of Her Majesty's 5th and 64th then took up the fire, which told with fearful effect on the densely-crowded defenders of the boats, who finding themselves unable to use their two guns, threw them overboard into the river. By this time the two guns under Lieutenant Gordon of the Artillery took up a position on the edge of the high bank overlooking the boats, and opened fire with round shot into the latter. This created an immediate panic, and the rebels rushing on deck from all sides precipitated themselves into the river, and endeavoured to escape by swimming down the stream. But showers of grape shot being rapidly discharged amongst them, and a terrific fusillade kept up by the Infantry and Cavalry, their efforts were unavailing: and but three survivors escaped to the opposite bank, to tell the tale of their unexpected disaster. About forty of our men had boarded one of the boats on the first rush of the enemy on deck, so that some few of the latter remained in the hold below; by one of whom their magazine was fired, but providentially only five men were seriously injured by the explosion: though several of them were more or less burnt.

Several stand of arms were found in the boats with new appointments all of the same pattern, which had evidently been very recently served out. Tidings were now brought to Major Eyre, that another party of marauders from Oudh had landed that morning at a ghaut four miles higher up the river, their numbers being reported at 300: in consequence of which Captain Johnson was despatched with the Irregular Cavalry to reconnoitre. He found the intelligence to be correct, but having heard the report of the engagement near Koondun Puttee, they had re-embarked and already regained the opposite shore. The police authorities of Koondun Puttee informed Major Eyre that but for the decisive blow which had thus been struck, and which would effectually terrify the Oudh borderers, the whole of the neighbouring country would have been overrun in two or three days; as threatening letters had been addressed to every police station, demanding their allegiance to the rebel government of Oudh. Having thus executed the duty entrusted to him, Major Eyre rejoined General Outram's camp by a forced march of twenty-four miles at Futtehpoor.

APPENDIX, No. 6.

List of Officers employed in the Province of Oudh, and Others, who were Killed, Died of Sickness, or were Wounded, during the Disturbances in that Province, from May to the end of November, 1857, exclusive of the Relieving Forces.

Regiment or Department.	Killed and Died of Wounds.	Died of Sickness.	Wounded.	Remarks.
	Name.	Name.	Name.	
Civil Employ	Sir Henry Lawrence, K.C.B.	....	....	Chief Commissioner and Brigadier General.
	Mr. M. C. Ommanney, C. S.	....	....	Judicial Commissioner.
	Major Banks	....	....	Commissioner of Lucknow, and Provisional Chief Commissioner.
	....	....	Mr. A. Boulderson, C. S....	Assistant Commissioner, Lucknow.
	....	Lieut. Fullerton, 44th N. I.	....	Assistant Commissioner at Duriabad.
	....	Mrs. R. P. Anderson	....	Wife of Captain R. P. Anderson, Assistant Commissioner.
	....	....	Mr. W. C. Capper, C. S. ...	Deputy Commissioner of Mullaon.
	....	Mrs. Edgar Clarke	....	Refugee from Gondah; wife of Lieutenant Ed. Clarke, Assistant Commissioner.
	Mr. Charles Cunliffe, C. S..	....	....	Deputy Commissioner of Bareytch; killed at Byram Ghaut.
	Mr. Arthur Jenkins, C. S...	....	....	Assistant Commissioner in Poorwah; killed at Cawnpoor.
	Mrs. Evans and children ...	....	....	Wife of Captain Evans, Deputy Commissioner of Poorwah; killed at Cawnpoor.

Regiment or Department.	Killed and Died of Wounds. Name.	Died of Sickness. Name.	Wounded. Name.	Remarks.
Civil Employ	Captain Fletcher Hayes	....	....	Military Secretary; killed near Mynpoory.
	....	....	Mr. G. H. Lawrence, C. S.	Deputy Commissioner of Gondah.
	Lieutenant Lester	....	....	Assistant Commissioner at Seetapoor.
	Mr. G. J. Christian, C. S., wife, and two children	....	....	Commissioner of Khyrabad; killed at Seetapoor.
	Mr. H. B. Thornhill, C. S., wife, and two children	....	....	Deputy Commissioner of Seetapoor; killed at Seetapoor.
	Sir Mountstuart Jackson, Bart.	....	....	Assistant Commissioner at Seetapoor; killed after the evacuation of Lucknow.
	....	Rev. H. Polehampton	....	Assistant Chaplain; wounded before.
	Mr. J. B. Thornhill, C. S.	....	....	Wounded before.
	M. J. Thomason, C. S.	....	....	Deputy Commissioner of Mohumdee; killed near Mohumdee.
	Captain P. Orr	....	....	Assistant Commissioner of Mohumdee; killed after the evacuation of Lucknow.
	....	Mr. Gonne, C. S.	....	Deputy Commissioner of Mullapoor, in the Nipal Turay.
	....	Captain Hastings	....	Assistant Commissioner of Mullapoor, in the Nipal Turay.
	Colonel Goldney	....	....	Commissioner of Fyzabad, at Begum Gunje.
	Mr. Adam Block, C. S. Mr. S. Stroyan	....	....	Deputy Commissioner at Sultanpoor. Assistant Commissioner of ditto. Both killed near Sultanpoor.
Military Staff	Brigadier Handscomb	....	....	In Cantonments on the 30th May.
	....	....	Captain James	In charge of Commissariat Department; at Chinhut.

			Lieutenant F. Birch	Aide-de-camp.
			Captain T. F. Wilson	Officiating Deputy-Assistant-Adjutant General; slightly.
		Captain Barlow		Brigade-Major, O. Irr. Force.
Engineers.		Major J. Anderson.		Chief Engineer.
	Captain G. Fulton.			Executive Engineer, afterwards Chief Engineer.
Artillery.	Lieutenant D. C. Alexander			
			Lieutenant Jas. Alexander	
			Lieutenant Bonham	Wounded three times.
		Lieutenant Bryce		Wounded before.
		Lieutenant Foster Cunliffe		Wounded before.
	Lieutenant Lewin.			
			Lieutenant McFarlan	
	Captain Simonds			Died of wounds received at Chinhut.
		Mrs. Thomas		Wife of Capt. Thomas, Madras Artillery.
	Major J. Mill			Drowned near Fyzabad.
	Lieutenant Ashe			Killed at Cawnpoor.
	Lieutenant R. Currie			Drowned near Fyzabad.
	Mr. Baxter			Conductor, Ordnance Department.
H. M.'s 32nd Regt.	Colonel Case			Killed at Chinhut.
	Captain Stevens			
	Lieutenant Thomson			
	Lieutenant Brackenbury			
		Captain Mansfield.		
			Captain Bassano	At Chinhut.
			Lieutenant G. Browne.	
	Captain McCabe.			
			Lieutenant Charlton.	
			Lieutenant Cooke.	
			Lieutenant Edmondstoune.	

Regiment or Department.	Killed and Died of Wounds. Name.	Died of Sickness. Name.	Wounded. Name.	Remarks.
H. M.'s 32nd Regt.	....	....	Captain Lowe.	
	....	....	Lieutenant Foster.	
	....	....	Lieutenant Harmer.	
	Captain Power.			
	Lieutenant Webb.			
	Ensign Studdy.			
H. M.'s 84th Regt.	....	....	Captain O'Brien.	
7th Regt. of Light Cavalry.	Lieutenant Arthur.			
	....	....	Captain T. F. Boileau.	
	Lieutenant Boulton	....	....	Killed at Cawnpoor.
	Captain Staples	....	....	Killed near Cawnpoor.
	Lieutenant N. Martin	....	....	Killed near Cawnpoor.
	Riding-Master Eldridge.			
	....	....	Lieutenant Farquhar	At Chinhut.
	Veterinary-Surgeon Hely.			
	Captain Radcliffe.			
	Cornet Raleigh	....	....	At Moodkipoor, on the 30th of May.
13th N. I.	Major Bruere.			
	....	....	Lieutenant Chambers	In Cantonments, 30th May,
	....	....	Captain Waterman.	
	Major Francis.			
	....	Ensign Green.		
	....	....		
			Lieutenant Cubitt.	
48th N. I.	Major Burmester	....	....	Killed near Cawnpoor.

	Ensign Farquharson	....	....	Killed near Cawnpoor.
	....	Lieut. A. J. Dashwood......	....	Wounded before.
	Ensign Dashwood.			
	....	....	Lieutenant Fletcher.	
	....	Mrs. Green	....	Wife of Captain Green.
	....	....	Lieutenant Hay.	
	....	....	Lieutenant Huxham.	
	....	Mrs. R. Ouseley and two children..................	....	Wife of Lieutenant R. Ouseley.
	Miss Palmer	....	....	Daughter of Colonel Palmer.
	....	....	Lieutenant O. L. Smith.	
	....	....	Ensign H. C. O'Dowda.	
	....	....	Surgeon Wells	Slightly.
71st N. I.	Lieutenant A. Grant.........	....	....	In Cantonments, 30th of May.
	....	....	Dr. Brydon.	
	....	....	Lieut. C. W. Campbell ...	At Chinhut.
	....	Colonel Halford.		
	....	....	Ensign R. L. Inglis	63rd N.I.
	Captain Maclean	....	....	At Chinhut.
	....	....	Captain Strangways.	
41st N. I.	Lieutenant-Colonel Birch ...	....	....	Killed at Seetapoor.
	Lieutenant Smalley	....	....	Ditto ditto.
	....	Lieutenant Graves.		
	....	....	Captain Kemble.	
	....	....	Lieutenant H. Inglis.	
	....	....	Ensign Hewitt.	
	....	Dr. McDonald.		
	....	Ensign McGregor.		
22nd N. I.	Lieutenant A. Bright .... Lieutenant A. F. English.	....	....	Killed near Fyzabad.
	Lieutenant T E. Lindesay	....	....	Killed in Goruckpoor, while flying from Fyzabad.

Regiment or Department.	Killed and Died of Wounds. Name.	Died of Sickness. Name.	Wounded. Name.	Remarks.
22nd N. I.	Lieutenant W. H. Thomas.	....	....	Killed near Fyzabad.
	Lieutenaut G. L. Cautley...	....	....	As Lieutenant Lindesay.
	Lieut. J. W. S. Anderson.	....	....	Killed near Fyzabad.
	Lieutenant T. J. Ritchie.			
Refugees from Shajehanpoor.	Captain Sneyd	....	....	
	Captain Lysaght and wife...	....	....	
	Captain Salmon........... ..	....	....	
28th N. I.	Lieutenant Key and wife ...	....	....	
	Lieutenant Robertson	....	....	
	Lieutenant Scott	....	....	
	Lieutenant Pitt	....	....	
	Lieutenant Rutherfurd	....	....	
	Ensign Spens..................	....	....	
	Ensign Johnston	....	....	
	Ensign E. C. Scott....	....	....	
	Quartermstr.-Sergt. Grant...	....	....	
	Mrs. Scott	....	....	Murdered near Aurungabad.
	Miss Scott	....	....	
	Mrs. Bowling	....	....	
	Mrs. Grant	....	....	
Vet. Estab.	Lieutenant Sheils and wife	....	....	
	Mrs. Pereira and 4 children	....	....	
	Mr. C. J. Jenkins, C. S. ...	....	....	Assistant to the Magistrate of Futtehgurh.
	....	Mr. Brand, merchant.	....	

1st Regt. Oudh Irreg. Cavalry.	Lieutenant Bax	......	......	Killed at Cawnpoor.
	......	......	Captain H. Forbes.	
	Lieutenant J. Graham.			
2nd Regt. O. I. Cavalry.	Major Gall......	......	......	Killed at Ray Bareilly.
	Lieutenant Shepherd.			
	Lieutenant Barbor	......	......	Killed near Mynpoory.
3rd Regt. O. I. Cavalry.	Lieutenant Alexander......	......	......	Killed at Allahabad.
	......	......	Lieutenant Graham.	
	......	......	Captain G. Hardinge	Since died at Sea.
2nd Regt. O. I. Infantry.	......	The wife of Lieutenant G. H. Hale.		
3rd Regt. O. I. Infantry.	Lieut. Longueville Clarke.	......	......	Killed at Byram Ghaut.
4th Regt. O. I. Infantry.	Captain Hughes.			
5th Regt. O. I. Infantry.	Lieutenant Gregor Grant.			
	......	......	Captain W. H. Hawes.	
6th Regt. O. I. Infantry.	Lieutenant Parsons	......	......	Drowned in the Ghogra River.
	Sergeant-Major Matthews.	......	......	Killed near Fyzabad.

Regiment or Department.	Killed and Died of Wounds. Name.	Died of Sickness. Name.	Wounded. Name.	Remarks.
7th Regt. O. I. Infantry.	Captain Graydon.			
9th Regt. O. I. Infantry.	Captain G. Gowan, wife and child …	…	…	
	Lieutenant O. Greene …	…	…	Killed at Seetapoor.
	Assistant-Surgeon Hill…	…	…	
	…	…	Lieutenant J. A. Vanrenen	
10th Regt. O. I. Infantry.	Captain Dorin …	…	…	
	Lieutenant Snell …	…	…	At Seetapoor.
	Mrs. Snell and child …	…	…	
	Lieutenant G. Burnes …	…	…	Since the evacuation of Lucknow.
	Mrs. Dorin.			
	Dr. Darby.			
	Quartermstr.-Sergt. Morton	…	…	Since the evacuation of Lucknow.
Uncovenanted Civil Service.	Mr. Jordan…	…	…	Extra Assistant at Bareytch; killed at Byram Ghaut.
	…	Mr. R. Garland.		
	…	Mrs. R. M. Collins …	…	Wife of Mr. R. M. Collins, Extra Assistant, Poorwah.
	Mr. Ramsey …	…	…	In charge of Electric Telegraph Office.
Department of Public Works.	Lieutenant Birch, 59th N.I.			
	Overseer Ryder.			
	…	…	Mr. Macrae …	Twice wounded.
	…	Mr. Casey …	…	Wounded before.

Merchants, Travellers, &c.	Mr. F. D. Lucas.	....	....	An Irish gentleman, travelling.
	....	Mr. E. Cameron.		
	M. Duprat.			
	Mr. R. Fayrer	....	....	Killed near Mynpoorie.
	Mr. Need.			
Shopkeepers and Tradesmen.	....	Mr. Cameron.	....	From Allahabad.
	M. Crabb.			
	Mr. Ereth.			
	....	....	Mr. J. Sinclair.	
Uncovenanted Service, including Clerks, &c.	....	....	Mr. A. Alone.	
	....	....	Mr. B. Alone.	
	....	....	Mr. G. Bailey.	
	....	Mr. Barrett.		
	Mr. Beale.			
	....	....	Mr. Bickers.	
	....	....	Mr. P. Blaney.	
	....	....	Mr. C. Blaney.	
	....	....	Mr. Blenman.	
	Mr. C. Brown.			
	Mr. J. Brown.			
	....	....	Mr. Brown.	
	....	Mr. O. Browne.		
	Mr. A. Bryson.			
	Mr. Clancey.			
	Mr. Dallicott.			
	....	....	Mr. Forester.	
	....	Mrs. Higgins.		
	Mrs. Horan.			
	....	....	Mr. Hyde.	
	Mr. Marshall	....	....	Opium Contractor.

Regiment or Department.	Killed and Died of Wounds.	Died of Sickness.	Wounded.	Remarks.
	Name.	Name.	Name.	
Uncovenanted Service, including Clerks, &c.	Mr. McAuliffe.			
	Mr. McManus.			
	Mr. Mendes.			
	....	....	Mr. Morgan.	
	....	Mrs. Nazareth.		
	....	....	Mr. Oliver.	
	Mr. Pigeon.			
	....	....	Mr. Rae.	
	....	....	Mr. Rutledge.	
	....	Mr. Schmidt.		
	Mrs. Sequera.			
	Mr. E. Sequera.			
	....	....	Mr. C. Sequera.	
	....	....	Mr. Thriepland.	
	Mr. Vaughan.			
	Mr. Wells.			
	....	Mrs. Wilkinson.		
	....	Mr. Wiltshire.		
	Mr. Edmund Wittinbaker.			

APPENDIX, No. 7.

List of Officers belonging to the Relieving Force, commanded by Generals Outram and Havelock, who were killed and wounded, from the 19th of September to the 25th of November, 1857.

Regiment or Department.	Killed and Died of Wounds.	Wounded.	Remarks.
Staff.	Brig.-Gen. Neill.		
	Brig. (Maj.) Cooper, Beng. Art.		
	Lieut.-Col. Bazeley, Beng. Art.		
	....	Major-Gen. Sir James Outram, G.C.B.	
	Capt. Andrew Becher, A. A. Gen.		
	....	Capt. Alex. Orr	Slightly.
	....	Capt. Dodgson, A. A.-Gen.	
	....	Lieut. Sitwell, A.D.C.	
	....	Lieut.-Col. B. Fraser Tytler, Dy. A. Qr.-Mr.-Gen.	
	....	Lieut. H. M. Havelock, Dy. A. Adj.-Gen.	
Engineers	....	Capt. Crommelin	Slightly.
	....	Lt. J. Russell, Brigade-Major, Engineers.	
	....	Col. R. Napier, Military Secretary.	
Artillery.	Lieutenant Crump, Madras Art.		
	Asst.-Surg. Bartrum.		
	....	Capt. Olpherts	Slightly.
Volunteer Cavalry.	....	Lieut. Lynch, H. M. 70th	Slightly.
	....	Lieut. Palliser, 63rd N. I.	Slightly.
	....	Lieut. Swanston, 7th Madras N. I.	
	....	Lieut. Birch, 1st Light Cavalry.	
	....	Ensign J. Hearsey, 38th N. I.	
12th Irr. Cavalry.	Lieut. Warren, H. M. 64th Foot.		

Regiment or Department.	Killed and Died of Wounds.	Wounded.	Remarks.
H. M. 5th Fusiliers.	Major J. E. Simmonds		
	Capt. F. W. L'Estrange		
	Capt. A. E. Johnson.		
	....	Capt. J. D. Adair.	
	....	Capt. A. Scott.	
H. M. 64th Foot.	Lieut. R. Bateman.		
H. M. 78th Highlanders.	Major Haliburton.		
	Capt. R. Bogle.		
	Lieut. J. Webster.		
	Lieut. M. Kirby.		
	Lieut. J. Swanson.		
	....	Capt. Lockhart.	
	....	Capt. Hastings	Slightly.
	....	Lieut. Crowe	Slightly.
	....	Lieut. Grant.	
	....	Lieut. Macpherson....	Slightly.
	Lieut. Joly	....	H.M. 32nd: doing duty.
H. M. 84th Foot.	Capt. R. Pakenham.		
	Lieut. Wm. Poole.		
	....	Capt. Willis	Slightly.
	....	Lieut. Barry	Slightly.
	....	Lieut. Oakley.	
	....	Lieut. Woolhouse.	
H. M. 90th Light Infantry.	Lt.-Col. R. P. Campbell, C. B.		
	Capt. H. Denison.		
	Lieut. A. Moultrie.		
	....	Lieut. W. Knight.	
	....	Assist.-Surg. Bradshaw.	
	Lieut. M. Preston.		
	....	Capt. P. Phipps.	
1st Madras Fusiliers.	Major Stephenson.		
	Lieut. Arnold.		
	....	Lieut. Bailey.	
	....	Lieut. Grant.	

APPENDIX, No. 8.

LIST OF OFFICERS BELONGING TO SIR COLIN CAMPBELL'S ARMY, WHO WERE KILLED OR WOUNDED IN THE OPERATIONS FOR THE RELIEF OF LUCKNOW, FROM THE 14TH TO THE 25TH OF NOVEMBER, 1857.

Regiment or Department.	Killed and Died of Wounds.	Wounded.	Remarks.
Staff.	Lieut.-Col. G. Biddulph, Intelligence Department.		
	Lieut. A. O. Mayne, D. A. Quartermr.-General.		
	....	Gen. Sir Colin Campbell, G.C.B........	Slightly.
	....	Brigadier D. Russell. .	Commanding 5th Brigade.
	....	Major A. Alison	Military Secrty.
	....	Capt. F. M. Alison ..	A. D. C.
	....	Capt. the Hon. A. Anson	A. D. C. to Gen. Grant; slightly.
	....	Lieut. C. J. Salmond. .	Orderly Officer to ditto; slightly.
Naval Brigade.	Midshipman M. A. Daniel	....	R. N.
	....	Capt. J. C. Gray	Royal Marines.
	....	Lieut. M. Salmon....	R. N.
	....	Midshipman Lord A. P. Clinton	R. N.
Artillery Brigade.	Capt. W. N. Hardy. .	....	R. A.
	....	Major F. F. Pennycuick	R. A.
	....	Capt. F. Travers	R. A.; slightly.
	....	Capt. H. Hammond..	B. A.
	....	Lieut. W. G. Milman	R. A.; slightly.
	....	Lieut. A. Ford	R. A.; slightly.
	....	Asst.-Surg. H.R. Veale	R. A.
Cavalry Brigade.	Capt. G. Wheatcroft	....	6th Drag. Gds.; doing duty with Military Train.
	....	Lieut. R. Halkett....	Hodson's Horse.
H. M. 23rd Welch Fusiliers.	....	Lieut. H. Henderson.	

Regiment or Department.	Killed and Died of Wounds.	Wounded.	Remarks.
H. M. 53rd Foot.	....	Capt. B. Walton.	
	....	Lieut. A. K. Munro.	
	....	Lieut. F. C. Ffrench.	
H. M. 82nd Foot.	Ens. W. T. Thompson.		
	....	Lieut.-Col. C. B. Hale.	
H. M. 90th Light Infantry.	Major R. Barnston.		
	....	Lieut. E. C. Wynne.	
	....	Ensign H. Powell.	
H. M. 93rd Highlanders.	Capt. J. Dalzell.		
	Capt. J. T. Lumsden	....	36th N. I.: doing duty.
	....	Lieut.-Col. Ewart	Slightly.
	....	Capt. F. W. Burroughs	Slightly.
	....	Lieut. R. A. Cooper.	
	....	Lieut. E. Welch.	
	....	Lieut. O. Goldsmith.	
	....	Lieut. S. E. Wood.	
	....	Ens. F. R. McNamara	Slightly.
1st Madras Fusiliers.	Lieut. Dobbs.		
2nd Regt. of Punjaub Infantry.	Lieut. T. Frankland		
	....	Ensign J. Watson.	
4th Punjaub Infantry.	Lieut. W. Paul.		
	....	Lieut. J. M. McQueen.	
	Lieut. F. F. Oldfield		

APPENDIX, No. 9.

NARRATIVE GIVEN BY ONE OF THE LADIES WHO ESCAPED FROM SULTANPOOR, AND AFTER FINDING AN ASYLUM WITH LALL MADHO SINGH, REACHED ALLAHABAD IN SAFETY.

On Saturday, the 6th of June, a native police trooper came in from Chanda, a town on the Jounpoor Road, and reported that a body of mutineer troops had reached that place, and were marching upon Sultanpoor. In consequence of this intelligence, all the ladies were sent up to the Irregular Cavalry lines, distant one mile from the rest of the station, about one or two o'clock of that day, and took shelter in Dr. Corbyn's house. They slept there that night, and went back the next morning to their houses. This occurred on Sunday, the 7th of June. About noon of that day Colonel Fisher came over; and said that he thought the ladies should all be sent off immediately. At the same time Mr. Block received a letter from Colonel Goldney, advising that the ladies should be sent off without delay to Allahabad. Sunday was occupied in preparations for their departure. The ladies packed up all their things, being kept in ignorance of the real extent of the danger.

About 5 P.M., Lieutenant Lewis, 8th O. I. Infantry, rushed into Mr. Block's house, stating that the sepoys of his regiment were demanding their pay. Messrs. Block and Stroyan accordingly went to the Treasury, to give them their pay. The sepoys were found surrounding the Treasury. The Treasurer had fled with his keys; and they could not therefore give out the money, and were obliged to return.

About two hours later, after sunset, the ladies drove down to Colonel Fisher's house, and found a party ready to escort them, composed of a troop of Fisher's Horse, and also of some police foot soldiers, provided by Luchmun Purshaud, Cotwal* of Sultanpoor. This man behaved well throughout. He was of much assistance in helping the ladies to prepare for their departure; and the men whom he sent with the party remained, the greater number of them, faithful, and attended the ladies as far as Beylah Ghaut.

It must have been 8 o'clock before they started. Dr. Corbyn, 15th Irregular Cavalry, was in charge of the party. Captain

* Head native police officer.

Jenkins, 8th O. I. Infantry, who had that day marched into the station from Lucknow with a wing of his regiment, which had escorted treasure into Lucknow, also accompanied it. The whole of the clerks and their families also left with the ladies. It had not been intended that the clerks themselves should go, but their families only. The men, however, would accompany their families; and though remonstrated with by the Deputy-Commissioner, Mr. Block, refused to remain at Sultanpoor. They were, they said, sure of being killed if they remained. Mrs. Goldney and family, Mrs. Block and child, Mrs. Stroyan, Mrs. Jenkins, Mrs. Bunbury, Mrs. O'Donel and Miss O'Donel, and a large number of clerks' wives and children, all left the station, conveyed in a long line of carriages a little after nightfall.

After proceeding about half an hour, an alarm was given that a mutineer cavalry regiment was approaching the party. The cavalry escort rode to the right and left, and drew up in groups, apparently as if in communication with some others. However, they were not attacked.

It was a terrible night. The road was rough and bad, and lay through a dhâk jungle. Every noise and every object, dimly seen at night, filled the ladies with terror. After a weary journey at a foot's pace all night, the day dawned upon them as they were crossing the Syee River, opposite to the Beylah Ghaut cantonment. While crossing the stream, they met a body of the Allahabad jail convicts, who had been released by the mutineers at Allahabad. They were shouting and making a noise as they went along, and at first it was not known who they were. They did not attempt to do the party any harm. At that time there only remained three of Fisher's horsemen with it. But the police guard sent by Luchmun Purshaud still remained, and walked alongside of the carriages. And their presence very probably prevented the convicts from attempting to do the party any injury.

On reaching the Beylah Ghaut cantonment, which is commonly known as that of Purtabgurh, the fugitives went to Captain Hardinge's bungalow there, and were most kindly received by Lieutenant J. A. Grant, Assistant-Commissioner, who was then engaged in raising a Native Infantry levy. With Lieutenant Grant was Mr. W. Glynne, a gentleman employed in the Customs' department, who also came forward to render assistance. At Beylah Ghaut, besides the new levies, which were being raised by Lieutenant Grant, there was also one troop of Hardinge's Oudh Irregular Cavalry.

Great was the excitement among the natives of the cantonment which was caused by the arrival of the party. A motley crew of Hardinge's sowars, Bunbury's police, and Grant's new levies, surrounded the bungalow in which the ladies alighted to take some refreshment and rest. Their arrival manifestly announced to the natives the fact that mutiny had occurred, or was imminent at Sultanpoor, and the men were grouped about, talking and whispering together. Mrs. Block was attended by a little native chupprassie, named Fyzoollah Khan, who rode by the side of the carriage the whole way, and eventually accompanied her to Allahabad. His conduct was most faithful, and nothing could shake his resolve to see her safely to her journey's end.

The ladies were dreadfully fatigued, and endeavoured to get some rest. One of them, Miss O'Donel, fell asleep upon a couch in a room in which Lieutenant Grant had procured a native to pull the punkah. Mrs. Block was attending to her infant in an adjoining chamber, when she saw the native let go the rope of the punkah, and approach the couch on which Miss O'Donel was lying. He glared upon the sleeping girl with so fiendish an expression, that Mrs. Block believed that he was going to kill her, and, screaming, sprung into the room. Miss O'Donel awoke, and the native retired with slow steps, and resumed his pull at the punkah.

While they were attempting to snatch some rest in this bungalow, an alarm was brought, that the Goreyts * were coming down in large numbers to demand their pay. It was said that they were coming with the intention of burning the bungalow and plundering the ladies. Hastily, therefore, they re-entered the carriages, and consulted what course to pursue. Lieutenant Grant advised that they should seek refuge with Golaubsingh, talooqdar of Turole, who had a house in the neighbouring town of Purtaubgurh. Mrs. Block's chupprassie, Fyzoollah Khan, gave the same advice. Mr. Block had been encamped in that neigh-

* These "Goreyts" were the village watchmen. They were almost all pâsies. They were in arrear of pay, and had some just cause of complaint. A liberal remuneration had been provided for them, by the settlement proceedings. The money had been collected, and had been paid over to the police department for issue. Great delay had however taken place in distributing the pay. The preparation of the Registers showing the names of the watchmen of each village was a work of time, and had been too much delayed. The pâsee watchmen were now, no doubt, afraid that if our Government were overthrown, they would lose their arrears of pay altogether. And this violent outbreak was probably intended to enforce immediate payment of that which was justly their due.

bourhood not long before; and had seen a good deal of this person. Accordingly, it was resolved to do so; and the party started for Golaubsingh's, but presently met the crowd of goreyts coming down, most of them armed with spears. The horses were put to the gallop, and the carriages tore along the road. The fellows tried to stop them, but the fugitives pushed along, flying for their lives. One of the men caught hold of the carriage, in which Mrs. Corbyn and Mrs. Block were conveyed, with his left hand; and hanging on by it, tried to aim a thrust with his spear at the ladies in the carriage. His spear just missed Mrs. Block, who moved to one side, and escaped it; then the man was forced to let go the carriage, and fell behind. In another carriage in which were seated Mrs. Goldney and Mrs. Stroyan, a spear was thrust in, and struck the carriage between the two ladies. Disappointed in their attempt to stop the carriages, some of the goreyts fell upon the elephants which accompanied the party; and plundered them. Others ran after the carriages, which were accompanied on horseback by Lieutenant Grant and Mr. Glynne. The wife of one of the serjeants was riding on an elephant. The insurgents pulled her and her children off; and made them prisoners. But she was afterwards rescued by Golaubsingh.

Proceeding on at a gallop, the party arrived at the enclosure of Golaubsingh's residence in Purtaubgurh, into which they had great difficulty in getting the carriages. Golaubsingh himself came out, and received them with great apparent civility; asked them to rest; had charpoys (or native beds) brought out for them to sit down upon, and gave them water to quench their thirst; and had the ladies fanned. They were thoroughly exhausted. The night's march and the excessive heat of the day had wholly worn them out, and they now hoped to obtain a little rest. Golaubsingh was himself a tall thin man, very advanced in years, and shaking with palsy. His words gave the refugees to hope that he would do all that he could to protect them. But while he was giving them these assurances, his people told the party that they must go. They declared that there were regiments of mutineers coming down upon the place from all quarters; and that Golaubsingh was not strong enough to protect them. Accordingly the ladies had not been inside his court-yard for more than one half-hour, before they were again turned out. By this time the insurgent pâsies or goreyts, who had been pursuing the carriages from Beylah Ghaut, had come up. The fugitives had the greatest difficulty in getting through them. The first carriage, in which were Mrs. Corbyn and Mrs. Block, got off better than the others, being better horsed. But they lost there most of their property. Mrs. Goldney's carriage was stopped by the men, who seized the horses' heads. Lieutenant Grant, however, threatening them with a pistol, induced them to let go. He at the same time urgently cautioned all the men of the party not on any account to fire a shot, lest a general slaughter should begin. At last Mr. Glynne succeeded in drawing off the mass of the goreyts, by promising to distribute among them a bag of money which he displayed before them. While they were so engaged, the ladies made off again, as fast as their tired horses could go. They did not know which road to follow. Dr. Corbyn wished to take the road towards Allahabad. But Lieutenant Grant, who had heard on the preceding day of the mutiny of the troops at that station, was much opposed to his doing so; and counselled that they should make off across country. The road towards Allahabad was, however, then the only one before them which seemed practicable for carriages; and the fugitives followed it. Proceeding along the road they met several sepoys with their uniform disordered, and themselves looking worn and tired, coming from Allahabad. They confirmed the fact of the mutiny having taken place at that station; but were civil, and said that they were going to their homes. There was nothing in their conduct or demeanour which would, otherwise, have indicated them to be mutineers. Mrs. Goldney being now assured that a mutiny had really taken place, ordered her coachman to leave the road and go across the country. But the attempt soon proved impracticable. The horses could not drag the carriage along; and she was obliged to return to the road. The horses soon after this became quite exhausted; and reaching a nullah where there was deep sand, could not drag the vehicles through. The ladies had, therefore, to get out, and push, all of them, at the wheels to propel the carriages.

M. de Hoxha, a French gentleman, who had been employed in the Road Department at Sultanpoor, and accompanied the party, now advised them to leave the high road, and seek shelter at a village on the left, at a short distance from the road, where he had before himself experienced civility. It was agreed to do so. The party turned off, and were kindly received by the poor villagers. They gave the ladies water; and at their request began to get ready some rice for their food. At this time, a horseman, in the uniform of Hardinge's Irregulars, was seen approaching at a gallop. His appearance filled the fugitives with dismay. They feared that others were following to attack them. The gentlemen took their arms and placed themselves in front; and the ladies were grouped behind them. He proved, however, to be no enemy; but was a faithful and staunch friend; and remained with the refugees to the last, and materially assisted their escape to Allahabad. His name is Seetulsingh.

It was then decided, on Lieutenant Grant's advice, that the party should go on to a small fort, belonging to a zemindar named Ajeetsingh, which was about one mile and a half off. Those whose horses were able to drag the carriages proceeded there in their conveyances. The rest walked. Ajeetsingh received them kindly; and gave them food cooked in the native fashion to eat. He pressed the ladies eagerly to partake of the food which was set before them. But worn, enfevered by the heat, and excited as they were, they could scarcely swallow a morsel. The carriages were all left outside the fort.

For three days the ladies suffered intense alarm and excitement. The gentlemen were endeavouring to ascertain whether the road was open to Allahabad; and sent out many messengers who brought in various news. But the road was evidently at that time impassable. M. de Hoxha and a Mr. Ames went down the road in person to ascertain its condition. They were attacked at a village called Mhow, and driven back. One night the ladies were alarmed by hearing that the females of Ajeetsingh's family had been sent away out of the fort. As this proceeding wore a most suspicious appearance, Lieutenant Grant remonstrated strongly with the zemindar, when the women were brought back again.

Golaubsingh, meanwhile, had rescued some clerks from the mob at Purtaubgurh, and sent to Ajeetsingh's fort a message, inviting the fugitives to return and take refuge with him. But this they would not do. The clerks afterwards joined the rest of the party at Ajeetsingh's fort.

On Friday evening, the 12th of June, a party arrived, consisting of a jumadar and a hundred men, with two elephants, sent from Gurh Ameythee by Lall Madhosingh. It appeared that this party had been first sent to Sultanpoor by Madhosingh, after the departure of the ladies, to offer to the Civil authorities their services as an escort: for the jumadar was the bearer of a letter from Mr. Block, in which he wrote that he believed Madhosingh to be faithful; and advised the ladies to accept his aid. Some suspicion having at the same time arisen about Ajeetsingh's readiness to send the party on to Allahabad, several of the ladies were disposed to accept the offer of an asylum which these people brought from Madhosingh. It was accordingly decided that Mrs. Goldney, Mrs. Block, and Mrs. Stroyan should leave Ajeetsingh's fort; and repair to the fort of Lall Madhosingh, at Gurh Ameythee. The jumadar in charge of the escort, who behaved then, and afterwards, admirably well, was named Seetul Pandey. He insisted that the ladies should be disguised as native women. Accordingly, they tore up their petticoats, and made their costume resemble the native dress. They were then mounted upon the elephants, and it was pretended that they belonged to a native marriage procession, going to Ameythee. As they passed near to villages, the natives who were escorting them began chaunting native marriage songs. And as soon as ever the village was left behind, the elephants were urged on at full speed. On one occasion they had stopped to drink water outside Purtaubgurh, at a well. There was a native at the well who penetrated the ladies' disguise, and said to Seetul Pandey that the ladies were European. The terror of the fugitives was extreme. The jumadar hurried on the elephants, and kept the man in conversation, for some time; and when at last he let him go, the ladies could see him running back to Purtaubgurh, to give the intelligence of their flight.

At another time, they passed through a number of pâsies or goreyts, who were sleeping outside a village, with their spears stuck in the ground near them; and were in an agony of fear lest they should be aroused. On this occasion, the native chaunt was sedulously kept up by their native companions.

The fatigue which these three ladies underwent on this journey was something fearful. Since the moment they had started on Sunday, they had had no real rest. They had never really slept. And the motion of the elephants, exhausted as they were, was almost unbearable. They would almost have been content to have been allowed to lie down under a tree, even to die.

Soon after sunrise on the Saturday, the 13th of June, they reached an empty small fort, belonging to Madhosingh. Here they were allowed to rest during the day; and here at last they got some sleep. They were, however, too exhausted to proceed on upon the elephants. And Mrs. Goldney and Mrs. Block were supplied with small native doolies, in which they again proceeded on at night-fall; and reached the fort of Madhosingh about midnight. Lall Madhosingh came out to meet them, and nothing could be kinder than his reception. He put them into an upper-storied room, containing beds and a few articles of furniture, which, after what they had recently. experienced, looked quite comfortable. During their stay there, he fed them with such food as the natives themselves generally partake of. But it contained too much impure ghee to be palatable to Europeans; and the ladies lived chiefly on boiled rice and buffalo's milk.

Madhosingh came every day to see them, and was always respectful and courteous. He forwarded letters from them into Lucknow; and safely delivered to them the replies received from Mr. and Mrs. Gubbins; and the articles which they had sent.

While there, the ladies saw the native extra assistant of Sultanpoor, Hursuhâe, who told them that he had been robbed of everything that he possessed. He appeared to be faithful to the British cause, and behaved with respect and civility.

The three ladies remained about a fortnight at Gurh Ameythee. During this time they received a letter, stating that the rest of the refugees had reached Allahabad in safety; and they became very anxious and impatient to be sent in themselves; the more particularly as Mrs. Block's infant had been taken dangerously ill.

Madhosingh had from the first represented the journey to be a very dangerous one. He said indeed that he could protect the ladies through his own villages; but no further. He now yielded to their solicitation: and promised to do his best to escort them back to Ajeetsingh's fort, which was on the road to Allahabad. He was himself at this time forcibly repossessing himself of all the villages of which he had been dispossessed at the settlement. And the ladies used to hear firing going on around them, all the day long, between his people and the villagers.

At last they started again, Mrs. Block in a native dooly, Mrs. Goldney, and Mrs. Stroyan, in a native cart; escorted by Seetul Pandey, and a party of more than 200 men; who took them back again to Ajeetsingh's fort. In passing through the country, they saw the villages burning in all directions. In one place they fell in with a party of dacoits, who had just set fire to a village, which was burning as they passed. The escort prevented their doing the ladies injury. The dacoits approached and inquired (this was at night) how many men the guard consisted of? It was a fearful scene. The burning village; the dark figures of the armed dacoits relieved against the flames; the equally rough ones of the escort! Seetul Pandey bade them keep off, or that his men would fire. And most fortunately the dacoits moved away.

Passing by Golaubsingh's residence at Purtaubgurh, Mrs. Goldney, who had lost much property there on the former occasion, went again inside the enclosure, and there saw a large quantity of the property which had belonged to the refugees, lying about. She also saw inside the inner yard some of the horses of which the party had been before robbed, when they first passed that way.

They at length reached Ajeetsingh's fort again in safety. It looked so empty, all the refugees being gone. The ladies had left it crowded with the European refugees: and now when they returned, there were only the empty carriages outside, and one or two horses left in it.

They passed that, and the succeeding day, in much discomfort in Ajeetsingh's fort. The heat was excessive; indeed, fearful. Ajeetsingh's people crowded round them impertinently, and they had much difficulty in keeping them off at all. As for Ajeetsingh, he made a variety of excuses about forwarding them on to Allahabad. At one time he declared that the villages along the road were in too disturbed a state to allow of the ladies passing. Then again he pleaded inability to obtain bearers to carry the doolies. And the bearers who had brought the ladies from Ameythee had been paid up, and dismissed. He appeared also to have some difficulty in collecting the necessary escort of one hundred men, which he was to furnish for their protection along the road. His excuses, most of which were probably feigned, alarmed the ladies much. They dreaded greatly being left to the sole care of Ajeetsingh. The Ameythee escort was to have accompanied them into Allahabad: but now hearing Ajeetsingh's excuses, they talked of leaving them, and going back. Mrs. Goldney, who was a perfect mistress of the native language, now remonstrated strongly with Ajeetsingh, and threatened vengeance whenever our Government should be restored, if he did not send them on. At last Ajeetsingh, on the second day, agreed to do so, and preparations were made accordingly. While here, a letter was received by the ladies from Lieutenant Lewis, 8th O. I. Infantry, dated from Newaubgunje, near Beylah Ghaut. He desired to go into Allahabad, in company with them. This officer had left Sultanpoor on Monday evening, the 8th of June, on the day before the mutiny broke out at Sultanpoor. He had learnt that the men disliked him, and had resolved that he should be killed. He therefore anticipated the outbreak, and left the station before it commenced. A reply was sent, that if he wished to accompany the party in to Allahabad, he must join it immediately. He did not do so, and it was afterwards heard that he had joined another party, and had got safe into Benares.

About nightfall of the second day after reaching Ajeetsingh's fort, Mrs. Block, Mrs. Goldney, and Mrs. Stroyan, started in doolies, disguised still as native women, escorted by Seetul Pandey the Ameythee jumadar, and his men; who were joined by Ajeetsingh himself with an escort of one hundred men. They passed along the road without accident, and in the morning reached the banks of the Ganges. In the low lands, adjoining the river, were a number of melon-fields covered with fruit. Ajeetsingh's men rushed off into the fields and returned laden with melons: pursued by the screaming peasants, loudly shouting complaints of this act of plunder. But though alarmed, the ladies were not molested in consequence. At the river bank they were detained some time, waiting for a boat. Here Mrs. Goldney received frightful abuse in the native language from a native, who was seated on the river bank watching the proceedings of the party. She was glad to retreat and hide herself inside her dooly. The escort crossed with them, and accompanied the ladies to the house of Mr. M. C. Court, C. S., the magistrate of Allahabad, which was one of the few which remained standing in the station. They were most kindly received by this gentleman, who paid rewards to Ajeetsingh, and to Seetul Pandey, jumadar, and let them go.

APPENDIX, No. 10.

Account of the Relief of Arrah, dictated by Major Vincent Eyre, Bengal Artillery.

On the 10th of July, No. 3 Horse Field Battery, with the 1st Company 5th Battalion Artillery attached, recently recalled from Burmah under command of Major V. Eyre, embarked at Calcutta for the Upper Provinces, to form part of the relieving army about to assemble at Allahabad. The horses not having yet arrived from Burmah, the battery was necessarily dependent on whatever means of draught the country might afford. On the evening of the 25th of July, the steamer ('Lady Thackwell') arrived at Dinapoor; where the three N. I. regiments, the 7th, 8th, and 40th, had on that morning broken into open mutiny. Major Eyre immediately offered his services to General Lloyd, by whose orders he landed three guns, pending the absence of Colonel Huish's battery, which had been sent in pursuit of the mutineers. Early on the following morning the guns were re-embarked, and Major Eyre resumed his voyage; having been authorized by the Assistant Adjutant-General, Major Lydiard, to exercise his own discretion as to the expediency of leaving a portion of his battery at Ghazeepoor, to assist in overawing the 65th Regt. N. I., stationed there. The Governor-General had recently evinced some anxiety for the safety of Ghazeepoor: which station was protected by only one weak company of H.M.'s 78th Highlanders, which had been sent there to hold in check the 65th Regt. N. I., which had not yet been disarmed.

On the 28th of July, Major Eyre reached Buxar; where he heard from the stud officers that the Dinapore mutineers had crossed the Soane unchecked, and were beleaguering the civilians at Arrah, in a fortified house in which they had taken refuge; and for whose safety intense anxiety was felt. Reports were spread during the day, that a portion of the mutineers had advanced within twenty miles of Buxar; with the intention of destroying the valuable stud property there. Major Eyre deemed himself justified, in consequence of these reports, in detaining the steamer until the following morning; when finding that there was no immediate ground for alarm, he considered it his duty to push on with all speed, to ascertain the state of affairs at Ghazeepoor. His avowed intention was, however, should all be found quiet at Ghazeepoor, to return to Buxar; and to advance to the relief of Arrah with the aid of such infantry as he might be able to pick up, from the detachments then proceeding up the river.

The steamer reached Ghazeepoor on the afternoon of the 29th, when Major Eyre had a consultation with Colonel Dames, H.M.'s 37th Regt., commanding the station; at whose earnest desire he landed two guns under Lieutenant Gordon. In return for these, Colonel Dames consented to detach twenty-five men of the 78th Highlanders with Major Eyre, to aid in the relief of Arrah. The Honourable Captain Hastings, superintending the stud at Buxar, had, in his anxiety for the safety of that station, preceded Major

Eyre on horseback to Ghazeepoor; to urge upon the authorities there, the expediency of adopting some decisive measures for the relief of Arrah. He returned in the steamer to Buxar, accompanied by Mr. Bax, C. S., Assistant Magistrate, who was deputed by the Magistrate of Ghazeepoor to assist Major Eyre at Buxar. The steamer anchored off Buxar at 9 P.M. on the same evening (the 29th); and Major Eyre was agreeably surprised to learn that a detachment of 160 men of H.M.'s 5th Fusiliers under Captain F. W. L'Estrange, had just arrived in the 'James Hume' steamer at Buxar. Major Eyre lost no time in requesting that officer's co-operation in the projected enterprise. This was unhesitatingly given; and at an early hour on the following morning, the 30th of July, three guns were landed, and 150 men of H.M.'s 5th Fusiliers; and a field force was organized. Thus reinforced, Major Eyre considered himself bound to send back the twenty-five men of the 78th Highlanders to Ghazeepoor. The field force was strengthened during the day by fourteen mounted volunteers, who were placed under the command of Lieutenant F. C. Jackson, 12th N. I., of the Karuntadee Stud. The Honourable Captain Hastings was appointed staff-officer of the force; and exerted himself during the day with great success in procuring the necessary carriage, and commissariat supplies. At 5 P.M. all was ready to start; the artillery ammunition boxes being carried on light carts, to avoid the delay attendant on extricating the waggons from the hold of the steamer. The 'James Hume' steamer was at the same time despatched to Dinapoor with intelligence of these proceedings, and to invite the co-operation of the authorities.

The force commenced its march a little after 5 P.M., and was joined about the sixth mile by four elephants, sent by the Dumraon Raja at the instigation of Mr. Bax. This was the only occasion on which that chief afforded the slightest assistance. The bullocks being fresh from the plough, occasioned great delay during the first march. And the road being also bad, the force did not reach its encampment at Nya Bhojepoor, distant only fifteen miles from Buxar, until daybreak on the 31st of July. During the march a mounted spy was shot by one of the volunteers. He was recognised as one of the confidential men of Baboo Kowursingh, the brother of the Dumraon Raja, who exercised extraordinary influence over the Rajpoots of Shahabad. This chief had, during a long lifetime, cultivated the friendship of the European gentry; who up to a very late period had placed implicit confidence in his fidelity. Of late years, however, his affairs had become much embarrassed, and his large estates in the Shahabad district had become extensively mortgaged. To this circumstance, and to Brahminical influence, his present treachery may probably be attributed. It has since been ascertained, beyond doubt, that the mutiny of the N. I. regiments at Dinapoor was instigated by him; and that he had been actively engaged in exciting rebellion in various other quarters. The Dinapoor mutineers had invaded Arrah by his invitation; and had with great pomp proclaimed him King of Shahabad.

At 4 P.M., on the 31st, the force resumed its march, and favoured by moonlight reached the village of Shahpoor by the morning of the 1st of August. There letters were received from Buxar, conveying the unexpected tidings that a force of 350 Europeans and 50 Seikhs, which had marched on Arrah from Dinapoor, had been entrapped into an ambuscade, and almost totally destroyed. It was also intimated by friendly natives, that several of the bridges between Shahpoor and Arrah had been destroyed, in order to delay the advance of the Buxar force. As no time was to be lost, the force resumed its march at 2 P.M., and at about the fourth mile, interrupted a party of hostile villagers, in the very act of cutting the roadway of a bridge. This caused an hour's detention, which was employed in restoring the roadway, and the force proceeded without further interruption to within a short distance of Gujrajegunje. Here it bivouacked for the night; and a party of fifty of H.M.'s 5th Fusiliers was sent forward to guard a bridge leading to the village. On the following morning, the 2nd of August, the force marched at daybreak; and had advanced about half a mile beyond Gujrajegunje, when bugles were heard sounding the assembly, in a thick and extensive wood about half a mile a-head, through which it was necessary to pass. This wood extended on either flank; and it was necessary to use great caution, to avoid being entirely hemmed in. Major Eyre, therefore, halted his force in order to reconnoitre. The enemy now began to show themselves in what appeared overwhelming force. Not content with occupying the wood to our front, large bodies were seen to extend themselves along the woods on either flank, with the evident intention of surrounding the little force opposed to them, To bring matters to a decisive issue, Major Eyre drew up his force on the open plain to the right of the road, and offered battle. The three guns opened fire to the front and flanks, causing the enemy to screen themselves as much as possible behind the broken ground, between the two positions. From this they opened a heavy fire of musketry, and Major Eyre ordered forward skirmishing parties of the 5th Fusiliers to retaliate. The superiority of the Enfield rifles now became apparent. Galled by their accurate fire, the enemy gradually fell back to the shelter of the woods. Meanwhile, Major Eyre directed the full fire of his artillery on the enemy's centre, with the view of forcing a passage through the wood. They scattered themselves right and left, leaving the road clear. And under cover of the Enfield rifles, the guns and baggage were promptly moved forward; and pushed through the wood, before the enemy could again close his divided wings.

Emerging from the woods, the road was an elevated causeway bounded on either side by partially inundated rice-fields: across which the baffled enemy could only open a distant fire. Finding their intentions thus frustrated, they hurried back to intercept the force at the village of Beebeegunje, distant about two miles a-head; where they had effectually destroyed a bridge, and completely commanded the approaches to it from breastworks, and the houses of the village. Major Eyre again halted his force to refresh the men and cattle, within a quarter of a mile of the bridge: and sent out scouts to search for a ford across the river, which separated him from the enemy. Here it was discovered that the Dumraon Raja's four elephants had taken fright in passing through the wood, and run away after casting their loads, consisting unfortunately of the great coats and bedding of the European soldiers. No ford was discovered. And as it was plainly impossible to effect a passage over the bridge, Major Eyre determined on making a flank march to the nearest point of the railway, distant only one mile, along which there was a direct road to Arrah. This movement was for a time masked by the guns, which opened a brisk fire upon the village, while the infantry and baggage pushed forward in the new direction. But no sooner did the enemy discover the manœuvre, than they hastened in great numbers to intercept the force, at the angle of a thick wood which abutted on the railway. En route Major Eyre discovered a ford, but, as his force had already passed it, he proceeded, followed up pretty closely by a large body of infantry and cavalry, being the raw levies of Kowursingh; while the three mutineer regiments pursued a course parallel to his own, on the opposite side of the stream. On reaching the railway, it became necessary to halt the force and assume a defensive attitude; until the mutineers could be dislodged from the wood, from which they opened a very galling musketry fire. For a whole hour, the force was hotly engaged at a great disadvantage, owing to the abundant cover which screened the enemy. Twice during this period, the mutineers, seeing the guns left almost wholly without support, (Captain L. Estrange's small body of infantry being occupied in skirmishing,) rushed impetuously upon them: and were driven back on both occasions by showers of grape. At this juncture the Honourable Captain Hastings brought word to Major Eyre that the 5th Fusiliers were losing ground, and that our position had become most critical. Major Eyre hereupon resolved on trying what a charge of bayonets would effect; and despatched Captain Hastings with an order to Captain L'Estrange to that effect. Unable immediately to find Captain L'Estrange, Captain Hastings at once most gallantly collected every available man, and himself led them on; Captain L'Estrange promptly joining, on learning the order which had been given. Rushing forward with a cheer they cleared the deep stream, now confined within narrow banks, at a bound; and charged impetuously an enemy twenty times their number. Taken completely by surprise, the mutineers fell back in the utmost disorder, the guns opening fire upon their retreating masses; and in a few minutes, not a man of them remained to oppose the passage of the force. Thenceforward an open road was available, which skirted the railway to within four miles of Arrah, where a little before nightfall the force was compelled to halt by a rapid impassable stream. The night was employed in endeavours to bridge this, by casting in the large piles of bricks that had been collected on the bank by the railway engineers; by which means the stream was narrowed sufficiently to allow the construction of a small bridge formed of country carts, over which the guns and baggage crossed in safety. And at an early hour on the morning of the 3rd of August, the force marched, without further opposition, into the civil station of Arrah; and the relief of the beleaguered garrison was accomplished. It would appear that after their defeat at the railway, the mutineers and Kowursingh had fled back with precipitation to Arrah; to remove their valuables, to the jungle stronghold of that chief at Jugdeespoor.

The relief of the garrison proved to have been most opportune; for their position had been so effectually mined, that a few hours' delay must have ensured their destruction. They numbered sixteen European civilians, and fifty of Rattray's Seikh Police. The position which they had so miraculously defended, against the three mutineer regiments aided by Kowursingh's levies, was a small upper-roomed house of substantial masonry, belonging to Mr. Boyle, District Railway Engineer, by whose skill and foresight it had been fortified and provisioned several days previous to the Dinapoor outbreak, in anticipation of some such crisis. But the strongest position is but of little avail, where stout hearts and an efficient leader are wanting to defend it. And in the present case such hearts and such a leader were forthcoming. To Mr. Wake, Civil Magistrate of Arrah, who possesses in a rare degree some of the highest qualities of a soldier, no less than to the unflinching fortitude with which his able efforts were supported by his brave associates, may be attributed the salvation of the garrison from the worst of fates. During eight days and nights, the garrison was incessantly harassed; and so closely watched, that not a loophole could be approached with safety. At one period their water failed; and they owed their supply to the prompt energy of the Seikhs, who in one night contrived with most inefficient tools to dig a well on the ground floor, twenty feet deep, whereby abundance of good water was obtained. During the last three or four days their position had been rendered doubly perilous, by the fire of three or four guns of small calibre, which the enemy had mounted within fifty yards of the house; the walls of which were perforated by their balls in all directions. Fortunately, the garrison possessed some excellent rifle shots, among whom was Mr. Littledale, the Judge, whose unerring aim had at an early day established a salutary dread; causing the enemy to conceal themselves behind every available cover. Not less than fifty or sixty of the enemy are believed to have been killed by the garrison. Yet strange to say, only two of the latter had been wounded!

The defence of Arrah may be considered one of the most remarkable feats in Indian history.

The main object of the expedition from Buxar had now been accomplished. But it seemed desirable to follow up the success that had been obtained, by attacking Jugdeespoor, whither the rebel Kowursingh, with the mutineers who still adhered to him, had fled; and which was generally considered to be a dangerous, if not desperate undertaking. Major Eyre, therefore, lost no time in applying to the military authorities at Dinapoor, for such reinforcements as could be spared. Meanwhile, he employed himself in restoring the country about Arrah to order. Martial law was proclaimed. The people were disarmed; plundered property recovered; and political offenders brought to trial by drum-head court-martial. About thirty wounded sepoys were brought in and hanged. Several native officials who had accepted service under Kowursingh were similarly dealt with. Among others the chief magistrate whom he had appointed to the district. Inquiries were instituted as to the extent of the recent disaffection; and it was ascertained that on hearing of the approach of the Buxar force, Kowursingh had summoned to his standard by beat of tom-tom in every village, not only the sepoys then on leave from various regiments, but also the pensioned sepoys of Government, of whom several hundreds obeyed the call! Among the slain in the engagement at the railway on the 2nd of August, there were found the appointments and distinguishing numbers of nine different regiments. And the total number of sepoys opposed to the force in that engagement may be safely estimated at 5000.

On the 8th of August, a reinforcement of 200 men of H. M.'s 10th Foot, under command of Captain C. D. Patterson, arrived at Arrah from Dinapoor. They had exchanged their old muskets for new Enfield rifles only just before starting, and had not yet been instructed in the use of their new weapons. Drill-instructors were therefore furnished to them from the 5th Fusilier detachment, in order to give them confidence in the use of the rifle. On the 9th of August, a further reinforcement of 100 of Rattray's Seikhs, under Lieutenant Roberts, of the 40th N. I., and Lieutenant Powis, joined the force. Lieutenant Jackson's body of Volunteer Cavalry was strengthened by eight of the Arrah garrison. Mr. Wake was appointed commandant of the fifty Seikhs, who had already served under him so well; and on the 11th, the force commenced its march at 2 P.M. for Jugdeespoor.

Passing over their old battle-field near Beebeegunje, where the marks of the bullets upon the trees sufficiently evidenced the fierceness of the conflict, a march of eight miles brought them to an open plain, where they bivouacked for the night. At day break on the following morning, the 12th of August, they moved on, the road becoming more and more difficult as they advanced. At 10 o'clock an hour's halt was given, to refresh the men and cattle. On advancing two miles further, the enemy were discovered, lining the belt of formidable jungle which covered the approach to Jugdeespoor. Along their front was a river, fortunately fordable. In their centre was the town of Dulloor, in front of which some breastworks had been raised. An advanced picket occupied the small village of Nuraynpoor, from which our skirmishers soon dislodged them. The mutineer sepoys held the town of Dulloor, and the right of the enemy's position: while Kowursingh's levies of horse and foot extended for some distance to their left. The mutineers were so screened behind broken ground and jungle as to be almost undiscernible, until the near approach of our skirmishers drew forth their fire; whereupon two 9-pounders immediately opened on them with grape, causing considerable confusion among them, and the whole body of them were seen to shift their position more to the right.

No sooner did the men of H. M.'s 10th Foot perceive this movement, than they became impatient to be led to the attack, burning as they were to avenge the death of their comrades, so recently destroyed in the ambuscade near Arrah. Major Eyre accordingly despatched Captain Hastings with an order to charge. Almost ere this could be delivered, they rushed forward, cheering loudly; and, nobly led on by Captain Patterson, charged to within sixty yards of the enemy, who fled for refuge before them behind the walls of the town of Dulloor, and the thickest part of the adjacent jungle. They were hotly pursued, both by the 10th, and the detachment of the 5th Fusiliers, under Captains L'Estrange and Scott, who had meanwhile been engaged in repulsing the enemy's left and centre.

Kowursingh's irregular levies on the left had meanwhile taken up a threatening position on our right flank, and were gradually closing in upon it, under cover of the jungle and broken ground. But they were held in check by the admirable fire of Captain L'Estrange's skirmishers, aided by Mr. Wake's Seikhs, and Lieutenant Jackson's Volunteer Yeomanry. They were finally driven back by the destructive fire of the howitzer, under the excellent management of Staff-Sergeant Melville, of the Artillery. After a contest of about an hour, the whole body of the enemy retreated on Jugdeespoor; a running fight being kept up through a mile and a half of the jungle, up to the walls of that place. Two guns were captured during their flight; and the force rapidly penetrated through the town, with but little further opposition, and entered the stronghold of Kowursingh in triumph at 1 P.M. This was an extensive mass of buildings, protected by lofty walls, with loopholes for musketry, and capable of making a formidable resistance, if properly defended.

Kowursingh's mansion was a conspicuous and handsome building, which, with his cucchery, afforded ample accommodation for the European troops. The town of Jugdeespoor having been deserted by its inhabitants, no accurate intelligence could be procured regarding the movement of Kowursingh and his followers, until the following day (the 13th), when it was ascertained that he had evacuated his stronghold only one hour before the entry of the British force, and had fled in the direction of Jutoora, distant seven miles to the south; where he had a favourite retreat in the midst of the jungle. Major Eyre accordingly detached Captain L'Estrange, with eighty men of the 5th Fusiliers, and the whole of the Volunteer Yeomanry, in pursuit; but on reaching Jutoora, they found that Kowursingh had hurried on towards Sasseram, with the remains of the 40th Regt. N. I., the only sepoys who now adhered to him; those of the 7th and 8th N. I. having proceeded westward in a state of complete disorganization. After destroying the place, Captain L'Estrange returned to Jugdeespoor. Meanwhile, Major Eyre had undermined every principal building in Kowursingh's stronghold, including a new Hindoo temple, whereon large sums had recently been expended. At 2 P.M. on the 15th of August, the force vacated their quarters: the mines were sprung; and the whole was reduced to a heap of ruins. Kowursingh had collected within his walls, stores of grain sufficient to have subsisted 20,000 men for six months. This the neighbouring villagers were allowed to remove; they having been reduced to great destitution by the licence and rapacity of Kowursingh's followers. Large stores of ammunition and material of war were also found, and much miscellaneous property; the former of which were destroyed. On the 16th of August, pending the receipt of instructions from the military authorities at Dinapoor, Major Eyre marched in pursuit of Kowursingh in the direction of Sasseram as far as Peeroo, from which place a practicable gun-road leads to Arrah. Here instructions reached him from Sir James Outram to return to Arrah, as every available European soldier would be required for the relief of Lucknow. Before leaving Peeroo; it was ascertained that Kowursingh had proceeded *viâ* Bijeegurh towards Reewah, with the ultimate intention of joining the mutineers at Dehli. The force reached Arrah on the 19th of August, and on the same night Major Eyre sent back the detachment of H. M.'s 10th Regt. to Dinapoor. On the following afternoon, at 3 P.M. he marched with the remainder of his force for Buxar, which he reached early on the 23rd, and found the fort occupied by a company of H. M.'s 90th Light Infantry. On the following day, he was visited by the

Dumraon Raja, who was upbraided for his backwardness in affording assistance to our troops. On the evening of the 24th, Sir James Outram arrived *en route* to take command at Cawnpoor, and was joined by Major Eyre's battery, and the detachment of H. M.'s 5th Fusiliers. And thus terminated the expedition "to Arrah."

Woodfall and Kinder, Printers, Angel Court, Skinner Street, London.

A

M. G. AVELINE.

Fairy Tales and Charades, for Acting.

By M. G. Aveline. Small 8vo, 2*s*.

MISS AUSTEN.

Novels of Miss Austen :

Emma, Sense and Sensibility, Pride and Prejudice, Mansfield Park, Northanger Abbey, and Persuasion. A Library Edition, in 5 vols. small 8vo, with Ten Illustrations, 15*s*.

"Miss Austen has a talent for describing the involvements, and feelings, and characters of ordinary life, which is to me the most wonderful I ever met with. Her exquisite touch, which renders ordinary commonplace things and characters interesting from the truth of the description and the sentiment, is denied to me."—*Sir Walter Scott*.

Anne Sherwood.

A Novel. 3 vols. post 8vo, 31*s*. 6*d*.

"Written in a style of bold and powerful invective that might have become a female Juvenal. It is a most remarkable novel."—*Press*.

"Its deep, passionate energy, is like Charlotte Bronte's 'Jane Eyre.'"—*John Bull*.

GEORGE BANCROFT.

History of the American Revolution.

By George Bancroft. 3 vols, 8vo. 31*s*. 6*d*.

"This work must take its place as an essentially satisfactory history of the United States. Mr. Bancroft's style is original and national, breathing of the mountain and the prairie. A strain of wild and forest-like music swells up in almost every line. The story is told richly and vividly. In his hands American scenery is full of fine effects. Steeped in the colours of his imagination, a thousand incidents, thought dull before, appear now animated and pictorial. In his narrative all is movement. His men glow with human purposes—his story sweeps on with the exulting life of a procession."—*Athenæum*.

T. HAYNES BAYLY.

The Songs, Ballads, and other Poems

of Thomas Haynes Bayly. Edited by his Widow. Post 8vo, with Portrait, 10*s*. 6*d*.

"Haynes Bayly's Songs are dramatic in a high degree. Associations by many tuneful firesides, with images of domestic tenderness and cheerful household enjoyment, they will doubtless rise to the reader's recollection, and be of greater force to recommend this pleasant volume than any praise of ours."—*Examiner*.

CUTHBERT BEDE.

Fairy Fables.

By Cuthbert Bede. Square 8vo, with numerous beautiful Illustrations by Alfred Crowquill. Handsomely bound, 4*s*. 6*d*.

"A pretty volume, full of short, fresh, and fascinating tales for the parlour and nursery fireside."—*Leader*.

"Pleasant tales of the right sort, with some clever pictures by Alfred Crowquill."—*Athenæum*.

JAMES BOSWELL.

Letters of James Boswell,

the Biographer of Dr. Johnson, to the Rev. William Temple. 8vo, 14*s*.

"Equally with the famous biography of Dr. Johnson, these Letters have the charm of sincerity—a charm which, as long as the world lasts, will be the greatest which the writings of one man can have for another. Boswell never disappoints us. He is an unfailing joke. Whether he writes about love, or riches, or literature, he is always the same, inimitable and inexhaustible. It is rarely that we come across a volume with so much to entertain us and make us laugh."—*Saturday Review*.

CHARLES L. BRACE.

Life in Norway and Sweden.

By Charles Loring Brace, Author of 'Home Life in Germany.' Crown 8vo, with Illustrations, 9*s*.

"A dashing, spirited book, and a welcome addition to the carpet-bag of all northern travellers."—*Athenæum*.

BENTLEY.

Bentley's Two Shilling Volumes.

It is Never too Late to Mend. By Charles Reade.

The Course of True Love. By Charles Reade.

Aspen Court. By Shirley Brooks.

Confessions of a Thug. By Captain Meadows Taylor.

The Initials. By the Author of 'Quits.'

The Cardinal. By Archibald Boyd.

Nearer and Dearer. By Cuthbert Bede.

Delhi; the City of the Great Mogul. By Mrs. Colin Mackenzie.

Roughing it in the Bush. By Mrs. Moodie.

Our Antipodes; or, Residence and Rambles in the Australasian Colonies. By General Mundy.

The Conquest of Canada. By Major Warburton, R.A.

Ghost Stories and Phantom Fancies. By Hain Friswell.

Any of these volumes can also be had, very handsomely bound in blue cloth, 3*s*.

"Mr. Bentley's far-famed Two Shilling Series."—*John Bull.*

Bentley's Five Shilling Volumes.

Prescott's Reign of Ferdinand and Isabella. 3 vols., with Illustrations, 15*s*.

Prescott's Conquest of Mexico. 3 vols., with Illustrations, 15*s*.

Prescott's Conquest of Peru. 3 vols., with Illustrations, 15*s*.

Prescott's Philip the Second. 2 vols., with Illustrations, 10*s*.

Prescott's Critical and Historical Essays. 5*s*.

Kaye's History of the War in Afghanistan. 3 vols. 15*s*.

Thiers's History of the Great French Revolution. 5 vols., with 41 exquisite Engravings, 25*s*.

These volumes are all beautifully printed in good legible type and on very good paper, and are handsomely bound.

The Bentley Ballads.

A Selection of the choice Songs, Ballads, etc., contributed to 'Bentley's Miscellany,' including the famous productions of Father Prout and Dr. Maginn. Edited by Dr. DORAN. Crown 8vo, with Illustrated Title, 5*s*.

Bentley's Edition of Ainsworth's 'Rookwood.'

With Illustrations, 3*s*. 6*d*.

Bulwer's Three Stories,

EUGENE ARAM, LAST DAYS OF POMPEII, and PAUL CLIFFORD. Bentley's Edition. 3 vols. 12mo, 15*s*., with Six Illustrations.

SHIRLEY BROOKS.

The Gordian Knot.

By SHIRLEY BROOKS. 8vo, with Twenty-four beautiful Illustrations by TENNIEL. Seven Parts are now ready.

REV. R. W. BROWNE.

History of Roman Classical Literature.

By the Rev. R. W. BROWNE, Professor of History at King's College, London. Second Edition. 8vo, 12*s*.

"Professor Browne is not only a classical scholar, but one of the most graceful of English modern writers. In clearness, purity, and elegance of style, his compositions are unsurpassed; and his sketches of the lives and works of the great authors of antiquity are models of refined taste and sound criticism. This is a work which for utility of design and excellence of execution may challenge comparison with any which the present century has produced; nor can we hesitate to regard it as a very valuable instrument for the instruction of the national mind, and the elevation of the national taste."—*Morning Post.*

REV. R. W. BROWNE.

History of Greek Classical Literature.

By the Rev. R. W. BROWNE, Professor of History at King's College, London. 8vo, 12*s*.

"One of those books that will extend the circle of Greek knowledge far beyond the limits which comprise those persons with whom classical studies are a profession. Mr. Browne's short biographies of the various Greek writers, his plots of tragedies and comedies, his well-chosen anecdotes, agreeably diversify his critical and historical disquisitions."—*Times.*

FRANCIS T. BUCKLAND.

Curiosities of Natural History.

By FRANCIS T. BUCKLAND, M.A., Student of Christ Church, Assistant-Surgeon, 2nd Life-Guards. Third Edition, in small 8vo, with Illustrations, 6*s*.

MRS. CASE.

Day by Day at Lucknow.

A Diary of the Siege. By Mrs. CASE, Widow of Colonel Case, 32nd Regt., Queen's. Post 8vo, 10*s*. 6*d*.

"Few will read without sympathy this unaffected, irregular, and thoroughly feminine narrative. We can imagine one of the escaped garrison reading it with proud emotion."—*Athenæum.*

"Every word in the volume appears genuine. It is a book of a hundred anecdotes, every one illustrating the tremendous character of the conflict waged, and the wondrous bravery, not of the garrison only, but of the besiegers."—*Leader.*

W. WILKIE COLLINS.

Rambles beyond Railways;

or, Notes taken afoot in Cornwall. By W. WILKIE COLLINS, Author of 'Antonina,' 'The Dead Secret,' etc. Square 8vo, with beautiful Coloured Lithographs, 10*s*. 6*d*.

"A very pleasant book, in which the most is made of a happily-chosen subject. The author takes us through all the rocky wonders and beauties of the Cornish coast, from St. German's to the Land's End."—*Times.*

MISS COSTELLO.

Memoirs of Mary, the young Duchess of Burgundy,

and her Contemporaries. By LOUISA COSTELLO, Author of 'A Summer among the Bocages and the Vines.' Post 8vo, 10*s*. 6*d*.

PROFESSOR CREASY.

The Fifteen Decisive Battles of the World,

from Marathon to Waterloo. By Professor CREASY. Ninth Edition, with Plans, 8vo, 10*s*. 6*d*.

"It was a happy idea of Professor Creasy to select for military description those few battles of which, in the words of Hallam, 'a contrary event would have essentially varied the drama of the world in all its subsequent scenes.' The decisive features of the battles are well and clearly brought out, the reader's mind is attracted to the world-wide importance of the event he is considering, while their succession carries him over the whole stream of European history."—*Spectator*.

PROFESSOR CREASY.

Rise and Progress of the English Constitution.

A Popular Account of the Primary Principles, the Formation and Development of the English Constitution, avoiding all Party Politics. By Professor CREASY. Third Edition. Post 8vo, 7*s*. 6*d*.

"An admirable summary of knowledge, which every well-educated Englishman ought to possess."—*Literary Gazette*.

PROFESSOR CREASY.

History of the Ottoman Turks,

from the Foundation of their Empire to the Present Time, chiefly based upon Von Hammer. By Professor CREASY. 1 vol. 8vo, with Maps, 15*s*.

"Of all the histories of the Turks this is by far the best."—*Spectator*.

"The author has added to his well-earned reputation by the care which he has bestowed on this history."—*Daily News*.

PETER CUNNINGHAM.

Letters of Horace Walpole, Earl of Orford.

Now first Chronologically arranged. With upwards of One Hundred New Letters. Edited by PETER CUNNINGHAM. 9 vols. 8vo, with Thirty-five exquisite Portraits, £4. 14*s*. 6*d*.

"Horace Walpole will be long known to posterity by his incomparable Letters—models as they are of every variety of epistolary excellence. But it is not only for the merits of his style that Walpole's Letters are, we think, destined more surely perhaps than any other work of his or our age, to immortality; it is because these letters are, in fact, a chronicle of every occurrence and of every opinion which attracted or deserved public attention, either at home or abroad, during one of the busiest half centuries of European history. This correspondence is, in fact, a perfect encyclopædia of information from the very best sources—politics from the fountain-head of parties—debates by the best of reporters—foreign affairs from an *habitué* of diplomatic society—sketches of public characters by their intimate acquaintance or associate—the gossip of fashionable life from a man of fashion—literature from a man of letters—the arts from a man of taste—the news of the town from a member of every club in St. James's Street; and all this related by a pen whose vivacity and graphic power is equalled by nothing but the wonderful industry and perseverance with which it was plied through so long a series of years."—*Quarterly Review.*

"Read, if you have not read, all Horace Walpole's Letters, wherever you can find them: the best wit ever published in the shape of letters."—*Sydney Smith.*

"Incomparable Letters."—*Lord Byron.*

"Walpole's great History of his own Times."—*John Wilson Croker.*

"Mr. Cunningham has been entrusted, and his peculiar knowledge justifies the selection, with the editorship of the first collected edition of an English Classic; and as this will no doubt hereafter be the standard one, Cunningham's 'Walpole' will henceforward be as regularly quoted as Tyrwhitt's 'Chaucer.' That Walpole is an English classic, who will gainsay? With the exception of James Howel, he was in point of time the first of English letter-writers. That he is first in literary rank the majority of readers will readily admit. With fancy and imagination enough for a poet, learning sufficient to have established his reputation as a scholar, wit equal to both, and a social position which put him in possession of all the gossip of the day, what wonder is it that Horace Walpole should shine pre-eminent as a letter-writer? His style, modelled upon those sparkling French writers whom he so delighted in, is perfect in its ease; and his pictures of society combine at once the truth of Hogarth and the grace of Watteau. When we add that in his delightful correspondence one may read the political and social history of England from the middle of the reign of George the Second to the breaking out of the first French Revolution, we do not risk damaging our reputation as prophets, when we predict that, great as has been the success of former publications of these Letters, yet greater success will attend the present edition. For be it remembered, this edition contains not only all the letters hitherto published, arranged in chronological order, and many now first collected or first made public, but also the notes of all previous editors, among whom are Lord Dover, Mr. Croker, the Misses Berry, and the Rev. John Mitford. Mr. Cunningham has come to his task, therefore, under very fortunate circumstances. He has been preceded by men familiar with the events and persons of whom Walpole writes, and one less practised in the duties of an editor, less intimate with the literature and history of Walpole's period, than Mr. Cunningham, could scarcely have failed in making a good book; no wonder, then, that with such materials he has produced the work by which he is destined to be remembered hereafter."—*Notes and Queries.*

The Crisis in India.

By CAUBULEE. 8vo. 1*s*. 6*d*.

SYDNEY DOBELL.

The Roman; a Dramatic Poem.

By SYDNEY DOBELL. Post 8vo, 5*s*.

"We have read this poem with delight. The Author touches with equal power the pathetic and the sublime; he brings a fancy which rivets by its boldness and enchains by its beauty. Should any one, after the extracts we have given, doubt whether we have a new poet amongst us, we should despair of his conversion."—*Athenæum.*

J. D'EWES.

China, Australia, and Islands of the Pacific,

in the Years 1855–56. By J. D'EWES, Esq. Post 8vo, with Illustrations, 10*s*. 6*d*.

"The account of the Chinese and China is by far the most valuable. Mr. J. D'Ewes had good opportunities of seeing the domestic economy of our princely merchants and their social relations with the Chinese."—*Spectator.*

DR. DORAN.

Habits and Men,

with Remnants of Records touching the Makers of Both. By Dr. DORAN. Third Thousand. Post 8vo, 7*s*. 6*d*.

"As old Burton makes melancholy and its many varieties a canvas wheron he may embroider whatever he thinks fit, so does Dr. Doran take up human attire. Nearly every page contains something amusing; and you may shut the book in the middle and open it again after a twelvemonth's interval, without at all compromising its power of affording enjoyment. We need scarcely add that Dr. Doran's book is not only amusing, but that it is full of strange information that every one would like to possess. Here, in fact, is the note-book of an intelligent, educated, and studious man, enabling the reader, by skimming over pages, to obtain, almost without a thought, an amount of knowledge for which the author has ransacked libraries."—*Times.*

DR. DORAN.

Table Traits and Something on Them.

By Dr. DORAN. Second Edition. Small 8vo, 6*s*.

"This entertaining work includes almost everything connected with the pleasures of the table. Dr. Doran exhibits a great amount of reading, very agreeable wit, and a refined scholarship."—*Manchester Times.*

DR. DORAN.

Knights and their Days.

By Dr. DORAN. Second Thousand. Post 8vo, 10*s*. 6*d*.

"Satirical, anecdotical, quizzical—full of most wise conceits and ridiculous stories—a book of knights of the stage and knights of the thimble—of mock knights and smock knights—of royal knights and knights of the road,—it is very laughable and very provoking. There is only one word to be said about it—*read* it."—*Athenæum.*

DR. DORAN.

Monarchs Retired from Business.

By Dr. DORAN. Second Edition, and Second Thousand. 2 vols. post 8vo, 21*s*. Two Portraits.

"Emphatically a book which will be liked by all classes. With information to recommend it to the studious, its liveliness will attract the desultory reader, and it cannot fail to delight both. It is altogether a very charming book."—*Gentleman's Magazine.*

DR. DORAN.

History of Court Fools.

By Dr. DORAN. Second Thousand. Post 8vo, 10*s*. 6*d*.

"Anything more quaint, subtle, and surprising than Dr. Doran's tale of the origin of court fools is scarcely to be found in the pages of the greatest and most genial humourist. Will not many of our readers, on so much acquaintance from our few extracts, desire a still more intimate knowledge of the 'History of Court Fools'?"—*Athenæum.*

DR. DORAN.

Queens of England of the House of Hanover.

By Dr. Doran. Second Edition, 2 vols. post 8vo, with Illustrations, 21*s*.

"These 'Lives' indicate afresh the wealth and variety of Dr. Doran's collections."—*Athenæum.*

"An extraordinary repertory of facts and anecdotes."—*Spectator.*

MRS. ELLIS.

Friends at their own Firesides.

By Mrs. Ellis, Author of 'The Women of England.' 2 vols. fcap. 8vo, 12*s*.

"The authoress here describes the social and domestic life of the Quakers. Mrs. Ellis, having been herself brought up in a Quaker family, is naturally very fit for such a task, which she executes with all the grace her pen has long been known to possess."—*Statesman.*

REV. J. EDWARDS, M.A.

The Andromache of Euripides.

With suggestions and questions at the foot of each page, intended to be read as a first Greek Play. By the Rev. J. Edwards, M.A., and the Rev. C. Hawkins, B.C.L., Ch. Ch. Oxon. Second Edition. Post 8vo, 4*s*. 6*d*.

"Every passage of the text is illustrated with an extent of erudition which renders the work of incalculable value to the student."—*Educational Times.*

MARIA FREEMAN.

A Friend in Need.

3 vols. post 8vo.

CHARLES E. FRANCATELLI.

The Modern Cook.

A Practical Guide to the Culinary Art in all its branches. Adapted as well for the Largest Establishments as for the use of Private Families. By CHARLES ELME FRANCATELLI. Fifth Thousand. 8vo. 12*s*.

"The destiny of nations depends upon their diet."—*Brillat Savarin.*

"There's no want of meat, Sir;
Portly and curious viands are prepared
To please all kinds of appetites."—*Massinger.*

REV. CHARLES FORSTER.

The One Primeval Language,

Traced experimentally through Ancient Inscriptions in Alphabetical Characters of lost Powers from the four Continents. By the Rev. CHARLES FORSTER, Rector of Stisted. This important work is now published in Three Volumes, demy 8vo, any one Volume of which can be had separately, price 21*s*. each, or the Three Volumes together, price 42*s*.

Part I. THE VOICE OF ISRAEL FROM THE ROCKS OF SINAI.

Part II. THE VESTIGES OF PATRIARCHAL TRADITION FROM THE MONUMENTS OF EGYPT, ETRURIA, AND SOUTHERN ARABIA.

Part III. THE MONUMENTS OF ASSYRIA, BABYLONIA, AND PERSIA. WITH A KEY TO THE RECOVERY OF THE LOST TEN TRIBES.

"The work before us lays claim to a great discovery. Mr. Forster has started a theory which deserves the attentive consideration of every Hebrew or Arabic scholar—for if his theory be verified, the result must be an immense accession of light to the whole field of Semitic philology. Mr. Forster thinks that he has already discovered Arabic to be or to contain the one primitive language. The theological value of the records of the miracles of the Exodus graven in the living rocks, by the hands of the very men who witnessed those mighty judgments, is perfectly incalculable."—*Guardian.*

"A very remarkable work. It is one of the most valuable contributions to Scripture evidences we have met with for some time."—*Daily News.*

"It exhibits extensive learning and great philological research; while the author's views, which are altogether novel on the subject, are supported by a mass of extraordinary and highly interesting evidence."—*Critic.*

REV. CHARLES FORSTER.

A Letter to Lord Lyndhurst

in Vindication of the Sinaitic Inscriptions, in Answer to the Rev. Arthur Penrhyn Stanley, M.A. 8vo. 5*s*.

FREYTAG.

Debit and Credit.

A Novel. From the German of FREYTAG. Translated by Mrs. MALCOLM. Crown 8vo, 6*s*.

"This novel has had an extraordinary circulation in Germany, approaching to that of 'Uncle Tom,' or Mr. Dickens's or Mr. Thackeray's novels in England. Mrs. Malcolm's translation is executed with fidelity and spirit, and with the sanction of the author."—*Times*.

"The most popular German novel of the age."—*Chevalier Bunsen*.

"We cannot here give any idea of the variety, vivacity, intensity of this admirable story."—*Statesman*.

LIEUT.-COL. GRAHAM

History of the Art of War.

Elementary History of the Progress of the Art of War. By Lieut.-Col. J. J. GRAHAM. Post 8vo, with Plans of Battles, 7*s*. 6*d*.

"A brief account of the composition of armies—the progress of the art of war from the earliest ages—maxims of modern military science, and a chronology of military events, illustrated by sketches, and the opinions of Frederick the Great, Napoleon, Cæsar, Gustavus, Turenne, Marlborough, and other great commanders, besides Jomini."—*Athenæum*.

MRS. GREEN.

Letters of Queen Henrietta Maria;

Including her Private Correspondence with Charles I. Edited by MARY ANN EVERETT GREEN. Post 8vo, 10*s*. 6*d*.

"On the history of the Civil War in the seventeenth century, these letters throw important light."—*Literary Gazette*.

EARL GREY.

An Essay on Parliamentary Reform.

By Earl Grey. 8vo, 7*s*. 6*d*.

M. R. GUBBINS.

The Mutinies in Oudh;

An Account of the Mutinies in Oudh and of the Siege of Lucknow Residency; with some observations on the Causes of the Mutiny. By Martin Richard Gubbins, Financial Commissioner for Oudh. One vol. 8vo. with Maps and Illustrations.

ARNOLD GUYOT.

Lectures on Physical Geography;

Or, Earth and Man. By Arnold Guyot. The only unabridged edition. Small 8vo, 2*s*. 6*d*.

"We have never seen the science of physical geography explained with greater clearness and elegance."—***Athenæum***.

M. GUIZOT.

Memoirs of my Own Time.

By M. Guizot. Vol. I., in 8vo, 14*s*.

"Will be devoured as a history of our own times by one of the most conspicuous men now alive, and will be referred to hereafter when much popular literature will have been devoured by the worms. Guizot is a man of genius—and genius is immortality. This is one of the few books that will mark the generation that gives it birth." —***Athenæum***.

M. GUIZOT.

Memoirs of Sir Robert Peel.

By M. Guizot. 8vo. 14*s*.

"The most impartial estimate of Sir Robert Peel we have seen."—***Athenæum***.

M. GUIZOT.

History of Charles the First

and the English Revolution. By M. GUIZOT. 2 vols. 8vo, 28*s*.

"The best history, both in thought and composition, of the Reign of Charles the First."—*Edinburgh Review.*

M. GUIZOT.

History of Oliver Cromwell

and the English Commonwealth. By M. GUIZOT. 2 vols. 8vo, 28*s*.

"M. Guizot has given us an admirable narrative, far more candid than any from an English pen."—*Times.*

"M. Guizot has unravelled Cromwell's character with singular skill. No one, in our opinion, has drawn his portrait with equal truth. M. Guizot's acquaintance with our annals, language, customs, and politics, is altogether extraordinary. He is an earnest and profound writer."—*Quarterly Review.*

M. GUIZOT.

History of Richard Cromwell

and the Dawn of the Restoration. By M. GUIZOT. 2 vols. 8vo, 28*s*.

"It is impossible to read this calm and noble work without feeling its unconscious pathos. M. Guizot here shows us the last act of a great drama, terrible in its interest and tragic at the close."—*Athenæum.*

"M. Guizot's narrative is masterly. Perhaps no period of equal importance could be less attractive as the subject of a history; yet these volumes are more interesting than most descriptions of brilliant and exciting times. The execution of the translation is excellent; M. Guizot has had ample justice done to the spirited and balanced language in which his thoughts are expressed. Generally the thoughts to which M. Guizot gives a distinct shape are profound and just; he especially excels in those statements—half fact, half reflection—in which the whole position and aim of a party is described and commented on."—*Saturday Review.*

M. GUIZOT.

Corneille and his Times.

By M. GUIZOT. 8vo, 10*s*. 6*d*.

M. GUIZOT.

Address to the French Academy:

Address delivered on the Admission of M. Biot into the French Academy in 1857. By M. GUIZOT. 8vo, 1*s*.

M. GUIZOT.

Shakespeare and his Times.

By M. GUIZOT. 8vo, 10*s*. 6*d*.

JAMES HAMILTON.

Sinai, the Hedjaz, and Soudan:

Wanderings round the Birthplace of the Prophet, and across the Ethiopian Desert, with Pictures of Arab Life. By JAMES HAMILTON, Author of 'Wanderings in Northern Africa.' Post 8vo, 10*s*. 6*d*. Maps.

"A work of great importance—a valuable contribution to the history and geography of a region associated with our earliest studies, and for the classical scholar invested by the oldest Greek historian with never-fading charms."—*Standard.*

MRS. HORNBY.

In and Around Stamboul.

By Mrs. EDMUND HORNBY. 2 vols. post 8vo, 21*s*.

"Mrs. Hornby was enabled to penetrate into all classes of society, Ottoman, Greek, and Armenian, and to explore the very innermost recesses of harem life."—*Leader.*

THOMAS INGOLDSBY.

The Ingoldsby Legends;

Or, Mirth and Marvels. 3 vols. post 8vo, with all the Illustrations of GEORGE CRUIKSHANK and JOHN LEECH. 21*s*.

The same work in One Volume, small 8vo, with Illustrated Frontispiece, 5*s*. This Five Shilling Edition contains the whole of the Legends, the Life of Thomas Ingoldsby alone being omitted.

"Abundant in humour, observation, fancy; in extensive knowledge of books and men; in palpable hints of characters, exquisitive grave irony, and the most whimsical indulgences of point and epigram: we doubt if even Butler beats the author of these 'Legends' in the easy drollery of verse. We cannot open a page that is not sparkling with its wit and humour—that is not ringing with its strokes of pleasantry and satire."—*Examiner.*

WILLIAM JAMES.

James's Naval History of Great Britain,

with a Continuation to the Battle of Navarino. By Captain Chamier. Embellished with 23 beautiful Portraits of the most distinguished Officers engaged in the late eventful War. 6 vols. demy 8vo, 42*s*.

"This book is one of which it is not too high praise to assert, that it approaches as nearly to perfection, in its own line, as any historical work perhaps ever did. The principal transactions narrated in it, and we trust by this time the narrative itself, are fortunately too well known to require a detailed notice of its contents. But a general sketch of its plan, and the manner of its execution, will, we think, convince our readers that the high character we have given of it is not exaggerated. Mr. James commences his work with a very useful Introduction, in which he briefly and clearly sketches the progress of Naval Architecture in Great Britain, and the origin of the principal improvements in the British Navy before the time of the French Revolution. The history itself opens with the declaration of war in 1793, and closes with the general peace of 1815.* Every year between these two periods occupies a separate division of the work; and every such division is subdivided under three heads, detailing respectively the movements of the hostile fleets, the encounters of single ships and boat attacks, and all colonial naval operations. The research necessary to procure materials for twenty-eight such abstracts, and the labour of composing them, must have been so great that they alone may be considered as a striking monument of industry. With a candour almost as uncommon as his accuracy, he never fails to notice any variation of consequence in the statements of the hostile party; and either to refute it by argument, or fairly to balance it with the opposing testimony. We cannot contemplate without admiration the impartial and unwearied zeal for historical truth, which alone could have supported him through his tedious and thankless labours."—*Edinburgh Review.*

* Since brought down to the Battle of Navarino.

J. W. KAYE.

Memorials of Indian Government.

By Henry St. George Tucker. Edited by John William Kaye. 8vo, 16*s*.

J. W. KAYE.

The Life of Henry St. George Tucker,

late Accountant-General of Bengal, and Chairman of the Hon. East India Company. By JOHN WILLIAM KAYE. 8vo, 16*s*. Portrait.

J. W. KAYE.

History of the War in Afghanistan.

By JOHN WILLIAM KAYE. 3 vols. 12mo, 15*s*.

"This vivid narrative is written with scrupulous and unflinching fidelity, whilst even the best-known details acquire the freshness of novelty from the skill displayed in weaving them into a narrative. Mr. Kaye's laborious researches seem to have been guided by a love of truth powerful enough to divest his mind of all personal partialities. His narrative flows on with a vigour and freshness which do him great credit. In short, the Afghan war is now presented to us with an approach to dramatic unity of form and purpose, the development of the plot subserving to the legitimate end of all dramatic composition—the enforcement of a great principle or moral truth."—*Quarterly Review*.

MISS KAVANAGH.

Madeline; a Tale of Auvergne.

By JULIA KAVANAGH, Author of 'Nathalie.' Second Edition. Small 8vo, Illustration, 3*s*. 6*d*.

"One of those rare books which at once touch the feelings by a simple and forcible truthfulness to nature. This book is destined to permanent popularity, and the name of the writer will be marked with those of Madame Cottin and St. Pierre."—*Atlas*.

R. B. KIDD.

The Primary Principles of Reasoning.

A Delineation of the Primary Principles of Reasoning. By ROBERT BOYD KIDD, B.A., Perpetual Curate of Botley, Suffolk. Post 8vo, 9*s*. 6*d*.

"I know the most eminent logicians existing, and I do not know Mr. Kidd's superior."—*Archbishop Whately*.

"I have read it with much admiration."—*Archdeacon Fitzgerald*, Professor of Moral Philosophy in the University of Dublin.

Katherine.

By the Author of 'Clara; or, Slave Life in Europe.' 3 vols. post 8vo, 31*s.* 6*d.*

"'Katherine' gives some pretty sketches of a sunny little market town."—*John Bull.*

"A good story, in which we have the quaint figure of the old Queen of the Market—the pretty Katherine, her daughter—the wild brothers, and the old maid, Clementine."—*Examiner.*

COLONEL LAKE.

The Defence of Kars.

Historical and Military Narrative of the Defence of Kars. By Colonel ATWELL LAKE, C.B. With numerous Lithographic Illustrations. 8vo. 15*s.*

"This work is a military study, and should become a class-book in military schools."—*Leader.*

COLONEL LAKE.

Our Captivity in Russia;

with an Account of the Blockade of Kars, including Letters of General Sir Fenwick Williams, K.C.B., Major Teesdale, and Capt. Thomson. By Colonel ATWELL LAKE, C.B. Third Edition. Post 8vo, 10*s.* 6*d.*, with Portraits of General Williams and Colonel Lake.

"A marvellous narrative."—*Daily News.*

"The story of Kars is one that will be fresh for ever."—*Globe.*

The Ladies of Bever Hollow.

By the Author of 'Mary Powell,' etc. 2 vols. small 8vo, 12*s.*

"This is a thoroughly English story. The incidents are slight, and not exciting; but the characters are well drawn, and the conversations being full of life and spirit, the interest never for a moment flags. The author of 'Mary Powell' has in this picture of country life proved herself a literary Gainsborough."—*Athenæum.*

"Simple and quiet is the new tale by the authoress of 'Mary Powell.' It is a half old-fashioned, half new-fashioned, tale of country life, and country love, and country gossipings."—*Examiner.*

M. DE LAMARTINE.

Memoirs of Remarkable Characters.

By Alphonse de Lamartine. 3 vols. 12mo, 18*s*.

"This work will materially raise the reputation of Lamartine. Along with the brilliancy of style and warmth of imagination which characterize all his writings, we find here gravity of thought and earnestness of purpose. The subject also is well suited to his peculiar genius and talents. As a sketcher of historical scenes and of historical characters, choosing his own subjects, suggested by his own tastes or sympathies, no living author is capable of greater or more successful efforts. In these volumes we have a gallery of illustrious portraits, drawn in bold and striking style, and glowing with life-like feeling and expression. The translation of the work has been prepared with care, and in several cases historical inaccuracies are pointed out and corrected."—*Literary Gazette.*

DR. LEE.

The Last Days of the Emperor Alexander

and the First Days of the Emperor Nicholas. By Robert Lee, M.D. Small 8vo, 3*s*. 6*d*.

M'CAUSLAND.

Sermons in Stones;

or, Scripture confirmed by Geology. By D. M'Causland. Fourth Edition, small 8vo, with Nineteen Illustrations, 4*s*.

The object of the author in this work is to prove that the Mosaic narrative of the Creation is reconcilable with the established facts of geology; and that geology not only establishes the truth of the first page of the Bible, but that it furnishes the most direct and sensible evidence of the fact of Divine inspiration, and thereby authenticates the whole canon of Scripture. The word of God is thus authenticated by His works.

LIEUT. MARTELLI, R.N.

Naval Officer's Guide

for Preparing Ships for Sea. By Lieut. Charles Martelli, R.N. Fcap. 8vo, 6*s*.

"A masterly exposition of those complex details on which the efficiency of our ships depends."—*United Service Journal.*

MRS. COLIN MACKENZIE.

The Great Day of Atonement;

or, Meditations and Prayers on the last Twenty-four Hours of the Sufferings and Death of our Lord and Saviour Jesus Christ. Translated from the German of CHARLOTTE ELIZABETH NEBELIN. Edited by Mrs. COLIN MACKENZIE, Author of 'The Mission, the Camp, and the Zenana,' etc. Post 8vo, 2*s*. 6*d*.

This work was written by the daughter of the honoured Pastor Rambach, about the middle of the last century, and was revised by the venerable Pastor Köllner, who, being in his 75th year, thanked God that he had been permitted to finish this revision.

LORD MAHON.

Letters and Works of Philip Dormer Stanhope,

Earl of Chesterfield. Including numerous Letters and Sketches hitherto unpublished. Now first collected. By Lord MAHON (Earl Stanhope). Five vols., 8vo, with Portrait, 56*s*.

"Of these famous letters it cannot be said that until now they had received even a decent measure of editorial care. Lord Mahon has reproduced them entire, and for the first time filled up names left in blank, and explained hints and allusions which the lapse of another generation would have condemned to hopeless obscurity. When we compare Lord Mahon's copy with what we had had before, it is hardly too much to say that he has given us a new work. Whatever could wound anybody's feelings had been omitted; in other words, a very large proportion of whatever could throw light on the secret history of parties and public men in Lord Chesterfield's time—very many letters entirely—the most striking paragraphs of half the rest. The *lacunæ* are now filled up as far as was possible, and the whole illustrated by notes brief and clear." —*Quarterly Review*.

GENERAL MARKHAM.

Shooting Scenes in the Himalayas,

Chinese Tartary, Ladak, Thibet, etc. By the late GENERAL MARKHAM, 91st Regiment. Imperial 8vo, with Lithographic Illustrations, 21*s*.

"These sporting adventures in the loftiest region of the globe are rapid, readable, varied, interesting, and never tedious from overdoing. The introduction of rare animals is accompanied by an account of them, and the narrative is relieved by pictures of the sublime scenery among which the pursuit led, as well as by anecdotes and sketches of the people. The character of the Colonel is well adapted to the style of the sportsman: frank, genial, and with fine spirits, he has also a wide knowledge of men and sporting."—*Spectator*.

THE EARL OF MALMESBURY.

Diary of the Earl of Malmesbury.

The Diaries and Correspondence of the Earl of Malmesbury. Edited by his Grandson, the present Earl. 4 vols. 8vo, 42*s*. Portraits.

"This mode of anticipating history has great charms. How much more delightful to us must be the sketches of George III. and George IV.—Queen Charlotte and Queen Caroline—Pitt and Fox—Canning and Windham (to say nothing of minor portraits)—all fresh, as it were, from the hand of a painter, their contemporary, and in some degree ours—than they will be in another generation. No extracts that our space would allow us to make could afford an adequate idea of the great mass of mingled gossip and history to be found in these volumes. To us nothing can be more attractive; we seem to be living our youth over again."—*Quarterly Review.*

REV. J. B. MARSDEN.

Dictionary of Christian Churches and Sects,

from the Earliest Ages of Christianity. By the Rev. J. B. Marsden, Incumbent of St. Peter's, Birmingham, Author of "The History of the Early and Later Puritans," etc. New Edition, in one handsome Volume. 8vo, 12*s*.

"Mr. Marsden's information is well digested, his judgment sound and impartial, his manner of statement not only clear, but with a sustained vividness. The work has somewhat the appearance of an Encyclopædia, but it is only in appearance. The exposition has the freshness of an original work. The philosophic impartiality of the author should not be passed over. He has, of course, opinions, but he indulges in no violence or harshness of censure. The arrangement is well adapted for the important point of conveying complete and full information."—*Spectator*.

The Netherwoods of Otterpool.

3 vols. post 8vo, 31*s*. 6*d*.

"A spirited novel. The story is interesting, and the interest arises from the development of character and the conflict of opposing qualities. Readers will seize on 'The Netherwoods.'"—*Athenæum*.

Notes on Noses.

Hints towards a Classification of Noses. With numerous Illustrations. 2*s*.

"Worthy of Lawrence Sterne."—*Morning Post.*

*** Nearly 6000 copies of this little book have been sold.

SIR CHARLES NAPIER.

The History of the Baltic Campaign of 1854.

From Documents and other Materials furnished by Vice-Admiral Sir CHARLES NAPIER, K.C.B. Edited by G. BUTLER EARP. 8vo, 16*s*.

MRS. NEWBY.

Margaret Hamilton.

By Mrs. NEWBY, Author of 'Sunshine and Shadow.' 3 vols. post 8vo.

"A most charming novel, worth a place in the memory for its simple, unaffected goodness, and keen common sense."—*Statesman.*

Philip Paternoster.

A Tractarian Love Story. 2 vols. small 8vo, 12*s*.

"A smart and slashing production, written with the intention of exterminating Puseyism, by making every Puseyite thoroughly ashamed of himself."—*Morning Star.*

W. H. PRESCOTT.

Reign of Ferdinand and Isabella.

History of the Reign of Ferdinand and Isabella of Spain. By WILLIAM HICKLING PRESCOTT.

In order to meet the demand of all classes, Mr. Bentley has prepared three Editions of this, and of all other of Mr. Prescott's works, as follows :—

Library Edition, in 2 vols. 8vo, 21*s*. Portraits.
Cabinet Edition, in 3 vols. 12mo, 15*s*. Portraits.
One Volume Edition, in post 8vo, 5*s*. Portrait.

"Written in a spirit and style worthy of Xenophon, and may rank among the first histories in the English language."—*Gentleman's Magazine.*

W. H. PRESCOTT.

History of the Conquest of Mexico.

With the Life of the Conqueror, Hernando Cortez. By W. H. PRESCOTT.

Library Edition, in 2 vols. 8vo, 21*s*. Portraits.
Cabinet Edition, in 3 vols. 12mo, 15*s*. Portraits.
One Volume Edition, in post 8vo, 5*s*. Portrait.

"It would be easy to fill our pages with sparkling quotations, with sketches of scenery worthy of Scott, with battle-pieces rivalling those of Napier, with pictures of disaster and desolation scarcely less pathetic than those drawn by Thucydides." —*Edinburgh Review.*

W. H. PRESCOTT.

History of the Conquest of Peru.

With a Preliminary View of the Civilization of the Incas. BY W. H. PRESCOTT.

Library Edition, in 2 vols. 8vo, 21*s*. Portraits.
Cabinet Edition, in 3 vols. crown 8vo, 15*s*. Portraits.
One Volume Edition, in post 8vo, 5*s*. Portrait.

"We can conscientiously recommend this work, as indispensable to complete that long line of English histories which is gradually appropriating to itself the most important events in the chronicles of mankind."—*Quarterly Review.*

W. H. PRESCOTT.

History of Philip II. of Spain.

By W. H. Prescott.

Library Edition, in 2 vols. 8vo, 28*s*. Portraits.
Cabinet Edition, in 2 vols. crown 8vo, 10*s*. Portraits.
One Volume Edition, in post 8vo, 5*s*. Portrait.

"Written with admirable art. Mr. Prescott brings together a profusion of original materials, collected from the principles libraries of Europe. . . . Mr. Prescott has a style of his own, vigorous, pointed and pictorial, exactly suited to an historian of the highest class."—*Leader*.

W. H. PRESCOTT.

Critical and Historical Essays.

By W. H. Prescott. Crown 8vo, Portrait, 5*s*.

Contents.

Cervantes.—Sir Walter Scott.—Chateaubriand.—Charles Brockden Brown, the American Novelist.—Asylum for the Blind.—Irving's Conquest of Granada.—Bancroft's United States.—Life in Mexico.—Molière.—Italian Narrative Poetry.—Poetry and Romance of the Italians.—Scottish Song, etc. etc.

Quits.

By the Author of 'The Initials.' 3 vols. post 8vo, 31*s*. 6*d*.

"Witty, sententious, graphic, full of brilliant pictures of life and manners, it is positively one of the best of modern stories, and may be read with delightful interest from cover to cover."—*Morning Post*.

Quinland; or, Varieties in American Life.

2 vols. post 8vo, 21*s*.

"Here we have every variety of American life; life in a clearing, life in an American village, and the fashionable life of large towns. We have farmers, storekeepers, and gentlemen; physicians, lawyers, and alchemists; hunters, horse-stealers, and usurers; roguish misers in council with keen attorneys; and ambitious senators bribing unscrupulous journalists."—*Press*.

CHARLES READE.

It is Never too Late to Mend.

By Charles Reade. Crown 8vo, 5*s*. edition, with Illustrations. Also square 8vo, 2*s*. Edition.

"Written with amazing spirit."—*Press*.

*** The sale of this work in all forms has reached 57,000 copies.

MRS. ROMER.

Filia Dolorosa.

Memoirs of the Last Dauphine. By Mrs. Romer. Second Edition, crown 8vo, 12*s*. Portrait.

"Exquisitely told."—*Daily News*.

"A more touching picture was never presented to the mind."—*Literary Gazette*.

LORD JOHN RUSSELL.

Memorials and Correspondence of Charles

James Fox. By the Right Hon. Lord John Russell, M.P. 4 vols. 8vo, 56*s*.

"No Englishman who desires to understand the history of his country from 1768 to 1807 can fail to read this work with advantage and pleasure."—*Edinburgh Review*.

The Ruling Passion.

Three vols., post 8vo, 31*s*. 6*d*.

"The plot of 'The Ruling Passion' is original, the characters well sketched, and the style good. It is beyond all question a novel of a high order."—*John Bull*.

Salad for the Social.

By the Author of 'Salad for the Solitary.' Post 8vo, 10*s*. 6*d*.

"The essence of a library, the information of a lifetime."—*Morning Chronicle*.

SIR W. H. SLEEMAN.

Journey through the Kingdom of Oude,

in 1849–50, by direction of the Right Hon. the Earl of Dalhousie, Governor-General; with Private Correspondence relative to the Annexation of Oude. By Major-General Sir WILLIAM H. SLEEMAN, K.C.B., Resident at the Court of Lucknow. 2 vols. post 8vo, 24*s*.

"These volumes give a faithful and most interesting picture of the unhappy state of Oude. General Sir W. Sleeman was one of the ablest and most distinguished of the military servants of the Company. He was strongly opposed to the annexation of Oude, and it is most instructive to see what were the objections urged by so very good a judge against it."—*Saturday Review.*

"This work, with every change of Indian events, rises in value as a storehouse of trustworthy facts."—*Examiner.*

LADY SCOTT.

Types and Antitypes

of the Old and New Testament. By the Hon. LADY SCOTT. Post 8vo, 5*s*. 6*d*.

"It is but justice to the author of the present volume to state that she has, on the whole, acquitted herself with much ability and sound judgment. Her book will be useful to the class of readers for whom it is principally intended, the young and the comparatively ignorant and uninstructed."—*John Bull.*

REV. W. S. SYMONDS, F.G.S.

Stones of the Valley.

By the Rev. W. S. SYMONDS, F.G.S., Rector of Pendock, Author of 'Old Stones,' and President of the Malvern Natural History Field Club. Foolscap 8vo, 5*s*.

"Notwithstanding Mr. Symonds's eminent position as a geologist, he has never lost sight of that simplicity in conveying instruction which renders his work admirably suited for the earliest students."—*John Bull.*

M. SIMON.

Natural Religion.

By JULES SIMON. Translated by J. W. COLE. Post 8vo, 6*s*.

"In France, this work has passed through three large editions. It is, indeed, a masterly performance, written with uncommon force and beauty."—*Press.*

"The brevity and force of the reasoning, and the singular aptness of illustration which abound in it, remind one of the most striking passages in Pascal."—*John Bull.*

MISS TILT.

The Old Palace.

By JULIA TILT, Author of 'May Hamilton.' 2 vols. post 8vo, 21*s*.

"The mystery of this story is resolved in an ending of considerable power."—*Spectator.*

M. THIERS.

History of the French Revolution.

By M. THIERS. 5 vols. crown 8vo, with 41 Illustrations. 25*s*.

Illustrations which accompany this Work.

VOL. I.—1. Attack on the Bastille.—2. Portrait of the Duke of Orleans (Égalité).—3. Portrait of Mirabeau.—4. Portrait of Lafayette.—5. Orgies of the Gardes du Corps.—6. Portrait of Marie Antoinette.—7. Return of the Royal Family from Varennes.—8. Portrait of Marat.—9. The Mob at the Tuileries.—10. Attack on the Tuileries.

VOL. II.—11. Murder of the Princess de Lamballe.—12. Portrait of the Princess de Lamballe.—13. Portrait of Madame Roland.—14. Louis XVI. at the Convention.—15. Last Interview of Louis XVI. with his Family.—16. Portrait of Louis XVI.—17. Portrait of Dumouriez.—18. Triumph of Marat.—19. Portrait of Laroche-Jacquelin.

VOL. III.—20. Assassination of Marat.—21. Portrait of Charlotte Corday.—22. Portrait of Camille-Desmoulins.—23. Condemnation of Marie Antoinette.—24. Portrait of Bailly (Mayor of Paris).—25. Trial of Danton, Camille-Desmoulins, etc.—26. Portrait of Danton.—27. Portrait of Madame Elisabeth.—28. Carrier at Nantes.—29. Portrait of Robespierre.

Vol. IV.—30. Last Victims of the Reign of Terror.—31. Portrait of Charette.—32. Death of the Deputy Feraud.—33. Death of Romme, Goujon, Duquesnoi, etc.—34. Portrait of Louis XVII. —35. The 13th Vendémiaire (5th October, 1795).

Vol. V.—36. Summoning to Execution.—37. Portrait of Pichegru.—38. Portrait of Moreau.—39. Portrait of Hoche.—40. Portrait of Napoleon Bonaparte.—41. The 18th Brumaire (10th November, 1799).

"The palm of excellence, after whole libraries have been written on the French Revolution, has been assigned to the dissimilar histories of Thiers and Mignet."—*William H. Prescott.*

"I am reading Thiers's French Revolution, which I find it difficult to lay down."—*Rev. Sydney Smith.*

ANTHONY TROLLOPE.

The Three Clerks.

By Anthony Trollope. 3 vols. post 8vo, 31*s.* 6*d.*

"Mr. Trollope amply bears out in this work the reputation he acquired by 'Barchester Towers.' There is a great field for amusing description in the varieties of London life brought before us through the various characters of Mr. Trollope's story. We regard the tenderness and self-sacrifice of Linda one of the most graceful and touching pictures of feminine heroism in the whole range of modern novels. We do not know any living writer who draws the portraiture of women more delicately or faithfully than Mr. Trollope."—*John Bull.*

"Here are scenes from family life, more true, more pathetic, and more skilfully sustained than any that can be found, except in the writings of family novelists."—*Saturday Review.*

A. WILLS.

Wanderings among the High Alps.

By Alfred Wills. Small 8vo, 8*s.* 6*d.* New Edition.

"The new edition of Mr. Wills's 'Wanderings' is a welcome book, not only for its agreeable home-reading as a description of scenery, and a narrative of adventures bravely undertaken and well sustained; but for its use as a stimulator to healthy exertion in a somewhat languid age, and as a companion-guide to those who may follow in the writer's footsteps. The form of the new edition is handy, and more fitted for a pocket companion than the original edition, with sketch-maps that save the trouble of reference. There is also additional matter, including a new chapter on the ascent of Mont Blanc."—*Spectator.*

MRS. WEBB.

The Martyrs of Carthage.

By Mrs. WEBB, Author of 'Naomi.' Second Edition. Fcap. 8vo, with Two Illustrations, 5*s*.

"A deeply interesting and most ably-written work."—*Morning Herald.*

MRS. WEBB.

Idaline.

A Tale of the Egyptian Bondage. By Mrs. WEBB, Author of 'Naomi.' Fcap. 8vo, with Illustration, 5*s*.

"A tone of earnestness and piety pervades this narrative."—*Morning Herald.*

A Timely Retreat from Meerut.

By TWO SISTERS. Second Edition. 2 vols. post 8vo. Illustrations, 21*s*.

"We have not had such a picture of Anglo-Indian daily life since the late Miss Roberts published her experiences. But these two volumes have an additional interest; it was a plucky undertaking, and the narrative is told with animation and truthfulness."—*Spectator.*

DR. WHATELY.

Mental Culture

Required for Christian Ministers. By RICHARD WHATELY, Archbishop of Dublin. 8vo, 1*s*.

DR. WHATELY.

Selections from Writings of Richard Whately,

Archbishop of Dublin. Fcap. 8vo, 5*s*., or bound in calf, 8*s*. 6*d*.

"This volume contains the pith, the cream, the choice bits of Archbishop Whately's writings. One of his great charms is his style, as clear as that of Cobbett and Paley." —*Athenæum.*

C. D. YONGE.

Latin and English Dictionary.

A New Phraseological English-Latin and Latin-English Dictionary. By C. D. Yonge.

Part I. English-Latin, 9*s*. 6*d*.
Part II. Latin-English, 7*s*. 6*d*.

Or the whole work complete in One Volume, strongly bound in roan, 15*s*.

It was suggested to Mr. Yonge, some years ago, to undertake this work. It has been submitted to the most eminent scholars and masters of schools in the kingdom (Dr. Goodford, Head Master of Eton; Dr. Moberly, of Winchester; Dr. Vaughan, of Harrow; Dr. Goulburn, of Rugby; and Dr. Jelf, of King's College, London), who all agree that a careful examination of Mr. Yonge's Dictionary has convinced them that it would fully supply the want so greatly felt.

They have, in consequence, authorized the book to be described as published "For the use of Eton, Winchester, Harrow, and Rugby Schools, and King's College, London," and ordered that it shall be, for the future, the only English-Latin dictionary used in those, the principal places of education in the kingdom.

"A very capital book, either for the somewhat advanced pupil, the student who aims at acquiring an idiomatic Latin style, or the adult with a knowledge of the language, who wishes to examine the differences between the structure and expressions of the English and Latin tongues by a short and ready mode. It is the best—we were going to say the only really useful—Anglo-Latin Dictionary we ever met with." —*Spectator*.

ON THE FIRST OF DECEMBER

MR. BENTLEY

WILL PUBLISH THE FIRST NUMBER

OF

A NEW QUARTERLY REVIEW,

TO BE PUBLISHED IN FUTURE ON

The* 1*st of December, the* 1*st of March, the* 1*st of June, and the* 1*st of September.

J. E. TAYLOR, PRINTER, LITTLE QUEEN STREET, LINCOLN'S INN FIELDS.